Campus Crusade for Christ Library

D1190977

Essays in

Biblical Culture

AND

Bible Translation

Jack Manning/New York Times

Essays in

Biblical Culture

AND

Bible Translation

HARRY M. ORLINSKY

Effie Wise Ochs Professor of Bible

Hebrew Union College—Jewish Institute of Religion

New York School

KTAV PUBLISHING HOUSE, INC.

New York

© COPYRIGHT 1974
HARRY M. ORLINSKY

Library of Congress Cataloging in Publication Data

Orlinsky, Harry Meyer, 1908-
  Essays in biblical culture and Bible translation.
  Includes bibliographical references. 1. Bible. O. T.—
Addresses, essays, lectures. 2. Bible. O. T.—Versions,
Jewish—Addresses, essays, lectures. I. Title.
BS1192.074   220.6   72-14069
ISBN 0-87068-218-0

MANUFACTURED IN THE UNITED STATES OF AMERICA

BS
1192
O 71

Campus Crusade for Christ Library

TABLE OF CONTENTS

13367

An Appreciation

Harry Orlinsky hardly needs my *haskamah* for his reputation as a scholar—one of the leading biblical scholars of his generation. He is his own superb *haskamah*.

To say that I was profoundly influenced by Professor Orlinsky during my days as a student at our New York School is very much to understate the case. But the influence he had on me—and, I am sure I may speak for them in this instance, on my fellow students—went far beyond that of a teacher and scholar. His influence as a creative and dedicated human being, a man of immense humor and *joie de vivre*, a deeply imaginative devoted Jew, his influence on us in these extra-scholastic respects, too, was and remains simply enormous. He had a capacity for making his students feel that their lives and careers were of genuine importance to him; and those who, like myself, were fortunate enough to be his students can never forget or underestimate his readiness to challenge them, or the value, the incalculable value, of that readiness on his part.

Others will pay a richly deserved tribute to Harry Orlinsky as a scholar. I want to pay a tribute to him as a teacher of rabbis. May he be rewarded with long life and splendid health for many years to come, and may Harry Orlinsky continue to impress apprentice scholars and rabbis with his rare human warmth as well as his exceptional intellectual vibrancy.

ALFRED GOTTSCHALK
President
Hebrew Union College—
Jewish Institute of Religion

Our Teacher

We, the former students of our beloved teacher Prof. Harry M. Orlinsky, are proud to have a share in the publication of this volume in celebration of his sixty-fifth birthday. While Prof. Orlinsky enjoys the merited reputation as one of the world's authorities in biblical philology, Septuagint, and Bible translation, his fields of specialty have by no means limited his interests or narrowed his sights. The range of subjects covered in this volume bear testimony to his broad vision and to a keen and prolific mind. As yet we have touched only on part of his writings! Far from being exhaustive, our intention has been to present a fair representation in convenient form of Prof. Orlinsky's more popular articles for the intelligent reader who may not be a scholar. It is our sincere belief that these writings constitute a significant contribution to the understanding of the Bible and of biblical history. We are therefore pleased to make these studies, heretofore found in professional journals, jubilee and anniversary volumes, yearbooks, and the like—indeed, five of the essays appear in print for the first time—available to a wider audience.

It was reported that when the famed Wellhausen had completed his formulation of biblical history he suggested to his pupils that they now turn their attention to other areas of knowledge, since all that needed to be studied about the Bible had already been adequately done by him. Today we tend to smile at this not-immodest claim, fully aware that men in each generation apply to biblical study *eisegesis* as well as *exegesis*. It is not so much a question of whether this is legitimate as it is a statement of fact that Bible study, as is true for other disciplines, is not divorced from the *Weltanschauung* and general conditions of life prevalent in a particular period of history. It is well known that in some non-Jewish circles the analysis of the Hebrew Scriptures is viewed as the pretext for the study of the text of the New Testament. Wellhausen's view of the Bible was refracted by the Hegelian interpretation of history. With the rapid advances in such disciplines as linguistics, anthropology, sociology, archaeology, and comparative studies of ancient civilizations, scholars have oftimes been tempted to interpret the Bible through their own particular prism. Needless to say, any view that tends to be monochromatic invites distortion. For the sake of upholding the integrity of biblical research Harry Orlinsky has steadfastly fought this; he would not permit any postbiblical ideas to be read back into the Bible any more than he would tolerate a biblical idea to impose itself mechanically on the postbiblical literature, be it Jewish or non-Jewish.

No modern Bible scholar has proved to be more sensitive to subjectivism and partisanship in biblical research than has Harry Orlinsky. Keenly aware, though, of the milieu from which he stems, and conscious of the religious, cultural, political, and economic influences exerted upon him, he has ardently striven to seek objectivity by asking relentlessly; "What did the author of the Bible mean to say?" It is this direct quest for truth, mixed with his sober sense of balance in drawing upon other disciplines, that can be described as his method. This approach he has passed on to his students, who in their own investigations of the Bible are prompted to ask at once: "What is the text really saying?" For this we remain grateful and indebted to Prof. Orlinsky; he has given us a fuller understanding of the biblical word. As for himself, his method has at times led Prof. Orlinsky to staunchly maintain views which ran counter to the mainstream of scholarly concensus. But he has also reaped the satisfaction of having such independent positions corroborated later by the research of other scholars.

To the world Harry Orlinsky will remain important as a scholar and thinker. For us, however, he takes on the added dimensions of a great teacher and friend. We who sat at his feet will not only remember it as an enlightening privilege but will also cherish it as a unique experience. In his inimitable warm and humorous manner he has bequeathed to us, beyond his knowledge, something of his inner humanity. His students have always had the distinct feeling that he has cared about each of them as an individual.

To paraphrase our rabbis, Harry Orlinsky does not require this volume to bring him honor, for his work and his person are their own testimonials. This volume, rather, is presented to him in the year of his sixty-fifth birthday as a heartfelt expression of our affection and friendship for him. May he remain productive and be with us for many more years.

MARTIN S. ROZENBERG—*Chairman*
HERBERT M. BAUMGARD
GUNTER HIRSCHBERG
LEIVY SMOLAR
BERNARD M. ZLOTOWITZ

STUDENT SPONSORS

Hebrew Union College—Jewish Institute of Religion
New York School

Meyer M. Abramowitz
Charles G. Agin
Philip M. Aronson
Henry Arrow
Albert S. Axelrad
Jeffrey L. Ballon
Henry Bamberger
Bernard Baskin
Herbert M. Baumgard
Jeffrey Bearman
Abner L. Bergman
Morrison D. Bial
Richard J. Birnholz
Reeve R. Brenner
Jay R. Brickman
Neil Brief
Gerald Brieger
Bernard M. Cohen
Norman J. Cohen
Bernhard N. Cohn
Michael J. Cook
Saul M. Diament
Joel C. Dobin
Israel S. Dresner
Frederick A. Eisenberg
Irwin H. Fishbein
Frank A. Fischer
Adam D. Fisher
Barry R. Friedman
Stuart A. Gertman
Bernard B. Goldsmith
David S. Goldstein
Bruce Goldwasser
Alfred L. Goodman
Joel S. Goor
Alfred Gottschalk
Jerome W. Grollman
Frederick H. Grosse

Joseph Gutmann
Max Hausen
Gunter Hirschberg
Lawrence A. Hoffman
Philip Horowitz
Marshall S. Hurwitz
Hirshel Jaffe
Sanford H. Jarashow
Earl A. Jordan
Leon M. Kahane
Ralph P. Kingsley
Bernard Kligfeld
William Kloner
Arthur Kolatch
Abraham Krantz
Paul R. Kushner
Jacob Lantz
Arthur J. Lelyveld
Paul H. Levenson
Richard A. Levine
Jerrold M. Levy
Eugene J. Lipsey
Lewis C. Littman
Irwin C. Lowenheim
Dennis Math
Ronald Millstein
Michael L. Morgan
Shimon Paskow
Norman R. Patz
Stephen Pearce
Bernard Perelmutter
James H. Perman
Marvin Petruck
Stephen H. Pinsky
Leonard H. Poller
Seymour Prystowsky
Gerald Raiskin
Israel Renov

Andrew J. Robins
James B. Rosenberg
Milton D. Rosenfeld
Harry A. Roth
Martin S. Rozenberg
Alvan D. Rubin
Lawrence H. Rubinstein
Peter J. Rubinstein
Benjamin Z. Rudavsky
Richard B. Safran
Elihu Schagrin
Edward Schechter
Irwin Schor
Robert D. Schreibman
Dannel Schwartz
David L. Schwartz
Mayer W. Selekman
Arnold M. Shevlin
Harold Silver
Allan L. Smith
Leivy Smolar
Rav A. Soloff
Edwin N. Soslow

Arthur Soffer
Ezra Spicehandler
David Spitz
Donald M. Splansky
Louis Stein
Paul M. Steinberg
Richard F. Steinbrink
Michael S. Stroh
David J. Susskind
Robert M. Syme
Herbert Tarr
Bernard Taylor
Morris M. Tosk
Milton Weinberg
Henry M. Weiner
Herbert Weiner
Richard H. White
Leo R. Wolkow
Ira S. Youdovin
Sheldon Zimmerman
Leonard Zion
Martin J. Zion
Bernard M. Zlotowitz

ESSAYS IN BIBLICAL CULTURE

1

Teaching Bible in a
Rabbinical School

TEACHING BIBLE in a Rabbinical School is not the same as teaching
Bible in the Semitics Department of a secular institution of higher
learning. In a Semitics Department, the primary purpose is to account
for the Bible in its historical setting: how and why it came to be. In
a Rabbinical school, the primary purpose is to account for the Bible in
its historical development: how and why the Bible—as a finished product—came to be used and interpreted.

For the proper comprehension of the Bible in its historical setting,
the Near East of the last two millenia B.C.E.—the period and region
in which the Bible came to be—constitutes the focus of study. However, for the correct understanding of the Bible in its historical career,
the Christian and Moslem countries of Asia, Europe, and North
Africa—and only recently also the countries of the western world—
during the first two millenia C.E., constituting as they do the period
and regions in which the Bible was widely used and regarded as the
basis of authority by every important stratum of society, make up the
area of our interest.

[Address delivered at the meeting of the Board of Governors of Hebrew Union
College-Jewish Institute of Religion, New York City, February 5, 1970.]

So it is two different Bibles that are involved in these two great, but different historical epochs. For we must realize clearly that the Bible became and remained a living force in Jewish (as in Christian) life precisely because it was lifted right out of the living conditions which had brought it into being and adjusted to the considerably different conditions of the Hellenistic, Roman, Christian, Moslem, Persian, and other cultures and societies of the Common Era. I use the term "adjusted" in its widest possible sense, excluding virtually no implications.

When studying the Bible in its historical setting, it is the languages and cultures and histories of Sumer, Babylonia, Assyria, Egypt, the Hurrians, the Hittites, Canaan, Moab, Ammon, Edom, Aram, Phoenicia, Philistia, and the like, that must be studied; and the archaeology of these lands and civilizations assumes major significance for the serious student of the Bible. For the study of the Bible in its historical development, however, it is rather the opinions and interpretations of Rabbi Akiba in the second century, of the Talmudic Rabbis and the Masoretes in the centuries that followed, of Saadia Gaon in the tenth century, of the incomparable Rashi in the eleventh century, of his grandson Rashbam in the twelfth, of the acute Ibn Ezra and of Radak —the greatest of the Kimchis—in the twelfth-thirteenth centuries, of Ramban in the thirteenth, Ralbag in the fourteenth, Abravanel in the fifteenth, and Sforno in the sixteenth centuries, down to Shadal and the Malbim and others in the nineteenth century—it is to these Jewish masters of Biblical exegesis that we must turn.,

In a rabbinical school it is not easy to combine the two approaches, though much of the problem would be solved if a post-graduate course in Bible leading to the Ph.D. degree were simultaneously available to the interested student. Lacking that, the student has to depend on his teacher and on the secondary literature—where he is usually limited to the English language—for information of extrabiblical origin.

Let me say a word about the traditional Jewish interpreters of the Bible. Professional Biblical scholars have tended to dismiss them as well-meaning and learned men who lacked the critical attitude that distinguishes the scientifically minded from the merely learned student of the Bible—as we say in Yiddish, *der gelernter* as distinct from *der vissenshaftlicher*. Of course the traditional Jewish commentators—

just like the non-Jewish prior to the nineteenth century—were not archaeologists, trained historians, cuneiformists, Egyptologists, and the like. But they knew the Bible. They knew Hebrew. They had a feeling for the nuances of a Biblical Hebrew expression. It is equally true that modern Biblical scholarship, mostly Protestant, has been nothing short of revolutionary in making us comprehend the Bible in a manner and to an extent that was impossible and unimaginable prior to the twentieth century; for this we must all be forever most grateful. Yet we can gain even deeper comprehension of the Bible if we study the medieval Jewish commentators increasingly systematically and critically, for they will supply us with considerable information and understanding that will go well with the extrabiblical data unearthed in more recent times. I say this, because of my experience in translating the Bible as a member of the committee that produced the Protestant Revised Standard Version of the Old Testament (1952) and of the committee that produced the new Jewish Publication Society's version of *The Torah* (1962). In the volume of *Notes on the New Translation of the Torah,* due to appear any day now [it appeared on March 4], I wrote, "A major consequence of this new (J.P.S.) translation is the realization that the traditional interpreters of the Bible—beginning with the earliest rabbinic literature and extending through Saadia, Rashi, Rashbam, Ibn Ezra, Radak, Ramban, Ralbag, Sforno, and Abravanel, to Luzzatto, Malbim, and others—command in vastly increased measure the respect and gratitude of modern critical scholarship. These traditional commentators gain our scholarly respect not from blind acceptance of their views but rather from a critical evaluation of their exposition in a manner that any modern commentator expects from his peers." And in an article on Jewish influence on Christian translations of the Bible ("Jewish Scholarship and Christian Translations of the Hebrew Bible," *Yearbook LXIII of the Central Conference of American Rabbis,* 1953, pp. 235–252), I dealt *inter alia* with the central role that Rashi's commentary—by way of the Jewish convert to Christianity, Nicolas de Lyra—played in the making of Martin Luther's great German translation and—through Luther— of William Tyndale's English version; with the influence of David Kimchi (Radak), so pervasive that, as put by Max L. Margolis in his fine little book on *The Story of Bible Translations,* it "may be traced

in every line of the Anglican (so-called King James) version of 1611";
with the way in which Abraham ibn Ezra influenced the translation
of the word *tsedakah* at Proverbs 8.18: "prosperity" instead of traditional "righteousness"; and the like.

There is so much more that I should like to tell you about teaching
Bible in our Rabbinical School. But I must stop; and having just
mentioned "prosperity" and "righteousness" in combination, this is as
good a juncture as any at which to stop. Thank you.

2

Moses

AMONG THE GREAT personalities in the long span of Jewish history, extending over a period of some four thousand years, Moses must invariably stand at the head. Already in biblical times, he had become so revered and so much a legend that when classical prophecy made its mark in Israel, more than half a millennium after Moses' time, he emerged as *the prophet* par excellence: "Never again did there arise in Israel a prophet like Moses, whom the Lord knew face to face" (Deuteronomy 34:10).

Israel Comes to Egypt

At the turn of the third millennium, about 2000 B.C.E., a Hebrew[1] named Abraham, accompanied by his wife Sarah and their worldly goods, started out on a journey that was to take them from one end of the Fertile Crescent to the other, from Ur in southern Mesopotamia

---

[Published originally as Chapter 1 in *Great Jewish Personalities in Ancient and Medieval Times* (= Vol. 1 in *The B'nai B'rith Great Book Series*, 5 vols.), ed. S. Noveck (New York, 1959), pp. 10-39, 333-335. Reproduced, without the notes and bibliography, in *Molders of the Jewish Mind* (B'nai B'rith, 1966), pp. 3-32.]

[1] While the terms "Hebrew(s)" and "Israel(ites)" are used interchangeably in this essay, the first is older than the second. It was during the period of the Judges (12th-11th centuries) that the term "Israelites" (Hebrew *bene yisra'el,*

to the southwestern border of Canaan, at Egypt. Abraham and Sarah had left family and friends in Ur, and in Paddan-aram too, in northern Syria, to make this trek; and although they and their offspring maintained their family and cultural ties with the place of their origin for some time, Canaan was to be their permanent home, and that of their descendants.

In the course of time, in the days of Ishmael and Isaac, of Esau and Jacob, and of their children and grandchildren—among whom the twelve sons of Jacob and his daughter Dinah are best known—many more Hebrews were to be found in the land, some of them as immigrants from the Syrian part of the Fertile Crescent and from the Arabian steppes. The first half of the second millennium was an exciting period, characterized by mass movements. People were being attracted in the thousands from their more primitive abodes in the grasslands and highlands to the more settled, sophisticated, wealthy, and comfortable towns and villages not far distant.

But drought and famine, also, were a common phenomenon in many parts of western Asia, and could change the historical direction of a people. It was one such period of desolation that brought Jacob and his family, and thousands of non-Hebrews as well, to Egypt, the country of full granaries. The periodic overflow of the Nile River, today no less than in the past, gave life to the land and helped regulate it as an agricultural society.[2] Thus a thirteenth-century Egyptian document tells how the semi-nomadic inhabitants of Edom, south of Palestine, left their homes in time of drought to come to Egypt, "to keep themselves alive and to keep their cattle alive." And just as Abraham and Isaac in an earlier period had been compelled by famine to go south (Genesis 12 and 26), so too did Jacob in his time have to send his sons to Egypt to purchase grain.

"children of Israel") came to replace the term "Hebrews," just as "Israelites" was later replaced by "Judeans" and "Jews" after the Exile in Babylonia. For further explanation, see Orlinsky, *Ancient Israel,* pp. 51-2

[2] A recent historian, J. A. Wilson, has designated the first two chapters of his study *The Burden of Egypt* (Univ. of Chicago Press, 1951), "The Black Land" and "Out of the Mud." This excellent work has now appeared in a Phoenix paperback edition, under the title *The Culture of Egypt* (1956).

Joseph, one of Jacob's sons, preceding his family to Egypt, had risen to high power, ranking next only to Pharaoh himself. When his father and brothers immigrated, they settled in the fertile Delta region of Goshen. This was the Eisodus, the "going into" Egypt.

The biblical tale concerns itself with the Hebrews alone. But in all probability the coming of the Hebrews to Egypt was part of a larger ethnic and military movement. During the first half of the second millennium Egypt had experienced an invasion and consequent degradation—reference to which was carefully, and, characteristically, avoided in its chronicles. A mixed group of Asiatics, apparently mostly Semites, and known generally as Hyksos (literally, "rulers of foreign countries"), appeared in the north, and in successive waves swarmed through Syria and Palestine. By about 1700 B.C.E. they had crossed the land bridge into Africa and conquered much of Egypt, a domination that was not to be completely broken until about 1550.

There appear to have been several points of contact between the Hyksos and the Hebrews during that century and a half. It is known, for example, that a certain Hyksos chieftain in Egypt bore the name Jacob-el (or perhaps: -har), which means "May El (or, Har—the mountain god) Give Protection." Another Hyksos leader was called Jacob-baal, "May Baal Protect." The verbal element Jacob, which means "protect," is identical with the name of the Hebrew patriarch who settled in Egypt.

Again, the historical kernel which resides in the dramatic story of Joseph's career in Egypt, of the coming to power of a Hebrew in the Egyptian royal court, could well have derived from the period of the Hyksos, when Semites, and in all likelihood Hebrews among them, were prominent among the new rulers of Egypt. It was not Egyptian habit to nourish the ambitions of strangers in their midst, and, furthermore, it would seem to be more than mere coincidence that in the Bible the Hebrews are said to have settled in the Delta, the very area which the Hyksos built up around their new capital, Avaris.[3]

---

[3] From H. M. Orlinsky, *Ancient Israel*, pp. 31-34. Wilson, *op. cit.*, has described this period in Chapter VII as "The Great Humiliation." [See now the map of the far-flung territory of the Hyksos, p. 50 of *Understanding the Bible*, etc., where Zoan represents Avaris, the later Tanis.]

Israel in Bondage: Birth of Moses

"And Joseph died, and all his brothers and all that generation," the Bible relates (Exodus 1:6-8), "and the Israelites were fruitful and prolific; they multiplied and increased very greatly, so that the land was filled with them. But a new king arose over Egypt, who did not know Joseph . . ." On the grounds that the Israelites were becoming too numerous and strong for the native government to handle, the new regime introduced a system of state slavery: "They set task-masters over them to oppress them with forced labor; and they built for Pharaoh store cities, Pithom and Rameses" (v. 11).[4]

At this point the findings of archaeology came to our aid, helping us to paint a broader picture than the biblical writers had deemed necessary. When the Egyptians finally succeeded in overthrowing their Hyksos oppressors, they drove many of them from the land and enslaved the rest. The ertswhile free rulers became captives of the state, subject to forced labor. It is now known that two centuries later, about 1300 B.C.E., Seti I of Egypt, who had done much to reorganize the empire in Palestine and southern Syria, began the rebuilding of Avaris, the old Hyksos capital. His son and successor, Rameses II, continued the building project on a much vaster scale, changing the name of Avaris to Rameses. This same Pharaoh also did much rebuilding at other sites, notably at Pithom. Slave battalions worked at all these places, and there is little reason to doubt that Hebrews were among them.[5]

At this point the biblical narrative introduces Moses. Pharaoh, the Bible relates, had given orders to drown in the Nile all Hebrew males at birth. But Moses' mother was able to hide her infant son for three months. At the end of that period, she placed the baby—who was of unusuallly striking appearance—in a waterproofed basket among the reeds by the bank of the Nile. A daughter of Pharaoh, coming down

---

[4] Biblical quotations in the essay, where they do not derive from the new, as yet unpublished Jewish Publication Society's Bible translation or from the Revised Standard Version of the Old Testament (Nelson), are the author's own versions.

[5] Cf. G. E. Wright, *Biblical Archaeology* (Westminster Press, Phila., 1957), Chapter IV, "Sojourners in Egypt," pp 53-68.

to the Nile to bathe, espied the basket. She sent a maid to fetch it, "and when she opened it, she saw that it was a child, a boy crying. She took pity on it, and said, 'This must be a Hebrew child' " (2:6).

Moses' sister, meanwhile, was stationed nearby watching for just such a development. She stepped forward and asked the Egyptian princess, "Shall I go and call you a Hebrew wet nurse to suckle the child for you?" And when the royal lady assented, she called her mother. When the child outgrew his mother's nursing and was brought back to the royal palace, the princess named him Moses (Hebrew *Moshe*): "because I drew him out (*meshitíhu*) of the water" (v. 10). So much for the biblical tradition.[6]

All peoples in antiquity were given to embellishing the circumstances of the birth of their great heroes, and so too did ancient Israel. A story similar to that of Moses was told of Sargon I (about 2300 B.C.E.), founder of the world's first empire, at Accad in Mesopotamia. The legend reads in part:

My (?) mother conceived me, in secret she bore me.
She set me in a basket of rushes, with bitumen she sealed my lid.
She cast me into the river which rose not over me.
The river bore me up and carried me to Akki, the drawer of water.
Akki, the drawer of water, lifted me out as he dipped his ewer.
Akki, the drawer of water, took me as his son and reared me.
Akki, the drawer of water, appointed me as his gardener.
While I was a gardener, Ishtar granted me her love.
And for four and (?) years I exercised kingship.
The black-headed people I ruled, I governed . . .[7]

---

[6] The Midrash waxes eloquent in its imaginative tales of the birth of Moses, his rescue from the water, and the like. See Louis Ginzberg's wonderful collection of *The Legends of the Jews* (7 volumes, of which 1-4 are the Legends, 5-6 the Notes, and 7 the Index), Vol. II, pp 262 ff. See the one-volume abridgment, *Legends of the Bible* (1956), "Moses," pp. 277-506.

[7] "The Legend of Sargon," translated by E. A. Speiser, *Ancient Near Eastern Texts Relating to the Old Testament* (edited by J. B. Pritchard), p. 119; the technical notes and signs have here been deleted.

While the biblical tale credits the princess with knowledge of Hebrew, scholars have long recognized the Egyptian origin of the common name-element Moses, meaning "offspring, born of." The name "Moses" is no less authentically Egyptian than such other contemporaneous biblical names as Miriam, Hophni, Phinehas, Merari, and Puti-el. And these names, in turn, help to authenticate the Egyptian locale of the biblical account of the principal heroes and events involved in this phase of Israel's career.

Midian: The Call of Moses

All that we really know for certain, therefore, is that Moses was born in Egypt. How he spent his formative years no one knows. The Bible, having brought Moses into the royal family as the princess' adopted son, took him out of it in the very next verse (2:10-11), telling us nothing whatever about his youth.

Grown to manhood—in all probability in the same environment as that of his enslaved Hebrew brethern—Moses was aware and conscious of his Hebraic origin, and ready to avenge the affliction of his people. His first positive act, understandable under the circumstances even if committed impulsively, was to strike down "an Egyptian whom he saw strike down one of his Hebrew kinsmen" (v.11).

Moses had to flee the land, for he had been seen—by two Hebrew slaves—beating the Egyptian. He went to the land of Midian, generally located south of Edom, in Arabia. There he met the seven daughters of Jethro, a Midianite priest, and married one of them, Zipporah.

This was the turning point of Moses' career, and that of biblical Israel. While tending the flocks of his father-in-law, Moses experienced his first contact with the God of his fathers. "When he came to Horeb, the mountain of God," the Bible reads (3:1 ff.), "an angel of the Lord appeared to him in a flaming fire out of a bush. He looked and, lo, the bush was aflame with fire, yet the bush was not consumed. And Moses said: 'I must turn aside and see this marvelous sight: why the bush does not burn up.' "

At this point the Lord revealed Himself to Moses: "I am the God of your father(s) . . . I have marked well the plight of My people in Egypt . . . I have come down to rescue them from the Egyptians, and to bring them out of that land to a good and spacious land, to a land flowing with milk and honey, to the region of the Canaanites . . . Come, therefore, I will send you to Pharaoh, and you shall free My people the Israelites from Egypt."

In this period, God's actions—and sometimes God Himself—were associated by the Hebrews with natural phenomena like fires, lightning, thunderstorms, mountains, and volcanoes. They believed that He manifested Himself and His will not merely by direct speech and in dreams, but also through these natural agents. Imbued as Moses was with the spirit of liberation and the desire to free his people at a time when the possibility of redemption was more favorable than before, it is understandable that he would see in natural phenomena, especially when they occurred unexpectedly or in unusual form, a theophany—that is, a visible appearance of God.

But Moses seems out of character in the dialogue that ensued. Rather than accept readily this mission from God to His people, he tried to find reasons why he should not become a spokesman for God (3:11-4:13). "Who am I?" Moses asked, "that I should go to Pharaoh and that I should bring forth the Israelites from Egypt? . . . What if they do not believe me or heed my voice, but say, 'The Lord did not appear to you'? . . . Please, O Lord, I have never been a man of words . . . for I am slow of speech and slow of tongue . . . Please, O Lord, send whomever else You will!" And Moses consented to go only after the Lord had assured him that his brother Aaron would be his spokesman.

In proper perspective, however, this biblically recorded conversation makes good sense. It was an ancient convention for one who felt himself chosen by God for a special mission to find reason for not responding at once and with eagerness to the call. Hesitancy, lack of confidence, fear of the consequences—these were conventionally attributed to God's chosen one when the call came. While Moses may have had a speech defect, and may also have felt some qualms about the enormity of the task, the biblical statement should not prevent us from recognizing in him a strong desire to lead his people out of slavery; for otherwise he would not have experienced the vision in the first place.

The Egyptian World in Moses' Time

What manner of civilization did Egypt constitute in this period so crucial to Israel? What were its material, artistic, and spiritual achievements?

The Near East, that quadrangle of land lying between the Mediterranean, Caspian and Red Seas, and the Persian Gulf, and connecting —at Israel and Sinai—Asia and Africa, is the birthplace of civilization. Egypt had long been one of the great powers in that part of the world. Indeed, during most of the third and second millennia B.C.E., Egypt was the principal power at the southwestern end of the Fertile Crescent, corresponding to the dominating regime at the northeastern end—Sumer, Babylonia, the Hittites, or Assyria.

The conquest at the hands of the Hyksos was Egypt's first full-scale and long-term experience as a subject people. Egyptian culture sank so low that this period has been described as "The Great Humiliation" (see note 2).

After the gradual expulsion of the Hyksos, the Egyptians began to devote their energies primarily to the reconquest of the neighboring regions, the rebuilding of the land, its army, shipping service, civil service, and temples. That accomplished, a decision had to be reached whether to venture into expanding imperialism or to remain essentially a localized economy. Queen Hatshepsut represented the latter view, her nephew Thutmose III the former. Ultimately, imperialism prevailed. And by the time that Thutmose had achieved his notable conquests (c. 1450 B.C.E.) Egypt was once more the greatest power in Western Asia. The revival that followed was on such a grand scale that the ensuing period of the New Kingdom, especially during the Eighteenth and Nineteenth Dynasties (down to shortly after 1200), has been called the Golden Age, and was the subject of a recent book suggestively titled *When Egypt Ruled the East*.[8]

Ikhnaton and Atonism

During the reign of Amenhotep IV (c. 1380-1360), a fundamental split developed between the royal house and its supporters on the one hand, and, on the other, the powerful priestly interests of the god Amon at Thebes. The latter group was apparently keenly interested in continued imperialist expansion and consolidation. The royal regime moved its headquarters from Thebes to a new site about three hundred miles to the north, and laid primary emphasis on another deity, Aton, the round disk of the sun. The king himself changed his name to Ikhnaton (Akhen-Aton, "He Who is Serviceable to [or "It Goes Well with] the Aton"), and named the new capital Akhet-Aton ("The Place of the Effective Glory of the Aton"), modern Tell el-Amarna. Art became more naturalistic than ever before. Women began to play a more prominent role in public life. Something of a democratization of social life was manifest in the public informality of the king, his wife, and their six daughters.[9]

The virtually exclusive worship of Aton by the royal household has led a number of scholars to assert that Ikhnaton was a monotheist, the first in the world. Some scholars, going even further, placed Moses in Ikhnaton's period, and claimed that he obtained his knowledge of monotheism, directly or ultimately, from Ikhnaton.[10] Sigmund Freud, in *Moses and Monotheism* (1939), made Moses an important Egyptian official in Ikhnaton's court who became a protector of the Hebrews, converted them to Ikhnaton's "monotheistic" religion, and led

---

[8] By G. Steindorff and K. C. Seele (Univ. of Chicago Press, 1942). Or see Wilson, *op. cit.,* Chapter VIII, "Far Frontiers," pp 166-205.

[9] The best treatment of this phenomenon is to be found in Wilson, *op. cit.,* Chapter IX, "Irrepressible Conflict," pp 206-235; the quotations in this section derive from Wilson. See also J. H. Breasted, *Cambridge Ancient History,* Vol. II (1924), pp. 109 ff.

[10] See J. H. Breasted, *The Dawn of Conscience* (New York, 1933).

them out of Egypt. According to Freud, those passages in the Pentateuch that stood in contradiction to this theory were to be dismissed as
invention and distortion; thus it was really Moses, not Abraham, who
introduced the custom of circumcision among the Hebrews. This study
of Moses by Freud is now regarded by many as a naive venture, constituting in reality a more important source of information for the
analysis of Freud himself than of Moses.

According to more reliable treatments of the subject, however, it
is clear today that Moses derived nothing from Ikhnaton's reign or outlook. Recent study has made it more than dubious that Ikhnaton was
really a monotheist, or that his views circulated outside his royal court
or subsequent to his death. What had been regarded by some as
monotheism, the recognition and worship of Aton alone, has on closer
study turned out to be a form of syncretism, a process by which several distinct gods came to be merged with a single deity so that all
their functions were attributed to him. Ikhnaton, it is true, initiated
a violent attack upon the god Amon, hacking the name out of inscriptions; at the same time, however, the many other less powerful and
important gods were rarely disturbed. Indeed, the entire matter becomes clear when it is realized that Atonism was basically not a
religious—let alone monotheistic—but an economic and political revolt against the powerful Amon interests.[11]

Another important factor differentiated Moses' beliefs from those
of Ikhnaton. Already in the preceding, patriarchal period, there had
come into being among the Hebrews a concept of deity which, while
not monotheistic in our sense of the term, was yet not polytheistic
either. In a sense, the patriarchs may be said to have practiced monotheism, but without defining it. While they probably did not think of
denying the existence of other gods, the patriarchs attached themselves to one God and worshipped Him alone. With Him, they entered
voluntarily into a covenant which was binding forever, never to be

---

[11] See note 9 above. See also R. J. Williams, "The Hymn to Aten" (pp. 142-150)
in *Documents from Old Testament Times* (Nelson and Sons, 1958), edited by
D. Winton Thomas

broken under penalty of severe punishment and, if only theoretically, of complete rejection. In sponsoring monotheism, Moses was therefore not actually introducing a new concept to the Hebrews. He had a familiar, developable Hebraic idea of monotheism with which to work. Even the covenant of Sinai represented not so much a change in kind as a change in degree from the old way of binding oneself to the deity. Moses and the Hebrews, therefore, had little need of Egyptian assistance—which was not forthcoming anyway—in this direction.[12]

The Age of Rameses II

Thanks largely to the findings of archaeology during the past few decades, evidence has been accumulating from various sources to indicate that the career of Moses is probably to be sought not in the reign of Ikhnaton but about a century later, in the decades following 1300 B.C.E., during the long reign of Rameses II (c. 1290-1224). It is quite certain that Israel was in Canaan in some force around 1250; excavations at several sites point to the Israelites as conquering Canaanite settlements at about that time. Indeed, around 1230 B.C.E., King Merneptah of Egypt celebrated his victory over numerous foes in an alleged campaign in Western Asia. And the Pharaoh boasted:

Israel is laid waste, its seed is not,
Palestine is become a widow for Egypt.[13]

If we add a few decades to 1250 to allow for the wilderness wandering under Moses, we arrive at a date well within the reign of Rameses II. It also seems clear that the store cities, Pithom and Rameses, said in the Bible to have been built by the Hebrews in bondage, were erected in the days of this same Rameses. All in all, one cannot be far wrong

---

[12] From Orlinsky, *op. cit.*, pp. 27-9, 41-2.
[13] See Wilson in *Ancient Near Eastern Texts*, pp. 376 ff.; or Williams, in *Documents from Old Testament Times*, pp. 137-41.

in dating Moses about 1300, and the Exodus during the thirteenth century.[14]

Rameses II could well be the vainglorious Pharaoh whose heart softened and hardened by turn. Rameses was the king-god who walked into a Hittite trap at Kadesh on the Orontes River in Syria, and then turned his feat in escaping from the ambush into a great personal triumph. On his return to Egypt, he outdid all his predecessors—and, it turned out, all his successors too—in covering the wall space in the temples with carved representations of his remarkable "victory." Steindorff-Seele describes him bluntly as the "greatest of Egyptian boasters."[15] The biblical Pharaoh of the bondage could scarcely be described better!

The Exodus

This was the Egypt to which Moses returned after his vision of God in Midian. His brother Aaron joined him, and the two together began the difficult and arduous task of persuading and organizing their fellow Israelites to leave their land of bondage. According to one version in the Bible, Aaron performed for them the signs that the Lord had commanded: he caused his staff to turn into a serpent and then into a staff again; he brought leprosy upon his hand and then cured it; and, finally, he poured on the dry ground some water from the Nile so that it became blood. "And the people believed," the Bible asserts (4:31), "when they heard that the Lord had taken note of the Israelites and that He had seen their plight; and they bowed in homage." But an-

---

[14] In general, see Wright, *op. cit.,* pp. 58-60 ("With Moses and the Exodus"). More details may be found in M. Noth, *The History of Israel,* pp. 109-119 ("The Deliverance from Egypt"); Y. Kaufmann, "The Biblical Age" in *Great Ages and Ideas of the Jewish People,* edited by L. W. Schwarz (Random House, 1956), pp. 14 ff.

[15] *When Egypt Ruled the East,* in the "Outline of Egyptian History," p. 275. Wilson, *op. cit.,* states (p. 247): "The fact remains that the arrogant bellowing of victory comes as an insincere ostentation similar to the bloated bulk of Rameses II's monuments or to his shameless appropriation of the monuments of his ancestors. Blatant advertising was used to cover up the failure to attain past glories."

other version has it that when Moses told the Israelites what the Lord had told him, "they would not listen to Moses, their spirits crushed by cruel bondage" (6:9).[16]

Pharaoh could hardly have been expected to consent to the release of so many thousands of unpaid workers. The biblical interpretation is different: God could readily have made Pharaoh free his captive Israelites; but He wanted to demonstrate for all time His power and glory. "The Lord said to Moses: Go to Pharaoh. For I have hardened his heart and the hearts of his courtiers, in order that I may display these My signs among them, and that you may recount in the hearing of your sons and your sons' sons how I made a mockery of the Egyptians and how I displayed My signs among them, that you may know that I am the Lord" (10:1-2).

And thus there began a series of ten events that have been retold by countless generations—the ten plagues. In the case of the first nine, neither blood nor frogs nor lice, neither insects nor pestilence nor boils, neither hail nor locusts nor darkness could stay Pharaoh from the swift completion of his appointed round. The tenth plague, however, brought matters to a head. "In the middle of the night the Lord struck down all the firstborn in the land of Egypt, from the firstborn of Pharaoh who sat on the throne to the firstborn of the captive who was in the dungeon, and all the firstborn of animals" (12:29). Pharaoh and his courtiers did not wait until morning. They arose in the night and summoned Moses and Aaron: "Depart from among my people, you and the Israelites with you! Go, worship the

---

[16] Biblical scholarship has long accepted the Documentary Theory, according to which the Pentateuch is made up, in the main, of four distinct Documents (or, sources), designated J, E, D, and P, deriving from about 10th-9th (J and E), 7th (D) and 6th (P) centuries B.C.E. Before World War I, scholars tended to regard much of these Documents as fictitious. But archaeology since World War I and closer analysis have reversed this attitude sharply; these sources are now generally regarded as substantially historical, preserving much that the careful and objective scholar may use with discreet confidence. See R. S. Driver, *Introduction to the Literature of the Old Testament* (1913; now reprinted as a Meridian paperback); or the excellent "Introduction" in the revised edition of his *Westminster Commentary on Genesis.*

Lord as you said! Take also your flocks and your herds, as you said, and be gone! And may you," the divine Pharaoh pleaded with these two men, "bring a blessing upon me also" (vv. 31-32).

For those who do not believe in miracles, the biblical account is understandable in natural terms. Scholars have long recognized that most of these plagues are natural phenomena that have afflicted Egypt throughout the ages. The Nile has long been known to acquire a reddish color. Frogs have on occasion plagued the country, their decomposition resulting in a vast multiplication of lice, insects, and pestilence. And what moderns explain as natural phenomena in aggravated form, the biblical writings accounted for in terms of God's direct and supernatural intervention in behalf of His people.

It seems clear that in the midst of some such upheaval, Moses and those slaves, non-Hebrew as well as Hebrew, who were courageous or desperate enough to follow him, made a dash for liberty. Their aim was to escape Egyptian territory to freedom. This they achieved. Thus Moses found himself at the head of an undisciplined collection of people—the Bible refers to the non-Hebrews as the "mixed multitude" and "rabble" (Exodus 12:38; Numbers 11:4)—numbering several thousand.[17]

Deliverance and the "Red" Sea

Moses' leadership was tested at once. Normally, he should have led the Hebrews directly to Canaan, the land that they believed God had promised the patriarchs to give to their descendants—and where, incidentally, some Hebrews had remained when the others went down

---

[17] According to the census lists in Numbers 1 and 26, said to have been taken right after the Exodus and at the end of the forty years of wandering respectively, the number of male Israelites who left Egypt under Moses, not including the Levites (or the wives, children, and cattle), came to just over 600,000. This figure can scarcely be taken seriously, for sundry and sufficient reasons. It is not unlikely that these lists originally belonged to a later period, perhaps that of David. In any case, scholars generally tend to guess at the number of people involved in the Exodus and Wandering at about 5,000.

to Egypt. But no. "God did not lead them by the way of the land of the Philistines," we are told (Exodus 13:17), "although it was nearer; for God said, 'The people may have a change of heart when they see war, and return to Egypt.'" In other words, the Philistines were settled in Canaan when the biblical account of the Exodus was being written down, but not yet when the Exodus took place. Moses realized full well that he dare not make directly for Canaan lest his people run head on into several Egyptian fortresses and garrisons en route. This road, so important for economic and military reasons, was always closely guarded. Instead, Moses led the Israelites roundabout, south and east, by way of the wilderness at the Red Sea—more correctly, Reed (or, Marsh) Sea.[18]

After a short period of wandering, the Hebrews found themselves up against the Reed Sea. In the meantime, an Egyptian force had set out—the biblical narrator states that in order to recapture the fugitive slaves Pharaoh himself "hitched up his chariot and took his men with him: he took six hundred of his picked chariots, and the rest of the chariots of Egypt, with reserves in all of them . . ." (14:5-9)—and they overtook the Hebrews encamped by the Sea.

At this point, tradition recounts, when panic and the urge to surrender to the Egyptians overcame many of the Israelites, Moses stepped forth and said, "Have no fear! . . . The Lord will battle for you, and you hold your peace!" (14:13-14). The following morning the curtain came down on the final scene of Israel's first great act in the drama of man's attempt to achieve and maintain freedom. A strong east wind backed up the waters of the Sea, "and the Israelites went into the sea on dry land, the waters forming a wall for them on their right and on their left. When the Egyptians came in pursuit after them into the sea . . . The waters turned back and covered the chariots

---

[18] The biblical term *yam suph* has been incorrectly translated "Red Sea." A clear discussion of this, as well as of the route of the Exodus, may be found in G. E. Wright-F. V. Filson, *Westminster Historical Atlas to the Bible* (revised edition, 1956), 38-9; or Wright, *Biblical Archaeology,* 60 ff. [More recently see H. M. Orlinsky, *Notes on the New (J.P.S.) Translation of the Torah,* p. 170 (at Ex. 15.4) with references to other discussions.]

and the horsemen of Pharaoh's entire host that had followed them into the sea; not one of them remained" (vv. 22-28).

The Song of Triumph

Then Moses, assisted by his sister Miriam and the Israelites, sang this song to the Lord (15:1 ff.):

> I will sing to the Lord, for He has triumphed gloriously;
> Horse and driver He has hurled into the sea. . . .
> The deeps covered them;
> They went down into the depths like a stone.
> Your right hand, O Lord, glorious in power,
> Your right hand, O Lord, shatters the foe! . . .
> The foe said,
> "I will pursue, I will overtake,
> I will divide the spoil;
> My desire shall have its fill of them.
> I will bare my sword;
> My hand shall subdue them."
> You made Your wind blow, the sea covered them;
> They sank like lead in the majestic waters.
> Who is like you, O Lord, among the mighty,
> Who is like You, majestic in holiness,
> Awesome in splendor, working wonders! . . .
> The Lord will reign for ever and ever!

Though Moses' song is ancient, it is scarcely his, for only one who had lived in Canaan and knew Canaanite poetic composition—from which ancient Hebrew poesy derived—could have written it. Exactly what transpired at the Red Sea can no longer be determined. We do know that it was invaders from the east Mediterranean, known as Sea Peoples—among whom the Philistines are the best known—who were largely responsible for the collapse of Egypt after about 1200. "The relentless surge of wave after wave of Sea Peoples," it has been noted (Wilson, 245), "shows one great folk-wandering . . . The Sea Peoples alone did not deal the vital blow to Egypt's proud position in the southeastern Mediterranean world, but they were one strong factor among many in sapping Egyptian power and shrivelling Egyptian spirit." One may wonder whether the biblical song of Israel's triumph at the Sea of Reeds, composed after the Philistines had become neighbors of the Israelites in Canaan, does not reflect something of the later battles between the Sea Peoples and the Egyptians.

To biblical Israel the Exodus became the greatest event in her history. If only for his leadership in the Exodus, Moses would have become immortal in Jewish history. The Israelites interpreted this single act as demonstrating that God had chosen them as His own. Time and again in the Bible the Exodus is referred to as the physical proof of God's selection of Israel out of all the peoples of the world. Thus, when the Judeans were in the Babylonian Exile (first half of the sixth century B.C.E.), the Isaiah of the Exile could comfort and urge on his fellow exiles with the argument of God's first Exodus, and the new Exodus soon to transpire (Isaiah 43:18 ff.). So it has been throughout the centuries, in the Diaspora, down to the several exoduses in our own time into the State of Israel from tyrannical countries in Europe, Asia, and Africa.

Passover, Matzot, and the Haggadah

Several later aspects of Israelite life in Canaan came to be associated with the Exodus. Such purely agricultural practices as sacrificing a lamb in the springtime, eating unleavened bread (probably in connection with the barley harvest), and dedicating everything firstborn —practices known in agricultural society from of old—came to be associated with Israel's coming forth from the Egyptian bondage. These nature festivals thus became historical feasts. And in time— especially when the Jewish people found itself exiled by Rome and again in need of an exodus—the Passover feast became the most popular occasion in Jewish religious life.

An essential part of the feast was the retelling (*Seder Haggadah*) of the Exodus and its by-products in accordance, of course, with the biblical account. The haste with which the Israelites had to leave was made responsible for the *matzot:* "And they baked unleavened cakes of the dough that they had taken out of Egypt, for it was not leavened, since they had been driven out of Egypt and could not tarry" (12:39); therefore, "seven days you shall eat unleavened bread (*maṣṣot*) . . . And you shall tell (*we-higgadta;* whence the term *Haggadah*) your son on that day, 'It is because of what the Lord wrought for me when I went free from Egypt' " (13:6-8).[19]

Journey to Sinai

The career of Moses was really hammered out in the generation-long wandering in the wilderness of Sinai. The period of his mature life coincided with the older generation of Israelites that was to die, and with the younger one that was raised in the stimulating but harsh environment of Sinai's rugged terrain. Only the determined and hardy could withstand—and thus in a way thrive on—the many trials. This phase of Israel's history affords an excellent example of challenge and response in man's struggle with his environment.

After traveling three days in the wilderness of Shur, the Israelites were without any water; and when they came to Marah (Hebrew for "bitter"), they found its water bitter. But by casting a log into the water, the Bible asserts, Moses made it sweet. Not long afterwards the Israelites found themselves without food in the midst of the wilderness of Sin, between Elim and Sinai, and they cried out in anguish, "Would that we had died by the hand of the Lord in the land of Egypt, when we sat by the fleshpots, when we ate our fill of bread! For you have brought us out into this wilderness to starve this whole congregation to death" (16:3).

This was the occasion for God to provide the people with "manna": "In the morning there was a fall of dew about the camp; and when the fall of dew lifted, there lay something fine and flaky upon the face of the wilderness, fine as frost upon the ground. The Israelites saw it

---

[19] See, e.g., "Passover," Chapter VII, pp 173-218 in J. H. Greenstone, *Jewish Feasts and Fasts* (Phila., 1945), or H. Schauss (Union of American Hebrew Congregations, 1938), *The Jewish Festivals,* "Pesach," Chapters V-IX, pp. 38-85.

and said to one another, 'What is it?'—for they did not know what it was. And Moses said to them, 'It is the bread which the Lord has given you to eat' . . . The House of Israel named it manna; it was like coriander seed, white, and it tasted like wafers in honey" (16:14-31).

On another occasion, the "rabble" (Hebrew *asafsuf*) urged the Israelites on: "and they said, 'O that we had meat to eat! We remember the fish we ate in Egypt free; the cucumbers, melons, leeks, onions, and garlic. Now our strength is dried up, and we have nothing before us but manna!" (Numbers 11:4-6). In response, the Lord brought on enough quail to keep the people busy capturing them for two days and a night. But when the people began to gorge themselves with quail, the Lord became angry and struck many of them down for their lust (vv. 31-35).

At Kadesh, in the wilderness of Sin, the people were once again overcome by thirst: "This is no place for grain, or figs, or vines, or pomegranates; and there is no water to drink" (Numbers 20:5). Moses struck a rock—though the Lord had instructed him merely to speak to it—and it gave forth water for the people and their cattle.[20]

Here again, what the ancients considered to be God's intervention in their behalf—sometimes by a miraculous act and sometimes by the miraculous timing of an act of nature—the modern scholar would explain more naturally. Quail fly over the vicinity of Sinai in large numbers every fall in their migration from Europe to Africa and Arabia. The limestone rock in Sinai has been known and Moses may have known this from his previous sojourn in Midian—to give forth water when struck, the broken surface exposing the soft and porous rock underneath. And the manna was almost certainly the honey-like substance found on the tamarisk: ". . . manna production is a biological phenomenon of the dry deserts and steppes. The liquid honeydew excretion of a number of cicadas, plant lice, and scale insects speedily solidifies by rapid evaporation. From remote times the

---

[20] Scholars generally agree that the Books of Exodus and Numbers have probably preserved varying versions of the same event. Thus Exodus 16:13 and Numbers 11:31-35 deal with the quail; Exodus 17:1-7 and Numbers 20:1-13 deal with obtaining water from a rock by striking it.

resulting sticky and often times granular masses have been collected and called manna." [21]

The Route of the Wilderness Wandering

To reach the Reed Sea, Moses led his people from Rameses to Succoth, "and they encamped at Etham, at the edge of the wilderness . . . Then the Lord said to Moses, 'Tell the Israelites to turn back and encamp before Pi-hahiroth, between Migdol and the sea, before Baal-zephon; you shall encamp facing it, by the sea' " (Exodus 13:20; 14:1-2).

This part of the Israelite itinerary can now be traced with fair certainty; previously, many thought it scarcely historical. Succoth has been identified with modern Tell el-Maskhutah (excavated since 1883, when numerous inscriptions were found), and Tell Defneh (Greek Daphne) is believed to be the modern site of ancient Baal-zephon. [22]

The route taken to Mt. Sinai, however, is not as certain, and the identification of Mt. Sinai itself is disputed. Tradition has long placed the holy mountain at the southern end of the peninsula of Sinai. Others, however, locate it farther east, across the Gulf of Aqaba, in Midian. Still others place it in the north-central part of Sinai. Had the Israelis been permitted to remain longer in Sinai after their campaign in 1956, a team of scholars might have been able to determine the site of the famed mountain. As of now, there is insufficient reason to give up the traditional location, except that what is conventionally called "Mt. Sinai" may in reality be a range of mountains rather than a single peak.

Moses and Jethro

Even before the great event at Mt. Sinai, Moses was playing something of the role of arbiter and lawmaker. When differences of opinion

---

[21] F. S. Bodenheimer, "The Manna of Sinai," *Biblical Archaeologist,* X (1947), pp. 1-6.

[22] On the route to the Red Sea and Mount Sinai, see Wright-Filson, *Westminster Historical Atlas to the Bible,* pp. 38-9; or Wright, *Biblical Archaeology,* pp. 60 ff.

arose, when disputes and recriminations resulted, even when simple inquiries had to be made, he acted as arbiter. Fortunately for Moses, Jethro, his Midianite father-in-law, came to the camp to see his daughter Zipporah and the grandchildren, and to congratulate Moses and Israel. "Blessed be the Lord," Jethro said, "who delivered you from the Egyptians and from Pharaoh . . . Now I know that the Lord is greater than all gods . . ." (18:10-11).

But when he saw how "Moses sat as magistrate among the people, while the people stood about Moses from morning until evening," Jethro advised his son-in-law as follows: "The thing you are doing is not good: you will surely wear yourself out, both you and this people with you, for the task is too heavy for you; you cannot do it alone. Now listen to me. I will give you counsel—and God be with you! . . . And Moses heeded his father-in-law," we are told, "and did all that he had said. Moses chose capable men out of all Israel, and appointed them heads over the people—chiefs of thousands, hundreds, fifties, and tens. And they exercised authority over the people at all times: the difficult matters they brought to Moses, and all the minor matters they decided themselves" (18:17-26).

There can be little doubt of the essential authenticity of this tradition. It is not likely that anyone would fabricate an Israelite dependence upon anything Midianite—the Midianites later became mortal enemies of Israel—especially one that involved Moses in relation to the administration of law. Then again, there is independent reason for recognizing an early and close relationship between some Midianites and the Israelites, e.g., by way of Hobab the Kenite, of the family of Moses' father-in-law (Numbers 10:29-32; Judges 4:11). Indeed, some scholars believe that the Lord, God of Israel, was originally the God of the Midianites (or Kenites), and that Moses adopted Him as God only after marrying into Jethro's family; this theory, however, is quite hypothetical.

Mt. Sinai: The Covenant

Israel was now ready for the corollary of the Exodus, the solemn establishment of the theocracy at Sinai on the basis of the "Book of the Covenant" (*sefer ha-brit,* Exodus 24:7), which consisted of the

Ten Commandments and a code of laws (chaps. 20-23). The two events together—for Exodus and Sinai are really inseparable—formed the basis of the national covenant (*brit*) between God and Israel, a pact around which the entire Hebrew Bible was to revolve. It is impossible to comprehend the biblical view of Israel's career without recognizing the central role of the covenant; the entire rabbinic view of Judaism derives wholly and directly from it. Indeed, early Christianity found it necessary to alter this covenant between Israel and God by proclaiming a New Covenant (or, Testament) that was to replace the Old, one which Jesus was to mediate and which was to involve all the nations of the world (Matthew 28:18 ff.; Hebrews 8:6 ff.).

The great event at Sinai, befitting its status as The Revelation, is majestically and vividly described in the Bible. It is true that much of the biblical account is the product of a later period; thus many of the laws derive from the experiences of a settled community long occupied in agriculture. On the other hand, since they associated God with awesome aspects of nature, it was natural for Moses and Israel to choose a setting like Sinai, amidst desert thunder and lightning, for the consummation of the act of covenant. Whether the Ten Commandments were introduced by Moses to Israel for the first time at Sinai, or were simply formally confirmed on that occasion—the fact seems to be that Sinai was a real event at Israel's coming into nationhood.

For three days the Israelites purified themselves. On the third day, "Mount Sinai was all smoking, for the Lord had come down upon it in fire . . . and the whole mountain trembled violently. The blare of the horn grew louder and louder. As Moses spoke, God would answer him in thunder . . ." (Ex. 19:18 ff.).

In this setting, "God spoke all these words, saying: 'I the Lord am your God who brought you out of the land of Egypt, the house of bondage. You shall have no other gods beside Me . . .' " (20:1 ff.) Then came the other nine commandments:

You shall not make for yourself a sculptured image . . .
You shall not utter improperly the name of the Lord your God . . .
Remember the Sabbath day and keep it holy . . .

Honor your father and your mother . . .
You shall not murder.
You shall not commit adultery.
You shall not steal.
You shall not bear false witness . . .
You shall not covet . . . anything that is your neighbor's.[23]

Accompanied by thunder and flashes, the blare of the horn and the smoking of the mountain, the people heard these words and agreed solemnly to the conditions of the covenant. The Israelites and their descendants voluntarily bound themselves exclusively to one God, who, in turn, obligated Himself forever to Israel. It was unthinkable that God, the incomparable, would fail to protect a law-abiding Israel and make it prosper; had He not already demonstrated by His acts His interest in Israel? But if Israel failed to heed God's commandments, then He could punish and even destroy her.

Yet over and above the letter of the law, another element was recognized in the covenant, namely, God's love for Israel and His devotion (hesed, traditionally rendered "lovingkindness") to her. It was believed that no matter how grievously Israel sinned and how undeserving she might be of God's protection, God would never cast her off completely. This concept is the core not only of the Written Law (the Bible), but also of the Oral Law (the Talmud, consisting of the Mishnah and the Gemara) and of the liturgy.

The concept of a covenant was not novel. Earlier, each patriarch had entered into a covenant with God. Abraham had entered into a mutually exclusive agreement with "the God of Abraham," whereby Abraham was to recognize and worship no other deity but God, and God was to watch over the welfare of Abraham and his family. When Isaac renewed the pact, God became "the kinsman (pahad) of Isaac." For Jacob, God was "the champion ('abir) of Jacob." [24]

---

[23] This version of the Decalogue is that of Exodus. The Book of Deuteronomy (5:6 ff.) offers a somewhat different version; cf. Driver, *Introduction to the Literature of the Old Testament*, 33-35.

[24] See Orlinsky, *op. cit.*, pp. 27-8.

This concept of covenant between two parties, it is now known, derived from earlier western Asia, where the covenant involved two equal rulers or a powerful ruler and a vassal. As in the case of the patriarchs, and later in the Mosaic period, the two parties of the covenant were bound by an oath, sometimes consisting specifically of blessings and curses; no legal means of enforcement was involved.

Significantly, however, only the patriarchs and their descendants are known to have entered into a covenant with a deity. They alone, it would seem, adopted a single god; but why they should have done so, in the midst of a polytheistic world, has not yet been determined.

In the wilderness, what had been a personal covenant involving God and an individual patriarch became for the first time a national covenant, one that brought together God and an entire people. As a result of the Exodus and Sinai, Israel came into being as a nation covenanted with God. The central figure and mediator in this epochal event was Moses.[25]

The Law

As part of the covenant, Moses proceeded to set before the Israelites some of the laws by which they were to live. Law, from the very outset, has constituted a necessary and useful brake against oppression of the weak on the part of the strong. Indeed, law marks the beginning, and the basis, of the trend toward a democratic society.

Western Asia, and Mesopotamia in particular, was the birthplace of law on earth. Three lawbooks, two written in Sumerian and one in Babylonian, have recently been discovered; preceding by about two to three hundred years Hammurabi's famous Code of about 1700 B.C.E., these are the oldest known lawbooks, and they antedate the earliest known codification of Roman law by more than fifteen hundred years.[26]

---

[25] See G. E. Mendenhall, "Covenant Forms in Israelite Tradition," *Biblical Archaeologist,* XVII (1954), pp. 50-76; Wright, *Biblical Archaeology,* pp. 98-100.
[26] See T. J. Meek, *Hebrew Origins,* Chapter II, "The Origin of the Hebrew Law," pp. 49-81; the chapters by E. A. Speiser and I. Mendelsohn on Meso-

Law in the ancient Near East—Egypt produced no lawbooks because the god-king was himself the source of law and authority[27]—reached its peak in the Bible. The constitution of ancient Israel was frequently called "the Torah of Moses" by the biblical writers. And while scholars today recognize several later strata, post-Mosaic layers of law, in the Torah, Moses came to be acknowledged as Israel's lawgiver, recipient of the Torah directly from God Himself.[28]

The collection of instructions (torot) that Moses is said to have set forth (Exodus 20-23), regulating the social and religious life of the people, was called (24.3,7) "The Book (or: Record, Document, Writ) of the Covenant." A better term could scarcely be found. Biblical law dealt with the individual's relationship to his neighbor—as an individual and as a member of society—and to God; all three parties, the individual, the state, and God, shared importance in the Mosaic code or covenant. Man's life, limbs, cattle, and fields (20:23 ff.) must be guarded and respected, according to the terms of the code, no less than the detail of the Tabernacle (or, Tent of Meeting), the Ark, and the sacrifices (25:1 ff.). Social and religious responsibility were the two complementary aspects of the covenant, a view never lost sight of in biblical tradition. Thus the prophet Isaiah asserted (Isaiah 1:2-4, 10-23) that no matter how many sacrifices and prayers the Israelites offer to the Lord, He will reject them all if the worshipper has failed in the commandments pertaining to man and society.

The Tabernacle and the Ark

Closely connected with the event at Sinai are the Ark and the Tabernacle (Hebrew mishkan). In the former, the acacia chest, Moses is

---

potamia (pp. 8-15) and Canaan-Israel (pp. 25-33) respectively in *Authority and Law in the Ancient Orient (Supplement* to the *Journal of the American Oriental Society,* No. 17, 1954); G. E. Mendenhall, "Ancient Oriental and Biblical Law," *Biblical Archaeologist,* XVII, pp. 26-46; J. B. Pritchard, *The Ancient Near East* (Princeton, 1958), pp. 133-170.

[27] See Wilson's chapter on "Ancient Egypt" in the above cited *Supplement,* pp. 1-7.

[28] All lawbooks in western Asia were said by their compilers or royal patrons to have emanated from the gods and been given to the rulers as a trust to uphold.

said to have placed the two tablets of stone on which the Ten Commandments were recorded; the latter was the movable shrine around which the political and religious life of the wandering Israelites revolved.

There can be little doubt that these institutions are the product of a nomadic or semi-nomadic society, even if later priestly writers embellished the original account considerably. Acacia wood—cedar, cyprus, or olive was later used in Canaan—ramskins, lambskins, cloth of goat's hair, and the like are all manifestations of nomadic existence. Again, while little is really known about many aspects of life among the nomads in antiquity, e.g., the religious—they left virtually no records—we do know that among some nomadic, pre-Mohammedan Arabs portable shrines (sacred tents) were employed.

The Tabernacle was to become later, after the conquest of Canaan, the "Tent of the Lord" at Shiloh, and it was ultimately replaced by the Temple that David planned and Solomon built. In the case of the Ark, Solomon placed it in the Holy of Holies in the Temple, and—except for a single unclear reference during the reign of King Josiah about two hundred years later (II Chronicles 35:3)—was heard of no more. It is clear that the Tent and the Ark were ancient institutions that played a more significant role in the wilderness wandering than they did in conquered Canaan.[29]

Desert Sojourn: Grumblings and Uprisings

Having received the covenant at Sinai, the Israelites were now ready to prepare themselves to enter the Promised Land. But problems still remained. At Rephidim, on the way to Mt. Sinai, the Amalekites, semi-nomadic desert folk, came and fought with Israel. Moses appointed a promising young man, Joshua, to lead a picked group of men in battle. In keeping with the manner in which the Bible interpreted history—combining the miraculous with the natural—Israel was victorious because God came to the aid of Moses, who kept his

---

[29] From Orlinsky, *op. cit.*, p. 38, with reference to F. M. Cross, Jr., "The Tabernacle," in *Biblical Archaeologist*, X (1947), pp. 45-68; Wright, *Biblical Archaeology*, pp. 65-67.

hands erect—with the aid of his brother Aaron and Hur of the tribe of Judah—until the sun set, thus ensuring the defeat of hated Amalek (Exodus 17:8-15).

At Hazeroth (Numbers 12), Miriam criticized her brother for having married an Ethiopian woman. Moses said nothing in defense. "The man Moses," the text reads, "was very humble, more than any other person on earth." But the Lord was vexed by this criticism. He summoned Moses, Aaron, and Miriam, but spoke only to the last two: "My servant Moses is entrusted with all My house. With him I speak mouth to mouth . . . Why then were you not afraid to speak against My servant Moses!" Then the Lord struck Miriam with leprosy, from which she was cured only after Aaron persuaded Moses to appeal to the Lord in her behalf.

This attempt on the part of Aaron and Miriam to reduce the total power and authority of Moses failed. But other revolts broke out against Moses (Numbers 16-17). A Levite named Korah, heading some two hundred and fifty chieftains, not all of them Levites, "assembled against Moses and Aaron and said to them, 'You have assumed too much! For the entire community, every one of them, is holy, and the Lord is in their midst. Why then do you exalt yourselves above the congregation of the Lord?' " (16:1 ff.). In defense, Moses bade them offer fire and incense to the Lord at the sanctuary, "and the man whom the Lord will choose shall be the holy one." As a consequence, "a fire went forth from the Lord and consumed the two hundred and fifty men offering up the incense."

At the same time, Dathan, Abiram, and On, all three of the tribe of Reuben, led another segment of the people in rebellion against Moses: "Is it a small thing that you have brought us up from a land flowing with milk and honey, to kill us in the wilderness, that you must also make yourself a ruler over us . . . ?" (vv. 13-14). Unlike the ecclesiastical revolt of Korah and his group, this was a rebellion of laymen against the civil authority which Moses claimed. Their punishment and end were dreadful.

The climax of the revolt and its collapse came the next day. "The entire Israelite community murmured aginst Moses and Aaron, saying,

'You have killed the people of the Lord!' " (17:6 ff.) The Lord then took matters into His own hands. He caused a plague to break out among the people, killing many of them (14,700 according to v. 14). Had not Moses intervened hastily, with an atonement offering of incense, the biblical text asserts, the people would have perished to the last man.

That many elements among the people at one time or another opposed Moses is certain; it is hardly likely that anyone gratuitously created in a later period such hostile sentiment against Israel's outstanding Founding Father. But what can never be clear is to what extent the opposition to Moses was justified under the circumstances. Later writers naturally tended to put Moses in the right, and use the divine acts as evidence against the guilty ones. If some of Moses' critics had actually been the victims of an epidemic, an earthquake, a fire, or a skin disease at about the time that they voiced their discontent, these occurrences were readily interpreted as indications and proof of God's view. It is more likely, however, that the biblical pattern of history-writing, in defending Moses, simply made use here of well-known natural phenomena.

Death in the Wilderness:
Punishment for Disobedience and Lack of Confidence

In the second year of the Exodus, Moses took the first positive action in regard to the conquest of Canaan by sending spies from the wilderness of Paran to the Promised Land (Numbers 13-14). "See what kind of country it is," they were instructed by Moses, "whether the kind of people that dwells in it is strong or weak, few or numerous; whether the cities are open or fortified."

The report that the majority of the spies brought back was far from favorable. True, the land "flows with milk and honey," they said, "but the people that inhabits the land is powerful, and the cities are fortified mightily . . . It is a land that devours its inhabitants . . ." And a final touch: we saw such giants there that we appeared in their eyes like grasshoppers.

Caleb, son of Jephunneh, however, supported by Joshua, son of Nun, gave a dissenting report. "If the Lord delights in us," they exhorted the people, "He will bring us into this land . . . Only do not rebel against the Lord, and do not fear the people of the land . . . The Lord is with us, do not fear them!" Caleb and Joshua were about to be stoned by the people when the Lord intervened (14:6-10).

To what extent this story is true cannot be determined.[30] But it was made, or, as some scholars would say, created to serve as the reason that so few of the erstwhile slaves in Egypt lived long enough to enter Canaan. The assumption is that had the people rejected the pessimistic view of the majority of the spies in favor of the confident outlook of the minority, relying utterly upon the power and protection of God, they would shortly have marched into Canaan and conquered it. Instead, God decided, except for such as Caleb and Joshua, only the children would live to reach Canaan; all the older folk, those who had been twenty years and over when the first census was taken, were going to die in the wilderness. Hence the forty years of wandering.[31]

If the facts preserved in the Bible are essentially true, then one may posit simply that the forty years—which is sometimes only a round number used in the Bible to indicate a generation—of wandering were made necessary by the urgent need to train and discipline the horde of slaves for the conquest of Canaan. Disaster clearly stared them in the face were an all-out invasion of the land undertaken prematurely.

Moses, too, and Aaron did not enter the Promised Land. The Bible gives two reasons, both in keeping with its religious interpretation of history: they, too, like the people, were disobedient and lacked confidence in God. In the older version (Deuteronomy 1:37),[32] Moses was excluded from Canaan along with the people because of their

---

[30] It has long been recognized that the biblical text is made up of two versions of the story, and the older one did not include Joshua at all (see Driver, *Introduction*, 62-3).

[31] A few scholars would reduce the total period of wandering to but a few years: cf., e.g., H. H. Rowley, *From Joseph to Joshua* (Oxford University Press, 1950); nowhere else will so full a bibliography on the subject be found.

[32] See Driver, *International Critical Commentary on Deuteronomy* (1896), pp. 26-28.

reaction to the pessimistic report of the spies (Numbers 13:20). According to the later version, when the people were overcome by thirst at Kadesh, in the thirty-seventh year of the Exodus, God had ordered Moses to take his staff, assemble the people, and "tell the rock before their eyes to yield its water" (Numbers 20:1-13). Instead, Moses used the staff to strike the rock. Whereupon the Lord told Moses and Aaron, "Because you did not believe in Me, by sanctifying Me in the eyes of the Israelites, therefore you shall not bring this congregation into the land that I give them." Why Moses is said to have struck the rock, instead of speaking to it as commanded, is for the folklorist to interpret; but if he had spoken to the rock, then the biblical writer would have had to look for another explanation.

Shortly afterwards Aaron died, on the top of Mt. Hor, on the border of Edom.

On the Eve of the Conquest of Canaan: Moses' Death

The people were now approaching inhabited territory. They had reached the land of Edom. Moses sent messengers to Edom's king for permission to go through his land. "We will not pass through field or vineyard," they assured the Edomite government (20:14 ff.), "neither will we drink water from a well . . ." But the king refused permission, and the Israelites had, once again, to take a roundabout route.

Farther north, in Transjordan, the people approached the territory of Moab, then dominated by the Amorites under King Sihon, who also refused to grant transit permission. Instead, Sihon attacked Israel; for his pains he and his forces were defeated, and the territory was occupied by the victors (21:21-32). North of Moab, in the territory of Bashan, King Og, too, attacked Israel and was vanquished.

At long last the Israelites found themselves at the border of Canaan (22:1). And Moses had now reached the point of neither return nor advance. His mission was accomplished. He had played the central role in effecting the Exodus from Egypt, in achieving the crossing of the wilderness in the peninsula of Sinai, and in preparing the Israelites, as a more-or-less united group bound by a national covenant to a single deity, for the conquest of Canaan. Even the vexing problem of successorship had been solved; no opposition seems to have arisen—among a people that was given so frequently to opposition—to Moses' selection of Joshua of the tribe of Ephraim as his successor.

After attributing to Moses a long review of his career just ended and a preview of his people's career about to begin (chapters 1-32), culminating in his famous blessing (33), the Book of Deuteronomy (chapter 34) tells us that "Moses went up from the steppes of Moab to Mount Nebo, the top of Pisgah, which is opposite Jericho," from which the Lord showed him Israel's land. After which "Moses the servant of the Lord died there in the land of Moab. And He buried him (or he was buried) in the valley of Moab opposite Beth-peor; but no man knows the site of his grave to this day. Moses was 120 years old when he died; his eyes were not dim, nor his natural force abated."

Jewish sources have embellished the story of Moses' death. Early legends differed as to whether Moses had experienced an unusual manner of dying or had simply not died at all. From the biblical text itself it is not clear whether God or someone else buried Moses. The Septuagint (Old Greek) translation reads "they buried him." Philo, the Alexandrian Jewish philosopher of the first century, in his essay on "The Life of Moses," wrote: "He was entombed not by mortal hands, but by immortal powers . . ." And Josephus, the Jewish historian and Philo's younger contemporary in Judea, asserted: "While, after having taken leave of the people, he was going to embrace Eleazar and Joshua on Mount Nebo, a cloud suddenly stood over him, and he disappeared, though he wrote in Scripture that he died, which was done from fear that people might say that because of his extraordinary virtue he had been turned into a divinity."

The Man and His Legacy

For the modern Jew, who may or may not accept the legends that have sprung up around Moses,[33] the patriarch remains the prime mover in the actions and decisions that led to the founding of Israel

---

[33] No biblical character has been able to compete with Moses in sheer quantity of legend in post-biblical times. In Louis Ginzberg's monumental collection of

as a nation. Even if it is not possible to delimit precisely his role, he alone was the leading personality and subjective factor among the objective conditions that made possible the Exodus from Egypt. In the wilderness of Sinai, not in Egypt, Israel was forged, hammered into the shape of nationhood amid appalling hardship. The weak and the weary perished, leaving the young and strong to drift yet another mile toward the Land of Promise, the ancestral home.

The struggle for power within the group that Moses led from Egypt was violent. Every faction in this group, religious and civil, including members of his own family, challenged the authority and wisdom of Moses. Only a man of iron will, patience, compassion for his people, and—above all—unlimited faith in his goal could have endured this endless bickering, scheming, and backsliding.

Moses comes through this struggle as a very human personality, revealing both positive and negative qualities. Several independent incidents would indicate that Moses had quite a temper. His act of beating an Egyptian to death for striking down a Hebrew is a case in point. When Dathan and Abiram accused Moses of authoritarianism, "Moses became incensed and he said to the Lord, 'Do not favor their offering! I have not taken a single ass from them, neither have I harmed a single one of them' " (Numbers 16:15). On several occasions he is also said to have betrayed indecision. At the "Red" Sea, with Pharaoh's superior forces approaching, the Israelites cried out to the Lord. "But the Lord said to Moses, 'Why do you cry out to me? Tell the Israelites to go forward . . . !' " (Exodus 14:15 ff.). At Marah, too (15:22-25), and at Rephidim (17:1), when the people thirsted for water, Moses "cried out to the Lord."

It was indeed a difficult struggle, and about a generation—the traditional "forty years" of wandering—had to elapse before Moses could weld the heterogeneous, inexperienced, and uncultured mass together into something of a unified force and social group.

Besides founding the nation, Moses taught the concept of mono-

---

The Legends of the Jews, the material on Moses fills more than one-third of the pages (611 out of 1728). Moses also played a prominent role in Christian and Muslim literature. [And see now J. C. Gager, *Moses in Greco-Roman Paganism,* SBL Monograph Series 16 (1972).]

theism to his people. It used to be generally thought in scholarly circles, as has already been pointed out, that monotheism did not come to Israel until the period of the prophets (eighth century), and that Israel had little substantial origin or existence during the second millennium B.C.E. The patriarchs were frequently regarded as the figment of a much later writer's imagination. And those who credited them with something of an existence usually attributed to them the beliefs and practices of polytheism. Thanks to archaeology, few scholars today would deny at least some historicity to the patriarchs; even fewer would refuse to grant some substance to the career of Israel in Egypt and to Moses.

There can now be little doubt that the patriarchs recognized the concept of covenant, each patriarch making his pact with God. It was under Moses that the covenant was made between a total nation and God.

This concept and act of covenant involving Israel and the Deity was an integral part of a second concept, that of monotheism. It is impossible to postulate the covenant between the two without belief in the One. The biblical tradition is clear and consistent that Moses was the individual most responsible for emphasizing and cementing Israel's alliance with God. This is precisely what the very first of the Ten Commandments asserts: "I the Lord am your God who brought you out of the land of Egypt, the house of bondage. You shall have no other gods beside Me . . .!"

It has long been recognized that Moses is not the author of the Torah. This is a far cry, however, from denying to Moses all responsibility for helping lay the basis of Israel's legal system.

Judaism came to recognize the Talmud, the Oral Law, as no less authoritative than the Written Law, from which it derived. And just as Moses was credited with receiving the Written Law from God on Sinai, so did he become the ultimate authority also of the Unwritten Law.

Thus, Moses, the lawgiver, was the midwife of the Israelite nation. In the extraordinary career of Jews and Judaism, his figure and personality stand out as brilliantly today as it did some thirty-two and a half centuries ago.

FOR FURTHER READING

There is no single work on Moses that is satisfactory; and unless—most unlikely—new materials of some substance come to light, none need be expected. The full-length biographies are essentially fiction. Of the shorter essays, the best are by James and Kittel, listed below.

[Much new data and analysis have appeared since this essay was written about fifteen years ago. The background of the Mosaic period is clearer and fuller than it had been, and the internal history of the Hebrews-Israelites in the period of the Patriarchs and Judges is better known. Withal, the strong reservations expressed here remain valid.

B. Mazar has edited the volumes *Patriarchs* (1970) and *Judges* (1971) in the series, *The World History of the Jewish People,* and the interested reader will find there more detailed discussion of a number of items dealt with in my essay. In *Patriarchs* may be noted, e.g., H. Tadmor, "Chronology of the Ancient Near East in the Second Millennium B.C.E." (pp. 63-101); B. Mazar, "Canaan in the Patriarchal Age" (169-180); M. Greenberg, "Hab/piru and Hebrews" (188-200); S. Yeivin, "The Patriarchs in the Land of Canaan" (201-218); and M. Haran, "The Religion of the Patriarchs: Beliefs and Practices" (219-245). In *Judges:* B. Mazar, "The Historical Development" (pp. 3-22); A. Malamat, "The Egyptian Decline in Canaan and the Sea-Peoples" (23-38); I. Mendelsohn, "Cultural and Religious Life" (39-51); and the chapters by B. Mazar, Y. Aharoni, and A. Malamat in Part II: Beginning of the Nation (pp. 69-179), to which may be added the chapter on "Law" by S. E. Loewenstamm (231-267). Most of these chapters are referred to, in their proper place, in my *Understanding the Bible,* etc., cited below.]

The Holy Scriptures (Jewish Publication Society, Philadelphia, 1917), pending the completion of the new translation [*The Torah,* 2nd ed. 1967; *The Five Megilloth and Jonah,* 1969; *Isaiah,* 1972-73; *Psalms,* 1972-73]; or *The Holy Bible: Revised Standard Version of the Old Testament* (Nelson & Sons, New York, 1952).

JAMES, FLEMING, *Personalities of the Old Testament* (Scribner's, New York, 1939), pp. 1-44.

KITTEL, RUDOLF, *Great Men and Movements in Israel* (Macmillan, New York, 1929), pp. 19-43. [Reissued by KTAV, 1971, with Prolegomenon by T. H. Gaster.]

ORLINSKY, HARRY M., *Ancient Israel* (Cornell University Press, Ithaca, N.Y., 1954). [See now the considerably enriched version, *Understanding the Bible through History and Archaeology* (KTAV, 1972.]

3

The Seer-Priest and the Prophet in Ancient Israel

A. DIVINATION AS A CRAFT IN THE ANCIENT EAST

DURING THE FIRST THOUSAND YEARS of its diversified and exciting career, covering the period of the Patriarchs, of the Eisodus and the Exodus, of the Judges, and of the United Kingdom, ancient Israel shared—more than it did during the several centuries of relative sovereignty that followed—many social, economic, religious, legal, and cultural features with the various peoples with whom it came into contact. It was really not until Israel had experienced a national life of its own for a few hundred years, from about 1100 to after 900 B.C.E., that its own genius came to express itself in these several phases of national activity.

An excellent case in point—indeed, it would be difficult to find a better one—is the common Egypto-Asiatic phenomenon of divination and how, in Israel alone, it came not to develop into, but to be opposed and largely replaced by, prophecy.

[Parts of this essay have been dealt with at greater length in my article "The Seer in Ancient Israel," *Oriens Antiquus,* 4 (1965), 153-74. This essay constitutes Chapter XII in *The World History of the Jewish People,* Vol. III, ed. B. Mazar, *Judges* (1971).]

39

All peoples in the ancient Near East practiced divination. How else could they stand up before the whim of the gods who controlled their destiny? The forces of nature, on which their very existence depended, and which they but ill understood, had to be brought under some kind of control; at least the attempt had to be made—and when unsuccessful had to be made again and again—to limit and perhaps even bend the otherwise unlimited will of the divine beings. The past had to be studied for the benefit of the present, and the future had to be foreknown and if possible even predetermined. J. A. Wilson's clear statement on Egypt holds true for the Near East generally: "Magic had always been an element of Egyptian life. Amulets are known from the earliest periods, and the Pyramid Texts are full of promotive or protective charms. This later period [ca. 1325-1100 B.C.E.], however, showed an increased reliance upon various magical techniques and powers. Insecurity brought a longing for greater protection through some kind of external potency. Men turned to magic scrolls and images of prophylactic power; they went through elaborate rituals when they recited charms. They tried to counteract the new fatalistic cast of life by summoning the gods for magical support. Man was no longer strong enough in himself."[1]

Divination took on many forms. It was a complex business. The beliefs and practices associated with the profession were so varied and intricate that one who wished to put them to successful use had to devote himself to studying them and working at them; there were, further, trade secrets and vested interests to be protected. And thus there arose throughout the ancient world guilds of diviners, after the pattern of guilds generally, with set rules governing masters and apprentices in divination as surely as if they were stonemasons or smiths. The novitiate in divination, like the worker in textiles or metals, had to spend many years of hard and closely supervised work in learning his trade. He had to memorize incantations of all sorts. He had to learn to interpret the flight of birds, the formation of livers (hepato-

---

[1] J. A. Wilson, *The Burden of Egypt* (Chicago, 1951), p. 243 (subsequently published as a Phoenix Paperback under the title *The Culture of Egypt*).

scopy) and entrails (extispicy), the lay assumed by sticks of wood, arrows, or stones cast out of a container, the casting of lots, the formation and direction of smoke (incense) emanating from a container (libanomancy) or of oil in a special cup or other vessel of water (lecanomancy), the significance of dreams and signs in general, the relative position and other aspects of the heavenly bodies (astrology); and the like. [2]

B. The Biblical Terms for Seer-Priest and Prophet

Ancient Israel, too, recognized the diviner in its midst. The Bible has preserved a number of references to the "visionary" (*hozeh*), "seer" (*ro'eh*), "man of God" (*ish [ha-] Elohim*), and "prophet" (*navi*). All four expressions, as technical terms, were employed by the diviner in the earlier period, before Hosea, Amos, Isaiah, and Micah of the 8th century appeared on the scene; but only the last-mentioned, the term *navi*, came to be used as a technical term for the exponents of classical prophecy. (See Excursus I, below, on the terminology for the biblical "seer-priest.")

Let it be stated at once what significant elements the seer-priest— for which the shorter term "seer" will usually be employed here [3]—

---

[2] There is a very considerable bibliography on our subject generally for the ancient Near East; but it is important to warn the reader that there is an urgent need of a detailed comparative account and analysis of the many forms of divination as they were practiced — or if they were not, why not — in Sumer, Babylonia, Assyria, the territory of the Hittites, Canaan, etc. Thus A. L. Oppenheim, *Ancient Mesopotamia: Portrait of a Dead Civilization* (Chicago, 1964), while noting that "the royal art of astrology is the method of divination for which Mesopotamia is famed," has observed that "study of the rise of astrology in Mesopotamian civilization has hardly begun" (p. 224). For literature on the subject, see the bibliography at the end of this essay.

[3] The term "seer-priest" is employed in this essay as a general expression covering the four terms used in the Bible for those endowed with uncommon powers in the earlier, pre-prophetic period: visionary, seer, man of God, prophet. The expression "diviner" would have been better, except that this term would recall — unnecessarily and misleadingly — too many of the practices of the ancient Near Eastern diviner (the Canaanite not least among them) to which the Israelite seer did not resort (see Excursus II, below); such terms as "diviner-priest" and "oracle-priest," though accurate, are perhaps somewhat clumsy for regular usage.

and the canonical prophet shared, and in what essentials they differed. Both the seer and the prophet experienced the phenomenon of ecstasy; they differed only in that the former practiced several recognized techniques to induce it that the latter did not. Unlike the prophet, the seer employed music, dance, and group participation to work himself up into a state of ecstasy, even frenzy.[4] Thus Asaph, Heman, and Jeduthun are said to be "visionaries" and also members of the musical guild under King David [5] (cf., for example, I Chron. 25:1 ff., where we are told of "the sons of Asaph, Heman, and Jeduthun, who were to prophesy with lyres, harps, and cymbals"; I Sam. 10:5 ff. mentions "a band of prophets" whom Saul would meet as they were "coming down from the sanctuary, led by harp, tambourine, flute, and lyre as they were prophesying"). The prophets of the Lord who gave advice to the kings of Israel and Judah—advice which the prophet Micaiah son of Imlah flatly contradicted—acted very little differently from the prophets of Baal (I Kings 22:9 ff.; 18:26 ff.); Elisha asked for a musician *(m^enaggen)* so that "the hand of the Lord" might descend upon him (II Kings 3:15), that is, that he might achieve ecstasy, and thereby God's message. In general, both the seer-priest and the prophet received directives from God in much the same way, through dreams, objects, and sounds.

Again—and this must not be overlooked—members of both categories spoke in the name of the same single God and practiced that

---

[4] It is unfortunate that scholars have permitted themselves to be misled by and to place such great emphasis upon the element of ecstasy. This was true even before — as well as in consequence of — the appearance of G. Hölscher, *Die Profeten* (Leipzig, 1914), chaps. I-III, as though ecstasy, or a special, frenzied brand of it, marked an essential difference between seer and prophet, or as though it was a special type of ecstasy that rendered the biblical prophet *sui generis* in all history. Thus J. Lindblom's *Prophecy in Ancient Israel* (Oxford, 1962), would have been a better work had it not been burdened with the "Supernormal Experiences" in chaps. I-III. Cf. the survey by H. H. Rowley, *The Servant of the Lord and other Essays on the Old Testament* (London, 1952), chap. III, pp. 91 ff., and *passim*: "The Nature of Old Testament Prophecy in the Light of Recent Study." The chapter appeared originally in *HTR*, 38 (1945), 1-38. See also on Wen-Amon, below (Section G, end).

[5] See W. F. Albright, *Archaeology and the Religion of Israel* (Baltimore, 1942), pp. 125-9.

same monotheism. That the Hebrew seer worked at what was a common craft in antiquity, whereas the prophet was uniquely a Hebraic product, should not obscure this important fact. Both groups in Israel declared themselves proponents of God's word; both asserted, and were much concerned to make the general population believe, that they received authority from God. When seer-priests differed with one another, or when the classical prophets denounced and scorned the seer-priests, or when the classical prophets differed among themselves (so that some prophets were denounced as "false prophets," to whom God had not really spoken), the basic causes of these differences derived from group interests which the seer-priest or prophet in question championed; the fact that the expressions and formulas employed in the sundry denunciations were couched in theological-covenant terms (how else could they then have been?)—so that the one who was criticized was accused of one kind or another of idolatry and covenant-breaking—should not blind the historian to the basic social-political-economic factors involved.

Finally, it is quite likely that already in the period of the Judges, as elsewhere in the Near East at the time, scribal activity was associated with the seer-priesthood and the shrines. Some half-dozen seers are specifically credited with having written royal chronicles: Samuel, Nathan, Iddo, Gad, Ahijah, and Shemaiah recorded something of the reigns of David (presumably something also of his predecessor, Saul), Solomon, Rehoboam, his son Abijah, and Jeroboam (I Chron. 29:29; II Chron. 9:29; 12:15; 13:22). However, as the seer-priesthood became increasingly a function of the royal court after the monarchical institution in Israel was firmly established, so did the scribe become independent of the seer-priesthood and a distinct functionary in the royal service; but at the numerous sanctuaries (bamot) in the land, the local seer-priest continued scribal activity for his clients round about.

C. THE DIFFERENCE BETWEEN THE SEER-PRIEST AND THE PROPHET

It is the points of difference, however, that stand out between the seer and the prophet. In the first place, the seer was usually a member of a guild or group, and he learned the craft from a master; the seer,

furthermore, was associated with a sanctuary. Thus Samuel was
trained under Eli the priest at Shiloh; the "band of prophets" to which
Saul attached himself was associated with a sanctuary (*bamah:* I Sam.
10:5); and Elisha was trained by Elijah (I Kings 19:21—"and he
became his *m^esharet.*" And see below, on the guilds). The prophet, on
the other hand, was individualistic[6]; there is no record of a prophet
having learned prophecy in association with or under another prophet,
or of having acquired his calling by enrolling in a guild of prophets.[7]
Indeed, there is reason to believe that membership in guilds of seer-
priests, as in guilds generally, was sometimes hereditary; thus Micah
(Micaiah) ordained one of his own sons to serve as seer-priest in his
"house of God" (Jud. 17:5), and Jehu the "visionary" was the son of
Hanani the "seer" (II Chron. 16:7-10; 19:2; I Kings 16:1, 7).[8] This
was so, because the craft of the father, providing as it did a ready
source of income and prestige, frequently attracted the son, whereas
the prophet, making a living from another source, was drawn into his
calling directly and (though only seemingly) against his will.

In his craft, moreover, involving individual Israelites and God, the
seer was the person to whom the people came for advice, to help them
in problems that a mere, untrained mortal, without special access to

---

[6] The "prophets" in A. R. Johnson, *The Cultic Prophet in Ancient Israel* (Cardiff,
1944), pp. 59 ff., are really "seers." It would seem that Lindblom, *op. cit.,* would
have been much clearer and more useful had he used the term "seer" (or diviner)
and "prophet" with greater discrimination. On W. F. Albright, *Samuel and the
Beginnings of the Prophetic Movement* (Cincinnati, 1961), see my comments on
pp. 93-4 of the chapter on "Old Testament Studies" in *Religion,* ed. by P. Ramsey
(Englewood Cliffs, N. J., 1965); M. A. Cohen, "The Role of the Shilonite Priesthood in the United Monarchy of Ancient Israel," *HUCA,* 36 (1965), 65 ff., and
notes 20-1.

[7] On *limmudai* "disciples" in Isa. 8:16, see Orlinsky, "The Seer in Ancient Israel,"
p. 156 note 7.

[8] Cf. A. Haldar, *Associations of Cult Prophets among the ancient Semites*
(Uppsala, 1945), pp. 34 ff.; I. Mendelsohn, "Guilds in Ancient Palestine," *BASOR,*
80 (1940), 17-21 (especially note 29); *idem,* "Gilds in Babylonia and Assyria,"
JAOS, 60 (1940), 68-72. Oded, the father of Azariah the prophet, who is mentioned in II Chron. 15:1 ff., may himself also have been a prophet; unfortunately,
verse 8 is corrupt at this point. The only other person in the Bible with the name
Oded is likewise a prophet (of Samaria) in the days of Pekah (II Chron. 28:9).

God, could not solve. For these services the seer was paid. One cannot imagine an Amos or Jeremiah or Deutero-Isaiah being approached thus and making a living in this manner. (See Excursus II, below, on the seer and divination.)

Again, fundamentally the Israelite seer predicted the future and attempted to control it. He performed miracles. The prophet, however, unreservedly opposed divination and miracle-making in every form. [9] He did not know the future; he did not predict it or try to control it. [10] He knew that Israel's transgression of its covenant with God called for punishment; but also that this punishment, in all or in part, could be prevented or mitigated not by magic or incantation—any more than by formal, insincere sacrifice and prayer—but by a heartfelt return to God. [11] Another and historically more correct and intelligible way of putting it would be: the prophet, claiming to speak directly and exclusively for Israel's God, warned those in power, both within and outside the government proper, that unless they acted politically and

---

[9] It is thus clear that Jesus as a miracle-worker is not to be associated with the classical prophets. In general, there was a resurgence in the belief and practice of magic and miracle-working, as well as the rise of an elaborate angelology, in the latter part of the Second Jewish Commonwealth (cf., for example, the Book of Daniel; the Apocryphal literature). This was due chiefly not to the influence of any holdover from the ancient, pre-prophetic past but to that of the new Persian-Hellenistic culture all about Judea; however, this is outside our present period of study.

[10] For some passages that would seem to indicate the contrary (Isa. 23:15-17; Jer. 25:11-12; 29:10), see Orlinsky, "The Seer in Ancient Israel," p. 156, note 10. Such passages (on Isa. 7:8, see, for example, Lindblom, *op. cit.*, p. 290, and note 116), where they are not *ex eventu,* are merely generalizations.

[11] M. Jastrow, Jr. put it very well in "Rô'ēh and Ḥôzēh in the Old Testament," *JBL,* 28 (1909), 56: "His [that is, the prophet's] main purpose is to speak out in the name of a Deity, to speak forth rather than to foretell. It is therefore a mistaken view of the later tradition which regarded the *rô'eh* as the prototype of the *nabî'.* The *rô'eh* is a diviner as is the *hôzeh* . . ." In time a number of scholars, such as R. H. Charles, *A Critical and Exegetical Commentary on the Book of Daniel,* Oxford, 1929, will call the diviner a "foreteller" and the prophet a "forthteller." It might also be said that the prophet represented a high-cultural tradition, as against the low-cultural tradition represented by the seer-priest (oral communication from M. A. Cohen).

socially in accordance with his proposals they would suffer defeat and even destruction.

In this difference between them, the seer was basically a man of action, the prophet a man of words. The former, a craftsman, did things: he offered sacrifices, he interpreted dreams, he predicted events, he performed miracles, and sometimes he was in charge of a shrine and of apprentices. The prophet on the other hand opposed everything that smacked of the seer as a craftsman. To have his way with his fellow Israelites, the prophet had to resort to another method. That method was argument, reasoning, exhortation—in short, words. And what the prophet did with words, and with the older concepts of monotheism, covenant, justice, and the like—the writings of the prophets from first to last bear the most eloquent testimony to their universal and lasting influence in the realm of religion, literature, law, and ethics. But this theme cannot be pursued here. [12]

D. THE SEER-PRIEST IN ANCIENT ISRAEL

It has scarcely been recognized that the diviner and the priest were one and the same in early Israel, as elsewhere in the Near East. Thus already Jastrow [13] recognized Samuel as "a priest and a diviner," and noted in that connection the role of the *bārû,* the Babylonian divining priest. An excellent example of this is provided by the account (widely accepted as old and authentic) preserved in Jud. 17-18. There we are told that a certain Micah (Micaiah) of the hill country of Ephriam owned "a house of God," that is, a local sanctuary, along with the appropriate equipment: a sculptured image, a molten image, an ephod, and household gods *(terafim);* and he ordained one of his sons to serve as priest (Jud. 17:4-5). Subsequently, an itinerant levite (that is,

---

[12] On the seer's intervention in the affairs of non-Israelites on foreign soil (for example, Elijah, Elisha) — an activity unknown to the prophet — see Orlinsky, "The Seer in Ancient Israel," pp. 159-60 and notes 16-18 (the last with reference to Jonah).

[13] Jastrow, "Rô'ēh and Hôzēh in the Old Testament," *loc. cit.,* 43 ff.

one who was associated with the craft of divination-priesthood),[14] who had left his home in Bethlehem of Judah to go seeking more attractive employment (verse 8), happened across Micah's shrine. When Micah learned that the traveler was a levite looking for work, he at once offered him the post of priest in his shrine (verse 10)[15]; for unlike the son who had been ordained *ad hoc* for the post, the levite was a professional diviner-priest.[16] The offer provided ten pieces of silver, the necessary garments, and food and lodging; and the levite accepted it. Micah then ordained the levite as his diviner-priest (verses 10-13).

Some time later, a group of Danites, in search of a homestead for their clan, also found itself at the house of Micah, and they recognized the levite by the sound of his voice (Jud. 18:3); apparently he had at

---

[14] Note that the term "levi(te)" has nothing to do here with the tribe "Levi" that allegedly existed along with eleven other tribes from the time that the Israelites settled in Canaan — "allegedly" because throughout the account in Jud. 17-18 the term "levi(te)" breathes no hint of anything tribal. The opposite is the effect one gets; cf., for example, Jud. 17:7, 10: "There was a young man from Bethlehem of Judah, from the clan seat of Judah; he was a levite and had lived there as a sojourner". . . . "I am a levite [not Levite!] from Bethlehem of Judah." It will be noted that Judah, too, does not constitute a tribe in these chapters, but rather a geographical designation. See Cohen's acute analysis of "The Role of the Shilonite Priesthood," *loc. cit.,* 59 ff. — one of the exceedingly few that comprehends the social forces that shaped Israel's early history — as well as his "Excursus on the Origin of the Tribe of Judah," *HUCA,* 36 (1965), 94-8.

Neither do the Danites constitute a tribe in Jud. 18; they are a petty clan of sorts. It is a pity that Israel's history in the period of the Judges has been terribly distorted by scholars who have uncritically accepted the later biblical statement that Israel then consisted of twelve tribes and who have even created for the non-existing twelve tribes an amphictyonic society; cf. H. M. Orlinsky, "The Tribal System of Israel and Related Groups in the Period of the Judges," *Oriens Antiquus,* 1 (1962), 11-20 (= *Studies and Essays in Honor of Abraham A. Neuman* [Philadelphia, 1962], pp. 375-87). [This essay follows immediately in this volume.]

[15] The text (Jud. 17:10) reads: "And Micah said to him, 'Stay with me, and be a father and priest to me.'" Whether the term *'ab* "father" is to be understood here honorifically, or as a formula of adoption, or as a corruption of an original *'ob,* a diviner of sorts, is immaterial for our purpose; verse 11 favors the first (and commonly accepted) interpretation: "So the levite agreed to stay with the man; and the young man became to him like one of his own sons."

[16] Cf. Jud. 17:13, "Then Micah said, 'Now I know that the Lord will make me prosperous, for the levite has become my priest.'"

one time worked also in their territory, being a poor itinerant diviner-priest. When they asked him what he was doing in Micah's house, he told them the circumstances under which Micah had hired him to be his priest (verse 4), whereupon they asked him to divine for them whether their mission would be successful or not. "And the priest said to them, 'Go in peace; the Lord looks with favor on the mission on which you are going' " (verses 5-6).[17] For the priest was a diviner and the diviner was a priest.

Let us go back to Samuel for a moment. It is true that Eli, the mentor of Samuel, is referred to only as a "priest," whereas Samuel is specifically designated "seer," "man of God," and "prophet"; but this should not obscure the basic fact that their functions were essentially identical, that Samuel the apprentice was simply following in the footsteps of Eli his master, and that, like him, he is also said to have "judged" *(shafaṭ)* Israel. Observe also that just as Eli's two sons, Hophni and Phinehas, were "priests" under their father at Shiloh (I Sam. 1:3; 2:11-17), just so was Samuel "girded with a linen ephod" (I Sam. 2:18); and he officiated at sacrifices (I Sam. 9:9 ff.; 16:5). As a matter of fact, however, a closer look at I Sam. 2:13, 35 indicates at once that the term "priest" *(kohen),* too, was applied to Samuel; for verse 13 describes the duties of the priest's assistant *(na'ar ha-kohen),* referring back to Samuel the assistant *(na'ar)* of Eli the priest in verse 11, and a priest is what Samuel would become when he grew up and succeeded Eli. This is precisely what verse 35 explicitly says in the name of God: "I will raise up for Myself a faithful priest," in place of Eli's two sons, to succeed Eli. The main difference between Eli and Samuel was that the latter was a much more powerful seer-priest than the former, and helped to raise the shrine at Shiloh to a level of authority it had not previously enjoyed in Israel. M. A. Cohen has put it well: "Samuel's importance derived not from his role as *shofeṭ* or military leader or from his role as a prophet, but from his actual position as the Shilonite seer-priest."[18]

---

[17] It may be noted that if any sacrifice was involved here, it was of too little significance to the biblical writer to merit attention.

[18] Cohen, "The Role of the Shilonite Priesthood," *loc. cit.,* 65.

Campus Crusade for Christ Library

That it has become necessary for the modern scholar to prove that Samuel, like Eli and others, was a priest as well as a seer is due to the fact that the old institution of seer-priesthood ceased to be correctly comprehended after the priestly group acquired power in postexilic Judah and supplied the literary framework in which the older materials (J, E, D, and the older parts of P) were brought together in their preserved form. Naturally, the hierocratically minded editors furnished the kind of data that gave their group antiquity, continuity, and authority; also, the "priest" element in the seer-priest of old became extremely blurred; and finally, the relationship between a "levite" and a "priest" was distorted beyond recognition, and the two were turned into members of an allegedly original tribe by the name of Levi. Hence one of the more important and urgent tasks in biblical research today —no less than in the pre-archeology days of the 19th century—is the attempt to reconstruct historically the growth of the P document and the role of the priest in ancient Israel, from the period of the Judges to the rise of the theocratic-hierocratic state of Judah in the 6th century B.C.E. [19]

That the seer and the priest in ancient Israel were really one should occasion no surprise; it would be surprising if they were not. For in the ancient Near East they were one, as the Semitist has long recognized. There, too, the priesthood was an organized guild of craftsmen, and there, too, the temples and shrines played central roles in the economy, politics, and culture of the country. The various categories and strata of the priesthood had their specific functions to perform. But, of course, the Mesopotamian and Egyptian social structures were more

[19] See, in this connection, the much-overlooked discussion by O. H. Gates, "The Relation of Priests to Sacrifice before the Exile," *JBL,* 27 (1908), 67-92. A good idea of the confusion in which our subject finds itself may be gained from the article by R. Abba, "Priests and Levites," *The Interpreter's Dictionary of the Bible* (New York, 1962), III, pp. 876b-89b; and cf. E. Nielsen, "The Levites in Ancient Israel," *Annual of the Swedish Theological Institute,* 3 (1964), 16-27. Several sound observations (e. g., Samuel as a seer-priest, prophetic gilds) may be found already in J. F. McCurdy's article on "Prophets and Prophecy—Biblical Data and Critical View" (§ I, pp. 213 f.) in the *Jewish Encyclopedia* (vol. X, 1905).

complex than was early Israel's polity, and far more is known of their priestly structure and functions than of the biblical. [20]

E. The Seer-Priest as a Member of a Guild.
Master and Apprentice

It is now widely recognized that the expression *b^ene ha-n^evi'im* (lit. "the sons of the prophets") means "members of the prophet's guild,

---

[20] Cf., for example, A. L. Oppenheim, *The Interpretation of Dreams in the Ancient Near East* (Philadelphia, 1956), § 5: "Interpretation and Interpreters," pp. 217 ff.; also his interesting chapter (III), "A Bird's-Eye View of Mesopotamian Economic History," in *Trade and Market in the Early Empires; Economies in History and Theory,* ed. by K. Polanyi, C. M. Arensberg, and H. W. Pearson (Glencoe, 1957), pp. 27-37; *idem, Ancient Mesopotamia,* chap. II, § "The Great Organizations," pp. 95-109; Wilson, *op. cit.,* Index, s.v. Priest, Priesthood, Priests; Haldar, *op. cit.,* chap. II, "Associations of Priests and Prophets in the O.T.," pp. 90 ff. — where, however, no distinction is made between the earlier seer and later prophet, and where conclusions are frequently reached too hastily; T. J. Meek, *Hebrew Origins,* rev. ed. (New York, 1950), chaps. IV, "The Origin of the Hebrew Priesthood," and V, "The Origin of Hebrew Prophecy," pp. 119 ff., 148 ff.

I do not include here such biblical figures as Joseph, Moses, and Joshua, not merely because they antedate Israel's settlement and consolidation in Canaan but because they were not professional seers. In their earlier period, the leading representatives of the Hebrews were believed to be able — with the direct intervention of God — to duplicate and even surpass the "super-human" qualities of their non-Hebraic counterparts. Thus Jacob, in his famous blessing (Gen. 49), could tell his sons what would befall them in days to come. His son Joseph had previously interpreted the dreams of Pharaoh's chief cupbearer and chief baker, and then the monarch's own two-in-one dream (Gen. 40-41. On the term for "interpret," *ptr,* Akkadian *pasaru,* see Oppenheim, *The Interpretation of Dreams,* pp. 217-22). Moses and Aaron could duplicate, and more, the wizardry of Pharaoh's magicians; indeed, Moses brought on Ten Plagues, he sweetened bitter waters by casting a log into them, he brought forth water from a rock by striking it, and he had cooperated with God in His dividing the waters of the Sea of Reeds (Ex. 7-17). Joshua caused the walls of Jericho to come tumbling down by magical rites that included the blowing of the shofar and various acts involving the potent number "seven"; and he later caused the sun and the moon to stop in their natural courses (Josh. 6:10).

In later times, in referring to Moses, Israel's outstanding founder of its nationality and its lawgiver, it was but natural to refer to him as "prophet" and "the man of God"; on the latter term, see — though with some reserve — R. Hallevy, "Man of God," *JNES,* 17 (1958), 237-44.

order." [21] This term, just like "visionary" [22] and "seer," is never applied to any of the literary, canonical prophets, for they did not constitute guilds or orders. And so, whenever a group of prophets is spoken of in the Bible, it is the seer-priests of the pre-classical prophetic period who are meant. Eli the "priest" in all probability, [23] just as Samuel after him, was the master of such a group associated with the shrine at Shiloh.

One of Samuel's signs and predictions in connection with the anointing of Saul as king was that "a band of prophets" *(ḥevel nᵉvi'im)* would be descending from the shrine *(bamah)* at Gibeah in prophetic ecstasy *(mitnabbᵉ'im)* to the accompaniment of instrumental music (I Sam. 10:5, 10)—an event that gave rise to the popular saying, "Is Saul also among the prophets?" (verse 11-12). [24] It would not be easy to imag-

---

[21] Cf. H. Junker, *Prophet und Seher in Israel. Eine Untersuchung über die ältesten Erscheinungen des israelitischen Prophetentums insbesondere Prophetenvereine* (Trier, 1927); and see note 8, above.

[22] Amaziah, priest at Beth-el, called Amos a "visionary." But the priest applied this term scornfully (Amos 7:12): "Visionary, off with you to the land of Judah, and eat bread [i.e. earn your living] there by prophesying there" — to which Amos retorted (verse 14): "I am neither a [professional] prophet nor a member of a prophetic guild" *(lo navi anoki wᵉ-lo ben navi anoki).*

[23] The account of Eli in the book of Samuel is very prejudiced. Thus the introduction to Eli's career is *via* the pre-natal career of Samuel; and the first reference to Eli is by way of his two wicked sons (I Sam. 1:3; this is so even if "Eli" stood in our text originally; cf. S. R. Driver, *Notes on . . . Samuel* [2nd ed.], Oxford, 1913, *ad loc.*). Samuel is made to be the "minister" *(mᵉsharet)* not of Eli — as, for example, Joshua was of Moses — but of God directly (I Sam. 2:11; 3:1), and he is said to have received the dream-call directly from Him. Again, Eli deserved to die as he did because of his two sinful sons; but Samuel died nicely at a ripe old age — even though he was also the father of two sinful sons — and he was never repudiated by Israel; it was God who was repudiated (I Sam. 2:27-36; 8:1-9; I Kings 2:26-27).

[24] On a later occasion, when David took refuge from Saul at Samuel's permanent shrine in Ramah (I Sam. 19:18-24) and Saul sent messengers to take David, they saw "the company *(lahaqat)* of prophets prophesying, with Samuel standing *(niṣṣav)* at their head." (On *lahaqat,* cf. J. C. Greenfield, *HUCA,* 29 [1958], 212-4; on *niṣṣav,* see Driver, *op. cit., ad loc.)* This so affected the three successive groups of messengers which the monarch had sent to take David that "the spirit of God came upon the messengers of Saul, and they also prophesied." And when Saul himself came to effect the capture, "the spirit of God came upon him also, and he went along prophesying . . . And he too stripped off his clothes . . ." This second event

ine a Saul prophesying in the manner of an Amos or Micah or Deutero-Isaiah!

It may well be [25] that Saul recognized Samuel's ghost, brought up by the woman of En-dor through necromancy, by the garment he was wearing (I Sam. 28:14; cf. 15:27; perhaps this is intended by the garment of Ahijah in I Kings 11:29 ff.). Zech. 13:4 is a clear reference to the "hairy mantle" that at least some prophets wore. Elijah was recognized by King Ahaziah by the description given him as one who "wore a garment of haircloth (or: was a hairy man), with a leather belt tied around his waist" (II Kings 1:8).[26] And it was through this mantle that Elijah transferred his authority to Elisha (II Kings 2:8, 13 ff.).

The seer, at least the wealthier or more important one, had an apprentice attendant about him *(na'ar; m^{e}sharet)* who sometimes succeeded him. Samuel was the attendant-apprentice of Eli,[27] and I Sam. 2:13 ff. describes some of the duties of the seer-priest's attendant *(na'ar ha-kohen)*. The references to such attendants are more numerous in connection with the careers of Elijah, Elisha, and others.[28] On the other hand, there is no record of a classical prophet, *qua* prophet, having such an attendant.

F. THE SEER-PRIEST AS AN INTEGRAL PART OF ISRAELITE SOCIETY

The seer-priest constituted an integral part of ancient Israelite society, usually playing a direct and important role in it; after all, his authority stemmed from the belief that he had direct access to God and some influence with Him. The preserved text of the book of Samuel is authority that the leadership of parts of Israel was in the hands of Eli, and then of Samuel. The unidentified "messenger *(mal'ak)* of the Lord" in Jud. 6:11 ff. chose Gideon as the military chieftain *(shofet)*

---

was then made to share with the first event the occasion for the origin of the proverb, "Is Saul also among the prophets?"

[25] See J. A. Montgomery, *A Critical and Exegetical Commentary on the Books of Kings* (Edinburgh, 1951), p. 350.

[26] See *ibid., loc. cit.,* on this "garb . . . of professional austerity."

[27] See note 23, above, on how God was made to replace Eli in this connection.

[28] See Orlinsky, "The Seer in Ancient Israel," *loc. cit.,* 166.

of Israel, following the Lord's condemnation through "a prophet" *(ish navi)* of their idolatrous practices (verses 7-11). Another nameless "messenger of God" (Jud. 13) predicted to the barren wife of Manoah the Danite that she would bear a son who would lead Israel in successful battle against its subjugators; Samson was that leader. The levite who became Micah's priest foretold the success of the military venture of the Danites against the inhabitants of Laish (Jud. 18:5). Samuel chose Saul as his successor in leadership (I Sam. 9), and—if I Sam. 16 is to be followed—David after him. [29]

The seer-priest's monopoly in the field of religion gave him, especially if he was the head of a shrine and a guild, considerable political, economic, and social authority. Like everyone else with a vested interest, the seer vigorously opposed any encroachment upon his domain, and was always on the alert to extend it. Hence, apart from religious considerations, the seer whose authority was bound up with the Lord (Yahweh) fought tooth and nail against the devotees of Baal or Asherah or Baal-zebub and the rest; indeed, the seers of the Lord fought no less violently among themselves when they presented clashing statements of the Lord's intentions, that is, when their interests clashed. Samuel could say—in the name of God—that the Lord brought about Eli's fall because of the wickedness of his two sons; but when his own leadership was repudiated by the people, Samuel—again in the name of God—was quick to blame not the wickedness of his own two sons but the people themselves, for they were repudiating God!

It is unfortunate that we no longer possess the data for reconstructing in detail the structure of ancient Israelite society and the precise roles played by the various groups in the period of the Judges and the early monarchy: the landowners, petty farmers, merchants, slaves, seer-priests and their shrines, craftsmen, money-lenders, and the like. Nevertheless, enough material is available for a reasonable attempt at comprehending the process of social forces at work even here.

---

[29] For additional data and references, involving Nathan the prophet and David in relation to Solomon, Ahijah and Jeroboam and "the man of God" from Judah, Shemaiah and Rehoboam, Azariah and Asa, etc., see Orlinsky, *ibid.,* 165-6.

About the middle of the 11th century B.C.E. the sundry tribes of
Israel, for the first time since their conquest of Canaan, found themselves in real trouble, for the military might of the Philistines threatened to crush them one and all. The hitherto politically and militarily
independent tribes,[30] each with its own city-states and governed by a
group of "elders"*(zᵉqenim),* now found themselves compelled to set up
a chieftain over them all, to lead them in organized battle against the
common enemy, the Philistines. Unwilling, however, to relinquish
more of their autonomy than was absolutely necessary, they sought
the means by which to keep under reasonable control the authority of
the new leader. This means was ready at hand in the form of the seer-
priesthood at Shiloh.

All the tribes acknowledged the authority of the Lord (Yahweh).
The seer-priest of the shrine at Shiloh, centrally located in Israel, was
considered a—if not the—major spokesman of the Lord. And at this
point the interests both of the tribal leaders and of the seer-priesthood
at Shiloh (that is, Samuel) coincided. This has been very well stated
by M. A. Cohen: "The divining-priesthood is the only supra-tribal
institution of the pre-monarchical period that is mentioned by the
Bible and therefore the only one capable of furnishing an ideology of
tribal unity . . . The priesthood [however] possessed no military power;
it therefore had to depend for support upon the leadership of the individual tribes. It had every reason to expect, and surely received, enthusiastic support. All the tribes, whatever their provenance, had attached themselves to the traditions of Yahwism. The leadership of each
tribe subscribed to the ideology of Yahwism. The loyalty of their subjects also derived from Yahwism. Yahweh, in turn, guaranteed tribal
autonomy and hence the positions of each tribe's leaders; at the same
time He transcended tribal limits and provided for a spiritual brotherhood of all Israel . . . It would have been too much to expect the old

---

[30] The idea that the Israelite tribes in this period constituted an amphictyony is
one of the scholarly fictions of our own making; see note 14 (end), above, for reference to my article on this. Cohen, "The Role of the Shilonite Priesthood," *loc. cit.,*
63, put it this way: "If an amphictyony existed, what kind of organization would
it be if it possessed no effective military power?" [See now chap. 4 below.]

guard leaders to abdicate all their power. They were compelled to invest the monarchy with sufficient strength to carry out its primary mission, that of defeating the [Philistine] enemy. At the same time, however, they. . . would insist on retaining for themselves as much power as circumstances permitted. This they could accomplish only by controlling the monarchy. They had at hand one institution, dependent and loyal, which was ideal for the purpose. This was the Yahwistic priesthood at Shiloh . . . The old guard leadership hoped that by subordinating the monarchy to the priesthood, it might be kept weak, and that if it should seek to increase its strength at their expense, the priests might hear Yahweh's voice dismissing the king from office. This is exactly what happened in the case of Saul . . ." [31]

The seer-priests located at the shrines and the roving bands (of the kind associated with Elijah and Elisha) depended for a living mainly on the relatively stable agricultural elements, the landed gentry, and the petty farmer; and when the monarchy came along, they were antimonarchical in principle, though in practice they would have to compromise with this new institution.

The seer-priest began to lose ground as first the United and then the Divided Kingdom established itself. This was true far more in Judah, where the Davidic dynasty became firmly established, than in Israel to the north, where the different circumstances prevented any dynasty from maintaining itself for more than a generation or two. Thus "Gad the prophet" was David's "visionary" (II Sam. 24:11), just as Nathan served the king as prophet, and Asaph, Heman, and Jeduthun were his "visionaries." [32]

It appears that the reign, and even the very person, of Solomon dealt the power of the seer-priests a very heavy blow. The Bible makes it clear (I Kings 3:5-15//II Chron. 1:7 ff.; I Kings 8-9) that this monarch himself constituted priest and diviner [33] (as well as merchant,

---

[31] *Ibid.,* 63-4, 69-70.

[32] For additional data, see Orlinsky, "The Seer in Ancient Israel," p. 168 and notes 32-5.

[33] On the incubation dream of Solomon at Gibeon (I Kings 3:5 ff. // II Chron. 1: 7 ff.), as well as the dream subsequent to the completion of the Temple (I Kings

government head, etc.), as witness his central role in offering sacrifices to God and in receiving dream-messages from Him. [34]

In the Northern Kingdom, however, where the landed gentry were too strong for a dynastic regime to establish itself and yet not strong enough to prevent the rise of monarchs, the seer-priests were content to settle for the clear-cut recognition of Yahwistic exclusivism and the monopoly control of the oracles and sacrifices by Yahwistic spokesmen. Hence Elijah was uncompromising and sought the support of those elements in society that were threatened by the urban-commercial-Baal orientation of the House of Omri. The Naboth incident (I Kings 21) was thus not primarily an ethical-moral issue, but one in which urban-commercial-Baal interests threatened the free peasant class and presumably other groups in the economic and social structure. And what Elijah sought and fought for, his disciple Elisha succeeded in achieving through the Jehu revolution. [35]

G. The Uniqueness of the Prophet in Israel

We are now, finally, in a position to relate some extra-biblical data to the biblical. Methodologically, it is possible to reconstruct the history of ancient Israel only in the light of the history of the peoples and cultures with which they had contact; and so the extra-biblical data that are constantly coming to light are most urgently needed and welcome. But an improperly understood biblical phenomenon must lead

---

9:1-9 // II Chron. 7:12 ff.), see Oppenheim, *op. cit.,* pp. 187 ff.; on other aspects, cf. *ibid.,* pp. 191, 193 (on how David "transmitted" to Solomon the pattern of the Temple). It is probably no mere coincidence that it is precisely from this period that reference in the Bible to the ark, the Urim and Thummim, and the ephod virtually ceases.

[34] The latest reference to diviners in our period (thus excluding the book of Daniel) — after the lapse of over one hundred and fifty years — deals with King Manasseh of Judah (II Chron. 33:18): "Now the rest of the acts of Manasseh, and his prayer to his God, and the words of the visionaries who spoke to him [*divrei ha-ḥozim ha-mᵉdabbᵉrim elaw*] in the name of the Lord, the God of Israel, are to be found in the Chronicles of the kings of Israel." The reference to *divrei ḥozai* (Septuagint: *ḥozim*) in verse 19 is obscure.

[35] From a private communication from Prof. Ellis Rivkin.

to utter confusion, both in the biblical and extra-biblical data, when applied to the larger body of data.

Scholars had long sought the pre-Israelite origins of prophecy (as of monotheism, the covenant, the concept of history, and the like) in some other culture in the ancient Near East, with but indifferent results—until the cuneiform texts (ca. 18th century B.C.E.) from the notable excavations at Mari began to appear. Similarities between the latter and biblical prophecy were at once noted. [36]

One text from Mari [37] tells of the reply that a king (presumably Zimri-lim) received from the priestly representative of the god Adad, in response to the king's request for information and advice. Whereas some scholars found in this text something of the origins and character of biblical prophecy, it is clear, as the biblical parallels collected by A. Lods indicate, [38] that it is only the period and career of the priest-diviner that is involved. The interests of the priesthood and temple of Adad are at stake, and the king is "influenced" to continue the alliance as before. [39] This interpretation is seen even more clearly in the light

---

[36] Cf., for example, M. Noth, "History and the Word of God in the Old Testament," *Bulletin of the John Rylands Library,* 32 (1950), 194-206; W. von Soden, "Verkündung des Gotteswillens durch prophetisches Wort in den altbabylonischen Briefen aus Mâri," *Die Welt des Orients,* 1 (1947-1952), 397-403. On these, see, however, H. M. Orlinsky, *Ancient Israel* (Ithaca, 1954), p. 144, note 4: "These articles have erred in connecting the Mari text with the later, uniquely Israelite phase of prophecy." See also H. H. Rowley, *Prophecy and Religion in Ancient China and Israel* (London, 1956), pp. 16 f., and note 4 (with references also to F. M. Th. de Liagre Böhl and H. Schmökel).

[37] A. Lods, "Une tablette intéressante pour l'histoire ancienne du prophétisme sémitique," in *Studies in Old Testament Prophecy Presented to . . . T. H. Robinson,* ed. by H. H. Rowley (Edinburgh, 1950), pp. 103-10 (translation and transcription of the text by G. Dossin). For a more recent analysis of this text, see A. Malamat, "History and Prophetic Vision in a Mari Letter" (Hebrew), *Eretz-Israel,* 5 (1958), 67-73 (English summary, pp. 86* f.); cf. *idem, VTS,* 15 (1966), 207 ff.

[38] Lods, *op. cit.,* pp. 108 f.

[39] See also the earlier study of this letter by A. Malamat, " 'Prophecy' in the Mari Documents" (Hebrew), *Eretz Israel,* 4 (1956), 74-84. The first four Letters discussed by Malamat (*loc. cit.,* 75-81), selected from *ARM,* II, III, VI (from among the correspondence of Kibri-Dagan and Bahdi-lim) make reference to the *muḫḫûm* (Letters 1-3) and *muḫḫûtum* (Letter 4), which are there rendered *navi* and *nevi'ah.* But this Hebrew term is misleading here; as noted by the author himself

of a second Mari text describing how the priesthood of the temple of the god Dagan in Terqa attempted to increase its prestige and income through a dream-message to King Zimri-lim. [40]

Hardly more pertinent for the role of the classical prophet, but fully parallel to that of the seer-priest and his period, is the 11th century B.C.E. Egyptian tale of Wen-Amon [41]: "Now while he (Zakar-Baal, King of Byblos) was making offering to his gods, the god seized one of his youths and made him possessed. [42] And he said to him: 'Bring up *(the) god!* Bring the messenger who is carrying him out! Amon is the one who sent him out! He is the one who made him come!'" This episode clearly bears no relationship to an Hosea or a Micah or a Jeremiah!

To sum up. Divination nowhere developed into prophecy, no more than polytheism developed into monotheism, or, to give a more recent analogue, no more than the guild system developed into trade unions. Divination was a common ancient Near Eastern phenomenon; prophecy is a uniquely Israelite phenomenon. The difference between divination and prophecy, clearly perceived, enables us to see how it is divination, and not prophecy, that finds its parallels in the Mari and other social structures and documents in the Fertile Crescent of old. [43]

(*loc. cit.,* 75), m^{e}shugga' "frenzied" would be a more appropriate correspondent (cf. the state of the "possessed" boy in the tale of Wen-Amon, below). It is the Israelite seer and his role, not the classical prophet, who corresponds to the *muḫḫûm* here.

[40] This letter is No. 5 in Malamat, *loc. cit.,* 81 ff. (For an English translation of the Letter, see Oppenheim, *op. cit.,* p. 195.) Note how Zechariah the son of Jehoiada the priest, in the role of seer ("And the spirit of God clothed [*lav^{e}shah* = took possession of] Zechariah"), exhorts the people, who had gone to worship at other shrines, not to abandon "the house of the Lord" (II Chron. 24:17-22).

[41] See the translation by J. A. Wilson, *ANET,* p. 26; see also *idem, The Burden of Egypt,* pp. 289 ff.; and cf., for example, Meek, *op. cit.,* pp. 155 f.

[42] On this word, Wilson has noted (*ANET,* p. 26 note 13): "The determinative [sign] of the word '[prophetically] possessed' shows a human figure in violent motion of epileptic convulsion."

[43] In his later discussion of "Prophetic Revelations in New Documents from Mari and the Bible," *VTS,* 15 (1966; Geneva Congress Volume), 207-27 (in Hebrew, *Eretz Israel,* 8 [1967], 231-40), A. Malamat has continued to overlook the basic

EXCURSUS I: ON THE TERMINOLOGY FOR "SEER-PRIEST"

The terms *hozeh* and *ro'eh* can hardly be differentiated in their biblical usage. One opinion[44] that the former was of Aramaic usage has now been upset by its use in Ugaritic-Phoenician. An earlier suggestion by Jastrow[45] had it that *"ro'eh* is the 'inspector' [cf. Bab. *bārû*] who looks for a sign and interprets it, the *hôzeh* is the one to whom a sign appears, and who recognizes its meaning when it manifests itself."

Nor is it possible to determine precisely the original meaning and usage of the term *navi*. It would seem that *navi* in the Bible meant approximately "spokesman," as when the Lord told Moses, "your brother Aaron shall serve you as spokesman "(*navi.'* Ex. 7:1; with which should be compared the term *peh* "mouth, spokesman" in Ex. 4:16). This is how the Jews themselves translated *navi* in the Septuagint ca. 200 B.C.E.; the Greek word which was there employed, *profētēs,* "declarer; interpreter," is the source of the English word "prophet." [46] Scholars generally are inclined to the view that the term *navi,* when employed for Abraham (Gen. 20:7; note the use of the verb *ra'ah* in verse 10), or Moses (Deut. 34:10; cf. Hos. 12:14; and cf. Num. 11:25-29 for Eldad and Medad), or Samuel (II Chron. 35:18; cf. I Sam. 3:20), or Nathan (II Sam. 7:2; 12:25; etc.), or an unnamed person (for example, Jud. 6:8—*ish navi*) is the product of later usage, as is similarly the term *nevi'ah* "prophetess," when employed for Miriam (Ex. 15:20) and Deborah (Jud. 4:4—*ishah nevi'ah).*[47] This accords

---

differences between the seer-priest of ancient Israel and the Near East and the Israelite prophet.

[44] M. A. van den Oudenrijn, "De vocabulis quibusdam termino *navi* synonimis," *Biblica,* 6 (1925), 304 f. A. R. Johnson, *The Cultic Prophet in Ancient Israel* (Cardiff, 1944), *passim,* discusses the etymology and usage of these and related terms. L. Koehler, *Lexicon in V. T. Libros,* Leiden, 1949, p. 284b, s.v. *hazah,* in recording "ug. *hdy*" as a cognate, proceeds to assert, *"the Aramaic word for Hebrew ra'ah, early used by the Hebrew";* the justification for this assertion is not apparent.

[45] M. Jastrow, Jr., "Rô'eh and Hôzeh in the Old Testament," *JBL,* 28 (1909), 53.

[46] Cf. T. J. Meek, *Hebrew Origins,* rev. ed. (New York, 1950), pp. 150 f.

[47] *Hozeh* and *ro'eh* as technical terms do not occur in Biblical Hebrew in the feminine form, singular or plural. Women do not seem to have taken a direct part in the cult worship in ancient Israel (pending determination of the exact meaning of *ha-sove'ot* in Ex. 38:8; I Sam. 2:22); but there were seers and prophetesses, for example, the woman of En-dor who divined by a ghost (I Sam. 28:3 ff.), Huldah (II Kings 22:14 ff. // II Chron. 34:22 ff.), and Noadiah (Neh. 6:14 — a "false" prophetess). The "prophetess" mentioned in Isa. 8.3 refers apparently to the prophet's wife.

with the editorial statement in I Sam. 9:9, "Formerly in Israel, when a person went to inquire of God, thus he said, 'Come let us go to the seer'; for he who is now called a prophet was formerly called a seer." [48]

It is likewise the consensus of scholarly opinion that the term "(the) man of God," [49] when associated with such early figures as Moses (Deut. 33:1; Josh. 14:6; Ps. 90:1; Ezra 3:2; I Chron. 23:14; II Chron. 30:16) and David (Neh. 12:24, 36; II Chron. 8:14), is the product of a later age. [50]

In the Book of Chronicles, as in the Septuagint and Targum, the terms *hozeh* and *ro'eh* are sometimes interchanged with "prophet" :1) *Ro'eh* is usually rendered by *ho blépōn* (but *ho profētēs* in I Chron. 26:28—Samuel; II Chron. 16:7, 10—Hanani) and *hezwayya* (but the Targum has, for example, *nevu'at* for *hazut* in Isa. 29:11). 2) *Hozeh* is usually reproduced by *ho orōn* (*ho blépōn* in II Chron. 19:2—Hanani; II Chron. 29:30—Asaph; II Chron. 35:15—Asaph, Heman, and Jeduthun; in I Chron. 25:1 they are described as *ha-nibbeim be-kinnorot* (and hence *ho anakrouómenos* for Heman as *hozeh ha-melek* in verse 5) and *hezwayya* (but *neviyaya* in Isa. 30:10). For *hazon* the Septuagint will employ both *profēteía* (used also for *nevu'ah*) and *hórasis* (used also for *massa*).

This usage in the Septuagint and Targum is natural enough, when in the Bible itself reference is made, for example, to Gad as both prophet and seer (II Sam. 24:11—*Gad ha-navi hozeh David*); to Asaph, Heman, and Jeduthun as "seers" and "who prophesy" (I Chron. 25:1, 5; II Chron. 35:15); to Shemaiah as "the man of God" (I Kings 12:22; II Chron.

---

[48] Most scholars would transpose this gloss to the word "seer" in verse 11. Yet note "the man of God" in verse 8, at which point the gloss is really just as pertinent.

[49] The term *ish* (*ha-*)*Elohim* (never *ish Yahweh;* or the plural *anshei* (*ha-*)*Elohim* or *Yahweh*) is to be distinguished clearly from *mal'ak Elohim* or *Yahweh* "messenger of God/the Lord; angel." If the being in human form (*ish*) is believed to be superhuman, he is then a *mal'ak Elohim* or *Yahweh*. This is clear from the story of Gideon (Jud. 6), where Gideon realizes that it was a divine being rather than a mortal that he saw face to face, and from the story of Manoah's wife (Jud. 13; where cf. the use of *mal'ak Elohim* or *Yahweh* and *ish ha-Elohim,* and the dialogue in verses 22-23). A. Haldar, *Associations of Cult Prophets among the Ancient Semites* (Uppsala, 1945), pp. 129 f. (in the section " 'Man of god' and 'messenger' "), has missed this completely, and has made the *mal'ak* a cult functionary. R. Hallevy, "Man of God," *JNES,* 17 (1958), 238 f., and note 7, is not clear in this distinction.

[50] Cf. *ibid.,* 243-4.

11:2) and "prophet" (II Chron. 12:5); to Samuel as all three: seer, man of God, and prophet. And so on.

If one must hazard an opinion, it would appear that the use of *hozeh, ro'eh,* and *navi* depends upon chronological-regional factors. Thus Samuel is called *ro'eh,* but never *hozeh.* And Hanani is the only other one to be called *ro'eh* (II Chron. 16:7, 10). Again, neither Elijah nor Elisha is ever referred to as *hozeh* or *ro'eh;* the former is either "the Tishbite" *(ha-Tishbi)* or *navi,* and the latter is either *navi* or (more commonly) *ish ha-Elohim.* Several persons are referred to as the *hozeh* of a king (for example, Gad, Heman, Jeduthun); but no one is either the *ro'eh* of a king or his *navi*—except for Aaron as the *navi* or *peh* of Moses, the *navi* can be only God's.[51]

EXCURSUS II: THE ISRAELITE SEER-PRIEST AND ANCIENT NEAR EASTERN DIVINATION

To what extent the Israelite seer practiced the same occult arts as his non-Israelite colleague is not certain. The Bible makes no mention of the seer, visionary, man of God, or prophet (the earlier, let alone the later) resorting to lecanomancy, libanomancy, necromancy, extispicy, bird-omina, star-gazing, hepatoscopy, and the like, to determine the future.[52] Indeed, it would appear that the injunction to burn the *lobus caudatus* of the liver

---

[51] When "seers" and "visionaries" (and "prophets" too) have ceased to flourish except in the memory of the people, it is easy to designate Hanani as *ro'eh* but his son Jehu as *hozeh* (II Chron. 16:7; 19:2); where Jehu is designated *navi* (I Kings 16:7, 12), it may well be that this term was added later (cf. J. A. Montgomery, *A Critical and Exegetical Commentary on the Books of Kings* [Edinburgh, 1951], *ad loc.,* pp. 282-3, 289) to distinguish our Jehu from King Jehu. The term *navi* was bandied about freely; in the case of Elijah, the Septuagint added in I Kings 17:1 "the reverential title 'the prophet' which he was not technically" (Montgomery, *op. cit.,* pp. 292-3); other uses of *navi* for Elijah are suspect (cf. *ibid.,* p. 311, on I Kings 18:36).

[52] A number of terms are found in the Bible for those who practiced forms of divination — though it is not yet possible to determine the precise meaning of most of the terms here listed, and several of the meanings given are but convenient guesses: *menahesh* "diviner"; *mekashef* "sorcerer"; *me'onen* "soothsayer"; *qosem* "augur"; *eshet ba'alat-ov* "necromancer"; *yidde'oni* "wizard"; *melahesh* "charmer"; *hover haver* "enchanter"; *holem* "dreamer"; **hartom* "magician" (on which, see A. L. Oppenheim, *The Interpretation of Dreams in the Ancient Near East* [Philadelphia, 1956], p. 238b), and the like. Cf. I. Mendelsohn, "Magic," *Interpreter's Dictionary of the Bible* (New York, 1962), III, pp. 223b-5a.

prevented its use in divination.[53] And it may well be that various forms of divination were banned simply because they were practiced in foreign modes of worship. Thus Y. Kaufmann would regard all forms of divination as foreign to, and, when in some periods imported from the outside (for example, Canaan-Phoenicia), incompatible with Israel's monotheism.[54]

It is clear that the Israelite seer-priest, who was believed to have direct and exclusive access to the Lord through an oracle—the ark, the ephod, and the Urim and Thummim come to mind at once—would oppose non-Yahwistic diviners and their means of divination. In any case, for whatever reasons, Saul had forbidden the use of necromancy in Israel on pain of death. But when Saul himself, in the midst of a crucial battle with the Philistines, failed to receive any reply from God, "either by dreams, or by Urim, or by prophets," he ordered his aides to find him a necromancer. And thus came about the dramatic event involving Saul, the woman of En-Dor, and Samuel's ghost (I Sam. 28:3 ff. Interestingly, Samuel rebuked Saul not for resorting to necromancy but for disturbing him by bringing him up; cf. verse 15). In the days of Elijah, Israelite kings (for example, Ahab) resorted to the divination of "the prophets of Baal," and King Ahaziah of Judah attempted to inquire of Baal-zebub at Ekron.[55] So that in whatever period divination was banned, segments of the Israelite population occasionally made use of it and were vigorously denounced by the prophets for doing so.

Yet it should be noted that this practice of divination did not neces-

---

[53] M. Jastrow, Jr., "Rô'eh and Hôzeh in the Old Testament," *JBL,* 28 (1909), 48, has argued that this "points to the knowledge of this form of divination among the Hebrews." Yet two significant facts stand out: a) In the list of various kinds of diviners in Deut. 18:10-11, there is no mention of hepatoscopy; b) clay models of livers have been found in Canaan (as in Mesopotamia), but this does not hold true for Israel. See also Jastrow, *ibid.,* for the possible significance of "on the roof . . . at sunrise" in I Sam. 9:25-26.

[54] Y. Kaufmann, *History of the Israelite Religion* (Hebrew; Tel-Aviv, 1937-1956), II, pp. 282 ff., 458 ff.; III, pp. 659 ff., 709 ff.; see M. Greenberg's abridgement and translation, *The Religion of Israel* (Chicago, 1960), chap. II, "Pagan Religion" (especially pp. 40 ff.). And see I. Mendelsohn, "Divination," *Interpreter's Dictionary of the Bible,* I, pp. 856b-8b.

[55] At the end of his long reign (about 870 B.C.E.), in the midst of his serious illness, King Asa of Judah (II Chron. 16:12) "did not inquire of the Lord, but of the physicians" (*rofe'im*), where *refa'im,* traditional "shades," may well have stood originally.

sarily entail transgression of monotheism, for the Lord could as readily be the Deity involved. Hence divination in Israel did not necessarily coincide with idolatry.

The Balaam oracles (Num. 22-24) need not be taken up here, for they are an example not of Israelite but of non-Israelite divination, involving a foreign (probably Mesopotamian) diviner.[56]

---

[56] See W. F. Albright, *JBL,* 63 (1944), 207-33, with special reference to S. Daiches, "Balaam — a Babylonian *bārū,*" *H. Hilprecht Anniversary Volume* (Leipzig, 1909), pp. 60-70 (= Daiches' collected *Bible Studies* [London, 1950], pp. 110-9).

BIBLIOGRAPHY

COHEN, M. A., "The Role of the Shilonite Priesthood in the United Monarchy of Ancient Israel", *HUCA,* 36 (1965), 59-98.

CONTENAU, G., *La divination chez les Assyriens et les Babyloniens* (Paris 1940).

————, *La Magie chez les Assyriens et les Babyloniens* (Paris 1947).

DAICHES, S., "Balaam—a Babylonian *bārū.* The Episode of Num. XXIII, 2—XXIV, 24 and some Babylonian Parallels," *Assyriologische und archeologische Studien. Herman v. Hilprecht . . . gewidmet* (Leipzig 1909), 60-70 (= S. Daiches, *Bible Studies* [London, 1950], 110-119).

GASTER, T. H., *"Thespis: Ritual, Myth and Drama in the Ancient Near East,* rev. ed. (New York 1961).

GATES, O. H., "The Relation of Priests to Sacrifice before the Exile," *JBL,* 27 (1928), 67-92.

HALDAR, A., *Associations of Cult Prophets among the Ancient Semites* (Uppsala 1945).

HÖLSCHER, G., *Die Profeten. Untersuchungen zur Religionsgeschichte Israels* (Leipzig 1914).

JASTROW, M., JR., "Rô'ēh and Ḥôzēh in the Old Testament," *JBL,* 28 (1909), 42-56.

————, *Aspects of Religious Belief and Practice in Babylonia and Assyria* (New York 1911), especially pp. 143-264.

JOHNSON, A. R., *The Cultic Prophet in Ancient Israel* (Cardiff 1944).

JUNKER, H., *Prophet und Seher in Israel. Eine Untersuchung über die ältesten Erscheinungen des israelitischen Prophetentums insbesondere Prophetenvereine* (Trier 1927).

LEXA, F., *La Magie dans l'Égypte antique,* etc., 3 vols. (Paris 1925).

LINDBLOM, J., *Prophecy in Ancient Israel* (Oxford 1962).

MEEK, T. J., *Hebrew Origins,* rev. ed. (New York 1950), chaps. IV ("The Origin of the Hebrew Priesthood"), V ("The Origin of Hebrew Prophecy").

MENDELSOHN, I., "Divination," *The Interpreter's Dictionary of the Bible,* I, 1962, 856b-858b.

————, "Magic(ian)", *ibid.,* III, 1962, 223b-225a.

OPPENHEIM, A. L., *The Interpretation of Dreams in the Ancient Near East* (Philadelphia 1956) = *Transactions of the American Philosophical Society,* New Series, XLVI, 3.

————, *Ancient Mesopotamia: Portrait of a Dead Civilization* (Chicago 1964), 171-227, 364-369, 385-386.

ORLINSKY, H. M., *Ancient Israel*² (Ithaca 1960), chap. VIII ("The Hebraic Spirit: The Prophetic Movement and Social Justice," 142-168) = *Understanding the Bible Through History and Archaeology* (KTAV, 1972), 248-276.

————, "The Seer in Ancient Israel," *Oriens Antiquus,* 4 (1965), 153-174.

ROWLEY, H. H., *The Servant of the Lord and Other Essays on the Old Testament* (London 1952), chap. III ("The Nature of Old Testament Prophecy in the Light of Recent Study") (= *Harvard Theological Review,* 38 [1945], 1-38).

THOMPSON, R. C., *Reports of the Magicians and Astrologers of Nineveh and Babylon in the British Museum,* 2 vols. (London 1900).

————, *The Devils and Evil Spirits of Babylonia,* etc., 2 vols. (London 1903-1904).

————, *Semitic Magic: Its Origin and Development* (London 1908).

VAUX, R. DE, *Ancient Israel: Its Life and Institutions* (New York 1961): Part IV, "Religious Institutions," pp. 271-517 (and the bibliography there, pp. 537-552).

4

The Tribal System of Israel
and Related Groups
in the Period of the Judges

DURING THE PAST QUARTER OF A CENTURY, largely due to the writings of Albrecht Alt and especially of Martin Noth in Europe, and, following them, of W. F. Albright on this side of the ocean, it has become all but axiomatic in the reconstruction of the period of the Judges in ancient Israel (Early Iron Age, about 1200–1000 B.C.E.) that the tribes of Israel constituted in that period an amphictyony, a confederacy of tribes established at and bound together by a central religious shrine.

In his well-known monograph on *Der Gott der Väter* (1929), Alt made passing reference to amphictyony in early Israel.[1] A year later

---

[This essay first appeared in *Studies and Essays in Honor of Abraham A. Neuman* (1962), pp. 375–387, and was reprinted in *Oriens Antiquus*, 1 (1962), 11–20 at the request of the editor.]

[1] On p. 59 Alt speaks of the unanswered "Frage, welche Gruppe der Amphiktionen von Mamre den Kultus des Gottes Abrahams in das gemeinsame Heiligtum eingeführt hat . . ." The monograph constitutes Heft 48 (Dritte Folge, Heft 12) in the series *Beiträge zur Wissenschaft vom Alten und Neuen Testament* (*BWANT*); reprinted in A. Alt, *Kleine Schriften zur Geschichte des Volkes Israel* (= *KS*), 3 vols (München 1953 and 1959), vol. i, pp. 1–78. *See also* Alt, *Die Landnahme der Israeliten in Palästina* (Leipzig 1925; = *KS*, vol. i, pp. 89–125); *idem, Die Staatenbildung der Israeliten in Palästina* (Leipzig 1930; = *KS*, vol. ii, pp. 1–65); and the article, "Israel, politische Geschichte," in *Die Religion in Geschichte und Gegenwart*, ed. H. Gunkel

Alt's outstanding disciple, Noth, published in considerable detail his reconstruction of *Das System der Zwölf Stämme Israels*,[2] which included amphictyonic data from the regions of Greece and Italy. A decade later, in his volumes *From the Stone Age to Christianity* (1940) and *Archaeology and the Religion of Israel* (1942),[3] Albright asserted his acceptance of this idea, and many scholars have followed suit.[4]

---

and L. Zscharnack, vol. iii (1929), cols. 437 f. Alt owed this theory directly to Max Weber, noted sociologist; *cf.* his *Gesammelte Aufsätze zur Religionssoziologie,* vol. 3 (Tübingen 1921), pp. 86 ff.; or his *Ancient Judaism,* translated and edited by H. H. Gerth and D. Martindale (Glencoe, Ill., 1952), pp. 77 ff. Weber seems to have been the first to connect the Judges period, as distinct from the patriarchal period, with amphictyony.

[2] Heft 52 in *BWANT;* and *cf.* his *The History of Israel* (New York 1958), ch. iii, pp. 85 ff. In the older literature, inspired by Greek example, scholars such as H. Ewald (*Einleitung in die Geschichte des Volkes Israel*[3] [Göttingen 1864], vol. i, "Die zwölf Söhne und Stämme Jaqob's," pp. 519 ff.; English translation by R. Martineau, *The History of Israel,* vol. i [1883], pp. 362–85), made much of the number 12 (and 6; and multiples of 12, *e.g.,* 24, 48)—as though this number or its multiples pointed to amphictyony; one could relate similarly most of the unrelated peoples of the world because of their common use of the twelve-month solar-system. Among those who followed Ewald—the patriarchal period alone was involved—were H. Gunkel, *Genesis*[3] (1910), p. 332 ("gewiss sehr plausibel"), who had recourse also to the work of E. Szanto, "Die griechischen Phylen," in *Sitzungsberichte der Wiener Akademie, phil.-hist. Klasse,* vol. CXLIV (1901), v. Abhandlung, pp. 40 ff. Apparently independently of Ewald, A. H. Sayce, "The Cuneiform Tablets of Tel El-Amarna, now Preserved in the Boulaq Museum," in *Proceedings of the Society of Biblical Archaeology,* vol. xi (1888–89), 326–413, had observed (p. 347), "In all probability the name of Hebron was derived from the 'confederacy' of the three or four nations (Hittites, Amorites, and Canaanites) who met around its great sanctuary, which accounts for the absence of the name in the Egyptian geographical lists."

[3] P. 215 in the former, pp. 102–5, 108 in the latter. In the meantime, several other scholars had adopted amphictyony for Israel in the period of the Judges, *e.g.,* T. J. Meek, *Hebrew Origins* (New York 1936 and 1950), pp. 25 f., 116, and passim (*see* Index, s. "Confederacy") H. S. Nyberg, "Studien zum Religionskampf im A.T.," *Archiv für Religionswissenschaft,* vol. 35 (1938), p. 367; K. Möhlenbrink, "Die Landnahmesagen des Buches Josua," *ZAW,* vol. 15 (1938), 238–268.

[4] *Cf., e.g.,* Danell, *Studies in the Name Israel in the O.T.* (Upsala 1946), p. 46 (with reference to Noth); S. Mowinckel, *Zur Frage nach dokumentarischen Quellen in Josua* 13–19 (Oslo 1946) pp. 20 ff. (who argues for a pre-Davidic ten-tribe amphictyony); L. H. Grollenberg, *Atlas of the Bible* (New York 1956), 57b; B. W. Anderson, "The Place of Shechem in the Bible," *Bib. Arch.,* vol. 20, no. I (1957), 13 f. Especially is this true of Albright's students, *e.g.,* G. E. Wright (-F. V. Filson) in *Westminster Historical Atlas to the Bible* (Philadelphia 1945 and 1957), p. 44b and *Biblical Archae-*

In *Ancient Israel* (Ithaca 1954), I wrote (pp. 58 f.), "Except for occasional brief emergency alliances, the Israelite tribes maintained complete autonomy during the Period of the Judges and recognized no central capital or shrine for all Israel . . ." Limitation of space prevented there elaborate defense of this anti-amphictyonic position; this article is meant to make good that lack.

The most important single source for our problem and period is still the book of Judges. In reading this Book carefully, one is struck time and again by several outstanding facts, which together help to make up a pretty clear and consistent pattern of tribal affiliation—or the lack of it. The facts are these. The "Judges" (Hebrew *shophetim*) were individual men who exhibited unusual military or physical prowess in time of dire circumstances for their kinfolk, leading them in victory over threatening non-Israelite invaders or in overthrowing the yoke of an enemy.[5] Ehud of the tribe of Benjamin,

---

ology (Philadelphia 1957), pp. 87 f. (although Wright does not seem to employ the term "amphictyony"); Jacob B. Myers, *The Book of Judges* (in *The Interpreter's Bible*, vol. ii, 1953), 685a; John Bright, *Early Israel in Recent History Writing* (= *Studies in Biblical Theology*, No. 19, London 1956), p. 84, "That the Israelite amphictyony with its Yahwistic faith was a going concern in the period of the Judges is, of course, beyond question . . ."; *A History of Israel* (Philadelphia 1959), pp. 142 ff. The only outspoken opponent of amphictyony in Israel was Yehezkel Kaufmann, whose reconstruction of Israel's early history precluded this structure; *cf.* his *Toledot ha-Emunah ha-Yisreelit* (Tel Aviv 1937-ff.), vol. iv, n. 60 on pp. 399 f.; or *cf.* pp. 256–8 of M. Greenberg's one-volume abridgment and translation entitled *The Religion of Israel* (Chicago 1960).

[5] It has now become a commonplace to attribute the quality of charisma to these "Judges"; it is doubtful that even Max Weber ever imagined to what extent this concept of his would be exploited by subsequent generations of scholars, so that *e.g.*, Roger T. O'Callaghan *Aram Naharaim* (*Analecta Orientalia* 26 [Rome 1948]), p. 122, following his mentor Albright (*From the Stone Age*, etc., p. 216), who followed Alt (especially his monograph on *Die Staatenbildung der Israeliten in Palästina*; *cf.* in n. 1, p. 1, above, = *KS*, vol. ii, pp. 1–65), who followed Weber (*see* his *Essays in Sociology*, translated, edited, and with an introduction by H. H. Gerth and C. Wright Mills [New York 1946], Index, s. "charisma" and "charismatic authority" (pp. 471 f.); *Ancient Judaism* (n. 1 above), Glossary and Index, s. "charisma," p. 465), would help explain the phenomenon in the Early Iron Age from its use in the New Testament over a millennium later. Actually it is most doubtful that the concept was part of Israel's religious outlook in the period of the Judges. When a man such as Jephthah the bastard demonstrated military acumen, or when Ehud assassinated King Eglon of Moab, people turned to them for leadership. No one recognized "the direct outpouring of divine grace" in anyone prior to an act of military or similar significance. It

Shamgar ben Anath, and Jephthah the son of a prostitute are cases in point. These military chieftains, brought into being by foreign pressures—never in peaceful times by domestic, inner-Israelite need— were not associated with any shrines.[6] And none of them was an amphictyon.[7]

---

clarifies nothing to introduce the concept and term "charisma" from postbiblical times and read it back into a period over one thousand years and many civilizations and social structures earlier.

[6] It is idle to compare—as everyone has long been doing (cf., e.g., Albright, From the Stone Age. etc., 216)—our shophet with later Carthaginian suf(f)ete(s) (see the Glossary in Z. S. Harris, A Grammar of the Phoenician Language [New Haven 1936], p. 153) so far as function and meaning are concerned; they are about a thousand years apart in time, and the historical circumstances and social structures were different. There is no evidence in the book of Judges that these "Judges" had anything to do with legal adjudication, for then it would have been internal, inner-Israelite needs that brought them into being. It was throughout external, military circumstances that created "Judges," and their function was to deliver (hoshí‘a) from the enemy the Israelites who were affected; then they "judged" (shaphetu), i.e., ruled as chieftans, those whom they had militarily delivered, cf., e.g., the use of shaphat in the tribes' demand to Samuel (1 Sam 8:5–6), símah/tenah lánu mélek le-shaphtḗnu, "Set up for us (Give us) a king to rule us," with the climax being reached in vv. 19– 20, where "The people refused to listen to Samuel, and said, '. . . We too will be like the other nations: let our king rule us (u-shᵉphatánu malkénu), going out at our head and fighting our battles.'" And the mishpat of the king (vv. 9, 11 ff.) has, of course, nothing to do with legal adjudication but with ruling and taxing the people with absolute power; the people needed and wanted a military leader against their external enemies, not a legal arbiter for themselves. (On Samuel—and his two sons—as judge rather than seer/prophet [8:1 ff.] as being due to later, Deuteronomic editorializing, see S. R. Driver, An Introduction to the Literature of the O.T. [1913 edition], pp. 175 ff. Otto Eissfeldt, Einleitung in das A.T.² [1956], pp. 323 ff., argues differently.)

It may be noted here that with all the confusion in his treatment of the shophetim and charisma, Weber yet asserted (Ancient Judaism, p. 86), ". . . politico-military decisions, not legal decisions or wisdom, were the specific function of charismatic shofetim." As to how and when the term shōphet in the Bible came to mean "adjudicate, adjudge"—that is a separate problem to be solved.

[7] Significantly, there is no term in the Bible for "amphictyon," any more than for "amphictyony" or "charisma." As for the term nasi' (cf. eg., Noth, Das System, etc., Exkurs III, "Gebrauch und Bedeutung des Wortes nasi'," pp. 151–162; whence, e.g., Bright, op cit., p. 98), it is indeed noteworthy that nowhere in the Book that is alleged to have sprung from an amphictyonic society, viz., the book of Judges, is the term nasi' found. And if wa-yehi/wat-tislah rúᵃh 'elohim/YHWH (e.g., Jud 3: 10 Othniel; 14:6 Samson) is interpreted as denoting "charisma" (cf., e.g., Bright, op. cit., p. 144), then not only does charisma become the property of many unlikely people in the Bible (cf. Mandelkern's Concordance, s. ruᵃh) but the persons generally desig-

It is significant, further, that no amphictyonic league ever met at a shrine to decide a course of action or to pick a "Judge."[8] One will go through all twenty-one chapters of the book of Judges and fail to find mention of Shiloh, or Shechem, or Bethel, or Ramah, or Beth-shean, or Gilgal, or any other shrine, at which a confederacy of two, or six, or twelve, or any number of tribes met as an amphictyony.[9] This is an outstanding anomalous phenomenon in the midst of an allegedly existing amphictyony, or of several smaller amphictyonies.[10] Thus Shechem is mentioned but once in the entire book of Judges, in chapter 9, and it would have gone unmentioned altogether had not its Israelite inhabitants set up there a shrine to the non-Israelite—or perhaps in this region and period, semi-Israelite—god Baal-berith, and

---

nated as amphictyons, viz., the *nesi'im*, are the very ones into whom the *rúªh* of God was never said to have entered.

[8] Let those who believe that twelfth-eleventh century B.C.E. Israel operated with the concept of charisma ponder over this fact: why, if a *shophet* was chosen because God's divine grace was recognized in him, did not the people perform the formal choosing of the leader at God's shrine? Incidentally, when God's "spirit" is said to have come over a man, he proceeded to go into action as a deliverer of his oppressed people (*e.g.*, Gideon, Jephthah, Samson, Saul); but nowhere does the text say that the people made that man a leader because they recognized in him something of the divine. It would seem that "charisma" and "amphictyony" are among several other concepts of nineteenth-early twentieth century sociology that require thoroughly fresh study.

[9] Numerous scholars have assumed or argued for amphictyonies of varying numbers of tribes in different periods at different centers: *cf., e.g.*, H. H. Rowley, *From Joseph to Joshua*, etc. (London 1950; The Schweich Lectures of the British Academy, 1948), pp. 125 ff. and the notes *ibid*. Thus Möhlenbrink (pp. 246 ff., *see* p. 2, n. 2 above) argues for a "Dreistämme-amphiktyonie" involving Benjamin, Reuben, and Gad. But the data are too glaringly inadequate to be overcome by scientific methodology, let alone by "scholarly guessing."

[10] There is a serious methodological error (so most recently Bright, p. 94) in assuming the existence of an amphictyonic league almost whenever and wherever a biblical Book records the existence of a shrine. Shechem, Shiloh, Bethel, Gilgal, Kadesh—all were shrines in the twelfth-eleventh centuries; what does that prove for amphictyony? All these sites were shrines in Canaanite, pre-Israelite times; did amphictyony obtain in Canaanite society? Note may also be made here of the attempt to prove amphictyony, in this case "centered about a sanctuary located at Shiloh," by the assertion that "archaeological evidence tends to support the biblical impression" and the footnote, "See Hans Kjaer, 'The Excavations of Shilo 1929,' *JPOS*, X (1929), 87–174" (Myers; *see* p. 2, n. 3 above). I fail to see how the dig at Shiloh demonstrates amphictyony.

had not Abimelech, one of the many offspring of Gideon, tried to become ruler of the area. Nothing amphictyonic appears in the entire chapter of fifty-seven verses.[11]

Again, in chapters 19–21, when some riffraff (*bene beliyá'al* is the Hebrew term, 19:22) in Benjaminite Gibeah raped and caused the death of a Levite's concubine, so that in the blood-feud that ensued the entire tribe of Benjamin was subjected to revenge and ostracization, it is to Mizpah that the avengers came to take counsel against the Benjaminites. A parallel, or supplementary, version has it that on the way to Gibeah—the geography here is not certain at all —the Israelites stopped off at Bethel to inquire of God as to which tribe should lead them in battle against Benjamin, and the reply was: Judah. The incidental statement is made there (20:27) that "the Ark of the Covenant of the LORD was stationed there in Bethel in those days"; even if this were so, and Shiloh was bereft of the Ark at the time, it is significant that Mizpah, and not Bethel, or Shiloh, is where the Israelite consultation took place.[12]

One final instance, though the book of Judges readily supplies several more. When the very critical struggle for existence had to be

---

[11] Yet Shechem has frequently been identified as the shrine around which the Israelite amphictyony revolved (cf., *e.g.*, Noth, *The History of Israel*, pp. 91 *ff*.; Bright, *A History of Israel*, pp. 147 ff.). Small wonder that this viewpoint has had to be defended by assuming and asserting that there were originally many references to Shechem (or Shiloh, or Bethel, or Gilgal, or Kadesh, etc.) as an amphictyonic center and that they were suppressed or excised from the biblical text; cf., *e.g.*, Hans-Joachim Kraus, "Gilgal, ein Beitrag zur Kultusgeschichte Israels," *VT*, vol. i (1951), 181–199, where Gilgal as the central shrine of an amphictyony is discussed; or, more recently, J. Dus, "Gibeon—eine Kultstätte des Sms und die Stadt des benjaminitischen Schicksals," *ibid.*, vol. x, (1960), 353–374. On the other hand, if there were no amphictyony, there was nothing amphictyonic to suppress or excise.

[12] Another unanswered question created by the "amphictyonists" involves this very incident. On the one hand it is stated, "In all probability the divine throne of the sacred ark formed the centre of worship . . ." (Noth, *op. cit.*, p. 91; *cf.* Bright, p. 146, "The focal point of the amphictyony throughout its history was the shrine housing the Ark of the Covenant, the throne of the invisible Yahweh . . ."), and on the other (Noth, *op. cit.*, p. 94, n. 3), "The meeting place of the tribes in this story was Mizpeh (Judges 20: 1 ff.), and the only [*sic*] part that Bethel plays in it is as the site of the Ark." But—as the Talmud would put it—*mim-mah nafshak* ("whichever position you take"): if the Ark "made" the amphictyony, then why was Bethel ignored; and if the Ark played no such role, then what "made" the amphictyony?

mounted against the Canaanite forces under Sisera, neither the poetic nor the prose version of this crucial event, in chapters 4–5 of Judges, makes mention of any central shrine, any religious focus, to which the Israelite tribes gathered for amphictyonic consideration.[13] And so it should come as no surprise when an objective reading of the book of Judges gives expression, more than once, to the statement that the period of the Judges was one in which there was no central authority in the land, and when each Israelite group did whatever it wished, without recourse to any central authority, religious or political. The Hebrew expression is: בַּיָּמִים הָהֵם אֵין מֶלֶךְ בְּיִשְׂרָאֵל אִישׁ אֲשֶׁר בְּעֵינָיו יַעֲשֶׂה (17:6; 21:25; in 18:1 only the first half of this expression is employed).

It is far from unlikely that this very situation obtained also in Transjordan, among the Ammonites, Moabites, and Edomites. It is true that prevailing opinion has it, largely since Alt's monograph appeared in 1930 on *Die Staatenbildung der Israeliten in Palästina,* that "the surrounding nations were all highly organized. Edomites, Moabites, and Ammonites all had kings who were much more than tribal emirs . . ." (Albright, *From the Stone Age,* etc., p. 221). Yet the evidence for this opinion is scarcely evident.

So far as the book of Judges is concerned, a contrary picture is clearly portrayed. Thus in Chapter 3 we are told that "King Eglon of Moab . . . mustered the Ammonites and the Amalekites, and went and defeated Israel, and occupied the City of Palms. And the Israelites served King Eglon of Moab eighteen years" (vv. 12–14). One may well wonder how highly organized, let alone powerful, was the land of Moab and Ammon, not to mention the elusive Amalekites, if it took the combined efforts of these three to subdue a portion of Israel, and if less than two decades later this part of Israel, under

---

[13] There would seem to be no justification for the assertion, "It is clear from the Song of Deborah (Jud. ch. 5) that the amphictyony was in full operation in the twelfth century" (Bright, *op. cit.,* p. 145; or *cf.* p. 144 on "the call to arms . . ."). In what verse is the amphictyonic shrine mentioned? And where was the Ark?

As for the fact that those tribal groups that did not bother to come to "the help of the Lord" were cursed (v. 23), how does this point to amphictyony? At what shrine were they cursed? Bright's note to this (p. 144, n. 37), ". . . The Hittite treaties discussed above required the vassal to respond to the call to arms," has no bearing on the problem of amphictyony. Does this aspect of the Hittite treaties indicate amphictyony among the Hittites?

Ehud, was able to evict the conquerors.

It is, furthermore, in this very period and general region that the Midianites were able to conquer a part of Israel for seven years (chapters 6–9), at the end of which period the Israelites of three tribes, Naphtali, Asher, and Manasseh, under the leadership of Gideon, drove out the Midianites from western Jordan, chased them across the Jordan into Ammonite territory, and destroyed the backbone of their organization forever. Regardless of how the details became embellished and garbled in the retelling of the event, and even if we do not include "the Amalekites and all the Kedemites" that the preserved Hebrew text mentions (6:33; 7:12; 8:10), is not really a highly organized Ammonite government that manifests itself in these chapters; rather do we get a picture of a considerable territory, quite sparsely settled, over which no one group had control. It is these very Ammonites that Jephthah is able to reduce with the help of but a few of the Israelite tribes (chapter 11). Clearly, we must be dealing here with but relatively small and essentially independent groups of Ammonites, Midianites, Israelites, Moabites, and the like, each led by a local chieftain. There is no hint of anything highly organized, of anything amphictyonic, of any kind of centralized authority, of any central shrine, on either side of the Jordan.

This picture, as the book of Judges appears to reflect it, seems likewise to be the very one that chapter 36 in Genesis and the archaeological data of Transjordan point to. In verses 31–39 of this well-known chapter we are given a list of "kings who reigned in the land of Edom before any king of the Israelites reigned." The number of kings listed is eight, and in all instances but two the city of his origin is given. Significantly, in not one single instance is a ruler succeeded by his son or by anyone from his own town. Not one of the six cities mentioned (Dinhabah; Bozrah; Awith; Masrekah; Rehoboth-on-the-river; and Pau. Husham came from "the land of the Temanites," and Baal-hanan's city is not given) ever became known as a "great central shrine," not even the best known of them, Bozrah. And nothing dynastic, or anything approximating centralized rule of monarchy, can be derived from this passage. On the contrary, the picture of Edom given here, in the period prior to King Saul (or, rather, David and Solomon), is exactly that of Israel itself during the period of the

Judges, prior to the rise of centralized authority under the monarchy
—one of petty chieftains, local military leaders, some of the rulers not
unlikely ruling contemporaneously in different regions of the land.
The fact that the biblical text refers to Edom's chieftains as *melakim*
should not impel the reader to jump to the conclusion that "king" in
the classical sense is meant, any more than biblical *shophetim* in the
book of Judges means "judges" in the classical sense.[14]

Transjordan, as is well known, has been combed topographically
very well by Nelson Glueck.[15] There are hardly any places of significance that remained untouched by him. The data compiled by him
shed much light on the clear picture drawn in the Bible. Nothing that
I have been able to determine would suggest a centrally organized
government in any of the Transjordanian countries during the period
of the Judges. I am aware that for Moab evidence was drawn from
two extra-biblical sources, "the Balu'ah stele of the twelfth century
and the Mesha Stone of the ninth . . ."[16]

The Mesha Stone, it is everywhere recognized, is of very considerable importance for conditions in Moab, but—and this is a very great
"but"—for the ninth century. It is fine supplementary material for
the biblical book of Kings; but its significance for our own problem in
the twelfth and eleventh centuries, the period of Israel's "Judges," is
all too little. It is like using the biblical book of Kings—in the absence
of the book of Judges—to prove that Israel was a monarchy and had
centralized government in the earliest phase of the Early Iron Age!

As for the Balu'ah stele, it may be that it is in origin a twenty-third
century or so B.C.E. product that was reused in the twelfth or eleventh

---

[14] G. E. Wright's recent observation (n. 5 on pp. 43 f. of his article on "Archaeology and Old Testament Studies," *JBL*, vol. 77 (1958), 39–51), referred to favorably
by Bright (p. 135, n. 21), is pertinent here, ". . . the rare use of the term 'king' for
God in Israel's earliest tradition should not necessarily be taken to mean that he was
not presented in monarchical form . . . 'king' (*melek*) in that particular Palestinian
environment meant the local princeling of a comparatively small city-state, one
among many . . ."

[15] *Cf., e.g., The Other Side of the Jordan* (New Haven 1940), chap. v, "Edom,
Moab, Ammon, and Gilead," pp. 114 ff., based upon the kind of material incor-
porated in his *Explorations in Eastern Palestine* (vols. 14, 15, and 18–19 of the
Annual of the American Schools of Oriental Research) and related publications.

[16] Albright, *From the Stone Age,* etc., p. 221.

century B.C.E.[17] The inscription on it, however, can no longer be read, the surface is worn so smooth.[18] As to how the Egyptianizing relief on the stone representing deities can point to centrally organized government in Moab, I do not know; surely similar reliefs carved on steles from other places in Syria, Phoenicia, and Palestine[19] do not indicate this political structure.

When we look back upon the nature of Israel's conquest of Canaan and the manner in which the Israelites worked out their *modus vivendi* after that, one may wonder how the concept of "amphictyony" occurred to anyone in the first place. There is nothing amphictyonic about the structure of Canaanite society before or during the period of Israel's Judges. The city-states of Phoenicia, of the Philistines in Canaan, of the Arameans north and east of Israel, did not constitute amphictyonies. There was nothing in this period in this area to influence Israel in this direction.[20]

Rather are we reminded of the Mari document cited by Albrecht Goetze[21] in which "one of the correspondents of the king of Mari writes his master . . . 'There is no king who is powerful on his own. Ten to fifteen kings follow after Hammurapi, the king of Babylon, a like number after Rim-Sin, the king of Larsa, a like number after Ibal-pi-el the king of Eshnunna, a like number after Amut-pi-el, the king of Qatanum, but after Yarim-lim, the king of Yamkhat, there follow twenty kings.' The[se] few lines describe admirably the political system before Hammurapi united Mesopotamia; it consisted chiefly of shifting

---

[17] *Idem, Archaeology and the Religion of Israel* (Baltimore 1942), p. 189, n. 53.

[18] Glueck, *The Other Side,* etc., p. 126, described the stele as follows, "One thinks also of the famous stele found at Baluah near the Wadi Mojib, assigned to the 12th century B.C., whose worn lines of inscription can unfortunately no longer be read (Fig. 66)."

[19] *Cf.* Albright, *op. cit.,* p. 43.

[20] Thus most recently Noth, *The History of Israel* (in dealing with "The Life of Ancient Israel in the Palestinian-Syrian World: I. The Self-Assertion of the Tribes in Palestine, §12, Their Connections with the Earlier Inhabitants of the Land"), pp. 141 ff., makes mention *passim* of the "Canaanite city-state system." Or *cf., e.g.,* Bright (pp. 109 f.), "Canaan was politically without identity . . . Palestine was a patchwork of (petty) states, none of any great size . . ."

[21] On pp. 119 f. of his Presidential address, "Mesopotamian Laws and the Historian", *JAOS,* vol. 69 (1949), 115–120; the Mari Document had appeared in *Syria,* 19 (1938), 117 f.

coalitions of small kings and sheikhs . . . It was the same from the Persian Gulf to the Mediterranean and the borders of Palestine . . ." Substitute David and Solomon, or Mesha, for Hammurabi, and the pattern in Israel and Moab, after consolidation of the conquest and cutting up of Canaan's land empire, is strikingly similar.

Interestingly, it may well be that the early Israelite conception of God provides additional proof that nothing amphictyonic obtained in their societal structure. Already in the patriarchal period the Deity was not localized. He accompanied the patriarchal household in its seminomadic wanderings, and made and renewed covenants with them in several different places. In the period of the Judges the Deity was worshiped in a large number of places. Shrines were plentifully scattered in virtually every populated site, and it is likely that but few persons had to cross tribal boundaries to offer up sacrifice and prayer to God. Amphictyony, a centralized shrine and cult, is scarcely part of this concept or need. And that must be one of the reasons why various rulers, most notably Josiah, failed to destroy the numerous independent shrines all over the country. None of Jerusalem—for a very long time—or Tirzah, or Bethel, or Samaria, or Shechem, or Shiloh, or any other capital or shrine, could achieve this kind of centralized authority. God could be, and always was, worshiped everywhere.

To sum up. Israel in the period of the Judges consisted of tribes and city-states that shared much in religious belief and practice and that spoke the same language; but their economic and geographical conditions, their disposition to commerce rather than to agriculture, the extent to which they were exposed to invasion and even conquest of varying might and duration—these were the factors that determined the actions of the tribes. The tribes and city-states came, or neglected to come, to each other's assistance insofar as they were, or were not, threatened seriously by the invading force. The concept and structure of amphictyony existed in Israel no more than it did in Transjordan or anywhere else in western Asia at the time.

[After completion of this study, there came to hand William W. Hallo's article on "A Sumerian Amphictyony," *Journal of Cuneiform Studies,* vol. xiv (October 1960), 88 ff. It would seem that the political structure of this phase of Ur III is to be compared with the Solomonic period in Israel, when (according to 1 Kings 4:7–5:8; *cf.*, e.g., J. A. Montgomery [-H. S. Gehman], *ICC on Kings* (1951), 119–128, with full bibliography) the national government imposed upon each of twelve *nesibim* ("governors" or the like) in turn monthly dues for the upkeep of the royal household (including probably the national religious center) in Jerusalem. The use of the number "twelve" here, or in Hallo's Sumerian data, or in the case of Esau's *'allufs* in Gen. 36, ought not, as such, call to mind the amphictyonic structure of Greece many centuries and epochs later, where the number "twelve" was only incidental to this structure (*cf.* n. 2 above). Perhaps the number "twelve" as such should now be studied as intensively as the more fortunate number "seven" has been, so as to be understood in its proper setting.]

[At this writing, April, 1973, the institution of amphictyony has been rejected by a number of scholars. *e.g.,* J. G. Vink (in *Oudtestamentische Studiën,* XV [1969]), G. W. Anderson (in the H. G. May Volume: *Translating and Understanding the Old Testament* (1970), pp. 135–151), and R. de Vaux (in *Harvard Theological Review,* 64 [1971], 415–436); and *see* J. R. Porter, "The Israelite Amphictyony: Some Questions" (in a forthcoming issue of *Journal of Theological Studies,* probably 1974.]

5

Nationalism-Universalism
and Internationalism
in Ancient Israel

OUR TOPIC IS PARTICULARLY PERTINENT for a volume that honors
Herbert Gordon May, for it has long been of major interest to him;
see, for example, his discussion of "Theological Universalism in the
Old Testament," *JBR* XVI (1948), 100-107. It is hoped that a close
reading of his article and the present essay that is warmly dedicated
to him will indicate that not infrequently it is a matter of definition
that marks our difference in attitude toward a biblical passage; on
such passages as Isa. 19:18 ff. and Mal. 1:11 we see eye to eye.

It has long been a commonplace, both in Jewish and in Christian
circles, among scholars no less than among laymen, that the authors
of the Hebrew Bible in general and the prophets in particular were
internationalistic in their outlook. It is widely asserted that their concept of God and of the non-Israelite, non-covenanted peoples of the
world embraced, quite beyond the population and boundaries of
ancient Israel, all mankind. Yet it is a fact that no one has attempted

[Published originally in *Translating and Understanding the Old Testament: Essays
in Honor of Herbert Gordon May*, ed. H. T. Frank and W. L. Reed (Nashville-New
York, 1970), pp. 206-236.]

to test systematically this universally assumed and accepted view. No one has gone directly to every pertinent biblical passage and examined it per se within its context, and then brought together all the individual conclusions reached in order to determine whether an integrated whole, a clear pattern, has emerged.

In the course of a paper read by invitation at the one hundred and third annual meeting of the Society of Biblical Literature (New York, December 29, 1967), I dealt with this matter under the general title, "Some Problems of Eisegesis and Exegesis in the Bible." I noted there at the outset that very few areas of scholarly research in the Humanities have been so exposed to outside, nonscholarly pressures as the biblical, both the Hebrew Bible and the New Testament. The Hebrew Bible has long constituted living reality to both the Jewish and Christian communities of the world, in a manner that ancient Mesopotamian or Egyptian or Canaanite or Greek or Roman religious texts have not been. No one devotes a lifetime of careful study to these writings conscious of anyone looking over his shoulder to see how he interprets them, that is, whether his interpretation of these texts will reflect favorably or otherwise on their original authors or on the society that produced them. There is no significant institution or group in existence today that has a vested religious interest in these texts and their interpretation.

Small wonder, then, that biblical research has long been a battlefield for the forces of eisegesis as against exegesis and, what is even more to the point, that hostile eisegesis has not always been recognized by scholarship for what it really is. It has, instead, been accepted as friendly exegesis. It is therefore incumbent upon biblical scholars, more than upon most others, always to be on the alert to recognize and practice the methodology that marks the study of, say, the ancient texts of Mesopotamia, Canaan, Egypt, Greece, and Rome.

It is significant that some half dozen passages constitute the parade examples for the internationalistic view attributed virtually unanimously to the Old Testament authors, and in every one of these passages it is clear, on close scrutiny, that incorrect eisegesis has been permitted to dominate correct exegesis.[1]

One of these passages, as everyone knows, is Mal. 2:10. This says[2]: "Have we not all one father? Has not one God created us?"[3] Yet it is a fact that non-Israelites are in no way involved in this passage. The prophet is addressing himself directly and exclusively to the sacerdotal elements (the priests and Levites) in restored Judah, and he is rebuking them vigorously for acting improperly and arrogantly vis-à-vis the nonsacerdotal, the lay elements in the Judean community, as though they were not equally the covenanted partners of God:

> "And now, O priests, this command is for you. If you will not listen, if you will not lay it to heart, to give glory to My name," says the Lord of Hosts, "then I will send the curse upon you. . . . So shall you know that I have sent this command to you, that My covenant with Levi may hold. . . . True instruction was in his mouth, and no wrong was found on his lips. . . . But you have turned aside from the way; you have caused many to stumble by your instruction; you have corrupted the covenant of Levi. . . ."   Mal. 2:1-8.

It is this denunciation of the priestly class which leads directly into our vs. 10. Indeed, the second half of our verse goes on to say: "Why then are we faithless to one another, profaning the covenant of our

---

[1] See the "Introductory Statement" in H. M. Orlinsky, *The So-Called "Servant of the Lord" and "Suffering Servant" in Second Isaiah, Supplements to VT* XIV (Leiden, 1967), pp. 3-4, where some pertinent passages from H. J. Cadbury's paper on "Motives of Biblical Scholarship" (*JBL* LVI [1937], 1-16) are quoted, and where further reference is made to essays by E. R. Goodenough and M. S. Enslin.

[2] The translations employed in this essay, where they are not my own, derive from *The Torah* (New York, 2nd ed., 1967), *The Five Megilloth and Jonah* (New York, 1969), or the RSV. In no case have I parted company with these translations when an important interpretation was involved.

[3] *ha-lo 'av 'eḥad le-khull-ánu//ha-lo 'el 'eḥad bera'ánu.* The system of transliteration employed in this essay has been simplified as much as possible without, it is hoped, loss of clarity. Thus *v* and *kh* (as distinct from *b* and *k*) represent spirant *beth* and *kaf*, whereas *g* and *d* do service for both spirant and mute *gimel* and *dáleth*. The length of the vowels has been disregarded, and only the penult accent has been indicated.

fathers?" It is only by suppressing this latter part of the verse, with its clear reference to "the covenant of our fathers" (*b*e*rith 'a*vothénu*) —which could embrace fellow Israelites only—that the first part, now wrenched wholly out of context, can be made to refer to all the peoples of the earth. This is a clear case of eisegesis.

In the process, one must also not forget that the only time a non-Israelite people is mentioned by Malachi is when Edom is referred to at the very beginning of the book. What the text says is this:

> The oracle of the word of the Lord to Israel through Malachi. "I have loved you," said the Lord. But you [namely, Israel] have said, "How have You loved us?" The Lord replies, "Esau is Jacob's brother; yet I have favored Jacob, and I have rejected Esau. I have made his hill-country a waste, and given his heritage to jackals of the desert." If Edom says, "We are shattered, but we will rebuild the ruins," the Lord of Hosts says, "They may build, but I will tear down, till they are called the wicked country, the people with whom the Lord is angry forever."
> Mal. 1:1-4.

That is what the text of the book of Malachi says about what its post-biblical readers assert to be an expression of internationalism.

It is rare for a verse to be made the basis for a creed. Yet Lev. 19:18 has been used in this manner with reference to internationalism and the "Golden Rule." This passage, traditionally rendered "You shall love your neighbor as yourself" (for a more precise and less misleading translation, see below) has long been used as the basis for the concept of world brotherhood.

Disregarding the implications of the negative and positive forms of expressing it, this concept reads "And what you hate, do not do to any one" in Tobit 4:15; "Just as you do not wish evils to befall you, but to participate in all that is good, so you should deal with those subject to you and with offenders . . . for God deals with all men with gentleness" in the Letter of Aristeas[4]; and "What is hateful to you,

---

[4] Section 207, in M. Hadas (ed.), *Jewish Apocryphal Literature* (Philadelphia, 1951), where additional reference is made, *inter alios*, to Isocrates (436-338 B.C.),

do not do to your fellow man. This is the whole Law (*Torah*); the rest is commentary" is credited to Hillel (first century B.C.) in the Babylonian Talmud, Shabbat 31*a* (in reply to the request of a heathen convert to Judaism for a brief exposition of his newly adopted religion). In similar manner, Jesus formulated the Golden Rule by "So whatever you wish that men would do to you, do so to them; for this is the Law and the Prophets" (Matt. 7:12; cf. Luke 6:31). And the answer he gave to the question, "Teacher, which is the great commandment in the Law?" is recorded in Matt. 22:37-40:

> "You shall love the Lord your God with all your heart, and with all your soul, and with all your mind [Deut. 6:5]. This is the great and first commandment. And a second is like it, You shall love your neighbor as yourself [Lev. 19:18]. On these two commandments depend all the Law and the Prophets."

Already Sirach (Ecclesiasticus; about 200 B.C.), at 17:14, had alluded to the Leviticus passage: "And He gave commandment to each of them concerning his neighbor." So did Paul several centuries later: "Now I Paul say to you. . . . For the whole Law is fulfilled in one word, "You shall love your neighbor as yourself" (Gal. 5:2, 14); with which compare Rom. 13:8-10: ". . . for he who loves his neighbor has fulfilled the Law . . . ," and subsequently James 2:8 ff.: "If you really fulfill the royal law, according to the Scripture, 'You shall love your neighbor as yourself,' you do well. . . ." Akiba, apparently a contemporary of James, likewise expressed the prevailing Jewish belief that Lev. 19:18 was the supreme principle in the Bible (see Sifra, *ad. loc.*).[5]

Nicocles 3:61 ("Do not do unto others that which angers you when others do it unto you"), and to the rabbinic and early Christian formulations mentioned by H. G. Meecham (*The Oldest Version of the Bible: "Aristeas" or Its Traditional Origin* [London, 1932], p. 292), and by H. L. Strack-P. Billerbeck (*Kommentar zum Neuen Testament aus Talmud und Midrasch,* I, "Das Evangelium nach Matthäus," 459-60).

[5] For additional data and discussions, the reader should consult the chapter on "The Greatest Commandment" in I. Abrahams, *Studies in Pharisaism and the*

There can be little doubt that early in the postbiblical period, first among the Jews and later among the Christians also, Lev. 19:18 became the biblical cornerstone of internationalism, of the concept of world brotherhood and the essential equality of all mankind. But is this outlook, noble and worthwhile as it may be, really what the text of Leviticus says? Alas, it requires no great learning or ingenuity, only objectivity—the determination to let the Hebrew text speak for itself—to read the text and its immediate, pertinent context and to note that its author had no one but fellow Israelites in mind.

In vss. 11, 15, and 17 he speaks of *'ᵃmithékha*, traditionally rendered "neighbor," the same as *re'ᵃkha*, but probably a more intimate (family?) term[6]; in vs. 16 he employs the term *bᵉne 'ammékha* "your countrymen" traditionally "your people"; in vs. 17 he uses the expression *'aḥíkha* "your brother, kinsman"; and in vs. 18, immediately preceding our own phrase, he asserts: *lo'-thiqqom wᵉlo'-thiṭṭor 'eth-bᵉne 'ammékha*, "You shall not take vengeance or bear a grudge against your countrymen" (RSV: against the sons of your own people). Reading the chapter as a whole, it is crystal clear that the author was addressing himself to fellow Israelites alone:

> The Lord spoke to Moses, saying: Speak to the whole Israelite community (*dabber 'el-kol-'ᵃdath bᵉne-yisra'el*) and say to them: You shall be holy, for I, the Lord your God, am holy. . . . You shall not steal; you shall not deal deceitfully or falsely with one another (*'ish ba'ᵃmitho*). You shall not swear falsely by My name, profaning the name of your

---

Gospels (KTAV reissue, New York, 1967), pp. 18-29 (with its reference to Philo, etc.); G. F. Moore, *Judaism in the First Centuries of the Christian Era: The Age of the Tannaim*, II (Cambridge, 1927), 79-88; G. B. King, "The 'Negative' Golden Rule," *JR* VIII (1928), 268-79; and see the comments by Malbim (Meir Leibush ben Yehiel Michael, nineteenth-century commentator on the Bible, author of *Ha-Torah we-ha-Miṣwah*) at Lev. 19:18, and by S. Zeitlin in "Love Your Enemies," pp. xxiii-xxvi of his "Prolegomenon" to the 1969 (KTAV) reissue of G. Friedländer, *The Jewish Sources of the Sermon on the Mount* (1911), as well as the chapter there (XVII) on "The Jewish Origin of the Golden Rule" (pp. 226-38).

6 While the dictionaries and commentaries generally adduce Akkadian *emūtu* as a cognate, the extra-biblical history of Hebrew *'amith* is hardly certain, and is in need of close analysis.

God: I am the Lord. You shall not defraud your fellow (*re'ᵃkha*) . . . .
You shall not render an unfair decision: do not favor the poor or show
deference to the rich; judge your kinsman (*'ᵃmithékha*). Do not deal
basely [meaning of Hebrew uncertain] with your countrymen (*bᵉ'ammékha*). Do not profit [meaning of Hebrew uncertain] by the blood of
your fellow (*re'ékha*): I am the Lord. You shall not hate your kinsman
(*'aḥikha*) in your heart. Reprove your kinsman (*'ᵃmithekha*), but incur
no guilt because of him. You shall not take vengeance or bear a grudge
against your countrymen (*bᵉne 'ammékha*). Love your fellow as yourself (*wᵉ'ahavta lᵉre'ᵃkha kamókha*): I am the Lord. You shall observe
My laws. . . .   Lev. 19:2-19.

As indicated above, it is not easy to find in the English language a
single word as the precise and clear equivalent for *ré'ᵃ*. The traditional
rendering "neighbor" lends itself too readily to misinterpretation, and
far too many readers of the Bible fail to recognize that " 'Neighbor'
in the Old Testament generally denotes a fellow member of the people
of the covenant; it is therefore similar to 'brother' . . ." (H. F. Beck,
"Neighbor," IDB III, 534-35). The term "fellow Israelite" expresses
the idea accurately.[6a]

Furthermore, it may be noted that in the covenanted Israelite
societal structure in the holy land of Israel, where all the inhabitants,
non-Israelite as well as Israelite, were subject to the laws of the covenant, the non-Israelite who lived in the land had numerous privileges
and responsibilities (see the convenient discussion of "Sojourner" by
T. M. Mauch in IDB IV, 397-99). Since our section of Lev. 19
involved Israelites only, it was necessary, later in the chapter, to make
special reference to the non-Israelites who resided (a better term than

---

[6a] The reader will understand that I do not exclude for *ré'ᵃ* elsewhere, where
applicable, the meaning of "neighbor" or "fellow man" in reference to a non-
Israelite. Thus in Ex. 11:2, "Tell the people that each man shall borrow from
his neighbor (*re'éhu*), and each woman from her neighbor (*re'uthah*), objects of
silver and gold," the neighbor is a non-Israelite Egyptian. In the same way, just
because *rú'ḥ* means "wind" in Gen. 1:2 doesn't mean that it cannot have the
meaning "spirit" elsewhere (e. g., when Pharaoh's "spirit was agitated" in Gen. 41:8);
see my discussion in either JQR, 48 [1957], 174-182 or on pp. 52-55 of my ed.
Notes on the New Translation of the Torah (JPS, 5730-1969).

"sojourned," which denotes a brief or temporary stay, a "visit") in the land; accordingly, vss. 33-34 read:

> When a stranger resides with you in your land (*w*e*khi-yagur 'ittekhu ger*), you shall not wrong him. The stranger who resides with you shall be to you as one of your citizens (*k*e*'ezrah mikkem yihyeh lakhem ha-ger ha-gar 'itt*e*khem*); you shall love him as yourself, for you were strangers in the land of Egypt: I the Lord am your God.

It is only because he resides among Israelites in the land of Israel that the non-Israelite receives this status; the same non-Israelite, were he a resident of Moab, or Ammon, or Assyria, or Egypt, or Edom, or Babylonia, etc., would have no such status, for the non-Israelite outside the land of Israel was outside the scope of the covenant between Israel and God.

A third classical case in point is the passage in Amos 9, where the statement is made (vs. 7):

> "You are to Me the same as the Ethiopians, O children of Israel," declares the Lord. "I brought up Israel from the Land of Egypt, and the Philistines from Caphtor, and the Arameans from Kir."

Amos is commonly understood to manifest here internationalism on the highest level: Ethiopians, Israelites, Philistines, Arameans—all are regarded equally by the God of Israel.

But does Amos really assert, or even imply, either here or anywhere else in his book, that the God of Israel is at the same time and equally the God of the Ethiopians and of the Philistines and of the Arameans? This is hardly what Amos says or implies in 2:4:

> Thus said the Lord:
> For three transgressions of Judah,
> For four, I will not revoke it,
> Because they have rejected the Teaching of the Lord
>   (*'eth-torath YHWH*)
> And have not kept His laws (*ḥuqqaw*).

None of the six non-Israelite nations mentioned previously (1:3-2:3—Arameans, Philistines, Phoenicians, Edomites, Ammonites, and Moabites) was accused of rejecting God's *torah* or of transgressing His *ḥuqqim*. How could they be, when they had no such obligation to Him in the first place?

Even more positive and pointed is Amos' statement in 3:1-2:

> Hear this word that the Lord has spoken concerning (or: against) you, O children of Israel, concerning (or: against) the whole family that I brought up from the land of Egypt:
>
> > You only have I recognized (or: acknowledged)
> > Of all the families of the earth;
> > Therefore I will punish you
> > For all your iniquities.

The fact that God brought up the Philistines from Caphtor and the Arameans from Kir in no wise indicated that these peoples and God had entered into a contract, as Israel and God had done previously. Indeed, God's contract with Israel was a mutually exclusive one, and forbade Israel to recognize and worship any other god—on penalty of various kinds and degrees of punishment—and barred God from recognizing any other people or from prospering it against Israel.[7]

As a matter of fact, the very phrase "I brought you up (*he⁽e⁾léthi 'ethkhem*)—or: "brought you out," "freed you" (*hoṣé'thi 'ethkhem*) —from the land of Egypt," frequently occurs in the Bible in place of the term *bᵉrith* ("covenant") to indicate God's exclusive covenant with Israel. Thus Amos employs this phrase three times (2:10; 3:1; 9:7) for the covenant relationship, whereas in its single occurrence (1:9) the term *bᵉrith* is employed in a less exclusive sense, concerning the "covenant of brotherhood" (*bᵉrith 'aḥim*) between Phoenicia

---

[7] Note, e.g., how often the *niph'al* form of *shabaᶜ*, "to swear, vow," is found in the Bible with God as the subject and His covenant with Israel as the context; see S. Mandelkern, *Concordance*, 5th ed. by (F. Margolin-) M. Goshen-Gottstein (1962), p. 1144. God could not act counter to His voluntary vow, unless Israel transgressed.

(Tyre) and an unnamed people which the former violated. Similarly, the expressions "I/He (God) led you (cf. 2:10, *wa-'olekh 'ethkhem*) through the wilderness (for forty years)," and "I/He (God) destroyed the Amorites/Canaanites (cf. 2:9, *we-'anokhi hishmádti 'eth-ha-'emori*) before you," and "I/He (God) dispossessed the Amorites/Canaanites (*wa-yóresh 'eth-ha'emori*) before you," are all expressions of the covenant relationship between God and Israel, never between God and any other people.[8]

What, then, is the relationship between God and the non-covenanted, non-Israelite peoples of the world, in view of the undeniable fact (e.g., Amos 1:3-2:3) that God, and none other, punishes them for transgressions? Further, what is the nature of these transgressions, seeing that God's *torah* and *ḥuqqim*, that is, His covenant, are not involved?

To the biblical writers, from first to last, God is not only Israel's God alone, exactly as Israel is God's people alone, but He is at the same time, and naturally so, also the God of the universe, the only God in existence in the whole wide world, the only God who ever existed and who will ever exist. As God of the universe, He is the sole

---

[8] James Muilenburg has made use of these expressions in his discussion of "The Form and Structure of the Covenantal Formulations," *VT* IX (1959), 347-65, though they hardly demonstrate an amphictyony; on the nonexistence of this institution in ancient Israel, see J. G. Vink, "The Date and Origin of the Priestly Code in the Old Testament" in *The Priestly Code and Seven Other Studies, Oudtestamentische Studiën*, XV (1969), 128 ff.: ". . . the idea of *amphictyony*. Recent studies tend to do away with the concept altogether. . . . An all-out attack on the amphictyonic hypothesis was launched by H. M. Orlinsky ('The Tribal System of Israel and Related Groups in the Period of the Judges,' *Oriens Antiquus*, 1 [1962], 11-20). . . . We agree with Orlinsky's view, not with Noth's widespread theory . . ."; and see further reference there to R. Smend, S. Herrmann, G. Fohrer, J. Maier, and others. H. G. May, in *The Bible in Modern Scholarship,* J. P. Hyatt, ed. (Nashville, 1965), p. 73, had expressed the opinion that ". . . deserving further discussion . . . is the amphictyonic organization of early Israel, almost axiomatic in contemporary biblical scholarship even though variously interpreted, and concerning which Orlinsky has raised serious questions." [See now the references to G. W. Anderson's and to R. de Vaux's complete rejection of amphictyony *apud* my above-mentioned essay printed elsewhere in this volume as chap. 4, pp. 66 ff.]

Creator and Master of all heavenly bodies (sun, moon, stars), of all natural phenomena (lightning, thunder, rain, drought, earthquakes), and of sky, earth, waters, and all living beings therein, human and animal. All natural phenomena, all heavenly bodies, all living creatures, all people, nations and individuals alike, are subject to His direct supervision and will. He is their Master in the fullest sense of the term.

And so, the God of Israel is at the same time the sole God and Master of the universe without being the God of any nation but Israel: the *national* God of biblical Israel is a *universal* God, but not an *international* God. With no people other than Israel did God ever enter into a legally binding relationship. To the biblical writers, God was never the God of Moab, or of Egypt, or Canaan or Assyria or Aram or Ethiopia or Philistia, *et. al.* He was the God of Israel alone; and just as Israel was to have no other god, just so was God to have no other people. However, as the God and Master of the universe, God did have a legal obligation to all His creation, embracing not only all non-Israelite peoples of the world, but also the living creatures of sky, earth, and waters, all the heavenly bodies, and the like.

What is this universal legal obligation of God's? According to the Bible (Gen. 8-10), after God destroyed the world (a world that had become too lawless to merit preservation) He assured the survivors (Noah and his family and all the animals with them, and their descendants forever) that never again would He bring destruction upon life on earth. But mankind, in turn, had to respect human life; wanton murder and the shedding of blood would not be tolerated. God further fixed the careers of all heavenly bodies, of the seasons, of the use of animals as food for man, and other matters that we have come to subsume generally under the term "natural law." As a result, while no nation other than Israel owes allegiance to God and His Teaching (*Torah*), and while God has committed and restricted Himself exclusively to the interests of His Chosen people, Israel, He has the power, as the God of the universe, to regulate and to interfere in the affairs of all peoples everywhere. He will not tolerate murder, excessive brutality, wanton conduct; such action is contrary to God's ordered universe, to what has aptly been called by the rabbis the "Noahide Laws."

J. H. Greenstone wrote a clear and compact article on this subject in the *Jewish Encyclopedia* in 1904.⁹ These are "Laws," he wrote,

> which were supposed by the Rabbis to have been binding upon mankind at large even before the revelation at Sinai, and which are still binding upon non-Jews. The term Noachian indicates the universality of these ordinances, since the whole human race was supposed to be descended from the three sons of Noah, who alone survived the Flood. Although only those laws which are found in the earlier chapters of the Pentateuch, before the record of the revelation at Sinai, should, it would seem, be binding upon all mankind, yet the Rabbis discarded some and, by hermeneutic rules or in accordance with some tradition . . . introduced others which are not found there. . . . They declared that the following six commandments were enjoined upon Adam: (1) not to worship idols; (2) not to blaspheme the name of God; (3) to establish the courts of justice; (4) not to kill; (5) not to commit adultery; and (6) not to rob. . . . A seventh commandment was added after the Flood—not to eat flesh that had been cut from a living animal (Gen. ix. 4). Thus the Talmud frequently speaks of "the seven laws of the sons of Noah," which were regarded as obligatory upon all mankind, in contradistinction to those that were binding upon Israelites only. . . . In another baraita . . . the seven Noachian prohibitions are enumerated as applying to the following: (1) idolatry; (2) adultery; (3) murder; (4) robbery; (5) eating of a limb cut from a living animal; (6) the emasculation of animals; (7) the pairing of animals of different species. . . .¹⁰

---

⁹ "Laws, Noachian," II, 648-50. This *Encyclopedia* was recently reissued by KTAV.

¹⁰ An interesting recent discussion of "Do Noachites Have to Believe in Revelation? A Passage in Dispute Between Maimonides, Spinoza, Mendelssohn, and H. Cohen: a Contribution to a Jewish View of Natural Law," by S. S. Schwarzschild, may be found in *JQR* LII (1961-62), 297-308; LIII (1962-63), 30-65. Incidentally, to Maimonides, the seven Noahide commandments are: the prohibitions of (1) idolatry, (2) the improper use of the name of God, (3) murder, (4) sexual immorality, and (5) theft, (6) the injunction to establish laws and courts, and (7) the prohibition to eat meat from a living animal. But whereas it had generally been held that (p. 301) "Everyone who accepts the seven Noachite laws and is careful to fulfill them is one of the righteous men of the nations of the world

Postbiblical rabbinic discussions apart, the fact remains that the Bible does tell us quite a bit about these universal laws. In Gen. 9:1 ff. we read:

> God blessed Noah and his sons, and said to them, "Be fertile and increase, and fill the earth. The fear and dread of you shall be upon all the beasts of the earth and upon all the birds of the sky ... and upon all the fish of the sea. . . . Every creature that lives shall be yours to eat; as with the green grasses, I give you all these. You must not, however, eat flesh with its life-blood in it. But for your own life-blood I will require a reckoning: I will require it of every beast; of man, too, will I require a reckoning for human life, of every man for that of his fellow man!
>
> > Whoever sheds the blood of man,
> > By man shall his blood be shed;
> > For in His image
> > Did God make man."

And God continues (vss. 9 ff.):

> "I now establish My covenant (*'eth-b^erithi*) with you and your offspring to come, and with every living thing that is with you—birds, cattle, and every wild beast as well. . . . Never again shall there be a flood to destroy the earth. . . ."

Or when Isaiah denounces King Sennacherib of Assyria and assures him ignominious defeat, it is because of his blasphemous treatment of God (II Kings 19:22 ff.//Isa. 37:22 ff.):

> Whom have you blasphemed and reviled
> > (*'eth-mi ḥeráfta w^e-giddáfta*),
> Against whom raised your voice
> And insolently raised your eyes?

---

and has a share in the world to come," Maimonides introduced the condition that the "Noachite" must also believe that these seven laws were revealed by God to Moses in the Torah, and that he thus merely reaffirmed an earlier injunction to Noah and his children.

Against the Holy One of Israel!
. . .
Because you have raged against Me,
And your tumult has reached My ears,
I will put My hook in your nose
And My bit in your mouth;
And I will take you back by the road
By which you came.

Turning back to Amos, chaps. 1 and 2, it is, again, God's universal, "Noahide" laws which have been violated by Israel's Gentile non-covenanted neighbors. Again, it is in His capacity as the God of the universe (not as the national God of Israel, since Israel was not the object of these violations) that He will punish the transgressors. In 1:3-5 it is the inhuman treatment that Damascus meted out to Gilead ("because they threshed Gilead with threshing sledges of iron") that will result in the former's punishment. In vss. 6-8, Gaza will suffer the consequences for "carrying off into exile a whole people." According to vss. 9-10, God will destroy Tyre "because they delivered up a whole people to Edom and did not remember the covenant of brotherhood"; while vss. 11-12 assert that God will devastate Edom "because he pursued his brother with the sword and cast off all pity." God will destroy Ammon and exile her leaders, say vss. 13-14, "because they ripped up women with child in Gilead"; and, finally, in 2:1-3, God will cut off the leaders of Moab "because they burned to lime the bones of the king of Edom."

All these crimes are clearly violations of the "Noahide" laws, the universal laws of nature, involving as they do mass murder, exile, and excessive and unnatural brutality—man's inhumanity to man. It is because God promulgated these laws that they exist (at least the biblical writers believed this to be so), and it is God alone who will punish the violaters. Indeed, who else is there to execute judgment—the "no-gods" of Syria, Philistia, Phoenicia, Edom, Ammon, and Moab? Then, after having hammered home to his Israelite audience the fact that Israel's God is the only and all-powerful Deity in the world, Amos turned directly to his fellow countrymen and warned them, as God's only covenanted people, that far and beyond their non-covenanted neighbors, they would be called to account "for having rejected the Teaching of the Lord and for not having kept His laws" (*al-mo'°sam 'eth-torath YHWH w*e*huqqaw lo' shamáru*)—for it is Israel alone upon whom the *torah* of God was binding. And this is exactly the import of 9:7. As the sole Deity of the universe, Israel's God is responsible for the migrations and careers of all peoples of the world, be it those of the Ethiopians, or of the Philistines, or of the Arameans, or others, as well as of those of His own chosen people. This did not, however, make Israel's God (nor is it ever so asserted in the Bible) also the God of the Ethiopians, or of the Philistines, or of the Arameans!

To prove that the expressions *'elohe ph*e*lishtim, 'elohe 'aram, 'elohe mo'av,* or *'ammon* or *'edom* or *'ashshur* or *bavel* or *miṣráyim*, etc., never refer to the God of Israel, it is scarcely necessary to refer to such a passage as Judg. 10:6: "The Israelites again did what was evil in the sight of the Lord. They served the Baalim and the Ashtaroth, and the gods of Aram, and the gods of Sidon, and the gods of Moab, and the gods of the Ammonites, and the gods of the Philistines; but they forsook the Lord and did not serve Him" (. . . *wa-ya'avdu 'eth-ha-b*e*'alim we-'eth-ha-'ashtaroth we-'eth-'elohe 'aram w*e*-'eth-'elohe ṣidon w*e*-'eth 'elohe mo'av w*e*-'eth 'elohe b*e*ne-'ammon w*e*-'eth 'elohe ph*e*-lishtim . . .*).

It is worth noting here that it may well be that the term *'elohe* in connection with, say, Moab and Ammon, ought to be translated "god" rather than "gods." The evidence that the Moabites and Ammonites regularly served more than one deity (more than, respectively, Chemosh and Milcom) is hardly any greater than that the Israelites regularly served more than one (YHWH). Thus the Moabite Stone and the Book of Kings, so far as monotheism is concerned, are not greatly different. What the term *'elohe* conveys here, and frequently elsewhere in the Bible, is not "gods" to indicate gross polytheism, but simply "a no-god," "an alleged god." So that the expression *'elohim 'aḥerim* may very often be rendered simply "another god" with even more justification than "other gods." The idea is simply that the biblical writers complained that God was not being obeyed, not that more than one other god was being worshiped. Whether the common expression accusing Israel of worshiping "other gods" (or perhaps "another god"; see Mandelkern's *Concordance*, s. *'aherim*) really constituted an accusation of idolatry or was, rather, a cliché expression for "You are not obeying God, whose spokesman I am and whose orders I bring you; obey Him by heeding my (i.e., His) words" (the speaker being anyone who claimed to be a spokesman of God: Moses, Samuel, Nathan, Ahijah, Elijah, or any of the prophets, etc.), is a very basic problem that I hope to deal with elsewhere. Be it also noted that just because a Gentile people worshiped only one god was no indication to the biblical writers that he was a real god and comparable to their own God, or that such a people was, like the Israelites, also monotheistic. Such a people was a heathen people that worshiped "a no-god."

In line with this understanding of the biblical concept of God (that is, that God was national and universal but not international), other passages such as Isa. 2:2-4, Mic. 4:1-4, and Isa. 56:7 fall readily and naturally into place. As the only real God in the world, and with Israel as His exclusive partner in covenant, the biblical writers believed that sooner or later the peoples of the world would come to recognize these two covenanted partners as representing the only true religious force. Thus Isaiah and Micah (perhaps deriving from a common source) declare:

> In days to come,
> The Mount of the Lord's House shall be established
> As the highest mountain,
> Rise above the peaks;
> And all the nations shall stream to it,
> And many peoples shall go and say:
> "Come, let us go up
> To the Mount of the Lord,
> To the House of Jacob's God,
> That He may instruct us in His ways
> And that we may walk in His paths."

For instruction (*torah*) shall come forth from Zion,
The word of the Lord from Jerusalem.
He will judge among the nations,
Arbitrate for many peoples;
And they shall beat their swords into plowshares,
Their spears into pruning hooks:
Nation shall not lift up sword against nation,
And never again train for war.

Whether this declaration is to be understood literally or figuratively, and even though the precise historical circumstances for it will hardly ever be determined, these two prophets expressed unequivocally the nationalism of God and the superiority—rather, the uniqueness— of His teaching (*torah*) which He gave to His people, Israel. Further, it is to Zion, and to no other capital city or religious center, that the peoples of the earth will stream, and it is from Jerusalem, and from no other spot on earth, that God's message (*davar*) will emanate. Yet strange as it may seem, this passage has been comprehended by nearly everyone as the very essence of internationalism, as though there were a single aspect of the beliefs and practices of any people in the world except Israel—the language, or the prayers, or the sacrifices, or the shrines, let alone the gods—that was worthy of the slightest consideration for incorporation into God's *torah*.

As for Isa. 56:7, "for My House shall be called a House of prayer for all peoples" (*ki bethi beth-t*^e*phillah yiqqare l*^e*khol-ha- 'ammim*), the whole passage, far from articulating internationalism, simply asserts that those non-Israelites (vss. 3-6 make mention of "foreigner[s]" *ben* [*b*^e*ne*]-*ha-nekhar* and "eunuch[s]" *saris*[*im*]) who adopt and demonstrate their obedience to God's commandments and institutions would be permitted to become members of His covenanted community in the land of Israel (vss. 1-8):

Thus said the Lord:
Observe what is right and do what is just,
For soon My vindication shall come,
My deliverance soon to be revealed.

Fortunate is the man who does this,
The person who holds fast to it:
Who keeps the sabbath and does not profane it,
And stays his hand from doing any evil.
Let not the foreigner say,
Who has attached himself to the Lord,
"The Lord will exclude me from His people,"
And let not the eunuch say,
"I am but a dry stick."
For thus said the Lord:
As for the eunuchs who keep My sabbaths,
Who choose what I delight in
And hold fast to My covenant:
I will give to them
In My House and within My walls
A monument and a name
Better than sons and daughters.
I will give them an everlasting name
Which shall never perish.
And the foreigners who attach themselves to the Lord,
To minister to Him and to love the name of the Lord,
To be His servants—
All who keep the sabbath and do not profane it,
And who hold fast to My covenant—
I will bring them to My sacred Mount
And let them rejoice in My House of prayer.
Their burnt offerings and sacrifices
Shall be accepted on My altar;
For My House shall be called
A house of prayer for all peoples.

Thus declares the Lord God,
Who gathers the dispersed of Israel:
I will gather still more to those already gathered.

Note that only those Gentiles—even eunuchs!—who have already
been observing the laws of the sabbath and fulfilling the covenant
in every respect are eligible for membership in God's select com-

munity, membership that takes effect when they have emigrated from
Babylonia to Judah and entered the service of God in His Temple in
Jerusalem.

Even a cursory examination of our section is sufficient to point to an
adherent of the priestly hierarchy in power in restored Judah as the
author. This is evident, for example, from the *combination* of the
following items: (1) The emphasis on the observance of the sabbath
(vss. 2, 4, 6) is typically priestly. The term *shabbath,* not part of
Second Isaiah's concern or vocabulary, is found otherwise only in
66:23, in a similarly late and specifically priestly context:

> "And from them (namely, the Gentile nations mentioned in vs. 19:
> Tarshish, Put (Pul, Heb.), Lud, Tubal, Javan, and the distant coasts)
> likewise I will take some to be levitical priests (lit., priests, Levites, *la-
> koh^anim la-l^ewiyyim*)," said the Lord.

> "For as the new heaven and the new earth
> Which I will make
> Shall endure before Me,"
> Declares the Lord,
> "So shall your seed and your name endure.
> And new moon after new moon,
> And sabbath after sabbath (*u-midde shabbath b^eshabbatho*),
> All flesh shall come to worship Me."

Note in this connection that the phrase *shabbath b^e-shabbatho* occurs
only here (in vs. 23) and in Num. 28:10 (a *P* passage); also that all
thirty-one occurrences of the plural form *shabbathoth* in the Bible are
found in *P* or otherwise late contexts: Exod. 31:13; Leviticus (eleven
times); Ezekiel (twelve times); Neh. 10:34; I Chron. 23:31; II
Chronicles (four times); and our Isaiah (56:4) passage.

(2) It is not acceptability of Gentiles or proselytism in general that
the author has in mind here (as one might argue, say, for Isa. 2:2-4
[Mic. 4:1-4]), but the legalization even of castrated Gentiles for sacred
work in the Temple of Jerusalem. This is contrary, for example, to
the older law (Deut. 23:2 [1]): "No one whose testes are crushed or

whose member is cut off shall be admitted into the congregation of the Lord." Indeed, even an animal with such defects is excluded as a sacrifice to the Lord, especially when offered by a *ben-nekhar,* "a foreigner" (Lev. 22:24-25): "You shall not offer to the Lord anything [with its testes] bruised or crushed or torn or cut; you shall have no such practices [i.e., mutilations or sacrifices] in your land. Nor shall you accept any such [animals] from a foreigner for offering as food for your God; since they are mutilated, they have a defect, they shall not be accepted in your favor."

(3) It is not easy to deny a direct connection between a passage such as Num. 18:1 ff. and our passage in Isa. 56. The Numbers passage reads:

> The Lord said to Aaron: You with your sons and your ancestral house shall bear any guilt connected with the sanctuary. . . . You shall associate with yourself your kinsmen the tribe of Levi, your ancestral tribe, to be attached to you and to minister to you (*wᵉ-yillawu ᶜalékha wi-sharᵉ-thúkha*), while you and your sons [serve] before the Tent of the Pact. They shall discharge their duties to you and to the Tent as a whole, but they must not have any contact with the furnishings of the shrine or with the altar, lest both they and you die. . . . No outsider (*zar,* i.e., an Israelite not of priestly-levitical stock) shall intrude upon you as you discharge the duties connected with the shrine and the altar. . . . I hereby take your fellow Levites from among the Israelites; they are assigned to you in dedication to the Lord . . . , while you and your sons shall be careful to perform your priestly duties in everything pertaining to the altar and to what is behind the curtain. . . . Any outsider (*zar*) who encroaches shall be put to death.

In Isa. 56:6 note the expression *u-bᵉne ha-nekhar ha-nilwim ᶜal-YHWH lᵉsharᵉtho* ("And the foreigners who attach themselves to the Lord to minister to him") in connection with vs. 2 in the Numbers passage reproduced above; and 56:7, *ᶜolothehem wᵉ-zivḥehem lᵉraṣon ᶜal-mizbᵉḥi* ("Their [viz., the foreigners'] burnt offerings and sacrifices shall be accepted on My altar") is to be noted for the contrast with vss. 3, 5, 7 in the Numbers passage.

A closer study may well uncover other associations that are pertinent. Thus, is *lo' yikkareth* in Isa. 56:5 (". . . I will give them [the
eunuchs] an everlasting name which shall never perish [lit., be cut
off]"), a deliberate play on *karuth,* "one whose member (or testicles)
is cut off" (Deut. 23:2 *keruth shaphkha; karuth* for animals in Lev.
22:24)? The eunuch's manliness may be cut off, but not his name!
Or when Isa. 56:6 talks of "(the foreigners who attach themselves to
the Lord to minister to Him . . .) to become His servants," should this
expression, *lihyoth lo(w) la-cavadim,* recall at once Lev. 25:55, *ki-li
vene-yisra'el cavadim cavaday hem,* "For it is to Me that the Israelites
are servants: they are My servants . . ."? It is significant that only
Israel and Israelites are God's servants (*'eved, avadim*) in the Bible,
with the sole exception of the eunuchs in this passage, and Nebuchadrezzar[11]; all other *avadim* are servants to mortals.

There is, of course, much more to the problem of "levitical priests"
than our immediate preoccupation with nationalism-universalism; for
example, the date of the sections quoted above and the period and
circumstances in which Aaron and the tribe of Levi (not the craft of
the levite, as in Judg. 17-18 [12]) were introduced in the Bible. But
enough argument has been presented here to indicate that, far from
being a model expression of internationalism, Isa. 56 presents the
clerical-nationalist interests of the priestly group in power in post-
exilic times, interests that are somewhat less than internationalistic.[13]

As a matter of fact, it is not certain that Isa. 56 is even universalistic,

---

[11] See chap. I, "The Biblical Term 'Servant' in Relation to God," pp. 7-11 in
H. M. Orlinsky, *The So-Called "Servant of the Lord," op. cit.,* with the "Additional
Note" on "King Nebuchadr/nezzar of Babylon, My Servant" in Jer. 25:9; 27:6;
43:10.

[12] See Section D, "The Seer-Priest in Ancient Israel," in my chapter (**XXIV**)
on "The Seer-Priest," *The Patriarchs and the Judges,* B. Mazar, ed., II, 144 ff., in
the series *The World History of the Jewish People* due to appear in English in
1969-70/5730. In the Hebrew version of 1967/5727, see pp. 290-96, 366-70, 387.
[See now the essay, "The Seer-Priest and the Prophet in Ancient Israel," reprinted
elsewhere in this volume as chap. 3, pp. 39 ff.]

[13] See the monograph by Vink (*op. cit.*) on the priestly treatment of history
and historical materials.

let alone internationalistic. The priestly element that came to dominate in little Judah in the post-exilic period manifested all the chief
characteristics that are usually associated with clerical interests: nar-
row political, social, and cultural views, an attitude of superiority
toward the nonclerical elements of the population, the kind of arro-
gance that comes from a belief that the priestly authority derives
directly and exclusively from God Himself, a ready reinterpretation
and rewriting of history and law codes to provide antiquity and
justification for what is really but contemporaneous priestly innovation and revision; and so on. The purpose of Isa. 56, then, is primarily
to justify and legalize the incorporation and use of what had been
palpably impermissible and illegal previously, specifically no less, but
no more, than the use of eunuchs and other aliens in the Temple
service of God. There was no universalistic—not to speak of internationalistic—ideology present in the priestly outlook, nor did it
develop such ideology in its subsequent career in power. Indeed, what
characterized its outlook was the vigorously nationalistic attitude
toward non-Judeans, precisely the attitude against which the authors
of Ruth and Jonah wrote so forthrightly and eloquently.

The nineteenth chapter of Isaiah has long been troublesome to
scholars. The whole first part of the chapter, vss. 1-17, speaks of the
crushing and humiliating defeat that Egypt will suffer at the hands of
God, and this theme is repeated in vss. 22-23 of the second part of the
chapter. But in the midst of these dire pronouncements, at the beginning of the second part, there appear statements in which, according
to many scholars, "Old Testament religion reaches its zenith and . . .
we find the crown of biblical theology." [14] Verses 18-25 read:

> In that day, there shall be five (or: several) cities in the land of Egypt
> speaking the language of Canaan and swearing allegiance to the Lord
> of Hosts. . . . In that day, there shall be an altar to the Lord in the midst
> of the land of Egypt. . . . And the Lord will make Himself known to
> the Egyptians; and the Egyptians shall acknowledge the Lord in that day

---

[14] H. G. May in *The Bible in Modern Scholarship,* p. 100.

and worship with sacrifice and burnt offerings, and they shall make vows to the Lord. . . . In that day, there shall be a highway from Egypt to Assyria. . . . In that day, Israel shall be the third with Egypt and Assyria, a blessing on earth, whom the Lord of Hosts has blessed, saying, "Blessed be My people Egypt, and Assyria the work of My hands, and Israel My heritage" (*barukh 'ammi miṣráyim u-ma'ᵃseh yaday 'ashshur wᵉ-naḥᵃlathi yisra'el*).

I regard this passage (along with the essential message of the books of Ruth and Jonah, on which see below) as evidence for the beginning of the development of internationalism as a flourishing factor in biblical Israel's outlook, and I should date this second part of Isa. 19 (vss. 18-25) to the Seleucid-Ptolemaic period in Judean history. It was then that an altar was actually erected to Israel's God on Egyptian soil, namely, the temple of Onias at Heliopolis. This historical setting is especially probable, if not indeed obligatory, if the preserved reading in vs. 18, *'ir ha-héres*—which is baffling as it stands (so that the entire phrase *'ir ha-héres ye'amer lᵉ-'eḥath* was left untranslated above, and is meaningless in the translations which reproduce it literally)—represents original *'ir ha-ḥéres* (with *ḥeth* in place of *he*), "City of the Sun"=Heliopolis. This reading is accepted by many scholars on independent grounds: a number of Hebrew manuscripts read *ha-ḥéres*, as do the Targum (on which see, for example, Rashi and David Kimchi), Symmachus, the Vulgate, and the Arabic translation of the Septuagint. On the overall background, see S. Zeitlin, *The Rise and Fall of the Judaean State*, I (Philadelphia, 1962/ 5722), 76-80, and n. 76 on p. 463.

This is the period and region—the commercial routes and the Mediterranean shores of Asia and Egypt, the heart of the Jewish diaspora at the time—which marked the beginning of genuine and consistent international thinking in ancient Israel. It is not the forced Exile in Babylonia, consequent on the destruction of Judah and Zion, that brought about this outlook. Nor yet is it the antinationalistic reaction of a considerable portion of the nonpriestly segment of the Judean population, as expressed by the authors of the books of Jonah and Ruth, that brought about this outlook. It was the presence of hundreds of thousands of Judeans in Egyptian and Syrian-Mesopo-tamian territory (*miṣráyim* and *'ashshur* in the Hebrew text) earlier conquered by Alexander. In these lands, Jews lived a relatively free life, free to remain where they were and free to return to Judea when-ever they wished and for as long as they desired. This would be the time and place for a new attitude, beyond the nationalistic-territorial-universalistic attitude of the prophets and of the pre-exilic period gen-erally, according to which God could be worshiped anywhere, not just on Zion in Jerusalem in the holy land of Israel. An Egyptian (let alone a Judean) could remain in Egypt and be a full-fledged Jewish worshiper of Israel's God; and even an altar could be erected in Egypt for sacrifice to God.[14a]

Contrast this new, late post-exilic attitude with the late pre-exilic attitude, as exemplified by Deut. 4:28 and Jer. 16:13. The former reads (Moses addressing his fellow Israelites):

(If ... you act wickedly and make for yourselves a sculptured image in any likeness ... the Lord will scatter you among the peoples. ...) There you will serve man-made gods of wood and stone, that cannot see or hear or eat or smell.

And Jer. 16:13 (Jeremiah addressing his fellow Judeans):

(You yourselves have acted more wickedly than your fathers. . . .) So I will cast you out of this land to a land you have not known, you or your fathers, and there you will (have to) serve other (or: alien) gods (*wa-'avadtem-sham 'eth-'elohim 'aherim*) day and night, for I will show you no favor.

[14a] Some few scholars connect Isa. 19:18-25 with the early post-exilic period, perhaps with the Jewish colony at Elephantine; for reasons that I cannot enter into here, I find this view quite inadequately supported. For some discussions, see P. Dhorme, *La Bible,* II (1959), p. 63, nn. 16 and 18; M. Delcor, "Le temple d'Onias en Egypte: Réexamen d'un Vieux Problème." *RB,* 75 (1968), 188-203 (with refer-ence, e.g., on p. 200, n. 40, to A. Feuillet, "Un sommet religieux de l'Ancien Testa-ment. L'oracle d'Isaïe xix [vv. 16-25], sur la conversion de l'Égypte," *Melanges Jules Lebreton, RSR,* 39 [1951], 65-87), followed by a "Post Scriptum" on pp. 204-205 by R. de Vaux.

In pre-exilic times, one of the most severe punishments that God's chosen people could suffer for transgressing the covenant with God was not alone the devastation of their homeland and the destruction of the Temple but, perhaps even more, exile from the holy land to an unclean land (cf. Amos 7:17), where they could not worship the Lord properly, that is, with sacrifice.[15]

It is wrong to lump together Isa. 2:2-4 and Mic. 4:1-4 on the one hand, with Isa. 19:18-25 on the other. The former insist that it is to Zion that all nations will come streaming, whereas the latter has it that an altar will be erected to God's worship in Egypt. It is the latter that is internationalistic, not the former.

Withal, my main purpose in quoting the latter part of Isa. 19 was not primarily to indicate the circumstances and period in which internationalism became a significant part of Israel's thinking. That would belong properly, it seems to me, to the domain of the competent scholar of the Second Jewish Commonwealth and the Hellenistic era. My intention was but to illustrate a basic aspect of methodology.

There are, literally, hundreds, not just tens and scores, of passages in the Hebrew Bible, from Genesis through II Chronicles, that assert positively or at least reflect the relationship of God and Israel as being purely nationalistic. Amos put it this way (3:1-2):

---

[15] The theory that the synagogue—as a house of prayer, not of assembly or sacrifice—originated in Babylonia during the Exile is quite without foundation; all the pertinent biblical, intertestamental, and early rabbinic literature, together with the results of archaeology, rule this out. See S. Zeitlin, "The Origin of the Synagogue," *Proceedings of the American Academy for Jewish Research,* III (1932), 69-81; E. Rivkin, "Ben Sira and the Nonexistence of the Synagogue: A Study in Historical Method," pp. 320-54 of *In the Time of Harvest: Essays in Honor of Abba Hillel Silver* (1963), with full bibliography; and I. Renov's (unpublished) doctoral dissertation (Hebrew Union College-Jewish Institute of Religion [New York, 1952]), *Some Problems of Synagogal Archaeology,* chap. II. "Development of the Ark," p. 58, and nn. 58-59 on p. 235. [Cf. now also J. Gutmann, "The Origin of the Synagogue: the Current State of Research," *Archäologischer Anzeiger,* 1972, Heft 1, 36-40.]

Hear this word that the Lord has spoken concerning (or: against) you,
O children of Israel, concerning (or: against) the whole family that
I brought up from the land of Egypt:

> You only have I recognized (or: acknowledged, *raq' ethkhem yadá'ti*),
> Of all the families of the earth (*mi-kol mishpᵉḥoth ha-'ᵃdamah*);
> Therefore I will punish you (*'efqod 'ᵃlekhem*)
> For all your iniquities (*'eth kol-'ᵃwonothekhem*).

Deut. 32:8-9 expresses it as follows:

> When the Most High gave nations their homes
> And set the divisions of men,
> He fixed the boundaries of peoples
> In relation to Israel's numbers.
> For the Lord's portion in His people (*ki ḥéleq YHWH 'ammo*),
> Jacob His own allotment (*ya'ᵃqov ḥével naḥᵃlatho*).

And Second Isaiah declares to his fellow Judean exiles (49:22-26):

> Thus said the Lord God:
> I will raise My hand to nations (*hinneh 'essa' 'el-goyim yadi*)
> And lift up My ensign to peoples;
> And they will bring your sons in their bosoms
> And carry your daughters on their shoulders.
> Kings shall be your attendants,
> And their queens shall serve you as nurses.
> They shall bow to you, face to the ground,
> And lick the dust of your feet. . . .
> I will make your oppressors eat their own flesh,
> And they shall be drunk with their own blood as with wine.
> Then all flesh shall acknowledge (*wᵉ-yadᵉ'u*)
> That I the Lord am your savior,
> The Mighty One of Jacob, your redeemer!

Similarly, as Herbert May has noted in the work previously cited, "the
post-exilic writer in Micah depicts the Gentiles licking the dust like
serpents . . ." (Mic. 7:16-17):

> The nations shall see and be ashamed of all their might;
> They shall lay their hands on their mouths,

Their ears shall be deaf.
They shall lick the dust like a serpent,
Like the crawling things of the earth;
They shall come trembling out of their strongholds,
They shall turn in dread to the Lord our God
And they shall fear because of You.

Or take as another example Isa. 14:1-2 (generally recognized as post-exilic) or Zech. 2:14-16. The former asserts that the alien may become attached to triumphant and restored Israel, whereas the Gentile peoples who had held them captive would become their slaves. The latter declares that only the Gentiles who join Israel in her restored homeland can become part of God's people and that only in Zion will God dwell. The text of Isa. 14 reads:

The Lord will have compassion on Jacob
And will again choose Israel,
And He will set them on their own soil;
And aliens shall join them (*we-nilwah ha-ger 'alehem*)
And cleave to the House of Jacob.
And the peoples (*'ammim;* the Gentiles) shall take them
And bring them to their homeland (*meqomam,* lit. place);
And the House of Israel shall possess them
On the soil of the Lord
As slaves and handmaids:
They shall become captors of their captors
And shall rule over their taskmasters.

And the passage in Zech. 2 reads:

"Shout for joy, Fair Zion! For lo, I come and will dwell in your midst," declares the Lord. "Many nations will attach themselves (*we-nilwu goyim rabbim*) to the Lord in that day and become My people, and I will dwell among you." Then you will know that the Lord of Hosts Himself sent me to you. And the Lord will take Judah to Himself as His portion in the holy land, and He will choose Jerusalem once more.

Such passages—it bears repeating—may be readily multiplied by many, many scores throughout the Bible. And if such other, allegedly internationalistic expressions as *navi' la-goyim n^{e}thatíkha* "I appointed (or: "designated") you a prophet concerning the nations" in Jer. 1:5; *w^e-'ettenkha livrith 'am l^e-'or goyim* "I will make you a covenant (of) people, a light of nations" in Isa. 42:6; and *u-n^{e}thatíkha le-'or goyim* "I will make you a light of nations" in Isa. 49:6, are not being dealt with here, it is only because I have discussed them in some detail in my study, *The So-Called "Servant of the Lord" and "Suffering Servant" in Second Isaiah.* The conclusions reached there may be cited here, in part (pp. 116-17):

> However such expressions as [the three passages cited above from Jeremiah and Second Isaiah] are translated, all the contextual data in these [two] Books make it amply clear that nothing international was implied in them. These prophets, God's spokesmen all, were not sent on any mission to any nation other than their own ... to God's covenanted partner, Israel. When they were not simply the means by which God punished His erring people, the pagan peoples were merely helpless witnesses—just like the heavens and the earth and the mountains—to God's exclusive love and protection of His people. This is the essential meaning of such passages as Jer. 26:6 and 4:2 ... i.e., the heathen nation shall say: May we be as prosperous and protected as Israel—if all goes well with Israel; but: Cursed shall you be like Israel—if Israel is in degradation at the hands of God for her sins.

> In a word: Israel will be "a light of nations" in the sense that Israel will dazzle the nations of her God-given triumph and restoration; the whole world will behold this single beacon that is God's sole covenanted people. Israel will serve the world at large as the example of God's loyalty and omnipotence.[15a]

Something ought to be said about the books of Ruth and Jonah in relation to our theme. I fully agree with the considerable majority of scholars who date both these books in the post-exilic Persian period. I understand these books to constitute a vigorous rejoinder to the

---

[15a] See now " 'A Covenant (of) People, a Light of Nations'—a Problem in Biblical Theology." reprinted elsewhere in this volume as chap. 9, pp. 166 ff.

views of the priestly establishment in power at the time, views clearly
set forth in the books of Ezra and Nehemiah. Thus it is hardly a
coincidence that in inveighing against the mixed marriages current
in restored Judah and their consequences, Ezra calls for the rejection
of the "foreign women" (*nashim nokhriyoth*) and their progeny (cf.
Ezra 9:12; 10:2, 10, 11, 14, 17, 18, 44). This stand Nehemiah
shared completely (Neh. 10:31; 13:1-3, 23-30). Ezra 10:10-11 puts
it forthrightly:

> And Ezra the priest stood up and said to them, "You have trespassed
> and married foreign women, and so increased the guilt of Israel. Now
> then, make confession to the Lord, the God of your fathers, and do His
> will; separate yourselves from the people of the land and from the foreign
> women."

And Nehemiah declares (13:23 ff.):

> In those days also I saw the Judeans who had married Ashdodite, Am-
> monite, and Moabite women. . . . And I contended with them and cursed
> them and beat some of them and pulled out their hair; and I made them
> take oath in the name of God, saying: "You shall not give your daugh-
> ters to their sons, or take their daughters for your sons or for yourselves.
> Did not King Solomon of Israel sin on account of such women . . . ?
> Foreign women made even him sin. Shall we then listen to you and
> do all this great evil and act treacherously against our God by marrying
> foreign women?"

The point of the book of Ruth is that a "foreign woman" (cf.
we-'anokhi nokhriyah in 2:10)—and a Moabite at that!—is not only
perfectly acceptable to God and to Israel, but she can be worthy
enough to become the ancestress of King David, Israel's greatest hero
and God's chosen ruler and founder of Judah's great dynasty. But
this is true only if she adopts wholeheartedly the beliefs and practices
of Israel. Within the short space of eighty-five verses, where the word
"Ruth" occurs a total of twelve times, the term *mo'aviyah* is employed
along with the name no less than six times (*ruth ha-mo'aviyah*: 1:22;
2:2, 21 [quite strikingly, in replying directly to her mother-in-law,

Naomi]; 4:5, 10; and cf. 1:4, *nashim mo'ᵃviyoth . . . wᵉ-shem ha-shenith ruth*). Also, in 2:6, one of Boaz' servants, in reply to his master's question, "Whose girl is that?" says, "She is a Moabite girl (*naᶜᵃrah mo' ᵃviyah hi*—not "She is Naomi's daughter-in-law" or the like) who came back with Naomi from the country of Moab." In 2:10, in thanking Boaz for his acts of kindness, Ruth says, "Why are you so kind as to single me out, when I am a foreigner (*wᵉ-'anokhi nokhriyah*)?" Boaz' reply is most revealing, in that it sets forth clearly the acceptability of a genuine convert—even a Moabite—to Israel's God and religion (vss. 11-12):

> "I have been told of all that you did for your mother-in-law after the death of your husband, how you left your father and mother and the land of your birth and came to a people you had not known before. May the Lord reward your deeds. May you have a full recompense from the Lord, the God of Israel, under whose wings you have sought refuge!"

No less significant in this connection is the blessing bestowed upon Ruth by the entire Bethlehemite community, after they bore witness to Boaz' acquisition of "Ruth the Moabite" in his role of levir (4:9-11):

> And Boaz said to the elders and to the rest of the people, "You are witnesses today that I am acquiring from Naomi all that belonged to Elimelech. . . . I am also acquiring Ruth the Moabite, the wife of Mahlon . . . , that the name of the deceased may not disappear from among his kinsmen. . . ." All the people at the gate and the elders answered, "We are witnesses. May the Lord make the woman who is coming into your house like Leah and Rachel, both of whom built up the House of Israel! Prosper in Ephrathah and perpetuate your name in Bethlehem!"

It is a considerable accolade to be blessed by God "like Leah and Rachel," and further to be described as a "daughter-in-law who . . . is better . . . than seven sons" (4:15)!

It is hardly for the purpose of discussing the institution of levirate marriage, or to tell a beautiful story about devotion or romance, or to provide David with a genealogy, or the like, that the book of Ruth was brought into being. Whatever the origin of the materials which our author employed, they were chosen and utilized for a purpose. That purpose could hardly have been anything other than a direct attack on one of the main planks of the program advanced by the Ezra-Nehemiah school of thought.

Likewise, the book of Jonah—also a product of the post-exilic period, a date accepted on various grounds by most scholars[16]—was hardly composed to tell the story of a shipwreck and a whale, or of a man who refused to accept God's call to be His spokesman, or of a great people and city becoming converts to Israel's God and a part of His covenanted people, or the like. Without going into detail, and admitting that here the data are less specific and clear, one can assert with some confidence that the primary purpose of the author of Jonah was to demonstrate that the entire world, man and beast, is God's creation and concern. Moreover, any non-Israelite people which repents of its wickedness—the kind of wickedness that deserves God's punishment (see above on Amos 1-2 and the Noahide Laws)—may be forgiven by God if it repents:

> The word of the Lord came to Jonah son of Amittai, "Go at once to Nineveh, that great city, and proclaim judgment upon it; for their wickedness has come before Me." (1:1-2.)

> The word of the Lord came to Jonah a second time, "Go at once to Nineveh . . . and issue to it the proclamation that I tell you." Jonah went at once . . . and proclaimed: Forty more days, and Nineveh shall be overthrown! (3:1-4.)

> The people of Nineveh believed God. They proclaimed a fast, and great and small alike put on sackcloth. When the news reached the king of Nineveh, he rose from his throne, took off his robe, put on sack-

---

[16] See the discussions and references in O. Eissfeldt, *The Old Testament: An Introduction,* trans. from the 3rd German ed. by P. R. Ackroyd (New York, 1965), pp. 403-6 and 477-83, with "Additional Literature and Notes" on pp. 760-61 and 765-66.

cloth, sat in ashes, and had the word cried through Nineveh: "By decree of the king and his nobles: Man and beast . . . shall cry mightily to God. Let everyone turn from his evil ways and from the injustice he has committed. Who knows but that God may turn and relent . . . so that we do not perish." God saw what they did, how they were turning back from their evil ways. And God renounced the punishment He had planned to bring upon them, and did not carry it out. (3:5-10.)

The Lord said [to Jonah], "You cared about the plant, which you did not work for and which you did not grow, which appeared overnight and perished overnight. And should I not care about Nineveh, that great city, in which there are more than a hundred and twenty thousand persons who do not yet know their right hand from their left, and many beasts as well!" (4:10-11.)

A close reading of Ruth and Jonah shows that the view of their authors is in keeping with the outlook of their pre-exilic predecessors. Once again a position is put forth which holds that God is Israel's God alone, and that He is the only God in the universe; in short, a national-universal God. In the latter capacity, He metes out punishment to all Gentile peoples who transgress the laws of the universe, but is ready to remit punishment if they repent. (Interestingly, the terms used in Jonah for the transgressions by the Ninevites, *ra'ah* [1:2; 3:8] and *hamas* [3:8], are the same as those employed in Gen. 6:5, 11, 13 for the generation that was responsible for God's decision to bring the Flood upon the earth.) In every essential respect, the concept of God in His relation to Israel and to non-Israelite peoples is the same in Ruth and Jonah as in Amos and all the other pre-exilic prophets. If Ruth and Jonah mention some specific events not found in pre-exilic literature, for example, the total acceptability of Ruth the Moabite or the cancellation of punishment for repentant Nineveh, it is simply because historical conditions brought on the presence of the one in one period and its absence in another; but there is no contradiction in basic concept.

Concepts do not originate and function in a vacuum. They are part of the social process, subject to social forces. The historian cannot be content with such generalizing statements as those of Eissfeldt[17]: "We may only say that the breadth of outlook towards another nation which appears here [in the book of Ruth] as in the book of Jonah is more readily intelligible in a later than in an earlier period"; and, "We can only say with certainly that the broad universalism and tolerant humanity which give the book [of Jonah] its attractive tone, belong to the compiler and his time. . . . In the pre-exilic period such far-reaching universalism and such unconditional tolerance are difficult to imagine." What is one to say, then, of the book of Esther, which is no less post-exilic than Ruth and Jonah, yet is hardly characterized by "broad universalism and tolerant humanity"? Indeed, Eissfeldt, and everyone who operates with abstract concepts in a vacuum, without regard to time and place, is so much the theologian and moralist, rather than historian, that he would insist that

> in the assessment of the book [of Esther], we must distinguish between its aesthetic and its ethical and religious value. As a narrative it deserves full recognition. . . . But Christianity, extending as it does over all peoples and races, has neither occasion nor justification for holding on to it. For Christianity Luther's remark should be determinative . . . : "I am so hostile to this Book [II Maccabees] and Esther that I could wish that they did not exist at all, for they Judaize too greatly and have much pagan impropriety." [18]

A scholar who moralizes demoralizes history.

The pattern of nationalism in the Bible, clear and pervasive, can be gauged from another angle. One may draw up a list of every Hebrew word or expression in the Bible that is used in describing the relationship between God and Israel on the one hand, and between God and non-Israelite peoples on the other; a student of mine, Frederick H. Grosse, wrote his ordination thesis on this subject in 1965. In the case, say, of the book of Isaiah (all sixty-six chapters), I have in

---

[17] *Ibid.*, pp. 483, 405.
[18] *Ibid.*, pp. 511-12.

mind *'elohe yisra'el* "the God of Israel" (not of any other people), *bore' yisra'el* "Creator of Israel," *yoṣer* (*yisra'el/ya'ᵃqov*) "He who fashioned (Israel/Jacob)," *mélekh* "King," *ṣur* "Rock," qᵉdosh "Holy One," *mᵉhoqeq* "Lawgiver" (for Israel), *ro'eh* "(Israel's) Shepherd," *ba'al* "be the Husband of, espouse," *'av* "Father," *ne'ᵉman* "Faithful One," *'ᵃvir* "Champion," *nish'an* the One on whom Israel alone can rely, etc. It is Israel alone whom God "chose" (*bahar*), "gathers" (*'asaf*), "glorifies Himself in" (*yithpa'er*), "ransoms" (*padah*), "redeems" (*ga'al*), "assembles" (*qabbeṣ*), "shields" (*magen*), "shows compassion to" (*mᵉrahem*), and a number of other terms. One will search in vain for such terms to be employed with reference to non-Israelite peoples, except in such a passage as Isa. 19:18-25, discussed above.

Instructive in this connection is the work compiled by Jesus son of Sirach. The Judean author of Ecclesiasticus, as is evident from a careful reading of his text, represents the priestly establishment in power in Judea in the third/second century B.C. His attitude toward the Gentiles is a direct continuation of the nationalism-universalism of his predecessors. It is not the internationalism manifest in the viewpoint of the author of Isa. 19:18-25. Sirach writes (16:24-17:32; after RSV):

Listen to me, my son, and acquire knowledge,
And pay close attention to my words.

. . .

The works of the Lord have existed from the beginning
    by His creation (or: judgment),
And when He made them, He determined their divisions.
He arranged His works in an eternal order,
And their dominion (or: elements) for all generations.

. . .

After this, the Lord looked upon the earth,
And filled it with His good things;
With all kinds of living beings He covered its surface,
And to it they return.

> The Lord created man out of earth,
> And turned him back to it again.
> He gave them few days, a limited time . . .
> . . . And granted them dominion over beasts and birds.
>
> . . .
>
> He filled them with knowledge and understanding
> And showed them good and evil.
>
> . . .
>
> He bestowed knowledge upon them,
> And allotted to them the law of life.
> He established with them an eternal covenant,
> And showed them His judgments.
> Their eyes saw His glorious majesty,
> And their ears heard the glory of His voice.
> And He said to them, "Beware of everything unrighteous,"
> And He gave commandment to each of them concerning
>   his neighbor.
> Their ways are always before Him.
>
> . . .
>
> He appointed a ruler for every nation,
> But Israel is the Lord's own portion.

Sirach conceives of God as the only God in the world, the God of the universe and everything and everyone in it. At the same time, He is the God of Israel alone, and of no other people. As 17:17 put it:

> He appointed a ruler for every nation,
> But Israel is the Lord's own portion.

After the first, and much briefer, form of this essay was read in public (see beginning of this essay), a question was asked from the floor: "What do you do with Mal. 1:11 in the light of your paper?" The verse reads:

> "For from where the sun rises to where it sets, My name is great among the nations, and in every place incense and pure oblation are presented to My name. For My name is great among the nations," said the Lord of Hosts.

The fact is that such representative scholars as S. R. Driver and Eissfeldt,[19] among many others, see nothing in this verse (at least, they make no specific mention of it) to upset or modify their view that Malachi, like Ezra and Nehemiah, emphasizes observance of the cult and national exclusiveness. How else is this passage to be taken in the context of both the chapter and the entire book if not as rhetoric? The same question can be posed for vs. 14*b:* "For I am a great King," said the Lord of Hosts, "and My name is feared among the nations."

But something more basic is involved here; namely, the very essence of scholarly research: the matter of methodology. It should be axiomatic that one must first deal with what is unequivocal and straightforward so as to comprehend as clear and consistent a pattern as possible. If such clear data are available in some abundance, so much the better. Then, and only then, does the scholar proceed with the difficult and less clear, the elusive passages, dealing with each passage in its own right. If this analysis brings forth a picture that is not consistent with that produced by the seemingly unequivocal and straightforward, the scholar must then proceed to determine whether the two patterns of thought existed side by side, at the same time and in the same region, but among different strata in the societal structure. Is the element of chronology involved, one outlook being later than the other? Or is it a matter of geography, different regions or countries? And so on. The investigator must look at various possible factors. Under no circumstances is it permissible to dismiss a clear-cut pattern in favor of an interpretation arising from elusive and unclear passages. Yet it is amazing how often in our field of research it is rather the principle of *ignotum per ignotius* that is followed. Exegesis is pushed out by eisegesis. More than one scholar blandly accepts Isa. 19:18-25 as genuinely Isaianic. It is described in such terms as: "The prophecy (is) Isaiah's last and noblest 'testament to posterity,' " "The prophecy is a remarkable one . . . for the grand catholicity of the picture . . .," and as "remarkable prophecy (which) has no equal in biblical litera-

---

[19] S. R. Driver, *Introduction to the Old Testament,* 9th ed. (London, 1913), pp. 355-58; Eissfeldt, *op. cit.,* pp. 441-43.

ture. . . ." Ignored in the process are all the other passages to the
contrary, overwhelming in quantity and in clarity, not only in the
Bible generally but in the book of Isaiah itself, including the group
of chapters (13-23) in First Isaiah that deal with the foreign nations:
Babylon, Assyria, Philistia, Moab, Syria, Ethiopia, Egypt, again
Egypt and Ethiopia, again Babylon, Edom, Arabia, and Phoenicia,
and, it should be noted, including the entire first part of chap. 19 itself.
So what is, to put it mildly, uncertain, namely, the presence of the concept of internationalism in the Bible as a whole and in Isaiah in particular, is explained by what is even more uncertain, namely, the
historical context of Isa. 19:18-25. This is hardly an acceptable
methodology.[20]

In this connection, it is worth repeating what Henry J. Cadbury
once wrote on "Motives of Biblical Scholarship":

> Another bias of our procedure is the over-ready attempt to modernize
> Bible times. This tendency . . . arises partly from taking our own men-
> tality as a norm and partly from a desire to interpret the past for its
> present values. . . . A third defect . . . arises not from a modernizing
> but from a conservative tendency. When new conceptions force us from
> old positions we substitute for the old positions imitations or subterfuges
> which are not better supported than their predecessors but which we
> hope are less vulnerable. . . . We are afraid to follow the logic of our
> discoveries and insist that we are retaining the old values under a new
> name.[21]

Very few of us biblical scholars, *qua* scholars, are free of the influence of our upbringing and general environment. The Hebrew Bible
means nowadays, as it has in the past, different things to different

---

[20] In the process, Amos, Isaiah, Jeremiah, Second Isaiah, and the rest, not to
speak of their audiences, are made to look foolish, contradicting themselves from
one statement to another. Thus Second Isaiah is made to say one thing in 49:1, 6
and the very opposite in climaxing the chapter in vs. 26. But then, I suppose, the
ancients, unlike ourselves, must have been primitive folk, gullible and illogical.
Or were they?

[21] Henry J. Cadbury, "Motives of Biblical Scholarship," *JBL* LVI (1937), 1-16.

people. Some would seek and find in it proof texts for post-biblical rabbinic interpretation. Others would like to see in it the kind of declarations that point to and demonstrate the truth of Christianity, each scholar understanding the term in his own way. [22] Still others would prefer to discover in the Bible, especially among the prophets, the most progressive and liberal ideas and ideals in all human experience. For one reason or another, nearly all who belong to these different groups would like very much to find internationalism, not nationalism, in the Bible. Certainly this is the temper of much of the world since World War II. And so if the biblical outlook is nationalistic-universal rather than internationalistic, biblical Israel is regarded as having been far behind our own times and our progressive outlook.

Apart from the fact that it is not the concern of scholarship to deal in judgment value and to mete out awards for backward- or forward-looking views, we tend to overlook all too readily that our own outlook in this area is still virtually identical with that of the Bible. We like to believe that we think and act internationalistically rather than nationalistically. Did we not, for example, create the League of Nations after World War I, and the United Nations after World War II? Yet who can deny that it was precisely the nationalistic interests of each member nation that brought the League of Nations into being and that determined the vote and actions of each of them? Was it not for self-protection and self-advancement that each nation joined the League and maneuvered within it, or did not join it, or voted to keep another nation out of it altogether? And finally the League of Nations died because of the clash of mutually exclusive nationalistic interests, and the United Nations was achieved. Yet how many would undertake today to seek to prove that pure unselfish internationalism motivated the joining, or not joining, or not being permitted to join, the United Nations? And if a nation, large or small, is too weak to

---

[22] See, e.g., H. J. Cadbury, "Gospel Study and Our Image of Early Christianity," *JBL* LXXXIII (1964), 139-45; C. T. Craig, *passim* in "Realized Eschatology," *JBL* LVI (1957), 17-26, and "The Identification of Jesus with the Suffering Servant," *JR* XXIV (1944), 240-45.

have its way, it will create or join one bloc of nations or another. This is not internationalism at all. It is nationalism pure and simple, not more and not less than biblical Israel's nationalism. When Isaiah and Micah looked forward to the transformation of swords into plowshares and spears into pruning hooks, it was surely because of their national-istic interests, because of the constant overrunning of their beloved land and people, that they looked forward to the cessation of war. Never again would an Asiatic power invade them (whether them specifically or simply en route to Egypt), nor would Egypt ever again overrun them (whether them specifically or en route to the conquest of Phoenicia-Syria-Mesopotamia). Their outlook and motivation were no different from our own today. Most of the European nations after World War I wanted war abolished because each of them had just experienced the brunt of it. Most of the nations of the world after World War II want war abolished because nuclear weapons can an-nihilate every one of them in a matter of minutes, no matter where they may be located. The motivation against war and for peace has long been and still is nationalistic. And if anyone wishes to designate biblical Israel a Founding Member of the League of Nations or of the United Nations, that is all right with at least one writer.[23]

---

[23] The main thesis of this essay is well expressed by David Kimchi (Radak; died 1235) in his commentary at Jonah 1:2: ". . . God Blessed-Be-He also concerns Him-self with the Gentile nations of the world when their wickedness and lawlessness becomes (too) great, as was the case with the Generation of the Flood and the people of Sodom (cf. Gen. 6:13) . . . For lawlessness brings harm to civilization, and God Blessed-Be-He desires the welfare of the world. But in the matter of other transgressions, they are not important to Him; Israel alone is—as it is stated (in Amos 3:2), 'You only have I singled out [or acknowledged, recognized] out of all the families of the earth,' as I have explained in the Prophetic Book of Amos." Or as Deut. 32:8-9 put it:

When the Most High gave nations their homes
And set the divisions of man,
He fixed the boundaries of peoples
In relation to Israel's numbers.
But the Lord's portion is His people,
Jacob His own allotment.

6

Nationalism-Universalism in the Book of Jeremiah

IN AN ESSAY on "Nationalism-Universalism and Internationalism in Ancient Israel" [1] I tried to demonstrate the proposition that the biblical writers regarded YHWH at one and the same time as their national God and as the only Deity in the universe; they did not consider Him the God of any other nation. The only God in existence had a mutually exclusive contract with Israel. As I expressed it there:

> To the biblical writers, from first to last, God is not only Israel's God alone . . . but He is at the same time, and naturally so, also the God of the universe, the only God in existence in the whole wide world, the only God who ever existed and who will ever exist. As God of the universe, He is the sole Creator and Master of all heavenly bodies (sun, moon, stars), of all natural phenomena (lightning, thunder, rain, drought, earthquakes), and of sky, earth, waters, and all living beings therein, human and animal. All natural phenomena, all heavenly bodies, all living creatures, all people, nations and individuals alike, are subject to His direct supervision and will. He is their Master in the fullest sense of the term.

[Reprinted from *Understanding the Sacred Text: Essays in Honor of Morton S. Enslin on the Hebrew Bible and Christian Beginnings*, ed. John Reumann (Judson Press, Valley Forge, Pa., 1972), pp. 61-83.

The two introductory paragraphs of the present essay may be skipped by those who have read the essay referred to in n. 1 immediately following.]

[1] In *Translating and Understanding the Old Testament: Essays in Honor of Herbert Gordon May*, ed. Harry T. Frank and William L. Reed (Nashville: Abingdon Press, 1970), pp. 206-236. (Reproduced immediately preceding the present essay.)

And so, the God of Israel is at the same time the sole God and Master of the universe without being the God of any nation but Israel: the *national* God of biblical Israel is a *universal* God, but not an *international* God. With no people other than Israel did God ever enter into a legally binding relationship. To the biblical writers, God was never the God of Moab, or of Egypt, or Canaan or Assyria or Aram or Ethiopia or Philistia, *et al.* He was the God of Israel alone. . . .[2]

In that connection I dealt with such notable passages as Malachi 2:10 ("Have we not all one Father? Has not one God created us?"); Leviticus 19:18 ("Love your fellow as yourself"); Amos 9:7 ("You are to Me the same as the Ethiopians, O children of Israel," declares the Lord. "I brought up Israel from the land of Egypt, and the Philistines from Caphtor, and the Arameans from Kir"); Isaiah 2:2-4//Micah 4:1-4 ("In the days to come, the mount of the Lord's House shall be established on the highest mountain. . . . and all the nations shall stream to [or: gaze on] it . . . and say: 'Come, let us go up to the mount of the Lord . . . that He may insruct us in his ways. . . .' For instruction [*torah*] shall come forth from Zion . . ."); and Isaiah 56:7 (". . . For My House shall be called a House of prayer for all peoples"); as well as such passages as Isaiah 19:18-25, Isaiah 14:1-2, Zechariah 2:14-16, Malachi 1:11, and the books of Ruth and Jonah. Elsewhere[3] I have discussed in some detail Jeremiah 1:5 ("I appointed [or: designated] you a prophet concerning [hardly "to," see below] the nations"); Isaiah 42:6 ("I have created you and appointed you a covenant-[or: of] people, a light of nations"); and 49:6 ("I will make you a light of nations"). The present essay is a study of the subject as it pertains to the book of Jeremiah.

The passages in Jeremiah that are clear-cut in their attitude toward God in relation to Israel and to the rest of the world are those that should be dealt with first; after a clear picture has been achieved, the

---

[2] *Ibid.*, pp. 87 ff. above.

[3] H. M. Orlinsky, *The So-Called "Servant of the Lord" and "Suffering Servant" in Second Isaiah* (Suppl. to *VT*, 14, 1967), Appendix: "A Light of Nations" (*ôr gôyim*) — "A Covenant of People" (*berith 'am*), pp. 97-117. (Reproduced below as Chapter 9, pp. 166 ff.: ". . . a Problem in Biblical Theology.")

passages that are less than clear may be dealt with. Unfortunately, too often the principle of *obscurus per obscurius* has been applied to the study of biblical problems such as ours.

A second point: Everyone recognizes the fact that Jeremiah is not the author of every verse of all fifty-two chapters of the received Hebrew text that bears his name, so that different—even conflicting— points of view might well be the result of multiple authorship. For our problem, it is methodologically preferable to treat the Book as a unit, as though Jeremiah were its sole author, in order to obtain a picture of the book of Jeremiah as a whole. If the picture obtained does justice to every part of the Book, then the matter of authorship —be it Jeremiah's or that of one or more additional writers—is of no concern for our problem. Only if problems arise that require close analysis of authorship need further study be made.

No part of the book of Jeremiah is without a reference to YHWH as the God of Israel. Thus the prophet, and whoever else contributed to the making of the Book, employed no less than about 70 times such expressions as "the Lord your/our God," "the God of Israel," and "their/its [viz., Israel's] God" when addressing or referring to his fellow Judeans.[4] Even Nebuzaradan, King Nebuchadnezzar's representative, recognized this when he is said to have told Jeremiah (40:2 f.), ". . . The Lord your God Himself pronounced this calamity upon this place. . . ."

In conjunction with this concept, the book of Jeremiah frequently puts in the mouth of God the term "My people" (*cammi*) in reference to Israel[5]; twice the term is "Your people" (31:7[6]; 32:21). In this connection, mention might be made also of the phrases "this people"

---

[4] I have noted 2:17, 19; 3:13, 21, 25; 5:4, 5; 7:3, 21, 28; 9:14; 11:3; 13:12, 16; 16:9; 19:3, 15; 21:4; 22:9; 23:2; 24:5; 25:15, 27; 26:13; 27:4, 21; 28:2, 14; 29:4, 25; 30:2, 9; 31:23; 32:14, 15, 36; 33:4; 34:2, 13; 35:13, 17, 18, 19; 37:7; 38:17; 39:16; 42:4, 6, 9, 13, 15, 18, 20, 21; 43:1, 10; 44:2, 7, 11, 25; 45:2; 46:25; 48:1; 50:4, 18; 51:5, 10, 33.

[5] See 2:11, 13, 31, 32; 4:11, 22; 5:26, 31; 6:14, 26, 27; 7:12; 8:7, 11, 19, 21, 22, 23; 9:1, 6; 12:14, 16 [*bis*]; 14:17; 15:7; 18:15; 23:2, 13, 22, 27, 32; 29:32; 30:3; 31:14 [13]; 33:24; 50:6; 51:45.

(*ha-ᶜam haz-zeh*)[6] and simply "the people" (*ha-ᶜam*),[7] both of which denote God's people.

As elsewhere in the Bible, no nation other than Israel is referred to as the "servant" (*ᶜébed*) of God; this is understandable if no people but Israel has a special relationship with God. The expression employed is *ᶜabdi yaᶜᵃqob*, "Jacob, My servant" (30:10; 46:27, 28).[8]

There are several passages in which the idea of Israel as God's people and of YHWH as Israel's God—to the exclusion of all other peoples and gods—finds expression: 7:23 (". . . this is what I commanded them [viz., your ancestors in Egypt]: Obey Me, and I will be your God and you shall be My people . . ."); 11:4 (". . . you shall be My people, and I will be your God [*wih-yitem li lᵉᶜam wᵉ-'anoki 'ehyeh lakem le'lohim*]"); 13:11 (". . . I brought close to Me the whole House of Israel and the whole House of Judah—declares the Lord—to be My people . . ."); 24:7 (". . . and they [viz., the Judean exiles] shall be My people, and I will be their God . . ."); 30:22 ("And you [viz., the restored Judean community] shall be My people, and I will be your God"); 31:1 [30:25] (". . . I will be the God of

---

[6] See 4:10, 11; 5:14, 23; 6:19, 21; 7:16, 33; 8:5; 9:14; 11:14; 13:10; 14:10, 11; 15:1, 20; 16:5, 10; 19:1, 11; 21:8; 23:32, 33; 27:16; 28:15; 29:32; 32:42; 33:24; 35:16; 36:7; 37:18; 38:4.

[7] Cf. 14:16; 19:1, 14; 21:7; 23:34; 26:7, 8, [*bis*], 9, 11, 12, 16, 17, 24; 28:1, 5, 7, 11; 29:1, 16, 25; 34:8, 10; 36:6, 9 [*bis*], 10, 13, 14; 37:12; 38:1, 4 [*bis*] 9 [*bis*], 10, 14; 40:5, 6; 41:10 [*bis*], 13, 14, 16; 42:1, 8; 43:1, 4; 44:15 [where *wᵉkol-ha- 'am hay-yoshᵉbim bᵉ-'éreṣ-miṣrayim*, "all the people who dwelt in the land of Egypt," denotes Judeans], 20, 24; 52:15, 28.

[8] It is unnecessary for our purposes to analyze the precise character of this relationship, i.e., what the term *'ébed* denotes specifically in connection with the God-Israel relationship: is it an economic-social term that derives from the lord-servant element in the Israelite economic-social (agricultural) structure — and so essentially an inner-Israelite development — or is it a political-diplomatic (=military) term that derives from treaty relationship, specifically vassal treaties? The past decade has witnessed the rise of "pan-vassal-treatyism," to the point where even data that are hardly comparable are used uncritically; I have drawn attention to this current obsession in my presidential address for the Society of Biblical Literature, "Whither Biblical Research?" *JBL*, 90 (1971), pp. 1-14 [reprinted as Chapter 11 in this volume]. Since the troublesome phrase "My servant, King Nebuchadnezzar of Babylon" (*N. melek-babel 'abdi*) in 25:9; 27:6; and 43:10 does not involve a people, it need not be discussed here.

all the [restored] families [or: clans, *mishpᵉḥot*] of Israel, and they shall be My people"); 31:31-33 ("Days are coming—declares the Lord—when I will make a new covenant [*bᵉrit ḥᵃdashah*] with the House of Israel and with the House of Judah . . . and I will be their God, and they shall be My people"); 32:38 (". . . they [viz., the restored Judean exiles] shall be My people, and I will be their God").

These bare references and quotations, however, receive their full import only when their respective contexts are fully comprehended, when it is realized that from the bondage in Egypt through the distant future, with no exceptions, it was always and it will always continue to be the exclusive God-Israel relationship that prevails: *tertium non datur*! (See further below.)

If God and Israel have a relationship that is not shared by any other people or deity, it should follow that expressions deriving from that exclusive relationship are not applied to others. This is borne out completely in Jeremiah. Thus God is referred to on three different occasions as the "hope" of Israel: 14:8 and 17:13, "the hope of Israel" (*miqweh yisra'el*); and 50:7, ". . . because they sinned against the Lord . . . and the hope [*miqweh*] of their fathers. . . ." Consequently, it is natural for Jeremiah, speaking for his fellow Judeans, to petition the Lord (14:22): ". . . no one but You, O Lord our God, and we hope in You [*u-nᵉqawweh-lak*]. . . ." In line with this, the prophet can extend to his people the hope that God will restore the Babylonian captivity: 29:11, "For I am mindful of the plans that I have for you—declares the Lord . . . to give you a hopeful future [lit., a future and a hope, *tiqwah*]." The same assurance is given in 31:17 (16), "There is hope [*tiqwah*] for your future, declares the Lord, and [your] children shall return to their territory."

Or take the root *qdsh*. Only "Israel was holy [*qodesh*] to the Lord" (2:3). And by the same token God is the "Holy One" of Israel, never of anyone else: 50:29, ". . . for she [Babylon] has acted presumptuously against the Lord, against the Holy One of Israel" (*'el-qᵉdosh yisra'el*); 51:15, "For Israel and Judah are not left widowed by their God, by the Lord of Hosts . . . by the Holy One of Israel." Since God, Israel, and the land of Israel constitute an inseparable unit in biblical thought, it is only the last named that will be graced by the term "holy": 25:30, ". . . The Lord makes His voice heard from His dwelling [*mim-mecon qodsho*]"; and of course Jerusalem-Zion, and no other site, will be called "Holy Mount" (31:23 [22]).

Terms of devotion, endearment, and kindness characterize God's attitude toward Israel, in contrast to that manifested to the Gentile nations. Thus in 31:9(8), in dealing with restored Israel, God is described as asserting: ". . . for I will be [or: have become] a father to Israel, and Ephraim is My first-born [*ki-hayiti leyisra'el le'ab we'efráyim bekori hu*]." The same term *'ab* "father" is employed also in 3:4 (". . . you have called Me 'Father' [*qara't li 'abi*] . . .") and 19 (". . . and I thought: you would call Me 'Father' . . ."). In contrast, note the bitter irony in 2:27 f., where God is said to taunt His people: "They said to wood, 'You are my father' [*'abi 'attah*]. . . . And where are those gods you made for yourself? . . ." In one Jewish tradition, 3:4 follows on 2:27-28 in the *haftarah* for the *sidrah Mas'e* (Num. 33-36).

Very moving is the description of God and Israel in 2:2 f.:

Go proclaim to Jerusalem: Thus said the Lord:
I remember[ed] fondly [or: in your favor; lit., for you] the devotion [*hésed*] of your youth,
Your love ['*ahabat*] as a bride:
How you followed Me in the wilderness,
In a land not sown.
³Israel was holy [*qodesh*] to the Lord,
First fruits of His harvest:
All who partook of it were held guilty;
Disaster befell them. . . .

And the same terms for "love" and "devotion" will be employed by the prophet to describe, in the opposite direction, God's feelings for Israel (31:3[2]):

I conceived for you [lit., I loved you] an eternal love ['*ahabat 'olam 'ahabtik*];
Therefore I extend (My) devotion [*hésed*] to you.

And in 33:11 God's *ḥésed* is bound up with the return of Judah's exiles: " 'Praise the Lord of Hosts . . . for His devotion [*ḥasdo*] endures forever, . . . for I will restore the fortunes of the land as of old,' said the Lord." These terms, *ḥésed* and *'ahab,* will not be found in passages involving God and a non-Israelite people.

The same holds true, for example, for *raḥam,* "have compassion." In 12:15 God is quoted as asserting that "After I have torn them out [viz., the people of Judah], I will take them back into favor [*we-riḥamtim,* have compassion on them]." In 30:18, "Thus said the Lord: 'I will restore the fortunes of Jacob's tents and have compassion ['*araḥem*] upon his dwellings' "; or compare 33:26, ". . . for I will restore their fortunes [viz., of the descendants of the patriarchs and David] and have compassion upon them [*we-riḥamtim*]"; 42:12, "I will have compassion upon you [viz., the Judeans under the Babylonian ruler] and he will treat you with compassion [*we-'etten lakem raḥᵃmim weriḥam 'etkem*]." God's relationship with the non-Israelite nations does not require the use of the term *raḥam.*

In a couple of instances God is said to be so angry with His people for their transgression of the covenant that His decision to punish them is irrevocable; he will not change His mind (*niḥam*); compare 4:28, "(²⁷For thus said the Lord: The whole land shall be desolate . . .) ²⁸ . . . For I have spoken, I have planned, and I will not relent [*we-lo niḥámti*] or turn back from it"; 15:6, "You cast Me off—declares the Lord—ever going backward. So I stretch out My hand to destroy you; I cannot relent [*nil'eti hinnaḥem*]." However, the reverse is asserted in several other passages. In 26:1-3 the Lord commands Jeremiah to stand at the entrance of the Temple in Jerusalem and tell the incoming worshipers to amend their evil ways: ³ "Perhaps they will give heed and turn back, each from his evil way, that I may renounce [*we-niḥamti*] the punishment . . ."; and similarly in v. 13, where Jeremiah pleads with his fellow Judeans: "Therefore mend your ways and acts, and heed the Lord your God, that the Lord may renounce [*we-yinnaḥem*] the punishment He has decreed for you." Or compare 31:13 (12), referring to the Judeans in exile whom He will restore to their homeland, ". . . I will turn their mourning to joy, and I will have compassion on them [w^e-*niḥamtim*] . . ." (For the use of *niḥam* in 18:8-10 in connection with non-Israelites, see below, pp. 133 f.).

Terms that indicate "joy" are part of the vocabulary that derives from God's covenant with Israel. On several occasions mention is made of the fact that "the sound of mirth and the sound of gladness [*qol sason* w^e-*qol simḥah*], the voice of the bridegroom and the voice of the bride" will either be banished from Judah because of her faithlessness to God (7:34; 16:9; 35:10) or "shall be heard again in this place" (33:10-11). Or compare the following passages: 31:7(6), "For thus said the Lord: 'Cry out in joy [*rannû . . . simḥah*] for Jacob . . .' "; vv. 10-13 (9-12):

> Hear the word of the Lord, O nations,
> And tell it in the isles afar,
> And say: . . .
> [11]. . . the Lord will deliver Jacob . . .
> [12]They shall come and shout in joy [w^e-*rinn^enu*]
> On the heights of Zion;
> They shall be radiant over the bounty of the Lord . . .
> [13]Then shall the maidens dance gaily [*tismaḥ . . . b^emaḥol*] . . . .
> I will turn their mourning to joy [l^e*sason*],
> I will comfort them and cheer them [w^e-*simmaḥtim*] in their grief.

In 32:41, the Lord assures the Judean exiles: "I will rejoice over them [w^e-*sasti*] . . .'"; in 33:9, again addressed to the captivity and Jerusalem restored, the Lord asserts that "It shall become for Me a symbol [lit., name] of joy [l^e*shem sason*], a praise and a glory, before all the nations of the earth. . . ." Contrast 50:11 ff., where Babylon, rejoicing in her victory over God's people, is assured by God of utter, irrevocable destruction—this as against the glorious future of His people as expressed in vv. 4-5, 19-20:

> [11]Though you rejoice, though you exult [*ki tism^ehi ki ta^calzi*],
> O plunderers of My heritage, . . .
> [12]Your mother shall be utterly shamed. . . .

¹³Because of the wrath of the Lord
She shall not be inhabited,
She shall be an utter desolation;
All who pass by Babylon
Shall be appalled. . . .
(¹⁹But I will restore Israel to his pasture,
And he shall graze on Carmel and Bashan;
In the hills of Ephraim and in Gilead
He shall satisfy his desire.)

Such terms as *ḥéleq* "portion" and *naḥlah* "allotment, inheritance, heritage, share," arising from the idea that God as the creator and master of the world had granted His favorite land to Israel and had apportioned it among her tribes, will occur for God vis-à-vis Israel and no other people: 10:16//51:19:

But the portion [*ḥéleq*] of Israel is not like these [gods],
For He is the creator of everything
And Israel is His own allotted tribe [*shebet naḥ^alato*]. . . .

One cannot refrain from noting the direct association of the foregoing with several passages in Deuteronomy, e.g., 32:8-9:

When the Most High gave nations their homes [*b^ehanḥel*]
And set the divisions of man,
He fixed the boundaries of peoples
In relation to Israel's numbers.
⁹For the Lord's portion [*ḥéleq*] is His people,
Jacob His own allotment [*ḥébel naḥ^alato*].

It is precisely the non-Israelite peoples and their gods who were denied this *ḥéleq* and *naḥ^alah*: Deuteronomy 4:19-20, ". . . These [viz., everything in the world that is worshiped as a deity] the Lord your God allotted (*ḥalaq*) to the other peoples everywhere under heaven; ²⁰but you the Lord took and brought out of Egypt, that iron blast furnace, to be His own allotted people [*lihyot lo l^{ec}am naḥ^alah*], as is now the case." And compare Deuteronomy 29:25 (26), "They [viz., violators

of the covenant in time to come] turned to the service of other gods
. . . whom He had not allotted (*w^elo ḥalaq*] to them."

To get back to these terms in the book of Jeremiah. According to
3:18-19, ". . . they [Judah and Israel] shall come together from the
land of the north to the land that I allotted [*hinḥálti*] to their fathers.
¹⁹ . . . and I gave you a desirable land, the fairest allotment [*naḥ^alat
ṣ^ebi*] . . ."; and 12:14 has it that "Thus said the Lord: Concerning all
. . . who encroach on the heritage which I allotted [*han-naḥ^alah
'^asher-hinḥálti*] to My people Israel. . . ." To these may be added the
use of *naḥ^alati,* "My [God's] portion," for the people Israel in such
passages as 2:7; 12:7, 8, 9; 50:11, and for the land of Israel in 16:18
and 17:4. (On *'ish l^enaḥ^alato* in 12:15, see below.)

All three standard terms denoting restoration of God's exiled people
—*qábaṣ* "gather in," *ga'al* "redeem," and *padah* "ransom"—are found
in 31:10-11 (9-10),

> Hear the word of the Lord, O nations . . .
> And say:
> He who scattered Israel will gather them in [*y^eqabb^eṣénnu*] . . .
> ¹¹For the Lord will ransom [*padah*] Jacob,
> Redeem him [*u-g^e'alo*] from one stronger than He.

In 50:33-34 the Babylonian captors are warned that Judah's God,
"their Redeemer [*go'^alam*], is strong . . . He will plead their case. . . ."

Jeremiah's usual term for "deliver, rescue" is *yasha^c,* and as with
the terms just mentioned, this word also refers to Israel as against
the Gentile peoples, never the reverse. Thus 30:10 (// 46:27)-11 (cf.
42:11) read:

> Have no fear, My servant Jacob—
> Declares the Lord—
> Be not dismayed, O Israel!
> For I will deliver you [*moshi^{ca}ka*] from afar. . . .
> ¹¹For I am with you . . .
> To deliver you [*l^ehoshi^{ca}ka*]. . . .

Or compare 14:8, "O Hope of Israel, / its deliverer [*moshi^co*] in time
of trouble . . ."; 31:7(6), "For thus said the Lord . . . 'Cry out in
joy . . . and say: Save [*hosha^c*], O Lord, Your people . . .' "; and 23:6
//33:16, "In his [//those] days [viz., of the restored dynasty of David],
Judah shall be delivered [*tiwwasha^c y^ehudah*]. . . ."

In keeping with the agricultural character of Israel's social structure,
God will be referred to as a "shepherd" (*ro^ceh*) in relation to His
people: 31:10(9), "Hear the word of the Lord, O nations, . . . He
will guard [Israel] as a shepherd his flock"; and God will see to it that
in restored Judah "there shall again be habitations of shepherds [*n^eweh
ro^cim*] resting their flocks" (33:12), that "[Israel] shall graze [*w^e-
ra^cah*] on Carmel and Bashan" (50:19), and that reliable "shepherds"
lead His people (3:15; 23:4). On the other hand, God is never the
shepherd of a Gentile nation, nor will He provide them with reliable
shepherds or enable them to graze in peace and prosperity; on the
"Noahide Laws," see the reference in n. 12a below. (On chaps. 48-
49, see below, toward the end.)

There are additional terms that shed light on our problem. Thus
the phrase *shab sh^ebut* "restore the fortunes" (traditional "captivity")
is used frequently for Israel: 29:14; 30:3 (*w^e-shabti et-sh^ebut ^cammi
. . .*, "and I will restore the fortunes of My people . . ."), 30:18;
31:23 (22); 32:44; 33:7, 11, 26. (On the use of this phrase for
Moab [48:47], Ammon [49:6], and Elam [49:39], see below toward
the end.) However, it is to the larger segments of the book of Jeremiah that we may now turn our attention.

In receiving the call from God as His spokesman, Jeremiah is
described as having heard this word of God (1:5):

Before I created you in the womb, I selected you;
Before you were born, I consecrated you;
I appointed you a prophet concerning the nations [*nabi la-goyim
n^etattika*].

Strange as it may seem, it has been essentially the last line—by being rendered "I appointed you a prophet to/for the nations"—that has been made to serve as the major evidence for the universally held belief that Jeremiah was an internationalist, that his message from God was directed not to his people alone but to all nations everywhere, to all mankind. As in the case, e.g., of Amos 9:7, Isaiah 56:7, and Malachi 2:10, not to mention Isaiah 42:6 and 49:6 (see the beginning of this essay), this phrase has been taken at its face value without being investigated further in the light of the rest of the book of Jeremiah. No one asked himself the natural, and crucial, question: precisely where in the Book does Jeremiah bring God's message to the Gentile peoples?

Indeed, immediately after receiving the call, Jeremiah replied (v. 6):

> Ah, Lord God!
> I don't know how to speak,
> For I am still a boy.

To which the Lord responded (vv. 7-8):

> Do not say, "I am still a boy,"
> But go wherever I send you. . . .
> ⁸Have no fear of them,
> For I am with you to deliver you. . . .

But whom did Jeremiah have to fear? From whose hands would God have to deliver him? Did Jeremiah have to go to Babylonia or Egypt to report to the government or to the populace the word of God, and thereby incur their wrath? Or, in Jerusalem, did he have to attack these foreign powers and depend on God to protect him from vengeance at the hands of their emissaries? But of course the answers to these questions are well known, if one bothers to look for them in this connection, because they are present in the text of Jeremiah, in the verses immediately following, vv. 17-19. After preparing Jeremiah for his career as His spokesman (1:9, "The Lord put out His hand and touched my mouth, and . . . said to me: Herewith I put My words into your mouth"),⁹ and advising him (v. 10),

See, I have set you (or: given you authority) [*hifqadtika*] this day over
the nations and kindoms,
To uproot and to pull down,
To destroy and to overthrow,
To build and to plant,

God tells him that He will soon bring in foreign nations with which
to punish Judah for her sins (vv. 11-19):

... ¹⁵For I am summoning all the peoples of the kingdoms of the north.
. . . They shall come and shall each set up a throne before the gates of
Jerusalem and against its walls round about and against all the towns
of Judah. ¹⁶And I will argue My case against them for all their wickedness. . . . ¹⁷But you, gird up your loins and go speak to them all that
I command you. Do not be dismayed by them [or: break down before
them], or I will dismay [or: break] you before them. ¹⁸And I, I make
you this day a fortified city, and an iron pillar, and bronze walls against
the whole land—against the kings of Judah, its officials, its priests, and
its citizens [lit., the people of the land]. ¹⁹They will attack you, but they
will not overcome you, for I am with you—declares the Lord—to deliver you.

It is clear, then, that it is not the foreign nations, even those on
Judean soil as victors, that Jeremiah is told by God not to fear in his
divine mission, but his fellow Judeans, and it is from their hands that
God assures him deliverance. Note also, in this connection, the same
phraseology in vv. 7-8 and 17-19:

⁷ וַיֹּאמֶר יהוה אֵלַי . . . וְאֵת כָּל־אֲשֶׁר אֲצַוְּךָ תְּדַבֵּר:

⁸ אַל־תִּירָא מִפְּנֵיהֶם כִּי־אִתְּךָ אֲנִי לְהַצִּלֶךָ נְאֻם־יהוה:

¹⁷ . . . וְדִבַּרְתָּ אֲלֵיהֶם אֵת כָּל־אֲשֶׁר אָנֹכִי אֲצַוֶּךָּ אַל־תֵּחַת מִפְּנֵיהֶם פֶּן־אֲחִתְּךָ
לִפְנֵיהֶם:

¹⁹ . . . כִּי־אִתְּךָ אֲנִי נְאֻם־יהוה לְהַצִּילֶךָ:

---

⁹ It has not been sufficiently noted that the resistance to becoming God's
spokesman (*nabi'*) to His people need not always and automatically be taken
literally. This "resistance" constitutes a stereotype throughout the Bible; cf.,
e.g., Elijah, Amos, Isaiah, Ezekiel, Jonah, and (retroactively) Moses. See my
study, *The So-Called "Servant of the Lord"* (cited above, note 3), pp. 56 f. and 57,
note 1.

The same phraseology, and the same context, may be found, e.g., also in 15:15-21 (see immediately below). (Contrast vv. 10-14, Judah and nations.)

This conclusion is borne out fully by everything in the Book that bears on Jeremiah's relationship with his own Judean countrymen, as well as on his experiences with the foreign nations; indeed, if Jeremiah appears from his Book as something of a "bellyacher," it is precisely because of this relationship with his fellow Judeans. One recalls readily such passages as 11:18-23

> [18] The Lord informed me, and I knew—
> Then You let me see their deeds.
> [19] For I was like a docile lamb
> Led to the slaughter;
> I did not realize it was against me
> That they fashioned their plots:
> "Let us destroy the tree with its fruit,
> Let us cut him off from the land of the living,
> That his name be remembered no more!"
> [20] O Lord of Hosts, O righteous Judge,
> You who test the thoughts and the mind,
> Let me see Your retribution upon them,
> For I lay my case before You.

> [21] Assuredly, thus said the Lord concerning the men of Anathoth who seek your life and say, "You must not prophesy in the name of the Lord if you would not die by our hand"—[22] Assuredly, thus said the Lord of Hosts, "I am going to deal with them: the young men shall die by the sword, their boys and girls shall die by famine. [23] No remnant shall be left of them, for I will bring disaster on the men of Anathoth, the year of their doom."

and 15:10

> Woe is me, my mother, that you ever bore me—
> A man of conflict and strife with all the land!
> I never lent to them

And they never lent to me,
Yet everyone curses me;

and verses 15-21 (where the last two verses read, "Against this people [viz., the Judeans] I will make you / as a fortified wall of bronze . . . For I am with you to save you and deliver you—declares the Lord [ki 'itteka 'ani lehoshicaka u-lehassiléka ne'um YHWH]. [21]I will deliver you [we-hissaltika] from the hands of the wicked . . ."); and 17:14-18 ([note the use of the root ḥtt, as in 1:17] [18]let them [viz., Jeremiah's opponents in Judah] be dismayed, and let not me be dismayed" [yeḥáttu hémah we'al-'eḥáttah 'áni]). Also 18:18-23; 20:1 ff. (cf. v. 2: "And Passhur had Jeremiah flogged and put in a cell . . ."), 7 ff. (cf. vv. 7-8: ". . . I have become a constant laughingstock, / everyone jeers at me. [8]. . . For the word of the Lord brings upon me / constant disgrace and contempt"), 14 ff.; 26:7 ff. (cf. v. 11: "The priests and the prophets said . . ., 'This man [viz., Jeremiah] deserves the death penalty, for he has prophesied against this city [viz., Jerusalem] . . .' "). Indeed, were it not for the intervention of Ahikam son of Shaphan, Jeremiah would have been killed just as his fellow ("true") prophet Uriah was (26:20-24); 26:14 ff.; 37:12 ff. (Jeremiah beaten and jailed and almost starved); 38:1 ff. (Jeremiah rescued from death by starvation); etc.

What is more: it is not the Egyptians whom Uriah feared when he fled to Egypt from his Judean opponents; and it is not to the Egyptians that Jeremiah prophesied when he was carried off by a group of his fellow Judean opponents, but to his fellow Judeans with him in Egypt or back home in Judah. Neither does Jeremiah prophesy to the Babylonian victors on Judean soil (chaps. 40-44). And when Jeremiah sends a message from Jerusalem to Babylonia (chap. 29), it is not to the Babylonians at all but "to the rest of the elders of the exile community—to the priests, prophets, and all the people whom Nebuchadnezzar had exiled from Jerusalem to Babylonia . . ." (v. 1).

One need merely render the prepositions le-, cal, and 'el naturally in context, that is, by "concerning, about" (sometimes "against" for cal or 'el), to do justice to the text of Jeremiah. When Jeremiah's rejoinder to the "false" prophet Hananiah in 28:8 is rendered "The prophets who lived before you and me in ancient times prophesied against [or: concerning; *'el*] many lands and great kingdoms of war and calamity and pestilence," the passage makes sense; and the standard English versions do so. If, however, *'el* were rendered here "to," then the truly—as well as unnecessarily—embarrassing question would be asked: which prophets, and to which lands and kingdoms?

The same is true, e.g., of 27:19 ff., where the standard English versions read, "For thus said the Lord of Hosts concerning [*'el*] the columns, the [*wᵉ-ᶜal*] tank, the [*wᵉ-ᶜal*] the stands, and the [*wᵉ-ᶜal*] rest of the vessels . . .," where "to" (or hardly even "against") would make no sense. Of special pertinence are the statements about the nations in chapters 46-50, where *ᶜal, lᵉ-*, and *'el* are all employed and where only "concerning, about" (or perhaps "against")—but never "to"—fits the context: "concerning [*ᶜal*] the nations" (46:1); "About/Concerning [*lᵉ-*] Egypt" (46:2); "about/concerning [*lᵉ-*] the coming of Nebuchadrezzar" (46:13); "c./a. [*'el*] the Philistines" (47:1); "C./A. [*lᵉ-*] Moab" (48:1); "Concerning [*lᵉ-*] the Ammonites" (49:1); "Concerning [*lᵉ-*] Edom" (49:7); "Concerning [*lᵉ-*] Damascus" (49:23); "Concerning [*lᵉ-*] Kedar" (49:28); "The word of the Lord that came to the prophet Jeremiah concerning [*'el*] Elam" (49:34); and "The word which the Lord uttered concerning [*'ªsher dibber YHWH 'el*] Babylon, concerning [*'el*] the land of the Chaldeans" (50:1).[10]

Yet with all these clear and ample data before them, scholars and translators have mechanically—and unnecessarily misleadingly—rendered (*nabi*) *la(-goyim*) *nᵉtattika* in 1:5 by "(I appointed you a prophet) to (the nations)." No one would have rendered *lᵉ-* here by anything but "concerning," were it not for the universally assumed

---

[10] It may be repeated here that the question of authorship of these chapters (46-50), as of any other passages in the book of Jeremiah, does not concern us here; scholars differ as to when who wrote what, and in many systematic studies and commentaries on Jeremiah it is often next to impossible to locate many passages without the use of an index. For our problem, the picture that emerges from the Book as a whole is clear and consistent.

notion that the prophets, including Jeremiah, were internationalistic, and hence the failure to ask oneself the obvious question: to what nations?

An additional point might be made here. A "diehard," insisting on rendering *lᵉ-* in 1:5 by "to" and disregarding the rest of the book of Jeremiah, might point to the book of Jonah as an instance where God sent a prophet to a Gentile nation—as though this one fact were decisive, and justified ignoring all the other evidence to the contrary. However, apart from the several serious problems with which the book of Jonah confronts the scholar (cf. pp. 108 ff. above, in my essay in the May volume mentioned in note 1 above; and see now Millar Burrows' essay in the same volume, "The Literary Category of the Book of Jonah," pp. 80-107), it should at least be recognized that— in contrast to the careers of the main heroes of the other prophetic Books—the career of Jonah is postexilic fiction, created when there was no Nineveh to which to deliver God's message. As long as Nine- veh was in existence—and it reached the zenith precisely during the *floruit* of Israel's prophets—there is no record of a prophet, even Nahum, who devoted his entire prophecy to Nineveh, going there or being sent there for any purpose. It might also be mentioned in pass- ing that such exilic prophets as Ezekiel and Second Isaiah had noth- ing to say *to,* but quite a bit *concerning,* even their Gentile "host" nation.

Not only is Jeremiah a prophet to his fellow Judeans and never to the Gentile nations, but the nations themselves have no independent existence for him. That is to say: whatever happens to the nations is of no concern to Jeremiah—in other words, is of no concern in the covenant between God and His people Israel—unless they are in- volved in some action between God and Israel. Thus, e.g., when warning the Judeans that God is omnipotent and that Judah is, in His hands, what clay is in the hands of the potter (18:1-6), Jeremiah says that just as God, master of the universe, can change His mind about any nation in the world if that nation deserves it, so will He act to- ward His people (vv. 7-11):

At one moment I may decree that a nation or a kingdom shall be up-rooted and pulled down and destroyed; ⁸but if that nation . . . turns back from its wickedness, I will change My mind concerning the punish-ment. . . . ⁹At another moment I may decree that a nation or a kingdom shall be built and planted; ¹⁰but if it does evil in My sight . . ., then I will change My mind concerning the good that I planned to bestow upon it. ¹¹And now, say to the men of Judah and the inhabitants of Jerusalem: "Thus said the Lord: 'I am shaping punishment for you . . . Turn back, each of you from your wicked ways, and mend your ways and your actions!' "

It is, again, but rhetoric when Jeremiah proceeds two verses farther on to argue and to rebuke (vv. 13 ff.):

> . . . thus said the Lord:
> "Inquire among the nations:
> Who has heard anything like this?
> Fair Israel has done
> A most horrible thing.
> ¹⁴Does one forsake Lebanon snow
> From the mountainous rocks?
> Does one abandon cold waters
> Flowing from afar?
> ¹⁵Yet My people have forgotten Me . . ."

just as it is but rhetoric in 2:10-13:

> Just cross over to the isles of the Kittim and look,
> Send to Kedar and observe carefully;
> See if aught like this has ever happened:
> ¹¹Has any nation changed its gods—
> Even though they are no gods?
> But My people has exchanged its glory
> For what can do no good.
> Be appalled, O heavens, at this;
> Be horrified, utterly dazed!
>   —declares the Lord.
> ¹³For My people have done a twofold wrong:

> They have forsaken Me, the fount of living waters,
> And hewed them out cisterns, broken cisterns,
> Which cannot even hold water,

and in 16:19-21 (the whole world will come to realize that Israel's
God alone is real). So that, when Jeremiah warns of the destruction
of the royal palace in Jerusalem (22:1-7) and says (vv. 8-9),

> And when many nations pass by this city and one man asks another,
> "Why did the Lord do thus to that great city?" [9]the reply will be,
> "Because they forsook the covenant with the Lord their God and bowed
>   down to other gods and served them,"

he is using "nations" in the same manner as "heavens" in 2:12 quoted
above ("Be appalled, O heavens, at this;/Be horrified . . .!"); surely
no one need argue that the "many nations" will hardly explain the
defeat as due to God's punishment for transgression of the covenant,
when the superiority of their weapons, men, god(s), and the like,
was so self-evident. Similarly, when Nebuzaradan, captain of the
Babylonian guard, is described as having said to Jeremiah (40:2-3),
"The Lord your God pronounced this calamity upon this place [3]. . . because you sinned against the Lord and did not obey Him . . .," this
is only a literary-psychological device to influence the Judean people
to believe that Jeremiah was the true spokesman of Israel's omnipotent
God.

This secondary and incidental role is one of the two main functions
that the nations, Babylonia among them, serve in the book of Jeremiah, viz., as a figure of speech, as a literary-psychological device;
the other main function is that of agents of God in His actions involving Israel. Sometimes, indeed, it is difficult to distinguish between
the two functions; in either case, however, the nations, whether only
rhetorically or actually, are but helpless pawns in God's plans.
Thus in chapter 27, Jeremiah relates that God said to him (vv.
2 ff.),

... Make for yourself thongs and bars of a yoke, and put them on your neck. ³And send them [better, with emendation, send a message] to the king of Edom, the king of Moab, the king of the Ammonites, the king of Tyre, and the king of Sidon, by envoys who have come to Jerusalem to King Zedekiah of Judah; ⁴and give them this charge to their masters: "Thus said the Lord of Hosts, the God of Israel: ... ⁵It is I who made the earth, and the men and beasts who are on the earth . . ., and I give it to whomever I deem proper. ⁶I herewith deliver all these lands to My servant, King Nebuchadnezzar of Babylon; I even give him the wild beasts to serve him. ⁷All nations shall serve him, and his son and his son's son, until the turn [lit., time] of his own land comes, when many nations and great kings shall subjugate him. ⁸The nation or kingdom that does not serve him . . . and does not put its neck under the yoke of the king of Babylon, that nation I will visit . . . with sword and famine and pestilence, until I have destroyed it by his hands. ¹⁰So do not listen to your prophets, augurs, dream[er]s, diviners, and sorcerers, who say to you, 'Do not serve the king of Babylon.' ¹¹For they prophesy falsely to you, with the result that . . . you shall perish. . . ."

Whether it was Jeremiah himself or a later writer who composed the above, and whether the statement is to be taken literally or symbolically[11]—that is, whether the yokes or the messages alone were or were not actually sent to the kings east and north of Judah who were involved in Nebuchadnezzar's western campaigns—the fact is that

---

[11] The precise character and function of these actions (e.g., the phrase "all the peoples of the kingdoms of the north . . . shall come and shall each set up a throne before the gates of Jerusalem" in 1:15 [see p. 129 above] to be understood literally, or as an expression for military victory, or both) are not our concern here. So whether Jeremiah did or did not purchase a linen loincloth, wear it, and then go to p*erat* and cover it up in a cleft of the rock (13:1 ff.) — and whether Perath is the Euphrates or an otherwise unknown place in or near Judah — our concern here is merely to note that only God's covenanted Judeans are involved in the symbolism. It need, further, scarcely be noted that if v. 23 reads,

"Can the Ethiopian change his skin,
Or the leopard his spots?
Just as much can you do good,
Who are practiced in doing evil!"

nothing international is involved in the use of the term "Ethiopian" (*kushi*) any more than in the parallel term "leopard."

the nations were arbitrarily and summarily being handed over to Babylonia, along with Judah; but whereas Judah had broken the covenant with God and was being punished for it by Babylonia, the other nations had done no wrong. They merely suited God's interests in the process of punishing Israel by means of Babylonia.[12]

The same may be said of Jeremiah's statement in 25:15-38:

> For thus said the Lord, the God of Israel, to me, "Take from My hand this cup of wine—of wrath—and make all the nations to whom I send you drink of it. [16]Let them drink and stagger about and go mad, because of the sword which I am sending among them." [17]So I took the cup from the hand of the Lord and gave all the nations drink to whom the Lord had sent me: [18]Jerusalem and the towns of Judah, and its kings and officials . . .; [19]Pharaoh king of Egypt, his courtiers, his officials, and all his people; [20]all the mixed [or foreign] peoples; all the kings of the land of Uz; all the kings of the land of the Philistines . . . [21]Edom, Moab, and Ammon; [22]all the kings of Tyre and all the kings of Sidon, and all the kings of the coastland across the Sea; [23]Dedan, Tema, and Buz . . . [24]all the kings of Arabia . . . [25] . . . and all the kings of Elam and all the kings of Media; [26]. . . all the kingdoms of the world which are on the face of the earth. And at the end, the king of Sheshach [traditionally regarded as a cipher for *babel* = Babylon] shall drink. . . . [28]And if they refuse to take the cup from your hand and drink, say to them, "Thus said the Lord of Hosts: You must drink! [29]If I am bringing the punishment first on the city that bears My name, do you expect to go unpunished? You will not go unpunished . . ."
> [31]. . . For the Lord has a case against the nations,
> He contends with all flesh.
> He delivers the wicked to the sword. . . .
> [32]. . . Disaster goes forth from nation to nation;
> A great storm is unleashed
> From the remotest parts of the earth.
> [33]In that day, the earth shall be strewn with the slain of the Lord . . .
> [38]. . . because of His fierce anger.

---

[12] Behind the statement in this chapter (18), as throughout the Book of Jeremiah and the Bible, lay the belief that, as the only Deity in the world, it was naturally Israel's God who was responsible for everything that happened to and among the nations, animals, heavenly bodies, .etc., of the universe. This is the point, e.g., in Amos 9:7 (cf. above at the beginning of this essay, p. 118, with reference to pp. 85 ff. above).

Two things are readily apparent: (1) whatever symbolism or sympathetic magic the "cup of wine, of wrath" was meant to represent, it is hardly likely that any of the wine was ever sent out to the nations; and (2) the nations, Babylonia included, are to experience calamity not because of any wrong that they have committed but because Judah has to be punished. Here is what the text of vv. 8-10 of the same chapter (25) says, "Assuredly thus said the Lord of Hosts: Because you [viz., Judah] would not listen to My words, [9]I am going to send for all the peoples of the North, and for My servant, King Nebuchadnezzar of Babylon, and bring them against this land and its inhabitants, and against all those nations round about. I will exterminate them and make them a desolation, an object of hissing—ruins for all time. . . ." And as for Nebuchadnezzar and his Babylonia (vv. 11-14), ". . . Those nations shall serve the king of Babylon seventy years. [12]When the seventy years are over, I will punish the king of Babylon and that nation for their sins . . . and I will make it a desolation for all time. . . . [14]For they too shall be enslaved by many nations and great kings; and I will requite them according to their acts and according to the deeds of their hands." One will look in vain for a serious description of the "sins" that merited such an end. Or compare 43:8-13, where Jeremiah is told by God to tell the Judean refugees in Egypt that God will bring Nebuchadnezzar to Egypt and destroy it; what the guilt of Egypt is, is not revealed.[12a]

Chapter 33 is another of the numerous typical statements in Jere-

---

[12a] In 1972, in a course on "The Concept of Sin and Punishment in the Late Preexilic and Exilic Prophetic Literature," the dozen students in the class were assigned the task of compiling and studying every passage in the Hebrew Text of Jeremiah insofar as (a) God and Israel and (b) God and the Gentile nations were concerned. My assertion that Judah was being punished for breaking the covenant whereas the Gentile nations experienced (or were threatened by) defeat and misery not because of wrongdoing but in consequence of being but tools of God in punishing Israel, was borne out fully by the mass of detailed factual data compiled and analysed by the students. On the "Noahide Laws" in relation to the Gentile nations (e.g., Amos 9:7), see my essay in the May Volume (reproduced immediately preceding this essay), pp. 88 ff. above.

miah concerning the status of Babylonia and the other nations (vv. 4-9):

> For thus said the Lord . . . concerning the houses of this city [viz., Jerusalem] and those of the kings of Judah which were torn down . . . ⁵whom I struck down in My fierce anger . . . because of all their wickedness. ⁶I will bring healing to them . . . ⁷I will restore the fortunes of Judah and Israel . . . ⁸I will purge them of all their guilt . . . ⁹And it [viz., Jerusalem] shall become to Me a name of joy, a praise and a glory before¹³ all the nations of the earth who, when they hear of the good that I do for them, shall fear and tremble because of all the good and all the prosperity that I provide for them.

Another of the clear-cut pasages which assert the uniqueness and universality of Israel's God and His exclusive covenant with Israel— and where Babylonia is only a temporary tool, to be discarded when no longer needed—is provided by 32:26-41:

> The word of the Lord came to Jeremiah: ²⁷"I am the Lord, the God of all flesh [ᵉlohe kol-basar]. Is anything too wondrous for Me? ²⁸Assuredly . . . I am delivering this city [viz., Jerusalem] into the hands of the Chaldeans . . . ³⁰because the people of Israel and Judah have done nothing but wickedness in My sight . . .," ³⁶Now therefore thus said the Lord . . . ³⁷"I will gather them from all the countries to which I banished them in My fierce anger . . . ³⁹I will give them one heart and one way to fear Me forever. . . . ⁴⁰And I will make with them an everlasting covenant [bᵉrit ᶜolam] . . . ⁴¹I will rejoice to do them good. . . ."

Babylonia as a mere tool is well described, e.g., in 51:7-8:

> A golden cup was Babylon,
> In the Lord's hand,
> Making all the earth drunk.
> Of its wine the nations drank,
> And so the nations went mad.
> ⁸Suddenly Babylon fell and was broken;
> Wail over her! . . .

---

¹³ The first part of v. 9 is clearly corrupt, and it is generally — and probably correctly — rendered so as to accord with the clear text and reasonable statement of the second half of the verse. Our rendering "before" for lᵉ(kol goye ha- ʾareṣ) follows such standard English versions as JPS (1917), RSV, JB, and NEB.

Poor Babylon, destined in the view of the authors of the book of Jeremiah to constitute only a passing incident in the long and eternal relationship between God and Israel! The author of 50:6-10 asserts,

My people have been lost sheep, led astray by their shepherds . . . [7]All who have come upon them have devoured them, and their enemies have said, "We shall not incur guilt, for they have sinned against the Lord . . ." [8]Flee from Babylon . . . [10]For Chaldea shall be plundered. . . .

Or as put by the author(s) of 51:15-24, speaking of God as the master of the universe, the covenanted partner of Israel and nemesis of Babylonia:

He who made the earth by His might. . . . [17]All mankind is stupid and witless, . . . for their images are false. . . .
[19]But not like these is the Portion [i.e., God] of Jacob,
for He is the one who formed all things,
and (Israel) is His very own tribe. . . .
[24]And I will repay Babylon and all the inhabitants of Chaldea for all the calamity that they wrought in Zion. . . .

More, much more, can readily be cited from Jeremiah in this vein; virtually every chapter provides several pertinent passages. But enough has been adduced for our purpose directly from the text of the Book, and the limitations of space in this [Morton S. Enslin] volume must be respected. Every passage in the book of Jeremiah, whether cited or not in this essay, derives from a specific historical circumstance and serves the interests of whatever group(s) may be involved. Further, the exclusive covenant between God and Israel, the only basis on which argument between God's prophets and His people is possible, must always be justified and explained.

So that if Nebuchadnezzar attacks Judah and her neighboring countries, it is because God is utilizing his Babylonian army; if Egypt will be destroyed, it is because this serves God's purpose in relation to His covenanted people; if, when the final editor of the statement about Moab in chapter 48 lived, Moab seemed destined to survive whatever calamity it was experiencing or had experienced, then v. 46, which is the culmination of the long prophecy against Moab and which reads, "Woe to you, O Moab! / The peopie of Chemosh are un-done. / For your sons have been taken captive, / Your daughters led into captivity," is supplemented by v. 47, "Yet I will restore the fortunes of Moab in the days to come—declares the Lord. Thus far the judgment of Moab." (As to why Moab should merit restoration— that is not explained. If Moab will be restored, it is because Israel's God wants it so.)

The same prospect of restoration is promised to the Ammonites (49:6), after the prophecy proper (vv. 1-5) had promised nothing but destruction—again without explanation. And similarly Elam (49:34-39). But no restoration of fortunes is promised to Edom (49:7-22), Damascus (vv. 23-27), and Kedar (vv. 28-33)—again without explanation. It is hardly possible to date with any confidence these several utterances, and their component parts, concerning the nations, since the precise historical circumstances are not known to us.[14] And the same is true of such passages as 12:14-17:

> Thus said the Lord concerning My wicked neighbors who encroach on the heritage which I allotted to My people Israel, "I am going to tear them up from their soil, and I will tear up the House of Judah out of the midst of them. [15]Then, after I have torn them out, I will take them back into favor, and restore them each to his own inheritance and his own land. [16]And if they learn the ways of My people, to swear by My

---

[14] A passage such as 3:17 ("At that time Jerusalem shall be called 'The Throne of the Lord,' and all the nations shall assemble there, in the name of the Lord of Jerusalem; they shall no longer follow the willfulness of their evil hearts") might be adduced here, except that the term *kol-hag-goyim,* generally rendered "all the nations," may actually — as I believe — refer only "to the house of Judah together with the House of Israel" in the verse immediately following (18), especially since the whole chapter otherwise (vv. 1-16 and 18-25) deals only with these two parts of God's covenanted people. The term *goy(im)* not infrequently refers to Judah-Israel in Jeremiah. And this, too, should be noted, that the phrase *sherirut leb,* "willfulness of heart," occurs in seven additional passages in Jeremiah (only in Deut. 29:18 and Ps. 81:13 elsewhere in the Bible) and always with reference to Judah.

name—'As the Lord lives'—just as they once taught My people to swear by Baal, then they shall be built up [or: incorporated] in the midst of My people. [17]But if they do not listen, I will tear out that nation, tear it out and destroy it," declares the Lord.

Most scholars now seem to agree that the date and authorship of such passages can no longer be determined; not only was this utterance not delivered to the nations round about Judah, but it holds out for these nations only the certainty of destruction unless they adopt Israel's God and way of life and become absorbed within the Judean community. In any case, Jeremiah is no prophet of theirs, and their role in the unfolding events involving God and Israel is not one of their choosing or one that they can in any way determine. This role is exclusively Judah's, and Jeremiah's function is to tell his fellow countrymen how God wants them to comprehend and play that role.[15]

---

[15] What Jeremiah and the group(s) whose views he shared really desired is a problem that only a trained historian can determine; neither the textual or the literary critic nor the theologian can comprehend this problem. Thus when God commands Jeremiah (7:2-3),

> Stand at the gate of the House of the Lord, and proclaim this word there: 'Hear the word of the Lord, all you of Judah who enter these gates to worship the Lord!' [3]Thus said the Lord of Hosts, the God of Israel: Mend your ways and your actions, and I will let you dwell (or, with change of vocalization: I will dwell with you) in this place,

with which, compare 26:2-3,

> Thus said the Lord [to Jeremiah]: Stand in the court of the House of the Lord, and speak to all the towns(men) of Judah, who are coming to worship in the house of the Lord, all the words which I commanded you to speak to them. Do not omit anything. [3]Perhaps they will listen and turn back, each from his evil way, that I may renounce the punishment that I am planning to bring upon them for their wicked acts (cf. also 36:6-7)

it is noteworthy that precisely those "who enter these gates to worship the Lord" are being denounced as evildoers. If then the "wicked acts" did not really involve sacrifices and prayers to other gods — i.e., did not really involve idolatry — they must have been political and economic and social acts which Jeremiah and his supporters opposed. So that while the terminology is religious (cf. 7:4 ff.), the significance of these terms is basically far more than religious. That is why, as put at the end of the address cited in note 8 above, "in his anal-

As a matter of fact, so dependent are the actions and experiences of the nations upon the covenant between Israel and God that the essence of the whole book of Jeremiah could be summed up fairly in the one single statement uttered by God to Jeremiah (36:2-3):

> Take a scroll and write on it all the words that I have spoken to you concerning [or: against] Israel and Judah and all the nations. . . . ³Perhaps the House of Judah, hearing of the harm that I plan to do to them, will turn from their wicked ways, and I will pardon their sinful wrongdoing.

Whether the phrase "all the nations" in v. 2 is original or secondary, the fact is that it is exclusively Judah's decision, by continuing in its conduct or by repenting, that will determine the fate of the nations, i.e., whether Babylonia will come and conquer and punish and, in the end, itself be destroyed, and whether the other nations will remain independent or be conquered by Babylonia.

---

ysis of the momentous events that befell Judah at the turn of the sixth century B.C., the historian will go seeking behind such terms as 'sin' and 'covenant' for the fundamental economic, political, and social forces that determined the use and content — and, so frequently, the utter disregard — of these terms. There is a great future for biblical research and the trained historian who devotes himself to it."

7

The Destruction of the First Temple and the Babylonian Exile in the Light of Archaeology

THE DESTRUCTION of the First Temple and the Babylonian Exile are two events that we all take for granted. You may wonder what there is about the Destruction and the Exile that we need archaeology for. Everyone knows about these events. Everyone knows that there was a Temple that was destroyed and that a Babylonian Captivity followed; so that archaeology can play but a relatively minor role here.

However, when I started out as a college student in Semitics, in the late twenties and the thirties, the Destruction and the Exile had come to be increasingly regarded by serious scholars as fictitious, and my teacher at the University of Toronto, Professor Theophile J. Meek, a

---

[This essay, worked up for a lecture delivered at the America-Israel Culture Foundation in New York City on June 5, 1968—a few hours after Senator Robert Kennedy was assassinated in Los Angeles—in connection with an archeological exhibition titled "From the Lands of the Bible," is a more detailed and updated version of an address given on January 7, 1945, in Yiddish, at the nineteenth annual Conference of the Yiddish Scientific Institute (YIVO) in New York City and published in *YIVO-Bleter,* 25 (May-June, 1945), 323–34, as *"Gâlus Bâvel in Shein fun Archeológiye."* Zvi Shimshi, father-in-law of Prof. Benjamin Maisler-Mazar, wrote a fine, lucid summary of the YIVO article in the Hebrew weekly *Ha-Olam* (XXXIII, 13; Dec. 6, 1945, p. 129), official organ of the World Zionist Organization, founded by Nahum Sokolow and edited at the time by Moshe Kleinman.]

person of very considerable knowledge and integrity, used to gloss over this period because he did not feel entirely secure with the data for it. The evidence for the destruction of the First Temple, the evidence for the Babylonian Captivity, and the evidence for the return to Judah and its Restoration were all rather unsubstantial. Simply because the Bible related these events was hardly enough assurance for a scholar that these events had actually taken place.

Just a few decades ago, in the thirties, there had developed a group of scholars in this country and in Europe—for example, Charles Cutler Torrey of Yale, Gustav Hölscher in Germany, and George A. Cooke in England, all outstanding and serious scholars—who were writing very bluntly that there never was a significant destruction of the First Temple, or of the country of Judah as a whole, in 586 B.C.E. Consequently, there was no great, meaningful captivity, no widespread exile to Babylonia. Hence, they concluded, there was no restoration of Judah, since there was nothing to restore, and the whole event was essentially fiction.

This attitude of scepticism to the Bible as a historical document was prevalent during the nineteenth century and the first two decades of the twentieth, until—as a consequence of World War I—the Ottoman Turkish Empire was destroyed, and France and England took over the Near East. Until the eighteenth century, the Bible had been universally accepted as a trustworthy history book of antiquity. Indeed, the Book was regarded as being literally true—the Creation, the Flood, Noah's Ark, the walls of Jericho, and all. But as the Age of Reason dawned, and in turn gave way to nineteenth-century philosophies of evolution and scientific materialism, the Bible, in common with the New Testament and all records of antiquity, Greek, Roman, and the rest, came to be very considerably discounted as reliable basis for the reconstruction of history.

The heroic doings of the patriarchs, Abraham, Isaac, and Jacob, as described in the book of Genesis, were discounted as mere myth. The very existence of Moses was doubted. Joshua was believed to have had little or nothing to do with the Israelite conquest of Canaan. David and Solomon were considered greatly overrated. And so on.

This negative attitude to the Bible was reflected in more recent times, for example, in the writings of the well-known social philosopher, Bertrand Russell, and the historiographer, R. C. Collingwood. What Russell wrote in 1944 in his popular *History of Western Philosophy* was (pp. 309–10):

> The early history of the Israelites cannot be confirmed from any source outside the Old Testament, and it is impossible to know at what point it ceases to be purely legendary. David and Solomon may be accepted as kings who probably had a real existence, but at the earliest point at which we come to something certainly historical there are already two kingdoms of Israel and Judah. The first person mentioned in the Old Testament of whom there is an independent record is Ahab, King of Israel, who is spoken of in an Assyrian letter of 853 B.C. . . .

So that, to Russell, the first reliable fact in the Bible is the reference in the First Book of Kings (Chapters 20–22) to the existence of King Ahab, for he is vouched for in an extrabiblical source.

The source is actually the so-called Black Obelisk of the Assyrian monarch, Shalmeneser III (858–824 B.C.E.), with its inscription of the king's war against an Aramean Coalition and the reference to the great battle of Karkar (853 B.C.E.). The text in question reads in part:

> In the year of . . . Daian-Ashur [853/852], in the month of Aiaru, the 14th day, I departed from Nineveh. I crossed the Tigris . . . I crossed the Euphrates another time at its flood on rafts of (inflated) goatskins . . . I received tribute from the kings of the other side of the Euphrates . . . I approached Aleppo . . . I received silver and gold as their tribute . . . I approached Karkara. I destroyed, tore down, and burned down Karkara . . . He [i.e., the head of the coalition] brought along to help him 1,200 chariots, 1,200 cavalrymen, 20,000 foot soldiers of Adad-idri (i.e., Hadadezer) of Damascus . . . 700 chariots, 700 cavalrymen, 10,000 foot soldiers of Irhuleni from Hamath, 2,000 chariots, 10,000 foot soldiers of Ahab the Israelite (*A-ḫa-ab-bu-*^{mat}*Sir-i-la-a-a*) . . . (altogether) these were twelve kings. They rose against me [for a] decisive battle. I fought with them with (the support of) the mighty forces of Ashur, which Ashur my lord has given to me, and the strong weapons which Nergal my leader has presented to me. [Ashur and Nergal are Mesopotamian deities.] I inflicted a defeat

upon them between the towns Karkara and Gilzau. I slew 14,000 of their soldiers with the sword, descending upon them like Adad when he makes a rainstorm pour down. I spread their corpses (everywhere), filling the entire plain with their widely scattered (fleeing) soldiers . . . (After A. Leo Oppenheim's translation of "Babylonian and Assyrian Historical Texts," in *Ancient Near Eastern Texts Relating to the Old Testament,* ed. J. B. Pritchard, Princeton University Press, 1950, pp. 278a–79.)

Subsequently there will be references to King "Jehu son of Omri" (*Ia-ú-a mâr Ḫu-um-ri-i*; see pp. 280–81) and, by Tiglath-pileser III (744–727 B.C.E.), to King "Jehoahaz (*Ia-ú-ḫa-zi*) of Judah (*Ia-ú-da-a-a*)" and to "Israel" (literally "house/land of Omri"—*Bît Ḫumria*); etc. (see pp. 282 ff.).

This same inscription of Shalmaneser (see the reproduction of the four panels of row II across pp. 120–121, and the enlargement of one of the panels at the top of p. 122, in J. B. Pritchard's companion volume, *The Ancient Near East in Pictures Relating to the Old Testament,* 1954; also the explanatory notes on pp. 290 f., from which the following is quoted) depicts how "Shalmeneser receives the tribute of 'Jehu, son of Omri,' who is upon his hands and knees, with his face to the ground . . . Four Assyrians—one bearded officer and three attendants—stand behind Jehu and precede the procession of thirteen Israelite porters. Each of these figures is bearded, wears the pointed cap and a long garment, over which is thrown a fringed mantle with tasseled ends, which are long enough to be thrown over the shoulder . . ."

As for Collingwood, he dismissed in less than one page the entire Hebrew Bible—in contradistinction to the New Testament—as theocratic history and myth, stories of one kind or another revolving about a single powerful deity. (See his posthumously published book on *The Idea of History,* 1945. On the problem as a whole, see the "Introduction" in my *Ancient Israel,* pp. 1–10.)

Archaeology can be a disconcerting, even chastening discipline. One never knows what he will excavate and how the freshly uncovered materials will affect his or anyone else's theories. As the late Professor Montgomery of the University of Pennsylvania put it, almost thirty years ago (p. viii of the Preface to his excellent *International Critical Commentary . . . on the Books of Kings*): "The marvelous results of modern archaeology have been recorded, however imperfectly, usually without more than reference to the authorities, who then may disagree among themselves, or whose opinions may be shattered by fresh discoveries, for Dame Archaeology has been a chastiser of theoretical reconstructions of literary and so of religious history."

Indeed, for reasons and in a manner that I cannot discuss here, our "Fickle Dame" was responsible in great part for the attitude of scepticism, and even cynicism, toward the Bible as a historical document, as expressed by the Russells and Collingwoods. Interestingly, it has been the same "Dame," more than any other factor, that has been responsible for the development of quite the opposite attitude toward the Bible.

Let us get to this evening's specific case in point. The most important Biblical material bearing on the Fall of Judah and the Babylonian Captivity is to be found in the last chapters of the Second Book of Kings, the books of Jeremiah, Lamentations, and Ezekiel, and Psalm 137.

In II Kings 24–25 reference is made to King Nebuchadnezzar's invasion and conquest of Judah, the destruction and despoilation of Jerusalem and the Temple, and the exile to Babylonia of the important strata of the population (the royal household, the military, civil service, government officials, craftsmen, etc.); as put in 24:14 and 25:12, "only the poorest of the people of the land remained . . . The [Babylonian] captain of the guard left some of the poorest of the land as vinedressers and plowmen." Also, the fate of the royal family in captivity and of the people of conquered Judah is briefly described. Jeremiah talks of the imminent exile, and chapter 52 parallels much of the last chapters of II Kings. In his book, the prophet Ezekiel tells of his experiences as a member of the Judean captivity at Tel Abib in Babylonia, beginning with the year 592 B.C.E. Finally, the book of Lamentations (1:1: "Alas! Lonely sits the city/ Once great with people!/ She that was great among nations/ Is become like a widow;/

The princess among states/ Is become a thrall") and Psalm 137 (v. 1, "By the streams of Babylon/ There we sat and wept/ As we recalled Zion") are traditionally regarded as compositions that resulted directly from the great national catastrophe of 586 B.C.E.

Ezekiel begins his story as follows (1:1–3):

> In the thirtieth year, in the fourth month, on the fifth day of the month, when I was in the community of exiles by the Chebar Canal, the heavens opened and I saw visions of God. [2]On the fifth day of the month—it was the fifth year of the exile of King Jehoiachin—[3]the word of the Lord came to Ezekiel son of Buzi the priest, in the land of the Chaldeans at the Chebar Canal, and the hand of the Lord came upon him there.

But objection was raised to the reliability of this passage: how could one accept as authentic a statement purported to have been made by a member (Ezekiel) of a defeated, captive community (Tel Abib), in exile in the land of its conqueror (Babylonia), in which chronological reference is made to the deposed and exiled King ("in the fifth year of the exile of King Jehoiachin"), on whose throne, back home in Jerusalem, the conqueror had set some one (Zedekiah) who would faithfully serve the foreign (Babylonian) master? This kind of recognition of the deposed king, and the more than merely implied rejection of the Nebuchadnezzar-appointed subservient king, would surely have been regarded as sedition, justifying even the death penalty. The Babylonian overlord would hardly have permitted such blatant treachery. Clearly, then, the superscription and the chronological framework of the book of Ezekiel are not original, but rather the work of an editor of a later period who probably lived in another country, say, Judah; these passages simply could not be used as evidence for the great events of 586 B.C.E.

Again, on two occasions Ezekiel refers to the Persians: 27:10 "([1]Proclaim a dirge over Tyre [Phoenicia]. Say to Tyre . . . :] Persia, Lud, and Put were your warriors in your army . . ."); and similarly in 38:5, in connection with Gog of the land of Magog. Elsewhere in the

Bible, Persia and the Persians are mentioned only in such later books as Esther, Daniel, Ezra, Nehemiah, and II Chronicles.

Now Ezekiel was supposed to be active in Babylonia from about 592 to about 570 B.C.E. But in the late twenties and early thirties, scholars were confronted by the fact that the Persians were not mentioned in any known Babylonian or other texts prior to about 560 B.C.E.; the Persians had simply not been significant enough before then to merit recorded mention. How then could Ezekiel know of them and mention them? Clearly, these passages are not Ezekiel's, but were composed after his time, perhaps by a person who added the superscription and chronological data mentioned above.

In chapter 14, in denouncing the people of Judah for their extreme wickedness and in proclaiming their resultant doom, Ezekiel twice makes specific reference to the righteous threesome, Noah, Daniel, and Job (vv. 14–20):

> [14]If these three men, Noah, Daniel, and Job, should be in it (Jerusalem), they will, by their just deeds, save only themselves . . . [16] . . . as I live—declares the Lord God—no sons or daughters will they save; they alone shall be saved, but the land shall be a waste . . . [20]Even if Noah, Daniel, and Job be in it, as I live—declares the Lord God—not a son or a daughter shall they save; they, by their just deeds, shall save only themselves.

In other words, unlike sinful Sodom and Gomorrah and all their inhabitants—which would have been spared had a minimum of ten just men (*saddikim*) lived there—Jerusalem and its inhabitants were so lawless that even the presence of such unique *saddikim* as Noah, Daniel, and Job could not save them; this notable trio alone would be saved.

But there is a difficulty here, a rather serious one. So far as Noah and Job are concerned, the passages are in the clear; these two have long been recognized by scholars as ancient worthies about whom stories were being composed in the Near East of patriarchal times; so that Ezekiel could readily have been familiar with the saga about them. Daniel, on the other hand, is a problem. It is true that tradition places the book of Daniel and its hero in the period of Nebuchadnezzar II (605–562 B.C.E.), thus making Daniel a contemporary of Ezekiel; scholars, however, have long agreed that the Book is rather the product of a much later period, in all probability that of the Seleucid-Maccabean conflict (after 200 B.C.E.). So that the references to Daniel (cf. Ezek. 28:1–3, "The word of the Lord came to me: ²O mortal, say to the leader of Tyre: Thus said the Lord God, Because you have exalted yourself and . . .³ you regard yourself wiser than Daniel . . .") could not have come into being in Ezekiel's days; it has no validity for the history of that period. Indeed, this section of the Book is to be dated some four hundred years later.

If Jerusalem and the Temple were captured and severely damaged, and if the country at large was devastated by the Babylonian army, one should expect archaeologists in the course of their work to unearth physical evidence of this catastrophic event. It is true that by the end of the twenties, only a few Palestinian sites that were pertinent to our problem had been excavated and the reports on them published; so that the archaeological data for 586 B.C.E. were rather scant. Among these few sites, Beth-shemesh was the most prominent, and it contained a stratum of destruction. But according to its excavators, this level of occupation had been destroyed about 700 B.C.E., in the course of the Assyrian King Sennacherib's invasion of Judah; and thus a site such as Beth-shemesh—which lay some twenty-five miles west of Jerusalem, and which would have had to be neutralized by any enemy force which wanted to make certain that it would not be attacked from the rear while it made its way east toward Jerusalem —provided no evidence of Babylonian destruction of Judah.

Finally, we are told in the last section in the Second Book of Kings (25:27–30; preserved also in Jeremiah 52:31–34) that

In the thirty-seventh year of the exile of King Jehoiachin of Judah, in the twelfth month, on the twenty-seventh day of the month, King Evil-merodach of Babylon, in his coronation year, released (lit., "lifted the head of") King Jehoiachin of Judah from prison. ²⁸He treated him kindly and set his throne above those of the other kings who were with him in Babylon. [29]His prison garb was changed, and for the rest of his life he always ate his meals at the king's table (lit., "before him"). [30]And his regular rations were provided for him by the king—a portion for each day—for the rest of his life.

This statement was hardly the kind that a critical scholar could accept at its face value. What power did a captive king from such a petty kingdom as Judah wield as to merit or justify elevation above all other kings? There could be little doubt that the Judean writer wished to glorify his king and people, and so concocted this tale.

By the same token, the statement in II Kings 24:16 (cf. v. 14) that King Nebuchadnezzar's army carried off to Babylonia (along with "[15]. . . Jehoiachin . . . the queen mother, the king's wives, his chamberlains, his officials, the nobles of the land . . . [16]and all the soldiers, seven thousand") "artisans and smiths," was not taken seriously by some scholars. After all, with its wealth of craftsmen and its tradition of fine craftsmanship, Babylonia hardly had need of the Israelite guilds whose members were relatively few in number and the quality of whose work was not exactly world-famous.

But unpredictable "Dame Archaeology" began to enter into the picture, and the study of the Bible was never again to be the same.

In 1930, a Jewish archaeologist at Princeton University and a specialist in Old Persian, Ernst Herzfeld, published an Old Persian text in which a great-uncle of Cyrus I refers to himself as "king of kings"; and a year later, Ernst Weidner of Berlin published an even older text, an Assyrian inscription of King Asshurbanipal (spelled Osnappar or Asenappar in Ezra 4:10), about 640 B.C.E., in which the grandfather of Cyrus I is mentioned. And thus Torrey's rejection of the "Persian" passages in Ezekiel, based as it was on argument from silence, itself had to be rejected: for if Persia and the Persians had become conquerors of importance already two generations before Ezekiel embarked on his exilic career, this prophet was certainly in a position to refer to them when and in the manner that he did.

The clarification of the chronological reference to King Jehoiachin in exile came a year later. In 1928, W. F. Albright (then Director of the all-important Jerusalem part of the American Schools of Oriental

Research) excavated at Tell Beit Mirsim (perhaps Biblical Debir, Kiriath-sepher; about twenty-eight miles southwest of Jerusalem) a jar handle stamped with a seal whose inscription read: "(Belonging) to Eliakim, steward of Yaukin" (*l*-'*elyakim ná'ar yaukin*). Two years later, two additional products of the same stamp were discovered, one at Beth-shemesh (about twenty-five miles west of Jerusalem) and the other at Tell Beit Mirsim. The important implications of this find for our problem at once struck Dr. Albright, and he published a brilliant article on "The Seal of Eliakim and the Latest Preëxilic History of Judah, with some Observations on Ezekiel" (in *Journal of Biblical Literature*, volume 51, 1932, pp. 77–106).

As summarized later by Albright himself ("King Joiachin in Exile," in *Biblical Archaeologist*, volume 5, No. 4, December 1942, pp. 49–55):

> Immediately after the find, the eminent Palestinian archaeologist, Father L. H. Vincent, identified the name "Yaukin" as an abbreviated form of "Joiachin" . . . All three stamps were made from the same original seal, indicating that Yaukin was a person of very high importance, probably king, since seals bearing a formula of this type have been proved to belong to kings of Judah and surrounding lands. It was possible to demonstrate . . . that Eliakim had been steward of the crown property of King Joiachin while the latter was a captive in Babylonia . . .

Now Jehoiachin was a young man of about eighteen when he succeeded his murdered father Jehoiakim as king of Judah (597 B.C.E.), and he sat on the throne a bare three months before succumbing to the Babylonian invaders and going off into captivity. His uncle Zedekiah, put on the throne by the alien conquerors, was hardly recognized by the native population as their king. So that while Zedekiah was accepted perforce as king in fact (*de facto*), it was Jehoiachin whom many of the people, if not the majority, continued to regard as their king by right (*de jure*).

During the three months that he reigned, Jehoiachin was cooped up behind the walls of Jerusalem, besieged and blockaded as the city was by the superior Babylonian army; he and his compatriots were unable to go out or come in. It could therefore not have been he who sent out his official jars, with his royal seal stamped on their handles, to such places as Beth-shemesh and Tell Beit Mirsim for the collection of taxes; this was done by his successor Zedekiah, under Babylonian control. And if Babylonia and its subject Judean king "recognized" exiled Jehoiachin—through the use of his royal stamp—in Judah proper, where an attempt at revolt and liberation would start first, surely it was possible, and legal, for Ezekiel to make use of the year of the exile—not of the accession—of King Jehoiachin. Indeed, any one composing chronological data in postexilic times, after Babylonia had gone the way of all governmental flesh, would automatically have chosen the accession year of the king for his chronological framework. And so Torrey's approach to the chronological data in Ezekiel was repudiated by the extrabiblical data uncovered by archaeology.

During this period, from 1929 on, excavation had begun and was continuing at Ras esh-Shamra, a site in Syria on the Mediterranean coast opposite the northeastern tip of Cyprus. Very considerable archaeological and written material was uncovered there, some of it of capital importance for a better understanding of ancient Israel and the Bible. Because the site was known as Ugarit in antiquity, the inscriptions have come to be known as the Ugaritic texts.

A prosperous and cultured Canaanite community inhabited Ugarit and environs, and—what is of especial interest for us—it had great impact on Biblical Israel. In one of the texts, published in 1936, we read of a king, dn'il (Danel or Daniel) by name, that

> He judges the case of the widow
> And upholds the cause of the fatherless
> (*ydn dn almnt = yadin din almanoth*
> *yṭpṭ ṭpṭ ytm = yishpoṭ sheᵉfot yathom*).

In the Bible, it is God and those who follow His teachings who are associated with this application of justice. Thus Deuteronomy 10:18 asserts that ". . . the Lord your God . . . upholds the cause of the fatherless and the widow" (*'oseh mishpaṭ yathom weᵉ-'almanah*); Psalm 68:6 describes God as "father of the fatherless and judge of the widows" (*ᵃvi yeᵉthomim weᵉ-dayyan 'almanoth*); and Proverbs 31:9

addresses a king: "Speak up, render a just decision, Give judgment to the poor and needy" (*pᵉtaḥ-pikha shᵉfaṭ-tsedek wᵉ-din 'ani wᵉ-'evyon*).

Noah and Job had long been acknowledged by scholars as models of justice going back to ancient times, and now the Daniel of Ezekiel joined their ranks. Daniel is not, in the book of Ezekiel, the hero of the book of Daniel but the ancient Near Eastern hero as revealed by the Canaanite texts from Ugarit. (Incidentally, and interestingly, the spelling of "Daniel" in all three passages in Ezekiel is originally *dn'l*, meaning "[The God] El has judged"; this is the spelling in Ugarit. In the book of Daniel, the spelling is *dny'l*, denoting "[The God] El is my Judge." This difference in orthography may point to Ugarit, rather than to the later book of Daniel, as the source of Ezekiel's Daniel.)

In the meantime, archaeological discoveries were being made in all parts of the Near East, especially on the west side of the Jordan. Probably the most sensational—and unexpected—discovery came out of the dig at Tell ed-Duweir, Biblical Lachish (about twenty-five miles southwest of Jerusalem and eight miles northwest of Tell Beit Mirsim). In 1934, while clearing the pre-Persian level of the site, the director of the British (Wellcome-Marston-Mond) Expedition, J. L. Starkey, came upon a room that had experienced terrible destruction by fire; that whole level constituted burnt debris about a meter thick. A number of ostraca (sherds used as writing material) were found in this room—eighteen were found in January, 1935, and three more a little later—several of which were meaningful as well as legible. These Lachish Ostraca at once became a prime source of information about the invading army of Nebuchadnezzar, driving down as it did along the edge of the hill country of Judah and neutralizing its fortified towns before proceeding to the heart of the country, the political and cultural center, Jerusalem. The ostraca were written only a few months before the capital city fell to the Babylonians. The last part of Ostracon IV reads:

> And let (my lord) know that we are watching for the signals of Lachish, according to all the signs which my lord has given, for we cannot see Azekah.

Not only Lachish, but Beth-shemesh too became prime evidence of Babylonian devastation of Judah in 586. For with the improved knowledge of pottery and other archaeological materials, it became evident that what had previously been considered the 700 B.C.E. level of (Assyrian) destruction was really the 586 level of (Babylonian) destruction. Indeed, since the early thirties, about a score of the many sites that have been excavated in Palestine-Israel exhibit clear evidence of widespread destruction precisely at the 586 level; such places—in addition to Lachish and Beth-shemesh—as Beth-zur, Bethel, Ras el-Kharrubeh (the Anathoth of Jeremiah), Gibeon, and Tell en-Nasbeh (probably Mizpah) come readily to mind. As put to me by one archaeologist: "The devastation was so complete that town after town was never reinhabited, and it was centuries before the country recovered."

The climax for our problem—if our problem required any after the excavation of Lachish and its Ostraca—occurred at the height of Nazi prestige and World War II. In the middle thirties, the Hitler regime had consolidated its hold on Germany enough to devote part of its organized efforts to prepare the basis for the worldwide and permanent destruction of the prestige and reputation that the Jewish people had built up in the course of its almost four-thousand year career of recorded history; the Nazis knew full well that to destroy the Jewish people without also defaming its name would not constitute real extermination. Thus early in 1936, the Reich Institute for the History of the New Germany announced that compulsory courses in scientific anti-Semitism would henceforth be taught in all German schools.

And so, well-oiled wheels were set in motion to gather from all over Germany, and from areas already or yet to be conquered, every bit of data pertaining to the career of the Jewish people since it appeared on the stage of human history; these data were to be assembled, classified, studied, and published to prove the infamous and degenerative character of this people. The operation grew into the "Institut zur Erforschung der Judenfrage" (1941) under Alfred Rosenberg.

Now let us go back a bit. In 1905, a German expedition excavating the ancient site of Babylon uncovered near the Ishtar Gate and the magnificent palace of the Royal House ("The House at which Men Marvel") a structure with fourteen vaulted rooms, in which were found some three hundred cuneiform tablets. These tablets were sent to the Kaiser Friedrich Museum in Berlin for proper disposition. But something went wrong; a funny thing happened in the Museum on the way to the cataloguer, and this horde of texts got misplaced, and for three decades they lay there, unknown and unread, as lifeless and lost in the dust of the Museum as they had been in the dust of Babylon for the two and a half millenia preceding.

In the course of the intensive search for documents relating to the Jews, Ernst F. Weidner of the Museum was informed that a batch of cuneiform tablets had been discovered in the basement of the Museum. Our lost find had been found—to prove once again that it is always worthwhile to dig your nearest museum first, before embarking on a dig many thousands of miles away.

When Weidner began to decipher the tablets, he became very excited. One of the things he did was to send off a letter to Albright at the Johns Hopkins University in Baltimore, telling him something of the sensational contents of a number of the tablets. But then World War II broke out, and virtually all academic contact was broken between Berlin and Baltimore. Naturally, Albright was not at liberty to divulge publicly the contents of Weidner's letter to him.

In 1941 and 1942 rumors spread in this country that Weidner's article had appeared, but no one had seen it directly. Then one fine day late in 1942, as I was sitting and working at my desk in the library of the Johns Hopkins, the librarian came over to ask me to help her catalogue a book that had come in to the Classics Department. I looked at the volume and became very excited. I rushed out with the as yet uncatalogued book to tell Albright about the utterly unexpected arrival of the volume. I burst into his office—I hope I did not forget to knock on the door first—and exclaimed "Here it is! Here it is!" After I calmed down, I told him that it was volume II of the *Festschrift* for the French scholar, René Dussaud (Mélanges Syriens offerts á M. René Dussaud; Paris, 1939), and that Weidner's article was in the volume. Albright then proceeded to write a popular article on "King Joiachin in Exile" for the very next issue of *The Biblical Archaeologist* (December, 1942).

So far as I know, this was apparently the only copy of the Dussaud volume that was to be found in the United States until after the war was ended. It was, I believe, sent out by someone in Switzerland.

Photostatic copies of the article were sent to scholars who requested it. I even sent out a microfilm of the article to Professor Sukenik at the Hebrew University in Jerusalem; but it was returned to me after the war, with the explanation: "Flammable." I suppose that the censors were right: this microfilm might have ignited something terrible in the midst of the otherwise calm events of World War II. The reader may find this letter of explanation to the censors of interest:

Harry M. Orlinsky
2518 Brookfield Avenue
Baltimore, Maryland
June 15, 1944

TO THE AMERICAN AND PALESTINIAN CENSORS:

The enclosed is a reproduction of an exceedingly important article. It deals with a Babylonian tablet which helps to prove that the Biblical account of the circumstances surrounding the Babylonian Exile is correct. The article appeared in a volume published in Paris late in 1939. It so happens that only one copy of this volume reached the U.S.A., at the Johns Hopkins University. Since no copy reached the Near East, Prof. E. L. Sukenik of the Hebrew University in Jerusalem, Palestine, wrote me on April 18, 1944, via Clipper Air Mail, asking that a reproduction of the article be made, if at all possible, and sent to the Hebrew University. To make sure that a copy gets there, I am sending out now a microfilm reproduction of the article, and a few weeks later I shall send out a photostatic reproduction.

Respectfully submitted,
(signed) Harry M. Orlinsky

The Johns Hopkins University

In his article, "Joiachin, König von Juda, in babylonischen Keilschrifttexten" (pp. 923–935), Weidner reproduced, transliterated, translated, and discussed the relevant passages of those of the nearly three hundred tablets that were pertinent to the Judean Exile. One of the tablets (written in 592 B.C.E.) contains the decree of King Nebuchadnezzar that daily rations of oil and grain be given to "Yaukin, king of the land of Yahud," his five sons, and other Judeans. This fact indicates that although conquered and in captivity, King Jehoiachin and his entourage were free to move about in Babylon. As to why he came to be imprisoned (later to be pardoned, in 561, by Nebuchadnezzar's son and successor, Evil-merodach), we know nothing definite. It may be that a planned revolt in Judah that was to be coordinated with an attempt by the Judean king to escape, brought about his incarceration. In any case, it would seem that even the Babylonian government itself regarded Jehoiachin as Judah's legal king, perhaps keeping him for possible restoration on the throne in Jerusalem if that should serve Babylon's purpose. However, if the Babylonian government at home referred to Jehoiachin as "king of the land of Judah," then his contemporary and fellow-exile, Ezekiel, could readily describe events in relation to the year of Jehoiachin's exile—as Albright had argued brilliantly a decade earlier on the basis of the seal impression on the broken jar-handles from Tell Beit Mirsim and Beth-shemesh.

Furthermore, mention is made in these tablets of sailors, musicians, gardeners, horse- and monkey-trainers, shipworkers, carpenters, and other craftsmen, from such varied and even distant places as Ashkelon (Philistia), Tyre, Byblos, Elam, Persia, Media, Judah, Egypt, Asia Minor, and Aegean Greece. Nebuchadnezzar, it is now known even more than before, initiated a vast building campaign in his capital city. The legendary "Hanging Gardens of Babylon" (really terraced or rooftop gardens that looked "hanging" from a distance) constituted one of the products of this campaign. For this, the king needed urgently craftsmen of all kinds, and he paid above average wages to attract them. Small wonder that he made it a point to have craftsmen of conquered countries (among them, e.g., "the artisans and smiths" of II Kings 24:16) brought to Babylon as forced labor.

In fine, ladies and gentlemen, there was a destruction of the Temple in 586, and a devastation of Judah, and a captivity, and an exile in Babylonia, and a Restoration in Judah.

It is not very often that archaeology can demonstrate a specific statement or event in the Bible in the manner that we have tried to do in this lecture. For the most part by far, archaeological discoveries in Israel and elsewhere in Bible lands do not bear directly on the Bible. However, it has become virtually impossible to look upon a factual statement in the Bible as unreliable simply because there is lacking an extra-Biblical datum to authenticate it; archaeology since World War I has seen to that.

To be sure, as I wrote in my *Ancient Israel* in 1954 (pp. 7–9), "Modern historians do not . . . accept every part of the Bible equally as literal fact. Yet they have come to accept much of the Biblical data as constituting unusually reliable historical documents of antiquity, documents which take on new meaning and pertinence when they are analysed in the light of newly discovered extra-Biblical sources. . . .

"This radical re-evaluation of the significance of the Bible has been necessitated by the archaeological discoveries of the past three decades. . . . The material, social, and religious configurations of the Sumerian, Egyptian, Babylonian, Hurrian, Assyrian, Canaanite, Hittite, and Aramaen societies can be delineated to an increasingly satisfactory degree. It is now possible to see the entire ancient Near East from a thoroughly new perspective, and so it has become necessary to re-examine the Biblical record in the light of our broadened understanding. . . ." The foregoing statements of sixteen years ago are even more pertinent today.

Let me close with this observation. The archaeological expedition that excavated the important Babylonian tablets that we dealt with in this lecture was German. The article about these tablets was written by a citizen of Nazi Germany and appeared in a book published in 1939 in France in honor of a French scholar a few months before World War II broke out between France and Germany. The book somehow got sent from Germany-controlled France to the United States, which was then already at war with Nazi Germany. And one of the important consequences of the article was the proof that it offered that the Bible constituted a first class repository of unusually reliable historical documents of antiquity. The people that Nazi Germany was determined to exterminate and whose reputation it planned to defame forever as the greatest falsifiers of history—this same people, thanks to the efficiency of the Nazis that resulted in the discovery of the tablets in the basement of a museum under their control, has emerged as among the most reliable writers of history, not only their own history but also that involving other peoples.

SELECTED BIBLIOGRAPHY

Albright, W. F., "The Seal of Eliakim and the Latest Preëxilic History of Judah, with some Observations on Ezekiel," *Journal of Biblical Literature*, 51 (1932), pp. 77–106.

———, "King Joiachin in Exile", *Biblical Archaeologist*, 5 (1942), 49–55.

Olmstead, A. T., *History of the Persian Empire* (University of Chicago Press, 1948; also in paperback), Chap. II (pp. 23 f., 31 ff.). Olmstead's uninhibited prejudice against modern Zionism vitiated significantly his chapters (XXII, XXV, XXXII) on the Restoration.

Orlinsky, H. H., *Galus Bavel in Shein fun Archeológiye* (*in Yiddish*) *YIVO Bleter* (*Journal of the Yiddish Scientific Institute*), 25 (1945), 323–334. Reproduced by Zvi Shimshi in Hebrew, in somewhat condensed form, in *Ha-Olam* (central organ of the World Zionist Organization), ed. Moshe Kleinman; XXXIII, 13 (Dec. 6, 1945), p. 129. [*Ancient Israel* now reissued, with addition of pictures, line drawings, charts, maps, passages from the Bible in vocalized Hebrew and modern English translation, as *Understanding the Bible through History and Archaeology*, KTAV, 1972.]

———, "Where Did Ezekiel Receive the Call to Prophecy?," *Bulletin of the American Schools of Oriental Research*, 122 (April, 1951), 33–35.

———, *Ancient Israel* (Cornell University Press, 6th printing, 1965; also in paperback, in reduced form), Chapter VI: "The Babylonian Exile and the Restoration of Judah" (pp. 118–141; also, see Index, s. Exile).

Rowley, H. H.: "The Book of Ezekiel in Modern Study," *Bulletin of the John Rylands Library*, 36 (1953), 146–190.

Spiegel, S., "Ezekiel or Pseudo-Ezekiel?," *Harvard Theological Review*, 24 (1931), 245–321.

———, "Toward Certainty in Ezekiel," *Journal of Biblical Literature*, 54 (1935), 145–171.

Torrey, C. C., *Pseudo-Ezekiel and the Original Prophecy* (Yale Oriental Series 18; New Haven, 1930).

———, "Ezekiel and the Exile, a Reply," *Journal of Biblical Literature*, 51 (1932), 179–181.

———, "Certainly Pseudo-Ezekiel," *Journal of Biblical Literature*, 53 (1934), 291–320.

[Torrey-Spiegel now reissued with Prolegomenon by W. F. Stinespring, in KTAV, *Library of Biblical Studies*, 1970, ed. H. M. Orlinsky.]

8

Where Did Ezekiel Receive
the Call to Prophesy?

IF THE CYCLE of Ezekiel studies in the past quarter century, one which differed sharply from the past by its extremely critical attitude toward the reliable character of the Book as an historical document, is beginning to come to a close, [1] there will be two important reasons

---

[This article appeared in the W. F. Albright issue of the *Bulletin of the American Schools of Oriental Research (BASOR)*, 122 (April, 1951), pp. 34-36, in honor of that great scholar's Sixtieth Birthday. The article is part of a paper ("Where did Ezekiel Begin and Continue to Prophesy?") read by title at the 86th Meeting of the Society of Biblical Literature, New York, Dec. 27, 1950.]

[1] Cf. S. R. Driver in the last (1913) revision of his excellent *Introduction to the Literature of the Old Testament*, p. 279: "No critical question arises in connexion with the authorship of the book, the whole from beginning to end bearing unmistakably the stamp of a single mind." Cf. also such surveys as S. Spiegel, "Ezekiel or Pseudo-Ezekiel?" (*Harvard Theological Review*, 24 [1931], 245 ff.); G. A. Cooke, *ICC on Ezekiel* (1936); R. H. Pfeiffer, *Introduction to the Old Testament* (New York, 1941), 525 ff.; W. A. Irwin, *The Problem of Ezekiel* (Chicago, 1943), 3-30; C. G. Howie, *The Date and Composition of Ezekiel* (1950, Vol. IV in the Monograph Series of the *JBL*), passim.

It should be recognized that a, if not the, paramount factor in this previously stable and consistent attitude toward Ezekiel's Book was the assumption that Wellhausen's conception of the Documentary Theory was essentially correct, and the Theory dated the P(riestly) Document in relation to the book of Ezekiel whose traditional date in the first half of the sixth century was then not seriously questioned.

for this newer outlook: (1) Archaeology has made it necessary to give up the attitude of extreme scepticism toward the essential reliability of much of the biblical writings for the reconstruction of the biblical period in history. For this quite radical change in outlook no single scholar is more responsible than Albright. (2) It seems to me that the first decisive argument against the tendency to look upon most of the book of Ezekiel as pseudepigraphic was the brilliant article by Albright in 1932 on "The Seal of Eliakim and the Latest Pre-Exilic History of Judah, with some Observations on Ezekiel" (*JBL,* 51, 77-106). More recently, his understanding of the book of Ezekiel may be discerned in the doctoral dissertation written by his student, C. G. Howie (see n. 1).

The preserved text of Ezekiel states explicitly that the prophet received his initial call in Babylonia:

> . . . When I was in the exile community by the Chebar Canal, the heavens opened and I saw visions of God . . . I looked, and suddenly a storm wind came out of the north—a huge cloud and flashing fire, with a radiance around it . . . This was the appearance of the likeness of the Presence of the Lord . . . And He said to me, "O mortal, I am sending you to the people of Israel . . . whether they listen or not . . . that they may know that there was a prophet among them." (1:1, 4; 2:3-5.)[2]

Many scholars, however, felt that this statement was not true, and that Ezekiel received his call in Judah and prophesied in that land; and the question whether he ever did prophesy in Babylonia became secondary in importance. [3]

Over six hundred years had elapsed since the Israelites had established themselves in a land of their own, and almost four hundred years

---

[2] Most scholars are agreed that there are two separate chronological materials in 1:1-2, and many interpretations of the "thirtieth year" in v. 1 have been offered (cf. the survey in Howie, Chap. II). However, our argument does not depend at all on the manner in which the problem of the "thirtieth year" is resolved.

[3] Cf. the survey in Howie, Chap. I (to which may be added Spiegel, JBL, 56 [1937], 403-8, "When did Ezekiel Go into Exile?" [in Hebrew; pp. 2-8 in the *Nissan Turoff Volume,* New York, 5798-1938]).

had gone by since Solomon had carried out David's intention to erect a dwelling place on Zion for the Lord. [4] While all the peoples and all the extremities of the world were ultimately subject to the Lord's will, Israel alone was His covenanted people, and the land of His dwelling place was uniquely holy. In all this period, no person outside of the Holy Land had received a "call" from the Lord, had experienced the spirit of God coming down upon him and into him, had been commanded in a vision to become His prophet. [5]

Ezekiel is the first person to become a prophet outside of God's holy territory. His call is thus utterly unique, and quite out of line with precedent and tradition. One could readily understand how a prophet who received his initial call in Babylonia would deny this fact, and claim instead to have received divine authority initially in Judah, on holy soil. It is inconceivable however that a prophet who received his call in Jerusalem, in Judah, would suppress this fact, and claim instead a foreign land as the birthplace of his prophetic career. So far as I am aware, no one who has rejected the biblical statement has attempted to answer the question: What could Ezekiel (or a redactor) have hoped to gain by shifting the locale of the initial call from Judah (if so it was) to Babylonia?

Reading the book of Ezekiel with no preconceived ideas, the initial

---

[4] One cannot overestimate the importance of this concept (now known strikingly also from the Ugaritic texts) in Israelite history and in the prophetic tradition. It was the primary concern of all the prophets before 587 that the Temple remain standing and functioning, and after 587 that the Temple be rebuilt (cf. Ezekiel, Second Isaiah, Haggai, Zechariah). Ezekiel's great concern with the rebuilding of the Temple derives directly from the fact that he is the first prophet in Israel to be active when God's Temple was no more.

[5] The rabbis were acutely aware of this fact; cf. the survey by Spiegel (§ 3 "Ezekiel or Pseudo-Ezekiel?"). As a matter of fact (*Mekilta*, ed. J. Z. Lauterbach, Vol. I, Tractate Pisḥa I, pp. 6-7; with which cf. the Targum at 1:3), ". . . Some say, He [viz., God] had already spoken with him in the [Holy] land, and then He spoke with him outside of the land . . . You can learn from the following that the Shekinah does not reveal itself outside of the land . . ." But surely no one would use this rabbinic statement (or Tractate Shirata in the *Mekilta,* Chap. VII [pp. 54-5 in ed. Lauterbach]) as the basis for the argument that Ezekiel received his prophetic call in the Holy Land.

call in Babylonia becomes perfectly clear and normal. Ezekiel did receive the same kind of authority to prophesy as his predecessors who were in the Holy Land. And in common with them, he received it directly from the Lord. There was only one difference between Ezekiel's call and theirs, one which derived from Ezekiel's presence in a foreign land, namely, the Lord came from Judah to Babylonia, and with His holy presence on foreign soil commissioned Ezekiel as His prophet. In fine, Ezekiel's call as described in Ezek. 1 is essentially the same as Isaiah's call as described in Isa. 6, except that whereas Isaiah came to the Lord, it was the Lord who, of necessity, came to Ezekiel.[6]

---

[6] While it does not affect our argument, I do not agree with those (e. g., Driver, *op. cit.,* p. 280; J. Morgenstern, *Hebrew Union College Annual,* 16 [1941], 65-7) who would see in the term *ṣaphón* in Ezek. 1:4 anything more than the conventional direction of one coming from Judah to Babylonia, even as one who comes to Judah from the region of Mesopotamia may likewise be said to come from the "north"; cf. the Malbim (which my friend Prof. Sidney B. Hoenig called to my attention), *loc. cit.;* D. H. Müller's very useful *Ezechiel-Studien* (Berlin, 1895), p. 28; H. G. May, JBL, 56 (1937), 317 and nn. 25-26.

9

"A Covenant (of) People, A Light of Nations" —a Problem in Biblical Theology

IT HAS LONG BEEN axiomatic among biblical scholars that when Second Isaiah used the expression (49.6) *u-n^ethattíkha l^e'or goyim* "I will make you a light of nations" (or cf. 42.6: *w^e-'ettenkha librith ^cam l^e'or goyim* "I will make you a covenant of people [or: a covenant-people], a light of nations"), he meant that he, the prophet, would serve as God's servant not only to restore the Judean captivity to its homeland but also to bring light and redemption to the heathen nations of the world.

TORREY, *The Second Isaiah*, 380 ff., has put it as eloquently and clearly as anyone: "This chapter may well occupy the central place in

---

[This analysis is a reworked version of my article "A Light of the Nations: A Problem in Biblical Theology," written for the 75th Anniversary Volume of *Jewish Quarterly Review* (1966). It was read originally before the Middle-Atlantic States Section of the Society of Biblical Literature, New York, April 4, 1965, under the title, "I Will Make You a Light of Nations." For a detailed analysis of the biblical data, see in this volume my essays on "Nationalism-Universalism . . ." reproduced from the May and Enslin Jubilee Volumes, and my study of *The So-Called "Servant of the Lord" and "Suffering Servant" in Second Isaiah* (*Supplements to Vetus Testamentum*, XIV [1967], 1-133)—hereafter cited simply as *Second Isaiah*.]

the book . . . It thus affords an excellent starting point for the study of (the prophet's) ideas in regard to the Servant, the 'restoration,' the conversion of the heathen nations, and the final status of the Jews and Gentiles in God's kingdom . . . The 'rescue' which had been promised to Israel, and which was the Servant's first mission (verses 5, 6) is to include the Gentiles as well; even the most remote nations are to be gathered in." JAMES SMART, "A New Approach to the 'Ebed-Yahweh Problem" (Expository Times, 45 [1933-34], 168a-172b)—one of the all too few analyses that breathes freshness and independence in the midst of stale and rehashed discussions—and KISSANE, The Book of Isaiah, vol. II, pp. 37, 128, interpret similarly.

On the other hand, SNAITH—who has long stood alone in his "nationalistic" interpretation of "The Servant of the Lord in Deutero-Isaiah" (in Studies in Old Testament Prophecy [the Theodore H. Robinson Volume], ed. H. H. ROWLEY, 1950, 187-200)—put it this way (p. 198): "But it is far too small a thing to bring back all the Babylonian exiles (the tribes of Jacob and the preserved of Israel). The servant's mission is to be 'a light of Gentiles,' i.e., a light through-out all the Gentile lands 'that my salvation may be to the end of the earth,' i.e., my salvation of Israel, since this is the only salvation in which the prophet is interested. The servant will be a light to guide every Israelite wanderer home. His mission is to gather in all exiles wherever they may be scattered." SNAITH received considerable sup-port from DE BOER's independent researches on Second-Isaiah's Mes-sage (1956), in the chapter (V) on "The Limits of Second-Isaiah's Message" (p. 94: "SNAITH observed rightly that the servant's mission is limited to his own people"). On p. 90 he asserted, "No other con-clusion can be drawn from our texts than the statement: Second-Isa-iah's only purpose is to proclaim deliverance for the Judean people . . . "; and he rendered 42.6b (pp. 9, 84), "(I, Yhwh . .)put you to a consolidation of the people, a light respected by the nations" (and cf. 92, "The renewed people will be set as a light, openly seen and respected among the nations le'or goyim, xlii 6; le'or 'ammim, li 4"). By berith 'am DE BOER understands (p. 94) ". . . the consolidation of the people after a period of disintegration."

But LINDBLOM, *The Servant Songs,* etc. (1951)—a fine antidote to some of the studies on this subject that have emanated from his Scandinavian colleagues—took issue with SNAITH (p. 27, n. 29). He would agree with the general view that (p. 26) "In this critical moment the prophet received a new revelation from Yahweh: he was told that he had been set apart to be a light to the nations, that is to say: he was to perform a missionary task in order that the Gentiles might be saved. The future of Israel is for the moment left out of consideration, the chief stress being laid on the new task in relation to the Gentiles . . ." This conventional view may be found also, e.g., in NORTH, *The Suffering Servant,* etc., 143 ff.; or in ZIMMERLI-JEREMIAS, *The Servant of God,* 29 f., ". . . the servant will be a light for the whole earth. His activity . . . glorifies the sole honour of Yahweh and thus becomes the light and salvation of the whole world"; or BLANK, *Prophetic Faith in Isaiah* (1958), 110 f. (and n. 85 on p. 221), 143 (and n. 4 on p. 223), and 157 (and n. 26 on p. 223).

On the generally accepted view, then, the prophet's message is one of internationalism, and on an unusually high level, a level that has not been achieved—for that matter, not even attempted—by any people in history. There is good reason, however, to believe that nothing of the sort was meant by the author; indeed, it is our contention that the prophet was here, as elsewhere in his argument, utterly nationalistic, and that the concept of internationalism was only later, over half a millennium later—after Jesus and his contemporaries had come and gone— read back into our passage and into Second Isaiah as a whole. In this, our prophet stood four-square in the biblical tradition, even if thus he disappoints modern scholars and theologians who would see in his statements the *Weltanschauung* of our own Twentieth Century supporters of the League of Nations and the United Nations.

Let us deal here with the terms *'or goyim* and *b^erith ^cam* in context, both the literary and historical context.

B

In 49.1 ff. (for the argument, see my *Second Isaiah,* pp. 79-89) the prophet proclaims to the whole world the fact that God has designated him from the outset as His spokesman to Israel, for the purpose of leading his fellow Judean exiles back to God. Up to this point, however, the prophet had labored in vain, for the condition of his fellow exiles had not changed. But now a new era was to begin: not only had God designated the prophet as His servant to restore His people to their homeland but, in addition, He would make him "a light of nations," with God's victory becoming a world phenomenon.

If one ignores what precedes and what follows this last assertion of verse 6 (*lihyoth y^eshu^cathi ^cad-q^eṣeh ha-^cáreṣ* "That My triumph[1] may reach to the ends of the earth"), then, I suppose, it is possible to assert that the prophet was to bring God's teachings to the heathen nations and thereby afford the entire world the rewards that derived from acknowledging Him as their Deity; and this is—as stated above— exactly what has been universally asserted. But this view is precluded by the context itself. For not only does verse 5a state that God had destined the prophet from birth to be His servant for the purpose of restoring His people Israel ("And now the Lord has declared—Who formed me in the womb to be His servant—That He will bring Jacob back to Him, That Israel shall be gathered to Him") but verse 7 no less clearly expresses what may be termed the other side of one and the same coin, viz.:

Thus said the Lord,
Redeemer of Israel, his Holy One,
To (or: Concerning) the one despised by men[2] (or: the despised one[2]),
Abhorred by nations,
The slave of rulers:
Kings shall see and stand up,

---

[1] Hebrew *y^eshu^cah* is best rendered "triumph, victory, vindication." Traditional "salvation" has become quite misleading with its almost wholly post-biblical theological overtones and associations.

[2] Israel in exile is clearly meant here. Note that whenever a major category such as "nations," "peoples," "ends of the earth," "ruler," "kings," "potentates," "princes," and the like is employed in Second Isaiah, the counterpart is "Israel"; see Chapter III, § B (pp. 23-51) of my *Second Isaiah,* where mention is made also of the hyperbolic use of these and other terms in relation to Israel.

> Princes, and they shall prostrate themselves—
> Because of the Lord, who is faithful,
> The Holy One of Israel, who chose you.

In other words, far from bringing "salvation" to the heathen nations, the prophet's task in the service of the Lord is to lead exiled Israel to redemption and thereby cause the nations and their leaders—who until then held the exiles in contempt—to acknowledge abjectly the omnipotence of Israel's faithful God. And the prophet continues (vv. 8-9, 13):

> (8) Thus said the Lord:
> In a time of favor I have answered you,
> In a day of triumph I have helped you;
> I have kept you
> And I have made you a covenant (of) people,[3]
> To restore the land,
> To allot the waste heritages,
> (9) To say to the prisoners,[4] "Go free!"
> To those in darkness, "Show yourselves!" . . .

> (13) Sing, O heavens, exult, O earth,
> Break forth into song, O mountains!
> For the Lord has comforted His people,
> Has shown compassion to His afflicted ones.

One could readily go on in this vein, not only for the rest of the chapter but throughout Second Isaiah, citing chapter and verse in every instance, to show the comfort that Israel in exile would receive from the Lord, in sharp contradistinction to the treatment that the heathen nations would receive in the process. In the light of the data

---

[3] For the expression *we-ettenkha librith ᶜam* see § E below.

[4] Such expressions as "prisoners," "those (who dwell) in darkness," and "the blind" always refer in Second Isaiah to Israel in exile; see chap. III, § B of my *Second Isaiah*.

offered in chaps. III-IV of my *Second Isaiah,* the following quotation
from the last five verses of our chapter will suffice here (vv. 22-26):

(22) Thus said the Lord God:
I will raise My hand to nations
And lift up My ensign to peoples;
And they shall bring your sons in their bosoms,
And carry your daughters on their shoulders.
(23) Kings shall be your attendants,
Their queens shall serve you as nurses.
They shall bow to you, face to the ground,
And lick the dust of your feet. . . .
(26) I will make your oppressors eat their own flesh,
They shall be drunk with their own blood as with wine.
And all mankind shall know
That I the Lord am your savior,
The Mighty One of Jacob, your redeemer. (49.22-26.)

In fine, it is but eisegesis—the clear perversion of the original and
plain meaning of the text—to make the prophet as "a light of nations"
mean that Israel was in exile in order to bring redemption to the world.
In point of fact, Israel was in exile only because she had transgressed
her covenant with the Lord, and she would be restored because—the
prophet maintained, as all the prophets did—God would never cast
her off.

C

Our expression "a light of nations" occurs also in 42.6. The prophet begins with the assertion (vv. 1-5) that God, creator of the world
and author of all life on it, has decided that the time has come for His
servant [5] to execute His judgment throughout the world. In the words
of the prophet (vv. 5-6):

---

[5] I have argued in chap. IV, § *A* (pp. 75-79) of my *Second Isaiah* that the servant in 42.1 ff. is the prophet himself (as against, e.g., Cyrus). However, our
analysis of the expression "a light of nations" is not affected by this problem.

(5) Thus said God the Lord,
Who created the heavens and stretched them out,
Who spread out the earth and what it brings forth,
Who gave breath to the people upon it
And life to those who walk on it:
(6) I the Lord have summoned you for triumph;
I have grasped you by the hand,
Have guarded you and made you (*we-'essorkha we-'ettenkha*)
A covenant of people [or: a covenant-people], a light of nations
(*librith ᶜam le-'or goyim*).[6] (42.5-6.)

Once again, as in 49.6 (§ B above), if this passage is isolated from the context of chapters 40-55 as a whole and from the verses immediately following in particular, one may, I suppose, agree with the virtually unanimous opinion of scholars that God had summoned His servant in order to achieve a covenant of all nations. Unfortunately for this—albeit universally held—view, it is flatly precluded by the verse immediately following (v. 7), one which is connected with it most intimately syntactically. For our prophet proceeds at once to assert vigorously and unequivocally that the function of God's servant is

To open the eyes of the blind,
To set free prisoners from confinement,
From the dungeon those who sit in darkness,

i.e., to liberate from captivity His people Israel. And it is scarcely necessary to add that—again as in the case of 49.6 ff. (§ B above)— the rest of the chapter, and what follows thereafter, is essentially but an elaboration of this theme; cf., e.g., vv. 8 and 13:

(8) I am the Lord, that is My name;
I will not yield My glory to another,
My renown to idols.

---

[6] For the argument and the pertinent Hebrew passages of this section, see conveniently chap. IV, § A (pp. 75-79) of my *Second Isaiah*.

> (13) The Lord goes forth like a warrior,
>   Like a fighter He whips up His rage;
>   He yells, He roars aloud,
>   He charges upon His enemies. (42.8, 13.)

Or finally, contrast v. 16, which describes God's restoration of exiled Israel, with v. 17, which asserts the utter discomfiture of the heathen nations:

> (16) I will lead the blind by a road they did not know,
>   I will make them walk by paths they never knew.
>   I will turn darkness before them to light,
>   Rough places into level ground.
>   These are the promises,
>   I will keep them without fail.
> (17) Driven back and utterly shamed
>   Shall be those who trust in an image,
>   Shall be those who say to idols,
>   "You are our gods." (42.16-17.)

D

Isa. 60.1ff. is pertinent for any discussion of our expression "a light of nations." Thus OTTO A. PIPER, in his article on "Light" in *The Interpreter's Dictionary of the Bible*, III (1962), has observed (p. 131a), ". . . thus faithful Israel is to become a light for the Gentiles (Isa. 49:6; 60:3, 5; 62:1)." Whether the author of 42.6 and 49.6 was also responsible directly for 60.1 ff. or only indirectly (i.e., the author of 60.1 ff. being influenced by him; cf., e.g., KISSANE, p. 255; LINDBLOM, p. 65 and n. 27) is immaterial at this point.

It should come as no surprise by now to learn that the internationalistic interpretation—read: eisegesis—of scholars to the contrary, the context of chap. 60, exactly as that of chapters 42 and 49, affords no support whatever for the view that Israel was something of a goodwill missionary to the heathen nations; the text of 60.1 ff. declares forthrightly against this:

(1) Arise, shine, for your light has dawned,
    The Presence of the Lord has shone upon you!,

(2) Behold! Darkness shall cover the earth,
    And thick clouds the peoples;
    But upon you[7] the Lord will shine,
    And over you will His Presence be seen.

(3) And nations shall walk by your light,
    Kings, by your shining radiance.

(4) Look up all around you and see:
    They are gathered all, are come to you;
    Your sons shall come from afar,
    Your daughters shall be carried on their shoulders.[8]

---

[7] Note the sharp antithesis syntactically between (*ki-hinneh ha-ḥóshekh yᵉkhasseh-'éreṣ wa-ᶜᵃrafel) lᵉ 'ummim* in the first part of the verse and *wᵉ-ᶜaláyikh (yizraḥ-YHWH)* in this second half.

[8] It need scarcely be noted here that it is the "nations . . . kings" in verse 3 immediately preceding who will do the carrying; that is why they are mentioned in the first place.

In this connection it may be noted that preserved *(banáyikh meraḥoq) yabó'u* probably harbors original *yabí'u,* "they (viz., "the nations . . . kings" *goyim . . . mᵉlakhim* in v. 3) shall bring (your sons from afar)." Our vv. 3-4 recall at once v. 9 below ("to bring" *lᵉhabi*), and 43.5-6 (where God addresses Israel in captivity):

(5) Fear not, for I am with you:
    I will bring *('abí')* your seed from the east,
    And I will gather you from the west;

(6) I will say to the north, "Give up!"
    And to the south, "Hold not back!"
    Bring *(habí'i)* My sons from afar
    And My daughters from the ends of the earth.

and 49.18, 22 f.:

(18) Look up all around you and see:
     They are gathered all, are come to you! . . .

(22) Thus said the Lord God:
     I will raise My hand to nations
     And lift up My ensign to peoples;
     And they shall bring *(wᵉ-hebí'u)* your sons in their bosoms,
     And carry your daughters on their shoulders.

(23) Kings shall be your attendants,
     Their queens shall serve you as nurses . . .

(5) As you behold, you will glow,
     Your heart will throb and thrill—
     For the sea's abundance shall pass on to you,
     The wealth of nations shall flow to you.
(6) Trains of camels shall cover you,
     Dromedaries of Midian and Ephah—
     All of them coming from Sheba . . .
(7) All the flocks of Kedar shall be assembled for you,
     The rams of Nebaioth shall serve your needs . . .
(9) Behold the coastlands await Me,
     With Tarshish-ships in the lead,
     To bring your sons from afar,
     And their silver and gold as well . . .
(10) Aliens shall rebuild your walls,
     Their kings shall wait upon you—
     For in anger I struck you down,
     But in favor I take you back.
(11) Your gates shall always stay open,
     Day and night they shall never be shut,
     To let in the wealth of nations,
     With their kings in procession.
(12) For the nation or the kingdom
     That shall not serve you shall perish;
     Such nations shall be utterly destroyed . . .
(14) Bowing before you shall come
     The children of those who tormented you;
     Prostrate at the soles of your feet
     Shall be all those who reviled you . . . (60.1-14.)
     Etc. etc.

E

So too, the expression *b^erith ^cam* in 42.6 and 49.8, however it be translated, must be understood strictly within the limits of Judean nationalism; the context—the same as that of *'or goyim*—precludes any broader interpretation.

In 42.6 (see § C above), it will be recalled, the prophet proclaims to his fellow exiles:

> I the Lord have summoned you for triumph;
> I have grasped you by the hand,
> Have guarded you and made you
> A covenant of people, a light of nations.

Exactly as in the case of "a light of nations," so do the verses that precede and follow our own make it amply clear that Israel alone is to benefit from God's actions; the purpose of the "covenant" is the liberation of captive Israel. As put in verse 7 immediately following:

> To open the eyes of the blind,
> To set free prisoners from confinement,
> From the dungeon those who sit in darkness.

Or in verse 16:

> I will lead the blind by a road they did not know,
> I will make them walk by paths they never knew.
> I will turn darkness before them to light,
> Rough places into level ground.
> These are the promises,
> I will keep them without fail.

The context in 49.8 is identical. As asserted in verses 8-9 (see § B above):

> (8) Thus said the Lord:
> In a time of favor I have answered you,
> In a day of triumph I have helped you;
> I have kept you *(wᵉ-'eṣṣorkha)*
> And I have made you a covenant (of) people *(wᵉ-'ettenkha librith 'am)*
> To restore the land,
> To allot the waste heritages,
> (9) To say to the prisoners, "Go free!"
> To those in darkness, "Show yourselves!" . . .

How much clearer could anyone wish the author to be in explicating "I have kept you And I have made you a *bᵉrith ᶜam*" than by following immediately with "To restore the land [of Judah, or Israel], To allot the waste heritages"? And note, further, how enthusiastic the prophet waxes in describing the return of the captivity in the verses immediately following (vv. 9 ff.):

> (9) To say to the prisonêrs, "Go free!"
> To those in darkness, "Show yourselves!"
> They shall pasture along the roads,
> On every bare height shall be their pasture.
> (10) They shall not hunger or thirst,
> Hot wind and sun shall not strike them;
> For He who loves them will lead them,
> He will guide them to springs of water.
> (11) I will make all My mountains a road,
> And My highways shall be built up.
> (12) Look! These are coming from afar,
> These from the north and the west,
> And these from the land of Sinim.

reaching a climax in v. 13 with an outburst of joy:

> Sing, O heavens, exult, O earth,
> Break forth into song, O hills!
> For the Lord has comforted His people,
> Has shown compassion to His afflicted ones.

Or we may read on a verse or two (14-15):

> (14) Zion says,
> "The Lord has forsaken me,
> The Lord has forgotten me."
> (15) Can a woman forget her baby,
> Or disown the child of her womb?
> Though she might forget,
> I never could forget you!

But there is hardly need to go on and on in this vein; Second Isaiah is full of it, from beginning (40.1-2, "Comfort, oh comfort My people,

Says your God. Speak tenderly to Jerusalem . . .") to end (55.12-13, "Yea, you shall leave [the Babylonian exile] in joy And be led home secure. Before you, mount and hill shall shout aloud, And all the trees of the field shall clap their hands . . .").

The same picture of b*e*rith is painted in chap. 55, where the "eternal covenant" (b*e*rith *c*olam) involves God and His people Israel (e.g., vv. 3-5): if only they will heed Him, He will make with them an everlasting covenant and fulfill the promise made to David to establish a powerful dynasty of his seed:

> (3) Incline your ear and come to Me:
>   Hearken, and you shall be revived.
>   And I will make with you an everlasting covenant,
>   The enduring loyalty promised to David.
> (4) As I made him a leader of peoples,
>   A prince and commander of peoples,
> (5) So you shall summon a nation you did not know,
>   And a nation that did not know you
>   Shall come running to you—
>   For the sake of the Lord your God,
>   The Holy One of Israel who has glorified you. (55.3-5.)[9]

---

[9] There is, clearly, some hyperbole in vv. 4-5; but scholars generally are not aware of hyperbole, a literary phenomenon that would interfere greatly with theology. I note this statement by LINDBLOM, who is one of the exceedingly few to recognize rhetoric in the Bible (cf., e.g., his chap. IV, "The Use of Figurative Language in Deutero-Isaiah," in *The Servant Songs,* etc.), p. 55, "As king David was a witness (*c*ed) to the peoples, a leader and commander of the nations, Israel will call upon nations it does not know, people who do not know Israel will run unto it, since they have realized the power of Yahweh, the God of Israel. In this passage (LV. 1-5), which deals with the spiritual empire of Israel, we meet with another expression of the idea of berith *c*am, the confederation of peoples with Israel as its centre . . . The idea of the conversion of the Gentiles is common to nearly all oracles of this group." I suspect that the author of our passage and his audience were more realistic, and less concerned about post-biblical theology and messianism and eschatology, than the interpreters of the post-biblical era have been. In the note (15) on his statement, LINDBLOM had asserted (p. 56), ". . . the expressions in vv. 1-2 seem to me to be entirely metaphorical . . ." In the first part of this same

And whoever be their author and whatever the source of their in-fluence, the statements in 59.20-21 and 61.9 can only make this theme even more crystal clear. In chap. 59 the prophet addresses him-self to purified Israel:

> (20) And He [viz., God] will come to Zion as a redeemer,
>   To those in Jacob who turn from transgression—
>   Declares the Lord.
> (21) As for Me, this is My covenant with them,
>   Said the Lord:
>   My spirit which is upon you
>   And My words which I have put in your mouth
>   Shall not depart from your mouth,
>   Or from the mouth of your children and children's children—
>   Said the Lord—
>   From now on and forever.

And in 61.8-9—again it is Israel that is addressed:

> (8) For I the Lord love justice,
>   I hate robbery with a burnt offering;
>   I will pay them their wages faithfully,
>   And I will make an everlasting covenant (u-$b^e$$rith$ '$olam$)
>   with them.
> (9) Their descendants shall be known among the nations,
>   And their offspring among the peoples;
>   All who see them shall acknowledge them,
>   That they are a people whom the Lord has blessed.

The expression *(w^e-'$ettenkha$ li)$brith$ ^{c}am)* has been variously trans-lated. The American (Chicago) Translation rendered "(I have made

---

note (p. 55) LINDBLOM had observed that "In his Commentary BENTZEN says that this is the first occurrence of the invitation to the eschatological Messianic meal"; LINDBLOM surely went far beyond the call of scholarly politeness in limiting his comment on this weird notion to little more than "I cannot agree . . ." The "Two Prophecies from 520-516 B.C." by JULIAN MORGENSTERN (*Hebrew Union College Annual*, 22 [1949], 365-431) constitute studies of our 55.1-5 and 60.1-3, 5-7.

you) a pledge to the people"; Revised Standard Version "(I have given you as) a covenant to the people;" La Sainte Bible (Jerusalem Bible) "(Je t'ai désigné comme) alliance du peuple." Perhaps "a people's (i.e., national) covenant" was intended. The rendering "a covenant-people," i.e., a covenanted people, would be acceptable but for the fact that this idea would more likely have been worded *leͨam be͏rith* in Biblical Hebrew. On EHRLICH'S view there is no problem in the first place; he emends *librith ͨam* in both instances to *lifduth ͨam (Randglossen,* IV, ad locc.), whence MOFFATT'S "(I have formed you) for the rescue of my people." Finally, out of the very many comments on our term, I should like to quote that of Rashi (at 42.6): *Qe͏ra'thíkha* (I have summoned you): *lishaͨyah hu 'omer* (He [God] is addressing [the prophet] Isaiah). *We͏-'eṣṣorkha* (And I created you): *zo'th haye͏thah maḥshabti* (this was My purpose), *shetashib 'eth-ͨammi librithi* (that you should bring back My people to My covenant) *u-le͏ha'ir lahem* (and bring light to them).[10]

F

Something should be said here about another expression, one that is quite pertinent to our own *u-ne͏thattíkha le͏'or goyim* of 49.6, viz., *nabi' la-goyim ne͏thattíkha* in Jer. 1.5. The whole passage reads (vv. 4-5):

(4) The word of the Lord came to me:
(5) Before I formed you in the belly, I selected you;
     Before you issued from the womb, I consecrated you;
     I designated you a prophet concerning the nations.

---

[10] It should be noted that Rashi goes on to identify the term *goyim* as Israel, citing from God's blessing of Jacob-Israel, Gen. 35.11, as a case in point, *goy u-qe͏hal goyim yihyeh mim-mékka,* "A nation, yea an assembly of nations, Shall descend from you." In general, there is too wide and mechanical an antipathy to identifying Israel with *goy-goyim* in the Bible; the equation needs fresh study.

One has but to proceed to read all of the book of Jeremiah—regardless of whether this or that passage or chapter is generally accepted by scholars as original with Jeremiah or of a secondary origin—to realize that Jeremiah was God's spokesman to Judah alone. [11]

Thus when Jeremiah protests—as was characteristic of God's spokesmen [12]—that he is but a youth and without skill as a speaker (v. 6), God's reply (v. 8) is, "Do not be afraid of them, for I am with you to deliver you." Whom did Jeremiah fear? From the hands of which nation would God rescue him? Clearly (cf., e.g., 1.17-19) it is his fellow Judeans of whom Jeremiah need fear, and from whom God stood ready to deliver him. Indeed, this was precisely the occupational hazard of every prophet: harm at the hands of his fellow Israelites, whom he had come to rebuke and threaten.

What follows is a series of declarations to Judah about what would happen to her if she persisted in her evil ways; but as to the heathen nations, they were nothing more than God's rod of anger and punishment, mere tools in His hands, against sinful Judah; cf., e.g., 1.14-16; 4.16-18; 5.15-17; 6.22-26; etc. Jeremiah will be ordered to proclaim "in the hearing of Jerusalem" (*be'ozne ye'rushaláyim*, 2.1-12), but never in the hearing of any heathen nation; God will tell Jeremiah to "speak" (*we'dibbarta*) . . . to his Judean countrymen (1.17; 7.22; 22.1 ff.; 26.2; 35.2), but never to any non-Israelite people; only Israelites —never any of the gentile nations—will be exhorted to "listen" (*shim'u* . . .) to God's word (2.4; 5.20-21; 7.2, 23; 10.1; 11.2, 4, 6, 7; 13.15; 17.20; 19.3; 21.11; 29.20; 42.15; 44.24, 26). Significantly, in each of the two passages in which *shim'u* is clearly associated with *goyim*, the "nations" are treated hyperbolically, exactly as when the "heavens" and the "earth" are called upon to be witness to God's message or action in regard to Israel; they are 6.18-19:

---

[11] This point is dealt with in great detail in my essay on "Nationalism-Universalism in the Book of Jeremiah" (reproduced above in this volume, chap. 6).

[12] Cf. pp. 56-7 and the notes there in my *Second Isaiah* on this aspect of the prophets' response to the call from God.

(18) Therefore, hear, O nations,[13]
      And know, O congregation,
      What will happen to them;
(19) Hear, O earth:
      I will bring harm upon this people . . .

and 31.9-11:

(9)   . . . For I am a father to Israel
      And Israel is my first-born.
(10) Hear the word of the Lord, O nations,
      And declare it in the distant coastlands.
      Say: He who scattered Israel will gather him,
      And He will guard him as a shepherd his flock.
(11) For the Lord has ransomed Jacob,
      Has redeemed him from hands too strong for him.[14]

---

[13] Mention should be made of the fact that the identity of the terms *goy(im)* and *mamlakhah* in Jeremiah is not always readily determined. Thus in 1.5 *goyim* is interpreted by RASHI as the Judeans; in 1.10 the phrase *ᶜal-ha-goyim wᵉᶜal-ha-mamlakhoth* is regarded by some scholars as secondarily derived from 18.7, where the context is wholly Judean. Scholars generally tend to overlook the frequency with which the term *goy(im)* is used in the Bible for the people Israel: this is probably a Jewish even more than a Christian prejudice. But the exposition of our problem, it will be noted, is based on the received text and the generally accepted interpretation of it.

[14] In 49.20 and 50.45, *goyim* is either, again, purely rhetorical (as also, e.g., in 18.13) or else is directed to the Judeans. In such a passage as 16.19,

> O Lord, my strength and my stronghold,
> My refuge in the day of trouble,
> To You nations shall come
> From the ends of the earth and say:
> Mere delusion our fathers inherited,
> Folly that can do no good,

it is naive to take the Hebrew literally, that nations will come from all over the world to Jerusalem to admit that the worship of any god but Israel's can do no good; neither Jeremiah nor his audience was that naive. All that Jeremiah meant— and was understood to say, *rhetorically*, was: the whole world will recognize God's uniqueness and omnipotence. Would scholars dare take literally such a similar expression as (Isa. 55.12) ". . . mount and hill shall break into song, And all the

Indeed, Jeremiah's attitude toward the nations is readily apparent from what he himself has to say, frequently. In 2.18 he declares scornfully:

> Now why are you on the road to Egypt,
> To drink the waters of the Nile?
> Why are you on the road to Assyria,
> to drink the waters of the Euphrates?

And far from being a prophet (i.e., God's spokesman) to the nations, Jeremiah warns his fellow Judeans (2.36):

> How lightly you gad about,
> Changing your way!
> You shall be put to shame by Egypt
> As you were put to shame by Assyria!

In 9.24-25, 10.1 ff., Jeremiah expresses outright contempt for the heathen nations and their ways:

> (24) Behold, the days are coming, declares the Lord, when I will punish all those who are circumcised and yet uncircumcised—(25) Egypt, Judah, Edom, the Ammonites, Moab, and all who dwell in the

---

trees of the field shall clap their hands"? (See on this LINDBLOM, p. 101, and his favorable references to ROBERT H. PFEIFFER, H. H. ROWLEY, and ALFRED GUILLAUME; cf. also DE BOER, pp. 89-90). If one wishes to take literally Jeremiah's rehetorical declaration (2.1):

> Cross over to the isles of the Kittim and see,
> Send to Kedar and observe carefully,
> (See if aught like this has happened:
> Has any nation changed its gods?
> —And they are not even gods!—...)

then he should also take literally the equally rhetorical statement in the verse following:

> Be appalled, O heavens, at this!
> Be horrified, utterly desolate!
> —declares the Lord.

desert that cut the corner of their hair; for all these are uncircumcised, and all the House of Israel is uncircumcised in heart.[15]

(1) Hear the word which the Lord speaks to (or: concerning) you, O House of Israel. (2) Thus says the Lord:

> Learn not the ways of the nations,
> Nor be dismayed at the signs of the heavens
> Because the nations are dismayed at them.

(3) For the customs of the peoples are false . . . (9.24-25; 10.1-3.)

And the chapter is climaxed by this passage (v. 25):

> Pour out Your wrath upon the nations that know You not,
> And upon the peoples that invoke not Your name;
> For they have devoured Jacob,
> Devoured him and consumed him,
> And laid waste his habitation. (10.25.)

G

Among the many additional passages that might be discussed in this connection, I may mention in passing Isa. 11.10-12:

(10) In that day,
> The stock of Jesse that has remained standing
> Shall become an ensign to peoples:
> Nations shall seek his counsel,
> And his abode shall be honored.

(11) In that day, the Lord will set His hand again to redeeming the remaining part of His people [viz., those outside the land of Israel-Judah] from Assyria, from Egypt, from Pathros, from Ethiopia, from Elam, from Shinar, from Hamath, and from the coastlands.

---

[15] The text (e.g., at the end of v. 24) is not in order; yet the general meaning seems clear enough.

(12)   He will raise an ensign to the nations
       And assemble the banished of Israel;
       He will gather the dispersed of Judah
       From the four corners of the earth.

Taken out of context, as has so often been done, one might assume
that the unnamed scion of the Davidic dynasty "shall become an
ensign to peoples" (v. 10) and that He (viz., God Himself; or "he",
viz., this same scion of David) will raise an ensign to the nations"
(v. 12), in the sense that something good will come to the gentile
nations through Israel's leader and through Israel's God. However,
one has but to read these expressions in context to see how completely
nationalistic the prophet—or whoever it was who composed these
verses—is. Thus in verses 1-9 the "shoot from the stump of Jesse" will
restore justice to the land of Israel, so that "it shall be filled with
recognition of the Lord." And everything that follows v. 12—indeed
the entire section from 10.32 through 12.6, which constitutes the
Haftarah for the Eighth Day of Passover—glorifies the deliverance of
Israel's exiles, the reunion of Israel and Judah, and Israel's God who
achieved it all.

To sum up. However such expressions as *u-nethattíkha le'or goyim*
and *we-'ettenkha librith ʿam le'or goyim* in Isaiah (49.6 and 42.6
respectively) and *nabï' la-goyim nethattíkha* in Jeremiah (1.5) are
translated, all the contextual data in these Books make it amply clear
that nothing international was implied in them. These prophets,
God's spokesmen all, were not sent on any mission to any nation other
than their own,[16] only to God's covenanted partner, Israel. When they
were not simply the means by which God punished His erring people,
the pagan peoples were merely helpless witnesses—just like the
heavens and the earth and the mountains—to God's exclusive love
and protection of His people. This is the essential meaning of such
passages as Jer. 26.6 and 4.2:

---

[16] On Jonah, see my essay on "Nationalism-Universalism . . . in Ancient Israel"
(May Volume), reproduced above, chap. 5, pp. 105 ff.

((4) Thus said the Lord:
     If you will not listen to Me . . .)
 (6) I will make this House [of Judah] like Shiloh,
     And I will make this city [Jerusalem] a curse
     For all the nations of the earth.
((1) If you return, O Israel,
     Declares the Lord . . .)
 (2) And if you swear "As the Lord lives"
     In true justice and uprightness,
     Then nations shall bless themselves in (or: through)
          him [viz., Israel],
     And in him they shall glory,

i.e., the heathen nations shall say: May we be as prosperous and protected as Israel—if all goes well with Israel; but: Cursed shall you be
like Israel—if Israel is in degradation at the hands of God for her sins.

In a word: Israel will be "a light of nations" in the sense that Israel
will dazzle the nations with her God-given triumph and restoration;
the whole world will behold this single beacon that is God's sole covenanted people. Israel will serve to the world at large as the example
of God's loyalty and omnipotence.

10

Who is the Ideal Jew:
The Biblical View

THE RECENT EMERGENCE OF THE STATE OF Israel and the subsequent need to define the precise status of the Jews outside of Israel who may claim entry to the State by right—i.e., by virtue of the fact that they are Jews—have brought to the fore once again the question: Who is a Jew? Naturally, Biblical passages have been adduced to justify one answer or another. One of the passages notably involved was Psalm 24:3 ff. This essay will attempt to elicit the plain meaning of the passage in question.[1]

It has become a commonplace among scholars, and rightly so, that the basic concept around which the Bible revolved was the Covenant. This was, it would appear, a mutually exclusive pact into which God

---

[This essay, republished from *Judaism*, 13, 1 (Winter Issue, 1964), appeared first in a Hebrew version, in the David Ben-Gurion Jubilee Volume, *'Oz (=77) le-David,* on the occasion of his 77th birthday—originally planned for the 75th—(Jerusalem, 5724/1963, pp. 521-28) under the title, *Mi Ya'aleh be-Har Adonay.*]

[1] The present writer is in the process of preparing a larger work that will deal in detail with a number of Biblical concepts in their historical development. The pertinent data for this essay will be made available in the major work. [See now the essays in this volume, reproduced from the May and Enslin Volumes, on "Nationalism-Universalism . . .," chaps 5 and 6.]

and Israel, as *equal* partners, voluntarily entered. Neither party coerced the other. In this altogether legal contract, the party of the first part, viz. God, promised on oath—for how else was a promise made binding?—to protect and to prosper Israel without limit, so long as Israel remained faithful to Him; and Israel, the party of the second part, in the knowledge that God was omnipotent and reliable, undertook to worship Him alone.

The pact was based on the principle of *quid pro quo*: reward for loyalty, punishment for disloyalty. And so the Bible constitutes the story, not of God alone, nor of Israel alone, but of God and Israel in relation to each other; the Bible is a history not of God's actions in general, nor of Israel's beliefs and practices in general, but of God's and Israel's actions and reactions within the framework of the contract which bound them to one another and which limited them in their respective careers.

After God created the universe, the Bible asserts, and started mankind on its career as a collection of distinct groups scattered the world over (*Gen:* 1-11)—naturally that part of the world of which the writers of *Genesis* had some knowledge—He settled down to His greatest single project thenceforth, viz, to take care of His chosen people, Israel. Thereafter, no people, no land, no person, no god, no event—no one and nothing came within the purview of the Biblical writers unless the people of Israel, in whole or in part, was involved. Egypt, the Hittites, the Hurrians, Babylonia, Assyria, Persia, the Canaanites, the Philistines, Aram, Moab, Ammon, Edom—these and all the others received mention in the Bible only when and insofar as they could not properly be left out from whatever account was being related about Israel. Egypt, for example, found mention only when—and because—it was involved with Israel; otherwise Egypt was passed over in silence. Indeed, were it not for the great Sojourn, Bondage, and Exodus—and such events as involved Egypt with the régimes, e.g., of Solomon, Rehoboam-Jeroboam, and Josiah—the land of the Nile would be little known to us from the Bible. It is the same with Assyria, Babylonia, Persia, and the others: as often and so long as Biblical Israel was caught up internationally with other nations, they provided subject matter for the Biblical writer; but not otherwise.

In the description of these international encounters, the foreign nations, incvitably, do not come off well. After all, to the Israelite writers they served only as the rod of God's anger and punishment upon Israel for her sins, for her transgression of the Covenant. These nations, great and not so great, had no independent power, or value, or interest, for the Biblical writer. The universe was but a stage on which God and His treasured people acted out their drama of covenant-relationship. When Israel failed to keep the Covenant, a local domestic form of punishment would result: drought, famine, thirst, epidemic. Or else, an international kind of punishment: one or another of the foreign nations would be brought in by God to execute judgment upon His sinful people. After playing out that role, the nation in question was immediately removed from the Biblical stage; it had no other significance for the authors of the drama.

Indeed, what other status could Biblical Israel accord the non-Israelite peoples and still remain true to the principles of its mutually-exclusive covenant with God? Israel recognized God as the only God in the universe. He was the Creator, the sole Creator, of the whole world: land, water, living things, sun, moon, stars—everything. He, and He alone, was responsible for the Egyptians, Assyrians, Babylonians, Arameans, Philistines, Ammonites—all peoples everywhere— coming into being.

Thus, when Amos says (9:7): *"Are you not like the Cushites to Me, O people of Israel?" declares the Lord. "Did I not bring up Israel from the land of Egypt, the Philistines from Caphtor, and the Arameans from Kir?"*, this did not mean—as it has so regularly been misunderstood to mean—that the Lord was the God of the Cushites and of the Philistines as He was the God of Israel. (Did God make a covenant with the Cushites and the Philistines?!) This would have constituted utter nonsense to Amos and his fellow-Israelites.

What Amos was saying was that everything in the universe was God's doing—what other divine Being was there?—and that all peoples and all persons everywhere were beholden and responsible to

Him. So that, e.g., if Damascus abused Gilead (*Amos* 1:3-5), or if Tyre acted deceitfully against Edom (vv. 9-10), or if Edom was guilty of treachery (11-12), who else, if not the Lord, would take note and act accordingly? But no people—other than Israel!—had a special claim upon Him; and God, in turn, had no exclusive claim upon any people, except upon Israel. That is why, when Amos arraigns his fellow countrymen (2:4):

> For three transgressions of Judah,
> For four—I will not relent,

he at once charges the accused with having violated the covenant with God:

> Because they have rejected the teachings of the Lord,
> Have not kept His laws.

God had a just case against Israel, for He had carried out His part of the covenant (2:9-10):

> "I, for My part, wiped out the Amorites for you

> *   *   *

> I, for My part, brought you up from the land of Egypt,
> And I led you through the wilderness forty years
> To occupy the land of the Amorites."

Or cf. 3:1-2:

> Hear this word which the Lord has spoken concerning you, O people of Israel, concerning the whole family that I brought up from the land of Egypt,

> "You alone have I recognized
> Among all the families of the earth;
> Therefore I will punish you
> For all your iniquities."

Scholars generally have failed to note—and this has misled them into quite erroneous conclusions—that there is a world of difference between God conceived as the Creator of all the world and as the God of the Gentile nations of the world; God had a pact with Israel alone, and an especial responsibility to her. Thus Second Isaiah (e.g., at 42:5), a thoroughly nationalistic prophet, talks of the Lord, the God of Israel exclusively, as the one

Who created the heavens and stretched them out,
Who spread out the earth and what it brings forth.

Exodus 19:3-6 put it this way, God speaking to Moses on Mt. Sinai:

Thus shall you say to the house of Jacob,
Declare to the children of Israel:
"You have seen what I did to the Egyptians,
And how I bore you on eagles' wings
And brought you to Me.
Now, if you will obey Me faithfully
And keep My covenant,
You shall be My treasured possession
Among all the peoples.
Indeed, all the earth is Mine,
But you shall be to Me a kingdom of priests
And a holy nation."
These are the words that you shall speak to the children of Israel.

In fine, the Lord was the Creator of the universe and the only God in it; but He was the God of Israel exclusively.[2]

The failure to recognize the plain meaning, the exegesis, of several pertinent passages in the Bible—a more historical way of putting it would be: the common and natural tendency of a much later period to read into the Hebrew text the viewpoint and interests of someone

---

[2] See the section on "Particularism and Universality in the Teachings of the Prophets" in my *Ancient Israel* (pp. 163 ff.).

else, in short, eisegesis—has played havoc with the correct under-standing of these passages. Thus, e.g., the famous passage in *Leviticus* 19:18, *You shall love your neighbor* [or: fellow; *re'aka*] *as yourself* has been made to mean that Israel was commanded to love his fellow-man (i.e., all human beings everywhere) as himself, in a word, to be internationally minded. In point of fact, however, the Hebrew term *re'a* means "fellow-Israelite, countryman," parallel to "(You shall not take vengeance or bear a grudge against) your kinsfolk" (*bene 'ammeka*) in the first part of the verse, "(You shall not hate) your kinsman ([*aḥika*] in your heart. Reprove) your neighbor [*'amiteka*], and incur no guilt because of him)" in the verse immediately preced-ing, as well as "(. . . judge) your neighbor ([*'amiteka*] fairly. Do not deal basely with) your fellows ([*'ammeka*]. Do not profit by the blood of) your neighbor ([*re'eka*]: I am the Lord.)" in verses 15-16 pre-ceding.

An even more extreme case of this eisegetical perversion of the text, no less famous than *Lev.* 19:18, is *Malachi* 2:10:

> Have we not all one Father?
> Did not one God create us?
> Why do we break faith with one another *('ish be-'ahiw)*
> And profane the covenant of our fathers?

Wrenched out of context, this verse has been made to mean that Malachi preached international equality and brotherhood. Yet noth-ing could be farther from the truth than this interpretation. All that Malachi was preaching was equality of all Israelites before the Lord, the ordinary Israelite on the one hand and the priests and Levites on the other. Attacking bitterly the members of the sacerdotal class in the rising priestly state for their evil doings in connection with both man and God (1:6 ff.; 2:1-8)—for the covenant provided laws for both these aspects of the worship of the Lord—Malachi specifically rebuked the priests for regarding themselves as above the law and superior to the secular Israelites (v. 10), and warned them that God would, in consequence, reduce them to a level below that of the com-mon people (v. 9): *So will I make you despised and abased before all the people, just as you have not kept My ways but have shown partiality in instruction.*

Not insignificantly, the only "international" element that marks the book of *Malachi* is the reference to Edom in 1:1 ff., where—in keeping with the Biblical view in general—that country is vigorously condemned.[3]

The duties of Israel in carrying out the covenant with the Lord, in other words, the worship of the Lord, were twofold: (1) the injunctions pertaining to God directly, and (2) the injunctions pertaining to fellow-Israelites. The two sets of injunctions were equally important; and all the Biblical writers—lawmakers, prophets, psalmists, authors of wisdom literature—all are unanimous in expressing this view.

It is true that scholars have tended to make a distinction between cult and social justice, between sacrifices and good deeds, in fine, between the priest and the prophet. This distinction is utterly unbiblical, and constitutes still another example of eisegesis, of reading back into the Bible views and interests of a later period. For what the proponents of this view have done is not alone to misinterpret the relatively few passages in the Bible that lent themselves to such distortion but also to emphasize them and to make them stand up as the norm, at the same time slighting or ignoring altogether the multitude of passages that clearly present the opposite view.

Let us take a few cases in point. In *Isa.* 1:11-14, the prophet, speaking for God, inveighs against those who bring sacrifices to the Temple:

---

[3] I am fully aware of the—significantly quite few—passages in the Bible which would seem to disprove the statements made here; indeed, these few passages have generally been made to serve as the basis for the opposite view, with all the other widespread and extensive data in the Bible being ignored. I have in mind not only the passages in *Amos, Leviticus,* and *Malachi* dealt with here (with which cf., e.g., *Isa.* 19, especially vv. 17-25), but — from another angle — the books of *Jonah* and *Ruth.* But all this will be treated at length in my larger work. In the meantime, see Chapter VII ("The Hebraic Spirit: The Prophetic Movement and Social Justice") of my *Ancient Israel.* [Also the essays on "Nationalism — Universalism," etc., in the H. G. May and M. S. Enslin volumes, reprinted in this volume, chaps. 5 and 6.]

"What need have I of your many sacrifices?"
Says the Lord.
"I am sated with burnt offerings of rams,
And suet of fatlings;
The blood of bulls
And lambs and he-goats
Is no delight to Me.
When you come to appear before Me—
Who asked this of you,
To trample My courts?
Bring no more futile sacrifices;
They are detestable incense-smoke to Me.
New moon and sabbath,
Proclaiming of solemn occasions—
I cannot abide
Iniquitous assemblies.
Your new moons and fixed occasions
I loathe;
They are become a burden to Me,
I cannot bear them."

With all too few exceptions, this forthright statement has been made by scholars to prove that the prophet opposed sacrifices. Significantly, however, the passage immediately following (v. 15) has not usually been brought into play by those who hold the anti-cultic view:

"When you spread out your hands,
I will close My eyes to you;
Even though you utter many prayers,
I will not listen—
Your hands are full of blood!"

For how could this passage be brought into the picture except—on the pertinent analogy of vv. 11-14—to be made to prove that the prophet opposed prayer! But since neither Christianity nor modern scholars tended to reject prayer as an essential aspect of divine worship of their own times, in other words, since their own religious *Anschauung* required the use of prayer, verse 15 was left out of consideration in connection with the analysis of the four verses preceding.

Not only that. The four verses in question were made to assert what the prophet never intended. He had stated clearly, and his original audience understood him equally clearly, that no matter how sumptuous the sacrifices to the Lord—just as no matter how many and prolonged the prayers—they were unacceptable to Him if the injunctions relating to the worshiper's dealings with his fellow-Israelites were not fulfilled; in other words, the "sacrifice" (*minḥah*) was "futile" (*shaw'*), the "incense-smoke" (*qetoret*) was "detestable" (*to'ebah*), the new moons and fixed occasions (*hodshekem u-mo'adekem*) were loathesome to God (*san'ah nafshi*), the prayers were rejected (*gam ki-tarbu tefillah 'enenni shome'a*)—as long as the worshiper's "hands" were full of blood" (*yedekem damim male'u*). If, on the other hand, they would heed the plea and injunction of verses 16-17:

> "Wash yourselves clean;
> Remove your evil acts
> From My sight.
> Cease to do evil,
> Learn to do good,
> Seek justice.
> Aid the oppressed,
> Uphold the rights of the orphan,
> Defend the cause of the widow,"

then the same sacrifices, and the same prayers, would be completely acceptable (v. 18):

> "Be your sins like crimson,
> They shall be white as snow;
> Be they red as dyed wool,
> They shall become like fleece."

Sacrifice and prayer were not—on Isaiah's view—to be belittled or neglected in favor of right deeds; the worship of God in the Temple was not to be brushed aside by social justice. The laws pertaining to

God and the laws pertaining to man were both equally valid, constituting the two sides of one and the same coin; one could not—on the prophet's view—exist without the other.

And this is precisely what Amos, e.g., asserted (5:21-23):

"I hate, I reject your feasts,
I delight not in your solemn assemblies.
Even though you present to Me
Burnt offerings and your meal offerings,
I will not accept them;
The offerings of well-being of your fatlings
I will not look upon.
Remove your noisy songs from My presence;
I will not listen to the melody of your lyres."

Like Isaiah, Amos told his fellow-Israelites that there was no use running to God's shrines at Bethel, Gilgal, and Beer-sheba (v. 5) to sacrifice and to pray to Him, if they transgress those laws of the Covenant that pertain to Israel's "human relations" (vv. 10-12):

They hate him who reproves in the gate,
They detest him who speaks the truth.
Therefore, because you trample upon the poor
And take from him exactions of grain,
Though you have built houses of hewn stones
You shall not dwell in them.

*   *   *

Your offenses are many,
Your crimes are countless—
You who harass the innocent, take bribes,
And subvert the rights of the needy in the gate.

Exactly as his contemporary Isaiah, Amos offers his people the identical solution to the problem (v. 24):

Let justice roll on like waters,
And right like a perennial stream.

That is to say, if only Israel will fulfill the terms of the Covenant in their dealings with their fellow-Israelites (*mishpaṭ u-ṣedaqah*), then, when they appear before God with sacrifice and prayer (*'olot u-min-ḥotekem . . . shireka we-zimrat nebaleka*), they will be accepted by God.[4]

Psalm 24 constitutes an excellent presentation of this view. The question, "Who is a good Israelite? What kind of Israelite is most acceptable to God?," finds ready and complete answer in this vivid composition.

The psalmist begins with the conventional recognition and assertion that God, because He is the sole Creator, is the sole Master of the universe (vv. 1-2):

---

[4] There are some passages in the Bible, e.g., verse 25 in this very chapter in *Amos* (if the definite article in *haz-zebaḥim* "The sacrifices [. . . you presented to Me in the wilderness . . .]" is understood as, or emended to, the interrogative *hazebaḥim* "Did [you present to Me] sacrifices [in the wilderness . . .?]"), or *I Sam.* 15:22 ("Samuel said: Does the Lord delight in burnt offerings and sacrifices as much as in obedience to the command of the Lord? Surely, obedience is better than sacrifice, compliance than the fat of rams.") or *Jer.* 7:21-22 ("Thus said the Lord of Hosts, the God of Israel: Add your burnt offerings to your other sacrifices and eat the flesh; for [or: yet] when I freed them from the land of Egypt, I did not speak with your ancestors or command them concerning burnt offerings or sacrifices"), where the statement is made that God never commanded Israel in the wilderness, when they were being led by Moses from Egypt to Canaan, to offer up sacrifices to Him. These very few passages have been made to prove that Samuel, Amos, and Jeremiah (or the persons who later composed these passages) opposed sacrifice as part of the worship of the Lord.

This is not the place to go into the problem in detail; it is self-evident, however, that a man who made a living as a priest, as Samuel did, would hardly have expressed opposition to sacrifice; or that anyone in the seventh-sixth centuries B.C.E., such as Jeremiah, several hundred years after the Temple had been in existence, would deny that sacrifice had been sanctioned by God. Rather, it would seem, did Jeremiah stress this urgent need (7:5-7): "But if you amend your ways and actions, if you execute justice one with another, if you do not abuse the stranger, the fatherless, and the widow, or shed innocent blood in this place, or follow other gods—to your own hurt— I will settle you in this place, in the land which I gave to your ancestors, for all time." In other words, unless Israel obeyed *all* the commandments of the Lord (cf., v. 23), then sacrifices alone would be of no avail, for it was not sacrifice alone that God enjoined upon Israel in the wilderness.

> The earth is the Lord's, and all that fills it,
> The universe and those who dwell in it;
> For He founded it upon the seas,
> Established it upon the rivers.

The author then proceeds to ask the rhetorical question—rhetorical because the answer has been known for many centuries (v. 3):

> Who may ascend the mount of the Lord?
> Who may stand within His holy place?

and immediately follows with the conventional answer (v. 4):

> The clean of hand and the pure of heart,
> Who has not given himself to anything improper,*
> Has never sworn to a lie.

That kind of person (v. 5):

> Will receive blessing from the Lord,
> Vindication from his God of deliverance.

But the rhetorical question has not always been understood correctly, and the verse has been made to indicate—in the manner that eisegesis was applied, e.g., to *Amos* 9:7; *Lev.* 18:19; *Mal.* 2:10; *Isa.* 1:11 ff.; and *Amos* 5:21 ff.—precisely what its author never intended. Many scholars have made the verse mean that anyone at all, non-Israelite as well as Israelite, may make a pilgrimage to the Temple in Jerusalem and offer sacrifices and prayers to God, if only his practices have been blameless.

But this brand of "ethical culture" on an international scale is utterly foreign to Biblical thought, and is, moreover, flatly precluded by v. 3 itself.

The Psalms of the Bible are prayers of one kind or another. They

---

[* I rendered "falsehood" in the original publication. See my edition of *Notes on the New Translation of the Torah* (J.P.S., 1969), pp. 175-76.]

were composed by Israelites for Israelites. Whatever be the specific circumstances of their origin, their *Sitz im Leben,* they became associated with services in the Temple. As with sacrifices, prayers were unacceptable to God in partial fulfillment of the requirements of the Covenant and of the worship of Him unless the worshiper had fulfilled the rules and regulations of the Covenant in the realm of man's obligation to man, i.e., unless the worshiper came with clean hands and pure heart. Sacrifice and prayer, the essential aspects of the worship of God in the Temple, were meant for Israelites alone; non-Israelites did not enter the Temple to worship the God of Israel. So that the term "Who" in v. 3 ("Who may ascend . . . who may stand . . .?") can only mean "Which Israelite"; and the whole concept can mean only, and exactly as Isaiah and Amos and the others had conceived it: Which Israelite may enter the Temple to worship the Lord, and be reasonably confident that his sacrifice and prayer will be acceptable to the Lord? He who has first fulfilled the laws of the Covenant with God so far as his fellow countrymen are concerned. The ideal Israelite in the Bible, worthy of "receiving blessing from the Lord," is he who, innocent of any wrongdoing against his fellow countryman, comes to the Lord's House to sacrifice and to pray to Him.

11

Whither Biblical Research?

IT IS NOT ALWAYS REALIZED, or kept in mind, that biblical research,
no less than any other branch of group activity, is subject to the
social forces—the term "social," of course, represents the longer
phrase and concept: social, economic, political, cultural, religious, and
the like—at work within the community at large. Thus the kinds of
interpretation of the Bible—both as a whole and even of specific passages in it—that prevailed in the last couple of centuries B.C. would
not have been possible in any environment but that of Hellenism as it
was adopted and adapted in the Jewish communities of the Diaspora
and Judea. The earliest specifically Christian exposition of what constituted the Bible differed markedly from that of the Jewish-Christian
period and community that preceded it, basically because the social
structure of the Roman Empire as a whole and the specific status of
the Christian and the Jewish communities within it had changed significantly from those that had obtained in the first three centuries A.D.,
before Christianity had become in rapid succession a tolerated and
then the official religion.

This principle of social forces, rather than the personal whim of a

[The Presidential Address delivered at the annual meeting of the Society of
Biblical Literature on October 26, 1970, at the New Yorker Hotel, New York, N.Y.
Reprinted from *JBL,* 90 (1971), 1-14.]

scholar here and there, being the decisive factor in the shaping of a discipline such as ours, applies of course to every epoch in history, be it the Middle Ages, the Renaissance, the Reformation, the demise of feudalism, or the birth of capitalism in Western Europe. But this point need not be belabored here, not because it has been dealt with adequately in various works on the subject—indeed, I do not think that it has been—but because it is chronologically not pertinent enough to the present discussion.[1]

During the nineteenth century and the first quarter of our own, i.e., before the consequences of World War I took real effect, biblical research—I shall be using the terms "Bible" and "biblical" sometimes to cover both the Hebrew and the Christian Scriptures and sometimes the Hebrew alone—followed generally the pattern of research in the classical field, which was more solidly and extensively established at the time. Textual and literary criticism and comparative linguistics—

---

[1] The interpretation of the Bible in the light of changing historical circumstances has remained essentially virgin soil for the inquisitive and trained scholar. To *describe* Philo's or Jerome's or Rashi's or Astruc's or Wellhausen's or S. R. Driver's manner of interpreting the Bible—basic as it is—is only preliminary to the systematic attempt to *account for* their kind of biblical exegesis. It is not easy to improve upon the descriptive approach of Beryl Smalley in her fascinating treatment of *The Study of the Bible in the Middle Ages* (1941; rev. ed., 1952; reprinted in paperback, 1964 [Univ. of Notre Dame]); what remains to be done is to account for the kind of biblical exegesis practised by the Gilbert Crispins and the Peter Abailards and the Hughs and the Andrews of St. Victor in the light of the historical developments in eleventh-twelfth century England. In more recent times, an inkling of the problem may be gained from a careful reading (sometimes between the lines) of the preface (pp. III–XXI) and addenda (XXV–XXXIX) of Driver's *Introduction to the Literature of the Old Testament* (rev. ed., 1913), where the learned and careful author has to defend his philosophy of biblical interpretation. An historical analysis of the attitude of the Church of England and its supporters toward Driver's kind of exegesis would constitute a major contribution to the history of the study of the Bible (e.g., why certain theories are regarded favorably by some groups and rejected in other circles, regardless of the cogency of the argumentation).

Formal—but really perfunctory—surveys of this aspect of biblical research may be found in such Introductions as R. H. Pfeiffer, *Introduction to the Old Testament* (New York: Harper, 1941), pp. 40–49 (Ch. 3: Historical and Critical Interest in the Old Testament); or O. Eissfeldt, *The Old Testament: An Introduction* (New York: Harper and Row, 1965), pp. 1–7 (§1: "The Nature of the Undertaking"); cf. the articles on "Biblical Criticism" (by K. Grobel, *IDB*, 1 [1962] 407–13) and "Biblical Criticism, History of" (by S. J. De Vries, *IDB*, 1 [1962] 413–18) and their bibliographies.

in those days involving almost exclusively Hebrew, Aramaic, Arabic, Syriac, and Ethiopic, and what Babylonian-Assyrian was known— were the norm. The standard works were the grammars by König, Gesenius-Kautzsch-Cowley, and Bauer-Leander; the lexicons employed were usually those of Brown-Driver-Briggs and Gesenius-Buhl; and Brockelmann's two-volume *Grundriss* was the sole claimant to respect in comparative Semitic linguistics.[2]

This state of affairs is easy to recall, because after all the hectic years since World War I it is still these same works that are standard today—except that Bergsträsser began a notable revision of Gesenius-Kautzsch-Cowley over half a century ago, but no one has followed up his effort after his untimely death in 1933. Koehler published a lexicon (1948–1953), which even Baumgartner's considerably revised edition is hardly able to improve upon so that it can seriously compete (in many respects) even with Brown-Driver-Briggs. (There is a good historical reason for this serious lack of progress, and I shall return to the problem below.)

Finally, the dominant philosophy of history then prevalent was Hegelianism or variations of it, so that the widely accepted reconstruction of biblical Israel's history and literary creativity was largely that of Wellhausen and S. R. Driver, as found in their standard introductions and commentaries, not to mention Wellhausen's *Prolegomena* and *Geschichte,* or Eduard Meyer's several works.

World War I, among other things, opened up western Asia, northeast Africa, and the eastern Mediterranean region generally to the world at large. The Ottoman Turkish Empire gave way to British and French domination, and also to uninhibited archeological and topographical investigation. This discipline gave new direction and emphasis to biblical research to the extent that it is no exaggeration to apply the term "revolutionary" to it. But revolution can be a bad as well as a good thing; and I believe that the negative and harmful consequences of archeology can and ought no longer to be denied or brushed aside.

---

[2] I have discussed some aspects of this in the chapter on "Old Testament Studies" (pp. 51–109) in the volume on *Religion* (ed. P. Ramsey; *Princeton Studies: Humanistic Scholarship in America,* Princeton, 1965).

But good things first. By the end of World War I biblical research had become stabilized, i.e., had gotten into a rut. Excellent as they were, and in many respects still are, the dictionaries, grammars, introductions, and commentaries mentioned above were not being significantly improved upon; no really new insights or breakthroughs were apparent. A major source of new data, the Sumero-Akkadian, had become available; but progress here was only gradual and accumulative. The Documentary Theory, as refined especially by Wellhausen on the Continent and by Driver in Great Britain, reigned supreme. The Pentateuch, as everyone knew, was composite; and the composers were J, E, D, and P. For lack of other approaches and new data, scholars delved even more intensively into these four sources, decomposing the composers into J_1 and J_2, E_1 and E_2, and the like. While sensitive to the frustrations confronting our colleagues of fifty and forty years ago, we regret that so much talent and energy were spent in helping to demonstrate the law of diminishing returns.

With all their secondary disagreements about the limits of J and E, or the character, if not the very existence, of J_2 and E_2,[3] scholars generally agreed not only in the matter of the four primary documents, J, E, D, and P, but also in something that was much more important, viz., that none of the four documents was to be treated as reliable material on which to base a serious reconstruction of biblical Israel's early career. Hence not only could J, E, D, and P be separated as essentially distinct literary creations, and not only could they be dated in their preserved form with some confidence—J and E as the products of the tenth-ninth centuries, D of the seventh (pre-exilic) century, and P of the sixth-fifth (post-exilic) century—but, and this was or should have been regarded as the most important aspect of the Documentary Theory—but they were considerably devoid of historical authenticity. Not one of the documents could the sober scholar use,

---

[3] I have used the term "secondary (disagreements)" deliberately; already Driver (*Introduction*, Preface, pp. IV–VI and n. * on p. VI) had something trenchant to say about how "language is sometimes used implying that critics are in a state of internecine conflict with one another . . . [so that] the results of the critical study of the Old Testament are often seriously misrepresented. . . ." Many of us today have heard people glibly assert that archeology has "confirmed" the Bible and demolished the Documentary Theory!

except with the greatest reserve, for the reconstruction of the patriarchal period, or of the Mosaic, or of that of the Judges.

The great and lasting merit of archeology is that it has made it
possible, and even necessary, to grant these documents considerable
trustworthiness; this constituted a *revolutionary breakthrough*. Pertinent parallels and other data were brought to light so that the Dark
Ages of Canaan-Israel in the second millennium (not to mention the
blackout of the region during the fourth and third millennia and the
prehistory before that) became the relatively well-known Middle and
Late Bronze Ages. In this connection, I need only mention in passing
such important excavations as that of Albright at Tell Beit Mirsim
in the Twenties and Thirties. There is hardly an aspect of biblical
research that has not benefited directly or indirectly, sometimes to a
remarkable degree, from archeology, be it linguistics, lexicography,
poetic structure, textual criticism, theology, history, chronology, social
and legal institutions, comparative literature, mythology, and so on.

Something too should be said about the fact that the material culture of ancient Israel is now known in vastly greater detail than before.
I have in mind not only the walls and houses and household articles
(especially pottery) and articles in trade, and the like, but also trade
and industry and the crafts in the large. And then there is archeology
as a discipline in its own right, regardless of whether it sheds any light
on the Bible—and far more often than not it does not. Naturally,
archeology in and about the Holy Land is important to biblical scholars "not so much . . . as a branch of science per se but as a handmaid,
a tool for the better understanding of the Bible and the Holy Land.
Unlike the Sumerologist, Akkadiologist, Hittitologist, Egyptologist,
and the like, who have been laying bare the history of their area from
the beginning of time to the end of the *floruit* of the civilizations that
interest them, the biblical scholar has been interested in archeology
mainly for its help in elucidating the Bible."[4]

This preoccupation with the biblical aspects of archeology has led
to a rather unbalanced view of what archeology has meant for the

---

[4] Orlinsky, "Old Testament Studies," p. 66. In this connection, H. J. Cadbury's
presidential address to this Society in 1936 is most germane, "Motives of Biblical
Scholarship," *JBL*, 56 (1937), 1–16.

Bible. Let us recall for a moment the historical background, which many, if not most of us present this evening, lived through, but sometimes tend to overlook in this connection. Ever since World War I, the depression of the early Thirties, the growth of various forms of totalitarianism in Europe and Asia, the horrors of World War II, the cold, hot, lukewarm, and warmed-over wars, domestic and international, of the past two decades, recessions and the fear of them, increasing automation and alienation, and the specter of unemployment —all this and more have convinced many that reason and science, the two major ingredients in the making of the Ages of Reason, Enlightenment, Ideology, Analysis, Science (in short, the Ages of Optimism) —were not able to bring our problems, international, national, group, or individual, significantly closer to solution. And so people began to come back to and seek out once again what had long been regarded as the Word of God, the Bible.

This Word, however, was no longer an isolated phenomenon in the midst of history; no longer was it a static event, independent of time and place. For archeology had changed all that.

So it was that the historical circumstances that had brought archeology into being, and had also brought the Bible once again to the fore of man's attention, led to an extraordinary increase of popular interest in the Bible in the light of archeology. Increasingly during the Forties and Fifties, and there is no sign of any appreciable let-up, people began to seek out the "truths" of the Bible as "proved" by archeology. What had been a bit of a rivulet immediately after the tomb of the late King "Tut" was cleared in 1922 became a veritable torrent of picture books on archeology, on the Bible, and on the Holy Land, a number of them good, some excellent, and many simply commercial potboilers—this apart from the daily press and literary magazines and lecture forums as a popular source of information (and misinformation and half-truths and melodramatic accounts)—of how archeology has "proved" the Bible right; as the title of a best-seller of the middle Fifties had it, *Und die Bibel hat doch Recht,* on which D. R. Ap-Thomas commented with refined British understatement (British *Book List,* 1957, p. 18), ". . . It will certainly have a large sale, although (perhaps in part because) the scholar would wish for a little more caution at some points . . ."[5]

The emphasis on archeology and the needs of the time made it all too easy for undisciplined journalists and popularizers not only to exaggerate beyond reasonableness the scope of substantiation but to take a giant, and utterly unjustified, step beyond that and assert that this substantiation demonstrated the Bible as the revealed word of God! Nothing could be more of a non-sequitur in disciplined reasoning than the juxtaposition of these two completely independent phenomena. This widespread confusion between the Bible as a religious document and the Bible as a historical document is a serious matter, and I shall touch on it below.

The rise of biblical archeology since World War I not only coincided with but has in part been responsible—to be sure, unwittingly—for the decline in biblical philology and textual criticism. In the general educational pattern of the United States and Canada, the humanities began to give way to the pure, the applied, and the social sciences. The number of students studying Greek and Latin in high school and college decreased considerably in the past two or three decades, and these subjects are generally not required for ordination even in theological seminaries; so most students, by the time they have acquired the B.A. or B.D. degree and decide to specialize in Bible, must *begin* the study of Greek and Latin, of Hebrew, Aramaic, Canaanite, Syriac, Arabic, Akkadian, or Egyptian. And since it is much easier to do original work in connection with such expanding disciplines as archeology and Akkadian and Northwest Semitic-Canaanite, it is these areas—especially in the form of parallels between them and between passages and phrases in the Bible—that have been attracting the research efforts of so many younger scholars who otherwise would have tended toward biblical philology. As a result, in 1947, E. C. Colwell, in his presidential address to this Society, was able to begin right off with the assertion, "Biblical criticism today is not the most robust of academic disciplines . . . [it] is relatively sterile today . . ."[6]

---

[5] Cadbury's *caveat* (p. 11), ". . . As experts we have some responsibility to help curb the morbid tastes of so many superficial lay book readers who prefer to hear from us some new guess than some old fact," certainly applies here.

[6] "Biblical Criticism: Lower and Higher," *JBL,* 67 (1948), 1–12.

This widespread inadequacy in the most basic of disciplines in any field of scholarly research, that of being able to handle a text, showed up especially in the study of the biblical portions of the Dead Sea Scrolls. It is no exaggeration, as it is no pleasure, to assert that all too many of the textual studies of these biblical documents hardly rated a passing grade. The Wellhausens and the S. R. Drivers, the George Foote Moores and the Max Margolises and the James Alan Montgomerys would have known how to deal with biblical texts and quotations, whether copied from a *Vorlage* or written down from memory or from dictation. Instead, that gold mine of misinformation and half-truths and of errors of omission and commission, and the like, viz., the so-called critical apparatus in Kittel's *Biblia Hebraica*[3], constituted the pay dirt for so many who used it when referring to or when basing arguments on the Septuagint or Targum or Syriac or Vulgate, etc., but who never saw these primary versions directly, or never realized the inner problems that not infrequently beset the primary versions. It will suffice here to reproduce the following statement from the survey article by Peter Katz(-Walters) in 1956, "Septuagintal Studies in the Mid-Century,"[7] ". . . Contrary to Lagarde's intentions they [Duhm and his school] confined their interest in the LXX to those passages which seemed hopeless in the Hebrew. One may say with truth: Never was the LXX more used and less studied! Unfortunately much of this misuse survives in BH[3]. I have long given up collecting instances. Ziegler, after ten pages of corrections from the Minor Prophets alone, rightly states that all the references to 𝕲 must be rechecked. H. M. Orlinsky who comes back to this point time and again is not very far from the truth when he says that not a single line in the apparatus of BH[3] is free from mistakes regarding 𝕲 " (p. 198).[8]

---

[7] Subtitled "Their Links with the Past and Their Present Tendencies," *The Background of the New Testament and its Eschatology In Honour of Charles Harold Dodd* (eds. W. D. Davies and D. Daube; Cambridge: University Press), pp. 176–208.

[8] The reference is to Part I ("Kritische Bemerkungen zur Verwendung der Septuaginta im Zwölfprophetenbuch der Biblia Hebraica von Kittel," pp. 107–120) of J. Ziegler, "Studien zur Verwertung der Septuaginta im Zwölfprophetenbuch," *ZAW*, 60 (1944), 107–131. There the concluding sentence reads, "Bei einer Neuausgabe der Biblia Hebraica des Dodekapropheton muss das gesamte Γ—Material, wie es die eben erschienene Göttinger Septuaginta-Ausgabe vorlegt, neu bearbeitet werden" (p. 120). For my own strictures against Kittel's *apparatus criticus*, see §§ I-II (pp. 140–152)

So far as the biblical texts among the Dead Sea Scrolls are concerned, it must be said that whatever be the consensus of scholarly opinion about their value for the textual criticism of the Bible, that consensus would have very little *a priori* standing in a court of law in which competent textual critics were the judge and jury. The consensus, whatever it be, would have to undergo the most detailed and searching methodological cross examination before it could hope to be cleared by the court. The fact that the biblical scrolls have come to enjoy a fairly widespread popularity among members of our scholarly guild makes that no more authoritative and useful than the fact that for decades the critical apparatus in BH³ also enjoyed that very status; the latter is a woefully weak link in the chain of the former.⁹

Another aspect of biblical research that the fruits of archeology have unfortunately helped to bring to the fore is the current vogue to equate "parallelism" with "proof," to substitute the citation of parallels for reasoned argument. I suppose that it is inevitable in the nature of things for anyone, as well as anything, to seek the level of least resistance. When the cuneiform texts of the second and first millennia B.C. were uncovered earlier in the twentieth century, what was more natural than for scholars to jump on the Hittite and other bandwagons and find parallels in the most unlikely as well as likely places? One may readily recall the Pan-Babylonian-Hittite school, and the obsession of Hugo Winckler; or the tracing back of almost every detail in the biblical version of creation to the so-called Babylonian Genesis, Enuma Elish; or the connecting of nearly every clause in the pentateuchal laws associated with Moses to the laws of Hammurabi. It is true that, by and large, we have subsequently learned differently. We dismiss good-naturedly Winckler's Pan-Babylonianism; and probably most scholars would now agree, e.g., with T. J. Meek's statement of twenty

---

of "The Textual Criticism of the Old Testament," *The Bible and the Ancient Near East* (Fest. W. F. Albright; ed. G. E. Wright; Garden City: Doubleday, 1965; paperback reprint, 1961, pp. 113–121), with considerable bibliography. Note especially the reference to the vain attempt of E. Würthwein to suppress the sharp criticism of Kittel's BH³.

⁹ See §§ II-III (pp. 145–157) of "The Textual Criticism of the Old Testament" (cited in n. 8).

years ago (*Hebrew Origins*[2], pp. 68–69), "There is no doubt but that there is great similarity between the Hebrew and Babylonian codes . . . , but the connection is not such as to indicate direct borrowing. No one today argues that. Whatever borrowing there was came indirectly, either through common inheritance or through Canaanite influence, or much more likely through both ways."

I think, however, that we must go into the matter more deeply than that, for the problem constitutes the very heart of the question posed in our title: Whither Biblical Research? Bluntly put, it is a fact, one that is generally not recognized, that virtually none of those who are engaged in serious work in our field has been trained to do research in history, that is, to seek to account for the important changes, or for the serious, even unsuccessful attempts at changes, or for the failure to attempt any serious changes, in the structure of a given society. And without being able to comprehend historical forces at work, it is simply impossible to understand how a social structure functions, why it comes into being, why it is maintained, why it is changed, sometimes radically.

Let us assume that some time in the future, out of the ground and rubble of civilization, several documents, none of them intact or complete, are excavated: they are what we today recognize as the Constitution of the United States, the Charter of the League of Nations, the Yalta Agreement, and the Charter of the United Nations. And let us assume further that very little is known in any detail about the events that brought these notable documents into being, or of the social forces that brought on those events; more specifically, we know the background of these documents no better than we know, say, the two centuries preceding 586 (or is it 587?) B.C. or the two centuries following the momentous event of that date.

The scholars of that future date begin to study the numerous fragments of those four documents, trying to fit the many pieces together. They devote years to the study of the terribly fragmented texts and contexts. They recognize word formations, phrases, meanings, and the like, which have association—whether directly or indirectly, they are not always sure—with what they know of Latin and Greek, and with the languages and dialects of countries that once in the long ago had been France, Germany, Italy, the United States, Canada, England,

Russia, and other such countries. The scholars have considerable difficulty in determining the precise nuance of numerous expressions; and
some even suggest that it would be worthwhile compiling special glos-
saries of legal terms, economic terms, and political terms. Of course,
a number of scholars will be busy working on the Form Criticism of
these fragmented documents, for their *Sitz im Leben*. Special groups
will be formed for this study, and foundations will be approached to
help finance these studies. Monographs will be published on the grammatical forms employed in these documents, whether it is, say, the
third or the second person that is employed, and on whether the
clauses are apodictically or casuistically formulated ("you shall" as
against "if one does . . . , then")—for then the documents may be
traced back to a British, or Russian, or American, or French, or other
prototype, or perhaps to a common ancestor for all four documents.
In that case, it might become possible to date these four documents
relatively (i.e., typologically), if not absolutely.

Naturally scholars will disagree in the matter of the relative, as well
as of the absolute, dates of the documents. Old words and phrases
will be found in all four documents, and so some scholars will jump to
the conclusion that the older the phrase the older must be the fragment in which it was preserved. It will also become apparent that
those scholars who ultimately derive from, or have an affinity to, the
region or people or culture of what had once been, say, Great Britain,
will tend to trace the origin and essential nature, and even the extraordinary worthwhileness of the documents—or of the Ur-Document—
to that sphere, as against those who will hold out for the North American, or Central European, or Russian spheres, depending on the
sphere to which they traced back their own cultural or physical
ancestry.

It is obvious that one could go on in this vein, for there are many
more areas and sub-areas of study in higher and lower criticism, in
linguistics, in literary structure and analysis, and the like, that could be
listed. But I have had something more in mind than a purely hypothetical situation in the future. What I have been leading up to is the
fact that there is hardly a member of our Society who would be content with the kind of studies that I have indicated—no matter how
scientifically they were done on these documents; and they would, of

course, be right. After all, is the significance of these documents to be found in their linguistic history and character? Or in their literary structure? Their primary importance, when all is said and done, their major raison d'être for scholars, as well as for laymen, lies in their historical value, in the use to which they are put for the explanation of not only what happened but *why* it happened. *Why* were these documents drawn up in the first place? Who had them drawn up, not merely the names of the countries but the powerful groups within each country? What motivated each of the signatories? Why did certain major powers decline to become signatories—for surely the reason that the United States did not become a signatory of the League of Nations will not be determined through literary, or linguistic, or archeological, or theological analysis.

It is for historical matters that these documents have significance, for it is about these matters that the welfare—sometimes the very existence—of the government and people of the signatory countries, and even of a number of non-signatory countries, revolves. One can just imagine how the scholarly and lay world, where it did not simply ignore, would hoot derisively at the virtually exclusively philological, literary, linguistic, archeological, theological, and similar studies of these documents; the silence that would greet these studies would truly be golden compared to the scorn with which they would be laughed at. And the world would be right: Is that all that these documents are useful for? Is that their true significance? Yet this is precisely what we members of our biblical guild have been doing since archeology began to provide us with a breakthrough in our field half-a-century ago. Literary patterns and—what is much worse, lexical and literary *parallels*—are what have been occupying the energies of so many of us and have been filling so many of the pages of our learned journals and books.

In the past decade especially, hardly an issue of our journal and of others in the field has appeared without an article or two and a book review or two, or more, that does not deal in part or in whole with a parallel, or an alleged parallel, between a biblical phrase or section on the one hand and an extrabiblical correspondent on the other. A decade ago the search for parallels in "the areas of rabbinic literature and the gospels, Philo and Paul, and [by then, especially] the Dead Sea

Scrolls and the NT" had reached such proportions that the presidential address to this Society in 1962 dealt with "Parallelomania." That was actually the title of the address; and the plea was made that "biblical scholarship should recognize parallelomania for the disease that it is . . . and which the scrolls have made an imminent and omnipresent one."[10]

I have alluded already to the handling of the biblical texts among the Dead Sea Scrolls both *per se* and in relation to the received Hebrew text and the Septuagint; this is a chapter in itself, not a very happy one. But I do wish to make specific reference to the current vogue, viz., the limitless and uncritical search for extrabiblical parallels to the concept and institution of covenant in the Bible. There is hardly a treaty or contract in any part of the Near East of the second or first millennium B.C. that has not been cited as a prototype of the biblical notion of covenant. Yet I am not aware of a single study of the concept and institution of the covenant in the Bible that a historian *qua* historian could accept methodologically. True, there is the basic factor, beyond the historian's immediate control, of being unable to date most of the biblical material. Imagine working on the Constitution of the United States, the Charters of the League of Nations and the United Nations, and the Yalta Agreement, and trying to reconstruct from them the history of their signatories without being able to date these documents relatively or absolutely. Yet that is exactly what we have been doing and tolerating, even accepting, in our field. All kinds of Sumerian, Assyrian, Babylonian, Hittite, and Northwest Semitic texts of all historical climes and periods are cited indiscriminately to prove that Israel and God had agreed to a vassal treaty. I am not really being facetious when I wonder out loud where the various historians, prophets, psalmists, and chroniclers—not to mention the glossators and redactors—who composed the Bible found the time to compose what they did when they were so busy reading and keeping up with and making use of the suzerain-vassal treaties that the Hittites and Babylonians and Assyrians and Northwest Semites were signing and, so often, breaking. In point of fact, I am not sure that

---

[10] S. Sandmel, "Parallelomania," *JBL*, 81 (1962), 1–13.

any scholar has ever proved—worse, I am not sure that any scholar has recently even thought of trying to prove—that the contractual relationship betwen Israel and God as presented in the Bible is actually one that involves an inferior and a superior in the manner of a vassal and a suzerain. My own impression is that the biblical concept of the contractual relationship between Israel and God, a relationship into which both parties entered freely and in which both are legally equals, derives ultimately—since God by the very concept of Him to begin with is the Lord, and Israel the servant—from the lord-servant (*'adon-'ebed*) relationship that characterized Israel's (and much of Western Asia's) economy at the time. And while biblical expressions may be clarified with the aid of extrabiblical texts, I do not see how this can prove that Israel's covenant with God derived from vassal-suzerain treaties. As a matter of fact, it may well be that the more numerous the "covenant" parallels between Israel and her Asiatic neighbors during the second and first millennia B.C. become, the greater becomes the probability that the biblical concept of the Israel-God covenant developed quite independently. So that, with Gertrude Stein, a parallel is a parallel is a parallel. . . . The pity of it is that in pursuing and collecting parallels, scholars think that they are writing history.[11]

The net result is this: when the overwhelming majority of us are not trained textually and are unable for the most part to handle a text properly, and when even fewer of us have been trained to get at the underlying forces that shape the structure of society, to comprehend the social process, that can mean only one thing—that our work is rarely taken seriously by historians in the classical, or medieval, or modern periods of research. The most frequently used history of biblical Israel, virtually our standard textbook, is described by its author as having "been prepared with the particular needs of the undergraduate theological student in mind"; and the author of a standard textbook in biblical archeology states frankly in his preface that "only readers concerned with the religious value of the Bible will find

---

[11] The "covenant" parallels may turn out to be very little different from the "Hammurabi" parallels, viz., essentially just parallels.

anything of interest in these pages. The volume has been written with a frankly and definitely religious interest. It has also, of course, been written from a particular point of view, that of a liberal Protestant Christian." Whatever else it may be that we are writing, it is not *history*.

Let us understand each other correctly. I am not opposed to Form Criticism, or to linguistic study, or to excavations, or to the seeking out of similarities—as well as points of difference—between Israel and her neighbors. Quite the contrary! I am all in favor of it, and more. But these disciplines, while each of them must be studied *per se* and not treated as but a handmaid to something else, cannot be re- garded as ends in themselves for the real comprehension of ancient Israel. A historical analysis of, say, the concept of covenant in biblical Israel's career will go quite beyond the citation and compilation of parallels between biblical and extrabiblical phrases; it will, instead, ask—and attempt to answer—such questions as, Why did the concept of covenant mean one thing to Jeremiah and something else to his opponents in the matter of pacts with Babylonia and Egypt? What did "covenant" really mean when Uriah "prophesied in the name of the Lord" against the policy of King Jehoiakim, had to flee for his life to Egypt, was brought back, executed, and denied proper burial (Jer. 26:20–23)? Why did "covenant" mean one thing to King Josiah in his attempted "reformation," and the opposite to those who cham- pioned the cause of the legitimate and non-idolatrous shrines all over the country (for we fall into a trap when we follow tradition mechan- ically and brand the *bāmôt* as idolatrous "high places")? Was it a question of conflicting economic and political interests couched in religious terminology—a phenomenon common to historians, espe- cially to those who study the Middle Ages. Only when all the data achieved by Form Criticism, archeology, textual criticism, the deter- mination of parallels, and the like, are brought into proper focus and play by the trained historian do they acquire life, worthwhileness, meaning.

In fine, as a consequence of a resurgence of textual criticism and philology in the broadest sense and by the introduction of the methodology and outlook of the trained historian, we shall not have to worry about a question like "Whither Biblical Research?" and preclude the withering of meaningful biblical research.

The full title of the presidential address had been "Whither Biblical Research: The Problem of 'Sin' as a Case in Point." Since time did not permit, the latter part of the title was not discussed on the podium of the Society's banquet. Here I shall but touch on the problem of the concept "sin" in the Bible, as I see it.

Discussions of "sin" in the Bible are almost as numerous as occurrences of sin; see, e.g., the recent study by R. Knierim, *Die Hauptbegriffe für Sünde im Alten Testament* (1965; 280 pp., with bibliography). It seems to me that without significant exception, the opening paragraphs of the article on "Sin" in *The Interpreter's Dictionary of the Bible* (IV, 361a–376a) represent very well the manner in which our guild of scholars understands the concept. They read:

> The Bible takes sin in dead seriousness. Unlike many modern religionists, who seek to find excuses for sin and to explain away its seriousness, most of the writers of the Bible had a keen awareness of its heinousness, culpability, and tragedy. They looked upon it as no less than a condition of dreadful estrangement from God, the sole source of well-being. They knew that apart from God, man is a lost sinner, unable to save himself or find true happiness.
>
> It is not difficult to find biblical passages referring to sin; as a matter of fact, there are few chapters which do not contain some references to what sin is or does. It might even be said that in the Bible man has only two theological concerns involving himself: his sin and his salvation. Man finds himself in sin and suffers its painful effects; God graciously offers salvation from it. This is, in essence, what the whole Bible is about.

It is my contention that this is precisely what the Bible is not about, and that the only way that one can begin to understand what sin, as well as the Bible as a whole, is all about is to try to comprehend it—naturally to the extent that our sources permit—in the light of the specific historical circumstances that prevailed at any given time. For instance, if one reads the book of Ezekiel, one gathers that the government and the people of Judah were on the greatest sinning binge in the history of Judah and Israel, if not in all of history. If only ten just men had been found living in Sodom and Gomorrah, those legendary centers of sin and all their sinful inhabitants would have been spared. But so great was the sin of Jerusalem and Judah that, even if those very models of justice, Noah, Job, and Daniel, were living there, they alone would have been spared; but all the other inhabitants would have been destroyed, along with the Temple, the great city itself, and the country as a whole.

Ezekiel, as is well known, has provided us with a most detailed description of sinful acts, some of them so perverse and striking that more than one person has been led to believe that much of the detail was due to "Ezekiel's Abnormal Personality."[12] But whether the acts of sin did or did not take place, no serious historian would permit himself to be drawn into a debate as to whether the sin of Jerusalem and Judah was greater than that of Sodom and Gomorrah, or whether such sin as Ezekiel described, regardless of its alleged quantity and quality, was responsible for King Nebuchadnezzar's decision to wage a military campaign against—*inter alia*—Judah. Rather, the modern historian would "seek—behind the religious terminology—the same kind of documented human story, with an examination of its underlying dynamics, that would be his proper objective in any other field. Otherwise he would achieve no more than a compilation of myths, chronicles, annals, oracles, autobiographies, court histories, personal apologia."[13] In dealing with the book of Ezekiel, the historian now has good reason to regard the Book as a whole as essentially reliable —unlike the situation in the late Twenties and early Thirties—thanks to the excavation of such sites as Tell Beit Mirsim, Beth Shemesh, and Lachish, and the publication in 1939 of the long-excavated and lost Babylonian texts of Nebuchadnezzar and Evil-merodach. But in his analysis of the momentous events that befell Judah at the turn of the sixth century B.C., the historian will go seeking behind such terms as "sin" and "covenant" for the fundamental economic, political, and

---

[12] E. C. Broome, Jr., *JBL*, 65 (1946), 277–92.

[13] From the writer's *Ancient Israel* (Ithaca: Cornell, 1954), p. 9 (p. 7 in the 2nd paperback edition, 1960).

social forces that determined the use and content—and, so frequently, the utter disregard—of these terms.[14] There is a great future for biblical research and the trained historian who devotes himself to it.

---

[14] The reader will do well to study carefully the methodology employed by M. A. Cohen in his discussion of "The Role of the Shilonite Priesthood in the United Monarchy of Ancient Israel" (*HUCA*, 36 [1965], 59–98) and in his analysis of "The Rebellions during the Reign of David: An Inquiry into the Social Dynamics of Ancient Israel," in the forthcoming volume of *Studies in Jewish Bibliography, History, and Literature in Honor of I. Edward Kiev* (ed. C. Berlin, New York: KTAV, 1971).

On "sin" as a cliché in the books of Isaiah and Jeremiah, see pp. 88 ff. of my essay on "Nationalism-Universalism . . . in Ancient Israel" (chap. 5 above) and p. 138 and n. 12a of my essay on "Nationalism-Universalism in the Book of Jeremiah" (chap. 6 above). On the background of the book of Ezekiel as history, see my essay on "The Destruction of the First Temple and the Babylonian Exile in the Light of Archaeology" (chap. 7 above).

ESSAYS IN JEWISH CULTURE

12

On Toynbee's Use
of the Term "Syriac"
for One of his Civilizations

LET IT BE STATED at the outset that this brief essay is not intended for the author of *A Study of History*. Whether he takes issue with the essay or not is quite irrelevant, since a perusal of his *Reconsiderations* makes it amply clear that it is hardly worth the effort to convince him that he may well be wrong in his views and that he might care to reconsider them. Rather is this essay meant for the general reader who might not read Toynbee in some detail or who finds himself unable to acquaint himself with how specialists regard this intrepid fact-collector.

The few specialists in the Ancient Near East who have bothered to read and comment publicly on A. J. Toynbee's discussion of that area and period in world history have been less than happy with what

[This essay appeared originally in the Silver Jubilee Volume, *In the Time of Harvest: Essays in Honor of Abba Hillel Silver on the Occasion of his 70th Birthday*, ed. D.J. Silver (New York, Macmillan, 1963), pp. 255–269.

In the discussion on pp. 222-26, I should have included reference to and made use of the devastating critique of Toynbee's *Study* in Henri Frankfort's penetrating analysis of *The Birth of Civilization in the Near East* (1951; Anchor Book, 1956), pp. 12–24. I should also have noted G. E. Grunebaum's interesting chapter on "Toynbee's Concept of Islamic Civilization" in *Intent of Toynbee's History*, ed. E. T. Gargan (Loyola University Press, Chicago, 1961.]

they have read. In this respect, they have not differed appreciably from the specialists in the other areas and epochs. But then the kind of "analysis" to be found in Toynbee's ten-volume *Study of History* was hardly calculated to win friends among scholars who study the materials at the source, and who do not tend to select data that fit perfectly into a pattern that had been created for them in advance.

For apart from other considerations, a student of the Fertile Crescent of old is hardly expected to take the time to read about his special field of interest something written by one who cannot read in the original a single source dealing with that period. The scribes of the great civilizations in question wrote in Sumerian, Egyptian, Babylonian, Assyrian, Hittite, Canaanite, Aramaic, Hebrew, and the like. But Toynbee had to depend upon secondary materials throughout for his own study of the "cradle of civilization." Everyone knows how unscholarly—indeed arrogant and less than responsible—such a procedure is, and how unreliable such analysis must be. This is especially true in the study of Western Asia and Biblical Israel, because of the rapidity with which discoveries and new analyses are made and the control that one must have over archeology and the written sources, each in its own right and in relation to each other. The writer of *A Study of History* lacked this control. It is in this connection that I often recall a conversation with a well known and authoritative cuneiformist in which I asked him whether he had read Toynbee on ancient Mesopotamia—after all, the Sumeric, the Hittite, and the Babylonic constitute no less than three out of his nineteen "societies"! —and receiving the laughing reply, "No, why should I read him? What does he know about it, and what can he tell me?"

In his comprehensive analysis of *The Burden of Egypt: an Interpretation of Ancient Egyptian Culture* (1951: now a Phoenix paperback, *The Culture of Egypt*), John A. Wilson, the noted Egyptologist of Chicago's Oriental Institute, wrote (p. 32, n. 12), ". . . In subsequent chapters it may be noted that we have not found some of Toynbee's concepts or principles sufficiently applicable to ancient Egypt to warrant detailed discussion. For example, we have difficulty in accepting the sequence of 'time of troubles' (First Intermediate Period), 'universal state' (Middle Kingdom), 'interregnum' (Hyksos invasion), and 'universal state reasserted' (Empire); for us, the effectively disturbing troubles which wrecked Egyptian culture grew ⌐ ˙ of the Empire and the attempt to maintain it. Even less valid seems uᵢₑ ˙oncept of the worship of Osiris as a kind of 'universal church created by an internal proletariat'; the Osirian religion was mortuary and could not be the genesis of a 'new society,' and it was originally created by and for Toynbee's 'dominant minority.' These criticisms do scant justice to Toynbee's enormously refreshing influence in assailing formerly fixed ideas. The thinking of this book owes much to him, even though his societal pattern for Egypt is rejected."[1]

In the same year Ephraim A. Speiser of the University of Pennsylvania published a paper on "The Ancient Near East and Modern Philosophies of History" (in *Proceedings of the American Philosophical Society,* Vol. 95, No. 6, December, pp. 583–588). It is to the fundamental changes that have occurred the world over since World War I, he noted, that "we owe so many contemporary or recent philosophies of history: those of Spengler and Toynbee, of Sorokin, Kroeber, and Northrop, among various others." The paper sought "to address itself to one serious defect that must leave the final conclusions in serious doubt. . . . [As] to the Near East . . . that unique and enormously significant testimony is no better than a blank in the comprehensive studies just mentioned. Toynbee and Kroeber, two

---

[1] Wilson's note pertains to Vol. I of Toynbee's *Study* (1935), pp. 302–315 (or pp. 68–73 of D. C. Somervell's *Abridgement* of Vols. I-VI, 1947).

In reference to ancient Egyptian culture, particularly in the matter of the Pyramids, Toynbee wrote (p. 30 of the *Abridgement;* cf. Vol. I, pp. 128 ff.), *"The Egyptiac Society.* This very notable society emerged in the lower valley of the Nile during the fourth millennium B.C. and became extinct in the fifth century of, the Christian Era, after existing, from first to last, at least three times as long as our Western Society has existed so far. It was without 'parents' and without offspring; no living society can claim it as an ancestor. All the more triumphant is the immortality that it has sought and found in stone. It seems probable that the Pyramids, which have already borne inanimate witness to the existence of their creators for nearly five thousand years, will survive for hundreds of thousands of years to come. It is not inconceivable that they may outlast man himself and that, in a world where there are no longer human minds to read their message, they will continue to testify: 'Before Abraham was, I am.' " Wilson quoted part of this statement in his *Burden of Egypt* (p. 310), but he went on immediately with this very (im?)pertinent query: "Of what importance to us is such a civilization, which was so long-lived and so immortal in its physical expression?"

authorities to whom we are especially indebted for penetrating insights, are no exceptions in this regard. They and the others make brief detours to Egypt . . . but what they come out with is a fragmentary account, out of focus and out of date and hence thoroughly misleading. . . . Even less satisfactory is the vestigial recognition, if any, that these works accord to the other areas of the Ancient Near East, especially Mesopotamia. There is, for instance, no tenable definition of civilization whereby Babylonia can be isolated from Sumer, as is done by Toynbee. On the other hand, Toynbee's Syriac society is a conglomerate of loosely assorted elements." And a footnote (n. 8) to this sentence reads, ". . . Toynbee's conclusions that the civilization of the Indus Valley was very closely related to that of the Sumerians . . . has only resemblances of a very superficial nature to support it."

In Chapter II of his book *From the Stone Age to Christianity* (1940), in the section on "The Encyclopaedic-Analytic Tendency in the Philosophy of History" (pp. 60 ff.), William F. Albright, after paying the usual tribute to Toynbee's literary style and clarity of

---

² It is of interest that scholars sometimes feel impelled to pay tribute to Toynbee as a scholar of great insight before they proceed to reject his scholarship altogether in their own field. The tribute is generally paid for "insight" in fields other than those in which the scholars have special competence. This is known in Yiddish as *gut far yénem* "[It is] good for someone else [but not for me]."

As for style and clarity, Toynbee has collected something of an autobiography on this too, in his *Reconsiderations* (II Annex, *Ad Hominem,* pp. 587 ff.), where he—gleefully, it would seem—flagellates himself publicly with references to and quotations from many of his critics. In reading this volume, I was reminded of A. Werner's review *(Jewish Quarterly Review,* 36 [1945–1946], pp. 207 ff.) of Jacob Klatzkin's book *In Praise of Wisdom,* where reference is made to Spengler and the "Spenglers" who "work hard to hide their simple and obvious ideas under a mass of verbiage . . . [and] examine every expression of theirs to make sure that it is sufficiently blurred."

Recently, the lamented S. F. Bloom of Brooklyn College, in his pungent review of *Reconsiderations* ("Toynbee on Toynbee: his *Reconsiderations* of *A Study of History,*" in *Midstream* 8 [1962], pp. 49–56)—where he hardly takes Toynbee seriously as a historian—described the author as one who—*inter alia*—"suffers from a kind of word-fetishism rare in educated men, and he has a strong appetite for provocation. . . ." Of course no one should take Toynbee's terminology—any more than, say, his lumping together of all kinds of data—seriously: why should he use the common term "Appendix" when "Annex" will lift eyebrows? Why resort to the clear and mundane term "Institution" when "slum" (!) can gain Toynbee so much wider publicity? (But see Bloom, pp. 50–55.)

presentation,[2] proceeds to indicate why Toynbee has so little value for the historian of the Ancient Near East in general and for Biblical Israel in particular: "The task of distinguishing cultural groups of mankind is by no means a new one. . . . It is not unfair to say that such divisions really exist, but they cross one another and change chronologically, geographically, and culturally to such an extent that they become rather useless as units of classification. . . . An attempt to take a common material culture (Islamic, Christian) or even a racial background (as in dividing Islam into two separate modern societies, the Iranic and the Arabic) in another can only lead to confusion . . . we consider this side of Toynbee's investigation as relatively futile. Unfortunately," continues Albright (p. 62), "the weakness of Toynbee's method does not end here. . . ."[3]

What constituted, however, a devastating criticism of Toynbee, though apparently not intended as such, is the opening sentence on p. 222 of his book, where Albright takes up the period of the Judges and the United Monarchy: "Though Toynbee seems to have overlooked the case of the Israelites between 1200 and 900 B.C., it would be difficult to find a better illustration of his principle of 'Challenge-and-Response under the stimulus of blows.' Under this stimulus the Israelites attained national unity in spite of the centrifugal forces operating to break up the confederation. . . ." Probably an even better and more dramatic example of this phenomenon is the Babylonian Exile and the subsequent Persian Restoration, when the Judeans were

---

[3] I do not understand the statement by Albright (pp. 63 ff.) that in the use of the principles "Challenge-and-Response" and "Withdrawal-and-Return" Toynbee was no innovator but that he "appears in both approaches to the problem of history as an old-fashioned spirit, acquiring the reputation of a great innovator and even of a prophet because he presents old but neglected principles with elaborate logical proof of their salient reality. All honor to him for reinstating forgotten truths!" The knowing reader, who has read Toynbee's critics directly (as usual, Toynbee has made some of the materials available, in *Reconsiderations,* e.g., pp. 573 ff., 606 ff.), will recall that those who used the term "prophet" or the like had in mind something pejorative. As for the principles in question, surely they have been neither neglected nor forgotten! Since Hegel flourished, hardly a day has gone by without a book or an article appearing by a Hegelian or a Marxist—or by an anti-Hegelian or an anti-Marxist—dealing with precisely these principles; except that the terms employed are something like "thesis, antithesis, synthesis" or "action and reaction" or "cause and effect" or "dialectic," rather than the pretentious terms that Toynbee is so fond of toying with.

literally "Withdrawn" and later permitted to "Return."

But of course Toynbee did not just happen to overlook "the case of the Israelites between 1200 and 900 B.C.," or the Babylonian Exile and Restoration, or several other pertinent events in Biblical Israel's career, for example, Judah in the Persian Period, or in the Hellenistic. Indeed, it can hardly be an accident that nowhere in his *Study* did Toynbee bother to adduce anything from Israel's rich and eventful history that would, at one and the same time, illustrate one of his principles and shed some glory on Israel.

And this leads directly to the matter of terminology. Eighteen (or twenty) out of Toynbee's nineteen (or twenty-one) societies (or civilizations) were given by him names that make sense in one way or another. The last paragraph on p. 34 of the *Abridgement* has this to say: "Our researches have thus yielded us nineteen societies, most of them related as parent or offspring to one or more of the others: namely, the Western, the Orthodox, the Iranic, the Arabic (these last two being now united in the Islamic), the Hindu, the Far Eastern, the Hellenic, the Syriac, the Indic, the Sinic, the Minoan, the Sumeric, the Hittite, the Babylonic, the Egyptiac, the Andean, the Mexic, the Yucatec and the Mayan. . . . Indeed it is probably desirable to divide the Orthodox Christian Society into an Orthodox-Byzantine and an Orthodox-Russian Society, and the Far Eastern into a Chinese and a Korean-Japanese Society. This would raise our numbers to twenty-one. . . ."[4]

Whether or not there is really justification for this system of societies, at least the names for them mean something to the student of

---

[4] Despite this statement, the reader will learn from Toynbee (*Reconsiderations*, "A Re-Survey of Civilization," pp. 546–561) that "In the course of the first ten volumes . . . I arrived at a list of twenty-three full-blown civilizations, four that were arrested at an early stage in their growth, and five that were abortive. . . . We are now in a position to draw up our revised list of civilizations . . .": 28 [of which three are qualified by "?"] Fullblown and 6 Abortive. There is nothing to prevent anyone from taking the new list any more seriously than the old one. But, in the creation of Civilizations, Bloom (p. 56) may have more justification than Toynbee when he comments wryly, ". . . *Reconsiderations* adds a Thirty-Third Civilization—Arnold J. Toynbee himself. . . ."

history—that is, for all the societies except the Syriac.[5] This is a curious name indeed, for under it was subsumed—along with the cultures of the Canaanites, Arameans, Ammonites, Moabites, and Edomites, among others—the great and unique culture of Biblical Israel. It would never have occurred to a student of the Ancient Near East in general, or of Western Asia alone, or of the eastern coastal area of the Mediterranean specifically, to designate this society as Syriac. It is a simple fact that the very term Syriac did not come into being until after the society onto which Toynbee grafted the term had virtually gone out of existence[6]—that is, all except that rambunctious fossil of Toynbee's, Judaism.

During the Hellenistic period, the term Syria came to refer to Aram (so, for example, in the Septuagint translation) as well as to other regions of Western Asia (so the Greeks themselves). Of course no one has argued that it was the region or the culture of the Arameans proper that was chiefly responsible for cultures that arose on both sides of the Jordan during the last two millennia B.C. Indeed, one would be hard put to describe the Aramaic culture of the second millenium B.C., for the simple reason that there is so little to discuss.[7] Contrast, on the other hand, the rightful place that Canaan and Israel hold in the civilization of Asia-on-the-Mediterranean. Both the Bible and archeology have made it abundantly—and in the case of Ugarit-Ras Shamra dramatically—clear how the culture of these two peoples dominated the central portion of the Fertile Crescent during so much of the second and first millennia B.C. Along with such lesser luminaries as the Ammonites, Moabites, and Edomites, it was Canaan

---

[5] Toynbee attempts to justify this term in Vol. I, p. 82, n. 2; *Reconsiderations*, pp. 393 f. The wisdom of employing this term does not appear to have impressed very many scholars.

[6] This statement is true regardless of how and by whom the term Syriac was first coined and applied. It has long been held that it was the Greeks who originated the term, by clipping off the first part of the well known name, Assyria. For another explanation (on which the name *Subria* became *Suria-Syria* by way of assumed *Suwria*), see apud R. T. O'Callaghan, *Aram-Naharaim* (*Analecta Orientalia* 26, 1948), p. 142 and n. 1.

[7] Cf., e.g., O'Callaghan's *Aram-Naharaim* (which is subtitled: *A Contribution to the History of Upper Mesopotamia in the Second Millennium* B.C.), Chapters V–VII (pp. 93 ff.), respectively: "The Aramaeo-Assyrian Period," "Israel and Aram," and "Aram Naharaim."

(later Phoenicia) and Israel that constituted and generated a society of their own, one that, with everything that it shared with—even derived from—Mesopotamia, could not possibly be confused with the other great societies to the east, north, west, and south. Surely, it is Canaan-Israel, not Syria, that deserved onomastic mention among Toynbee's nineteen (or twenty-one, or thirty-four) societies.

Even more. In dealing with two of his societies, the Orthodox Christian and the Far Eastern, Toynbee was quite willing, because "it is probably desirable," to make two societies out of each of the two: an Orthodox-Byzantine and an Orthodox-Russian out of the Orthodox-Christian, and a Chinese and a Korean-Japanese out of the Far Eastern. Regardless of whether these terms and divisions are acceptable to specialists in those complex areas, it is utterly beyond comprehension—at least to the historian—how anyone could take himself seriously and cause cultures and peoples by the score in every part of the world to come into being, to flourish (or to abort), and to vanish, with or without progeny—and persist in denying existence to an Hebraic-Jewish society in the southwestern part of Asia; and let us not quibble whether it was full-blown, or arrested, or abortive.

Confronted by some facts that refuse to disappear in the swamp of verbiage that characterizes so much of his *Study,* Toynbee will admit (*Reconsiderations*, pp. 394 f.) that "The most fateful single event in all Hellenic history was the ideological and religious collision, in Coele Syria [read: Judea!] in the second century B.C., between Hellenism and Judaism. . . . The Hellenic World was eventually converted to a religion of Jewish origin that was, and remained, essentially Judaic in its inspiration and its principles. . . . And this conversion of the Hellenic World to Christianity was the end of the Hellenic Civilization. As a result of the conversion, Hellenism lost its identity." So once again a little David of little Judah conquered an Aegean Goliath; but for Toynbee neither of the two Davids was a Judean—both were but Syriac products!

What is fascinating in this connection is that while he devotes an entire chapter (XIII, pp. 393–461) of his *Reconsiderations* to "The Configurations of Syriac History," Toynbee squanders still another entire chapter (XV, pp. 477–517) on the Jewish people alone, under the high-falutin title: "The History and Prospects of the Jews." It is most curious that Toynbee devotes here to the Jews more space than he does to the two chapters immediately following (XVI and XVII) combined: "The History and Prospects of the West" (518–536) and "Russia's Place in History" (536–546). So much does the Jewish people "bother" Toynbee that the East and the West—in combination! —receive less attention here than a people and a culture whose existence as a civilization he denies.[8] Toynbee will grant this prestige status to the Hittite civilization (satellite of Sumero-Akkadian), to the Iranian (satellite first of Sumero-Akkadian, then of Syriac), to the Mediaeval Western City-State (abortive), to the Nestorian Christian (abortive), to the Monophysite Christian (abortive), etc., etc.— see the chart on p. 558 of *Reconsiderations*—but he will not bestow it upon a (*pace!*) civilization that not only brought an end to Hellenism but—believe it or not!—can save the whole world from destruction if only it wills: ". . . the Jewish diaspora [*sic!*] might win converts to a denationalized and defossilized Judaism among the gentile majority around them. What the Romans did on the political plane, the Jews could do on the religious. They could incorporate gentiles in a Jewish religious community by converting them to the religion of Deutero-Isaiah. The greatest of the Prophets up to date, though not necessarily the last of them, would be, not Muhammed, but a Jewish seer who inspired his fellow Jews at last to dedicate themselves to their universal mission wholeheartedly. The World has been waiting for this

---

[8] One maye add the 15 pages devoted to "Islam's Place in History" (Chapter XIV in *Reconsiderations*), and he will find that Toynbee devoted 40 pages to the Jews, as against a grand total of 43 pages to Islam, the West, and Russia combined, all within four successive chapters! How fossilized can one get?

This obsession of Toynbee's reminds the present writer of a joke that has been making the rounds. A Jewish mother was telling her friends proudly that a son of hers had achieved remarkable success in the field of his endeavor and had become so wealthy that he was paying a doctor a hundred dollars for thirty minutes, twice a week, just to listen to him talk. This talking, she continued, had been going on for several years, so that her son was obviously in the upper brackets in income. One crony then asked the mother, "But what does he talk about? What is it that is of such importance to your son that he sets aside so much time and money to talk about?" To which the mother replied, bursting with pride, "Me!"

prophet for 2,500 years" (p. 517).[9] As the Yiddish saying goes: *Halevai volt es émes geven* ("If only this were true!").

It would seem clear by now that Toynbee, first and above all, simply refused to use any and all forms of any such terms as Hebrew or Israel or Jew, contrary to every justification for it even on his own approach. This same willfulness is apparent in his refusal—colossal ignorance would not be involved here[10]—even to make mention of the significant things that the Jewish society did and created during the past nineteen hundred years in the Diaspora—on which see Maurice Samuel's brilliant polemic, *The Professor and the Fossil* (1956).[11]

Toynbee has asserted (see the references in n. 5 above) that the Greeks gave him the idea of using the term Syriac for the civilization of Asia-on-the-Mediterranean. I wonder, however, whether the idea for the term does not derive from quite another, much later source than the Greek, the Islamic.

In one of his numerous exhibitions of self-flagellation, Toynbee writes (*Reconsiderations*, pp. 596 f.), "A second dim spot, of which I am aware, is my neglect of Israel, Judah, the Jews, and Judaism. I

---

[9] One is reminded of an address that Toynbee gave in England, one which was widely referred to in the Yiddish and Anglo-Jewish press in this country as a retraction and reconsideration of his solemn view that the Jewish people constituted a fossil. But when the complete text of this address reached this country—not without significance it was the American Council for Judaism that circulated it ("Pioneer Destiny of Judaism," 1960, 14 pp.)—the careful reader saw at once, behind the verbiage and sanctimonious sympathies, a malicious attack on world Jewry: unless the Jews outside of Israel give up all association with Israel and unless they proceed energetically to spread their Jewish religion among the peoples of the world so as to prevent the destruction of the world in the Atomic Age—the Jews will bear responsibility for having failed to help save the world! What is one to say about such monstrous and warped "reasoning"!

[10] In his *Reconsiderations* (p. 596), Toynbee writes, "I am ignorant . . . of the Jewish philosophy that flourished in an early Islamic and a medieval Western cultural environment," with the note (6), "Samuel points out . . . that I do not mention the Talmud, the Mishnah, the Midrashim, or any Jewish philosopher—not even Spinoza." But I prefer my own statement about Toynbee to Toynbee's.

[11] I am in a position to appreciate Mr. Samuel's confession (pp. 18 f.) that "My [time of?] troubles began quite early . . . on page 35 of Volume I (of Toynbee's *Study*) . . ." and before too long "It began to dawn on me that, incredibly enough, the man was quite serious. . . ."

have neglected these out of proportion to their true importance. . . . I am ignorant of the Rabbinical Jewish literature . . . I know the Pharisees . . . through the denunciations of them in the Gospels. . . . Worst of all, I have never learnt even a smattering of Hebrew. Since childhood, Hebrew has left me cold, whereas I have had a passionate desire to learn Arabic. This partiality is evidently irrational . . . I cannot account for my acquiescence in this particular dim spot, though I am none the less conscious of its being there." More recently, we may recall Toynbee's hatred for Zionism and the State of Israel, his concern for the Arabs who left Israel in 1948 in the hope of returning shortly to a land without Jews, and the like.[12]

Let us see what role the term Syria has played in Islamic terminology. In 1950 P. K. Hitti, Professor of Arabic at Princeton University—and not known for Zionist or Israeli sympathies—published a rather large book of some 750 pages under the title *History of Syria, Including Lebanon and Palestine*. Dr. Hitti is a specialist in matters Islamic and Arabic, not Biblical or Ancient Near Eastern. In writing this book, and in choosing the title that he did, the author manifested a lamentable unconcern for matters Biblical and Jewish, so that, as a Christian reviewer noted, "To the history of the Hebrews from the Exodus to Alexander only fifty pages are devoted, and to Herod and his father only a single page."[13] Of course, Dr. Hitti was using the term "Syria" in the manner that Arabs used it, viz., the eastern coastland of the Mediterranean. For the Land of Israel, as such, was regarded as but an appendage to Syria. Such cities as Jerusalem and

---

[12] I wonder whether this concern (pro-Arab as against anti-Zionist) is any more genuine than his tears for the six million Jews obliterated by the Nazis and their collaborators. I note his specific assertion, "In the Jewish [to distinguish from the Christian?] Zionists I see the disciples of the Nazis" (*Reconsiderations*, p. 628). I am not aware that Toynbee has employed the expression "disciples of the Nazis" for any of the many—alas, so many!—Christians (and Moslems) who assisted, or hoped to be in a position to assist, in the fiendish Nazi holocaust. Solomon Zeitlin ("Jewish Rights in Eretz Israel [Palestine]," *Jewish Quarterly Review,* 52 [July 1961], 31), in his devastating rejoinder (pp. 12–34) to Toynbee's denial of "Jewish Rights in Palestine" (*ibid.*, pp. 1–11), commented on this intentionally provocative expression of Toynbee's: "*Pace,* Professor! How many Zionists put Christians into gas chambers?"

[13] H. H. Rowley, in 1951 *Book List* of the British Society for Old Testament Study.

Hebron had special sanctity for the Moslems; but the Land as a whole did not.

Among the numerous Moslem guidebooks to the holy places in Palestine, C. D. Matthews selected as "the two most interesting and typical" *The Book of Arousing Souls to Visit Jerusalem's Holy Walls* by Ibn al-Firkah (1262–1320) and *The Book of Inciting Desire to Visit Abraham the Friend*, etc., written in 1351 by Abu 'l-Fida', and made them available in English translation under the rather startling title, *Palestine—Mohammedan Holy Land*, published in 1949 in Yale's *Oriental Series* (*Researches*, Vol. XXIV). I say startling, because the simple fact is that Palestine was not to the Mohammedans the Holy Land, any more than, say, it was to the Christians; and in these two guidebooks it is only Jerusalem and Hebron in all of Palestine that were taken up.

What Matthews did was to make the original Arabic manuscripts say what they never did! Thus, for example, whereas al-Firkah called his Chapter XII "On the Merits of Jerusalem in Summary," Matthews arbitrarily added "(and Palestine)"—and this in spite of the fact that this chapter begins with the clear statement: "On the authority of Abu Umamah it is related: The Apostle of Allah said, The Koran was sent down unto me in three places, Mecca, Medina, and Syria—which means Jerusalem, as Walid says." Or when he mentioned (p. xxiii, note 6) al-Maqdisi's *Inciter of Desire to Visit Jerusalem and Syria* (written in 1350) as an "Arabic document of Moslem veneration of Palestine," Matthews has, without justification, not only substituted "Palestine" for "Jerusalem" (al-Quds) but even inserted after his "Jerusalem," in the English translation of the title, the words: "(or Palestine)." Again, when he commented ·on the term "Syria" in A. Guillaume's *Traditions of Islam* (1924), Matthews himself adds to the Traditions on the religious merits of Syria the words: "including Palestine and Jerusalem"! But Dr. Matthews—who became an employee of an oil company in the Near East—was writing in a period when Arab and Jewish claims to Palestine were in conflict, and he was moved in the twentieth century to attribute to a couple of pious

Moslem pilgrims of the thirteenth-fourteenth centuries a concept that they did not themselves manifest.[14]

Again, when Sherif Hussein of Mecca and Sir Arthur McMahon of Great Britain exchanged secret letters in 1915–1916 on the distribution of the spoils of the Ottoman Empire, Palestine as such was not even mentioned in the correspondence. But then, why should that territory—for that is virtually all that it was to the Moslems—have been spelled out by name when the term Syria was understood to include it? And that is why, for example, statistics for Palestine are so difficult to come by for the period prior to the British Mandate; the statistics for Syria, the head and the body of the state of which Palestine was but the tail, automatically included and absorbed those of the region to the south of it. But it is hardly necessary to pursue the matter here.

Now let us get back to A. J. Toynbee. We had noted previously in his *Reconsiderations*[15] the "confession" to a "dim spot . . . I am ignorant of the Rabbinical Jewish literature . . . my neglect of Israel, Judah, the Jews, and Judaism. . . . Since childhood, Hebrew has left me cold. . . . This partiality is evidently irrational. . . ." (Of

---

[14] For additional references, see my review of Matthew's book in *In Jewish Bookland,* March, 1950, p. 2. See also, e.g., S. Zeitlin, "Jewish Rights in Palestine," *Jewish Quarterly Review,* 38 (Oct., 1947), 119–134.

[15] This is as good a place as any to note that Toynbee's title is something of a misnomer, and Arthur Schlesinger, Jr., has driven home this point rather well in his review of the book (*New York Post,* May 14, 1961, Book Review page): ". . . For a moment, one is involuntarily impressed by the apparent openness of manner, by the eager interest in new evidence, by the asserted readiness to change views when proven wrong. Yet after a time, one begins to wonder. Toynbee's very intensity of concern with his critics, his microscopic analysis of their objections, his almost compulsive turning of the other cheek—and all combined with a stubborn adherence to his original views—begin to rouse suspicion . . . one feels more than ever in his work, despite the stylistic gestures of diffidence and openmindedness, the presence of a ruthless and gigantic intellectual imperialism deeply persuaded that all history can be subjugated to his private network of categories and generalizations. 'I have,' Dr. Toynbee writes, 'a passion for unity,' by which he means, among other things, for 'a unitary vision of human affairs and of all other phenomena.' It is on this altar that he has sacrificed the writing of history. In the end, one cannot escape the conclusion that, as William James wrote of Hegel, such a passion turns its practitioner into a philosophic monster."

course, one who is ignorant of an entire civilization and irrationally partial against it ought not write about it.) This confession comes as no surprise even to one who might have read only the "Acknowledgements and Thanks" in Vol. X of the *Study* (pp. 213–242; "large parts" of this section were reproduced in *The Saturday Review*, October 2, 1954, pp. 13–16, 52–55, under "I Owe My Thanks"). In this bit of autobiography[16] Toynbee gives thanks to such diverse people, books, etc., as: I. To Marcus (Aurelius) for teaching me to return thanks to my benefactors . . . II. To my Mother, for making me an Historian . . . IV. To People, Institutions, Landscapes, Monuments, Pictures, Languages, and Books, for exciting my curiosity . . . V. and VI. To People and Books, for teaching me Methods of Intellectual Work . . . [and] Methods of Literary Presentation . . . VII. To People, Monuments, Apparatus, Pictures, Books, and Events, for giving me Intuitions and Ideas . . . VIII. To People and Institutions [not "Slums"?], for showing Kindness to me.

In section IV Toynbee specifies, among numerous persons and books, his great-uncle, Robert Browning, Heyerdahl's *Kon-Tiki*, E. Creasy's *The Fifteen Decisive Battles of the World*, the four-volume *Story of the Nations*, Col. G. F. R. Henderson's *Stonewall Jackson*, "My Mother's account of her conversation with the disgruntled custodian of the deserted royal palace at Hanover, when she visited it during her stay in Germany in A.D. 1885, made me realize, even as a

---

[16] Toynbee's obsession with himself has been noted notoriously; a normal person finds himself feeling uncomfortable in the presence of this constant exhibitionism. Bloom, e.g., has commented, ". . . In Mr. Toynbee's case . . . the personality and the purpose—it is perhaps not too much to speak of his mission—all but overwhelm the interpretation and dictate to the material. This has been said before, but the chief value of the twelfth volume of *A Study* is to dramatize the role that Mr. Toynbee plays in his own 'history.' " In the section *"Ad Hominem"* (*Reconsiderations,* II Annex, pp. 573–657) Bloom has noted that Toynbee "presents a full self-portrait as an appendix of 84 pages supported by 266 footnotes. He himself is the subject of the longest entry in the index: 373 references to the text, many of them to passages of several pages . . . a sample of the items . . . : Toynbee, A. J., . . . as a furniture-shifter, . . . attempts the impossible, . . . birth of [five references], . . . hypocrisy, accused of, . . . insight of, . . . not anti-Semitic, . . . openness of his mental horizon, . . . the self-destructive bent of his thought, . . . stimulating effect of his work, . . ." (pp. 735–736 of the *Index*). It is not easy to suppress a smile, and more, while perusing this entry.

child, that all was not well under the surface in Prussia-Germany"—
and, in the midst of all these and the others, "The Genealogy of the
descendants of Noah's three sons in the tenth chapter of the Book of
Genesis. . . ." From among the very many hundreds of books and
articles that Toynbee had read and had been influenced by, one would
think that the Old Testament stood somewhere at the top of the list.
He was seven years old, he tells us, when he came across Genesis 10
in a lesson in school: "I was excited to find myself, as I supposed,
being admitted to an inside view of the panorama of the unfolding
of human history from the bud." Apart from a reference to "The
Gospels and Herodotus . . ." and "The Authorized Version of the
Bible, made in the reign of King James I . . .' (in Section VII), this
is all the Acknowledgments and Thanks that Toynbee owes the Bible!
And one may well marvel: Did not Moses, or David, or Elijah, or
Hosea, or Isaiah, or Amos, or Micah, or Jeremiah, or the Psalmist, or
Job, among others, arouse in him something to remember and recall
thankfully? Could it really have been only the genealogy in Genesis
10, out of the entire Hebrew Bible, that he can recall with thanks?
Interestingly, *The Saturday Review* (p. 54) reproduced the following
paragraph under the caption, *Toynbee on History:* "What do we mean
by History? The writer would reply that he meant by History a vision
—dim and partial, yet (he believed) true to reality as far as it went—
of God revealing Himself in action to souls that were sincerely seeking Him." Is not this the very essence of the Hebrew Bible?[17]

---

[17] Of course theology is not yet history; and while Biblical Israel was the first to
produce historians (e.g., the authors of the books of Samuel and Kings), over twenty-
five centuries ago, the quotation here cited from Toynbee does not mark him a historian. G. Mattingly noted this in his review of Toynbee's *Civilization on Trial* (1948;
in *Journal of Modern History*, Vol. 21, No. 4 [Dec. 1949], pp. 360–361): ". . . This
is not quite the same Toynbee who wrote the first six volumes of the *Study*. . . . He
now stands his former thesis (the gist of which is that the higher religions are subsidiary to civilizations . . .) on its head, holding that civilizations are subsidiary to
religion and that the whole of history has meaning only as it has pointed to one far-
off divine event, the universal triumph of Christianity, which will be strengthened
and advanced by the sufferings consequent upon the collapse of Western civilization.
. . . No new 'higher religion' will arise from the ashes of the West, because no religion
higher than Christianity is possible. Even the institutional organization of its ultimate
triumph is prepared. It is 'the Church in its traditional form . . . armed with the
spear of the Mass, the shield of the hierarchy, and the helmet of the Papacy' . . .

And the litany of the saints that Toynbee compiled, with which to bring the main text of his ten-volume *Study* to a close! This is an extraordinarily grotesque mishmash even for a theologian. The prayer begins (*A Study*, X, pp. 143 f.):

"Christe, audi nos.

Christ Tammuz, Christ Adonis, Christ Osiris, Christ Balder, hear us, by whatsoever name we bless Thee for suffering death for our salvation.

Christe, Jesu, exaudi nos.

Buddha Gautama, show us the path that will lead us out of our afflictions.

Sancta Dei Genetrix, intercede pro nobis.

Mother Mary, Mother Isis, Mother Cybele, Mother Ishtar, Mother Kwanyin, have compassion on us, by whatsoever name we bless thee for bringing Our Saviour into the World."[18]

The prayer ends:

"Sancta Maria Magdalena, intercede pro nobis.

Blessed Francis, who for Christ's sake didst renounce the pride of life, help us to follow Christ by following thee.

'So,' he [viz. Toynbee] says at the end of his preface, 'history passes over into theology.' And one can only sigh, 'Again!' "

I don't suppose that Toynbee is any better at theology and prophecy than he is at history, since he has now given up Christianity as the source of salvation for mankind and has substituted for it—it is almost embarrassing to mention it—that good old fossil of his, no, not the Parsees, or the Monophysite Christians, or the Nestorian Christians, or the ex-Nestorians, or the Lamaistic Mahayanian Buddhists, or the Hinayanian Buddhists, or the Jains, but—the JEWS!!!

[18] The prayer goes on to invoke Michael and Mithras ("fight at our side in our battle of Light against Darkness"), Angels and Archangels and "All ye devoted bodhisattvas," John the Baptist and "Noble Lucretius," *"Omnes Sancti Patriarchae et Prophetae"* and "Valiant Zarathustra, breathe thy spirit into the Church Militant here on Earth," St. Peter and "Tenderhearted Muhammad . . . ," St. Paul and "Blessed Francis Xavier and Blessed John Wesley," John and "Blessed Mo-ti," the Apostles and the Evangelists and "Strong Zeno . . . Pious Confucius," Stephen and "Blessed Socrates," Martyrs, Gregory and "Blessed Açoka," Augustine and Jalal-ad-Dīn Mawlãna, "singing reed," *Sancta Pater Benedicte* and Epicurus, *Sancte Antoni* and Marcus, and Monks and Hermits.

Most of this litany was reproduced in H. A. Grunwald's article, "The Mapping of a Great Mind," for *Life* (Nov. 29, 1954, pp. 87–90, 95–98). Even in this sympathetic, journalistic article, the litany is described as "a strange conglomeration."

Omnes Sancti et Sanctae Dei, intercedite pro nobis;
For *ilayhi marji'ukum jami'an:* to Him return ye every one. (Qur'ān x. 4)

Finis
London, 1951, June 15, 6.25 P.M., after looking once more, this afternoon, at Fra Angelico's picture of the Beatific Vision."

Two acts are noteworthy here for us: (1) Not one specific person in the entire Old Testament is invoked, with or without an *intercede pro nobis.* Squeezed in between John the Baptist and Lucretius on the one hand and Zarathustra and Peter on the other are "the patriarchs and prophets." (2) The litany closes with a passage from the Quran, not from the Hebrew Bible, which happens to abound with sentiments of this kind.

It is clear that Toynbee is irrationally disposed against the Jewish people, ancient, medieval, and present. He was not able to overcome this irrationality and, within his scheme of things, recognize the Jewish people as a Society. Having thus precluded the use of any form of any of the terms Hebrew, Israel, and Jew, he set about finding a term that would cover over this notable Society. In all probability he hit on the term Syriac from its significance in Moslem literature. The simple fact that the Ancient Near East never knew a Syriac Society and that no competent scholar today recognizes such a Society—in short, the truth—was of secondary account. The whole concept is but the figment of the imagination of one who recognizes virtually no good in the remarkably long and varied and fruitful career of Israel.

Shushan Purim, 5722 (March 20, 1962)

This essay was completed on Purim Day. I could not go to a museum to look at a painting, say, Chagall's Rabbi of Vitebsk or one of Rembrandt's Jews; but in my mind there did run through the thought that, just as Haman is remembered on this day only by the Jewish people, it may, ironically, well be that many, many years from now the author of *A Study* will be remembered not as a historian, or even as a theologian or a prophet, but as a—confessedly "ignorant" and "irrational"—disparager of the Jews, and remembered only by the Jews.

[Ten years after this essay first appeared, one may well ask, "Does anyone read Toynbee anymore as a historian?"

A pity indeed that the serious study of history had to be set back even for a few years by the success of the Madison Avenue publicity gimmicks in promoting Toynbee's *Study*. It should have been evaluated on essentially the same level that Toynbee's *Amazon* was noticed in the Book Review Magazine of the New York *Times,* Sunday, Nov. 6, 1967, p. 32. The four-paragraph notice, from which I quote the following, said everything that had to be said:

> Twenty-three pages into this undistinguished and overpriced travelogue, Arnold Toynbee offers this socio-economic comment: "I do not know what the truth is about the Church's past social record in North-Eastern Brazil. But the number and beauty of the churches in Recife are evidence that, in the past, the Church did not distribute all its funds to the poor." He then proceeds to discuss, not the social record, but the beauty of the churches. That, alas, is typical of the book. Toynbee descends on Latin America like a leaky Colonel Blimp, and gives off mostly gas.
>
> More time is spent chronicling the perils of air-travel and the derring-do of his pilot than examining the problems of the eleven countries he visits. And when he does attend to business, he is usually banal or wrong: "Salvador may be poor, but it is smiling." . . .
>
> . . . Then, at the end, he proposes dumping all the statues of San Martin, O'Higgins, and Bolivar into the Atlantic, Pacific and Caribbean, and substituting for them "replicas of the Christ of the Andes and pictures of the Virgin of Guadalupe." Latin America needs a little something more than Toynbee provides here. . . .]

13

The Story of Hanukkah—
What Really Happened

To MANY JEWS the Story of Hanukkah is a simple story about the religious persecution in Judea by a villain named Antiochus, the Syrian King, and of the heroic resistance led by the Hasmonean family, Mattathias and his five sons. The truth is, however, that the origin of the Hanukkah story is more complex than that. History as a rule is a complicated affair, involving national and international, political and economic factors, as well as religious ones.

The history of Hanukkah, as it has come down to us, is found, of course, in the Books of the Maccabees and in the writings of Josephus. Recent researches, however, especially by Prof. Solomon Zeitlin of Dropsie College in Philadelphia, and Avigdor Tcherikover of the Hebrew University in Jerusalem, help to reconstruct for us the Maccabean story in its true historical perspective.

_____

[During his brief tenure as Registrar of the Jewish Institute of Religion—he was its Instructor in Education from 1945 until his untimely passing in 1955—Rabbi Michael Alper conceived the idea of having members of the faculty write popular articles on timely subjects; he would then see to it that the articles, constituting a service to the Jewish community, reached the Anglo-Jewish press of the United States and Canada for publication—and for favorable publicity for the Institute. This account of "The Story of Hanukkah," written in November, 1947, is one of these articles, and it was reproduced rather widely in the Jewish press.]

Judea Caught Between Two Empires

After Alexander the Great, who conquered the Near Eastern world, died in 323 B.C.E., the vast Hellenistic (or Greek) Empire fell apart. One of Alexander's generals, Seleucus, came into control of Southwest Asia with headquarters in Antioch in Syria, and another general, Ptolemy, took over Northeast Africa with headquarters at Alexandria in Egypt. This happened 2,250 years ago.

Judea, the small Jewish state situated between these two rival empires, became a pawn in their hands. In the course of their struggle for power, the Seleucid and Ptolemaic dynasties entered into various treaties with one another and with others. Thus, by a treaty of 303 B.C.E. Judea and coastal Phoenicia were ceded to Ptolemy of Egypt. Two years later, however, in 301 B.C.E., in accordance with a new treaty, these two lands were ceded to Seleucus of Syria. Thus the Jewish people in Palestine were caught up in an imperialistic tug of war. How did they react to this situation?

Two Groups Among the Jews

One group of Jews, whose leader was the High Priest in Jerusalem, believed in playing off one imperialist power against the other, while working vigorously at the same time to preserve and develop the Jewish way of life. This pro-Jewish group was economically powerful, partly because the High Priest's office controlled the market of Jerusalem and through it much of the city's economy.

The Temple in Jerusalem derived its revenue not only from the Jews in Palestine but also from the Jews in the Diaspora. Ever since the beginning of the Babylonian Exile in 586 B.C.E. and even after the Edict of Liberation issued in 538 B.C.E. by Cyrus of Persia who conquered Babylonia, the bulk of dispersed Jewry was to be found in the areas north and east of Palestine, the territory that came to be governed later by the Seleucid dynasties. However, over the centuries a notable shift in Jewish population occurred. By 190 B.C.E. the Jews of Egypt, especially of Alexandria, had increased considerably in population and influence. Not only that, but the increasing disintegration of the Syrian Empire made travel for gift-bearing Jewish pilgrims to the Temple in Jerusalem a hazardous and forbidding affair.

For these reasons, the ruling group in Judea as represented by the Temple officials began to side more and more with the Ptolemaic court in Egypt, rather than with their political rulers, the Seleucid court in Syria.

The Hellenist Jews

However, there gradually grew up in Judea another group of "substantial" Jews who were anxious to exercise political power befitting their economic status. They were the tax-collectors led by the Tobias family, with headquarters in Jerusalem. They waxed economically powerful by ruthlessly collecting the heavy taxes (ceded by Antiochus III to Ptolemy V of Egypt after 192 B.C.E.) imposed by the Ptolemaic government of Egypt on the peoples of Judea and nearby lands. For payment they received a sizable share of these taxes.

The Jews of this group were in constant contact with the Ptolemaic and Seleucid courts whose favor they curried. And so they acquired the Hellenistic outlook on life, changed their names from Hebrew to Greek and spoke Greek instead of Hebrew. They became fond of the athletics which were so prominent a feature of Hellenistic life and they wanted very much to build a gymnasium in Jerusalem. It was not that they were so much interested in sports. More than that was involved. According to the law of that time, a city which received permission to erect a gymnasium could also strike its own coinage, and those who frequented the gymnasium were regarded as citizens.

But despite their amassed wealth, this Hellenizing group could not gain the political power which the pro-Jewish group held. So one of their representatives bribed King Antiochus IV of Syria with a considerable sum of money and thereby got Jason (Greek for Joshua) appointed High Priest in place of his brother, Onias III. Subsequently they erected a gymnasium in Jerusalem and struck their own coinage. Moreover, they then became "Citizens of Antioch" instead of members of the Jewish nation.

This assimilationist movement gained momentum. Jason, who proved to be somewhat on the conservative side, was soon replaced by Menelaus (Greek for Onias), a member of the Tobias family. By 170 B.C.E. the Hellenization and suppression of Judaism was in full swing. Judaism might gradually have disappeared in this period, but as fate would have it, Antiochus IV of Syria became an instrument for Jewish survival. In 169–168 B.C.E. the Syrian regime embarked upon the conquest of Egypt. In the process they overran Jerusalem and Judea and resorted to force in an effort completely to Hellenize the country. They prohibited the observance of the Sabbath, the dietary laws, circumcision, and daily sacrifices in the Temple. They defiled the Temple by ordering swine and other unclean animals to be sacrificed on the altar.

Thus the policies of the wealthy Hellenizers, the assimilationists who started out by exploiting their own people in behalf of a foreign imperialist power, led to the total enslavement of the entire people, not only economically and politically, but culturally and religiously as well. These wealthy assimilationists were the quislings of the time, serving their masters abroad to the detriment of their own people.

The Hasidim

Many Jews, however, refused to become paganized. They defied the commands of Antiochus and the quislings. They continued to observe the Sabbath, the dietary laws, the rite of circumcision. These loyalists, known as Hasidim, "the Pious," would rather die than give up their religion. Many of them did make the supreme sacrifice. They were the first martyrs in recorded history.

The Hasidim, however, were rebels but not revolutionaries. They argued that it was a sin to bear arms on the Sabbath, even though the fate of the Jewish people and their religion was at stake. It was then that Mattathias, the son of Hasmoneus, a priest of Jerusalem who lived in the nearby town of Modin, entered the scene. Mattathias argued that the Sabbath was made for the Jews and not the Jews for the Sabbath, and that to transgress a Sabbath was as nothing if it made possible the observance of all the Sabbaths thereafter.

The Hasmonean revolt, especially under the astute leadership of Mattathias' son, Judah the Maccabee, gained some initial military successes. The road to Jerusalem was opened up. Parts of Judea and of Jerusalem were liberated; and exactly three years after it had been defiled, the Temple was purified and rededicated to God. This was on the 25th day of Kislev, 165 B.C.E.

The chief general of the Syrian army, Lysias, took over personal command, and set out to punish the rebel Jewish forces. In the meantime, however, the Syrian King, Antiochus IV, died, and Lysias was compelled to make a hasty peace with the Jews and return to Syria at once in order to prevent a rival general from gaining the throne.

Two Views on Peace Terms

The peace terms offered by Lysias made provision only for religious freedom, not for economic and political independence. The Hasidim had never shown interest in more than religious freedom, so when the peace terms of Lysias granted them that freedom, they gladly accepted the terms.

Judah and his faction, however, held out for political and economic independence, but he was outvoted; so he and his forces withdrew from Jerusalem to continue the struggle.

The Hasidim Betrayed

Within a few years after the celebration of the first Hanukkah, and with Lysias scarcely out of sight, the new High Priest appointed by Lysias, Alcimus (who preferred this Greek form of his Jewish name, which was Eliakim), removed from office most of the Hasidim, and had some 60 of them executed. Those who had been Hellenizers, or their supporters, were brought back into power. Only then did the Hasidim realize the terrible mistake they had made when they accepted Lysias' terms. In desperation, they turned to Judah for leadership a second time. Once again civil war broke out in Judea, between the upperclass Hellenizers and the common people who had the sweet fruits of victory cruelly snatched from their hands.

Fearful that his group would not defeat those who sided with Judah, Alcimus called upon Syria for help. A powerful Syrian army came, defeated Judah's forces, and killed Judah himself on the battlefield. This happened in 160 B.C.E., a short five years after the first Hanukkah.

The Struggle Prolonged

If all was not yet lost, it was due largely to the wisdom of Judah's brothers, Jonathan and Simon. They knew that the great mass of Jews would now, more than ever before, refuse to submit to the Syrian yoke which the Jewish Hellenizers were helping to tie around their necks. The now popular Maccabean-led forces kept harassing their own Jewish betrayers and their Syrian overlords.

At that time, civil war, with the blessings of Rome and Egypt, broke out in Syria also. The Jews took full advantage of this development to press hard against the enemy. Jonathan came to power in 150 B.C.E., and nine years later, in the year 141 B.C.E., the Jewish people convened a Great Synagogue, voted a Declaration of Independence from the Syrian yoke, constituted themselves a Jewish Commonwealth, and appointed Simon as the head.

Thus, we see that liberation for the Jewish people in Judea 2,088 years ago did not come about merely from a rededication of the Temple. The loyalists among the Jews had first to break the political and economic shackles imposed upon them by foreign powers and simultaneously had to destroy the sources of power of their own quisling assimilationists, before they could establish true religious freedom. The Hanukkah or rededication of the Temple was merely an incident and a symbol of a faith triumphant.

14

The Dead Sea Scrolls
and Mr. Green

IT WAS ABOUT NOON on Thursday, July 1, 1954. My wife and I had
driven in earlier that morning from our home in Bensonhurst, Brooklyn, to Grand Central Station in Manhattan, with our two sons, Velvel
and Zeke, and saw them off for their summer at Camp Derry in Lon-
donderry, Vermont. Our car was now packed with the sundry things
that we'd need for a fortnight's trip to Toronto, my wife was seated
in the car, and I was closing the door with key in hand to lock it when
the telephone rang. (Everyone knows that it usually does in such
circumstances.) We looked at each other: should I answer the phone
or not? We were impatient to get away, and we had made reservations
at a motel in Red Hook, N.Y. for late afternoon. After the third or
fourth ring, I went back to answer the phone.

It was Yigael Yadin, speaking from the office of Avraham Harman,
Consul-General of Israel in New York City. He was overjoyed to be
able to reach me. I must come over to the Consulate at once. It was
something extremely important and urgent.

But I was less than enthusiastic about the idea. What could be so
important that only I could perform whatever service it was that Yadin
and Harman had in mind? Could it be that Yadin wanted me to take
over the rest of his United Jewish Appeal or Israel Bond or similar

lecture tour in the country? Nothing like that. I then asked, face-tiously, whether I was needed for some military action; the reply was that it was more important than that. I must come over immediately! I told Yadin that I'd need a minute or two to talk it over with my wife, while he held the phone. My wife and I decided that if Israel needed me for whatever it was, we had no choice but to give it the benefit of any doubt that we might have. I told Yadin that we were coming over at once—unless the phone rang again—and we were assured that another reservation would be made for us for the night en route to Toronto.

We arrived at 11 East 70 St. in Manhattan at about 1 p.m. I advised my wife to take a walk or go shopping for about an hour, and I entered the building of the Israeli Consulate. Harman and Yadin were waiting for me impatiently, and they took me up to the main office on the second floor to tell me what the matter was all about. The matter was about the Dead Sea Scrolls; and once again my wife's intuition proved correct. She had thought of the scrolls as the reason for the telephone call from Yadin, but I had dismissed this as too unlikely.

Exactly a month earlier, on Tuesday the 1st of June, Monty Jacobs, the (London) *Jewish Chronicle* Staff Correspondent in New York, was told by an American colleague that he had seen "a small announcement tucked away in the advertising columns" of that day's issue of the *Wall Street Journal.* On p. 14, under the heading " 'Miscellaneous For Sale,' among scores of other commercial and business advertisements, was a small two inch by two inch paragraph." The advertisement ran:

THE FOUR DEAD SEA SCROLLS

Biblical manuscripts dating back to at least 200 B.C. are for sale. This would be an ideal gift to an educational or religious institution by an individual or group. Box F. 206, the WALL STREET JOURNAL.

Unable to get any additional information about the advertisement from the Executive Editor of the *Journal,* and reminding himself that Yadin and his wife had just arrived in this country on a speaking tour for the United Jewish Appeal, Jacobs telephoned Yadin and asked him whether he had seen or heard about the advertisement, and what did he think of it. Yadin became excited by the news. No, he knew nothing about it. Would Jacobs come up at once to his room, on the thirtieth floor of the St. Moritz Hotel, and bring a copy of the *Journal* with him.

As soon as he read the advertisement, Yadin decided that he must acquire these four scrolls, that the only proper home for them was Israel. He had frequently thought of them, ever since his father, Prof. Eleazar Lippe Sukenik, founder and head of the Hebrew University's Department of Archaeology, had "experienced" them, and several others along with them, in the late Forties. For it was in the very midst of those historic months in 1947-48, when the British were abandoning Palestine and its Jewish inhabitants to the Arab population and the Arab nations round about, and when the Jews were preparing desperately to fight not alone for a Jewish State within the country but at the same time for their very lives—it was then (beginning with Sunday the 23rd of November, 1947) that Sukenik first learned of the scrolls, and on several occasions thereafter he literally endangered his life to examine them and acquire them. Yadin relates (pp. 19 f.) how he reacted when his father asked him whether he ought to go to Bethlehem to examine the scrolls; this was on Friday, Nov. 29:

> What was I to tell him? As a student of archaeology myself, I felt that an opportunity of acquiring such priceless documents could not be missed. On the other hand, as Chief of Operations of Haganah, I knew perfectly well the dangers my father would be risking in travelling to Arab Bethlehem. And as a son I was torn between both feelings. I tried to hedge, but, before leaving, son and soldier won and I told him not to go. I bade him and my mother *shalom* and left for Tel-Aviv. Fortunately, my father disregarded my advice and next morning left for Bethlehem. But I did not discover this until later.

At this point it is worth quoting a bit from Sukenik's private journal (as recorded by Yadin, pp. 21 ff.):

> I had planned to meet my Armenian friend again on November 28, and go with him to the Arab antiquities dealer [in Bethlehem]. But

my wife had been particularly adamant against my going, in view of the danger. . . . my son, Yigael . . . too, indicated, though not as vehemently as his mother, that perhaps it was not too wise . . .

Later in the evening I listened to the radio and heard that the United Nations, which had been expected to vote on that day, had postponed its decision. Here I thought was my chance. For I believed that the Arab attacks would begin immediately after the vote . . . I therefore resolved to make the journey [to Bethlehem] next morning, the 29th, and this time I decided not to tell anyone.

Next morning I telephoned my Armenian friend and told him that I was coming over to see him right away. Armed with my pass I entered Zone B once again . . .

We took the bus. I was the only Jewish occupant. The rest were Arabs. All of us felt the tension in the atmosphere. My friend told me later that he had been really scared stiff . . .

When we arrived in Bethlehem, we made straight for the attic of the Arab house in which the antiquities dealer, Feidi Salahi, lived . . . He . . . brought out two jars, in which the bundles [of scrolls] had been found, which he offered for our inspection. They were of a shape unfamiliar to me. He then carefully produced the leather scrolls. My hands shook as I started to unwrap one of them . . . I . . . told the dealer that I was much interested, would probably wish to buy, but I should like to take them home for further scrutiny . . . He agreed and wrapped the scrolls in paper. Tucking them under my arm we parted with friendly salaams.

Descending from the attic, my Armenian friend and I made our way to the Bethlehem market place where the Jerusalem bus was filling up. All around were groups of Arabs, some sullen and silent, others gesticulating wildly. I don't think it was imagination that made me sense a heightened tension in the atmosphere, but there was no incident. The package under my arm must have looked like a bundle of market produce. We entered the bus and reached Jerusalem safely. At the Jaffa Gate we got off and my companion let out a deep sigh of relief . . . I went home and sat reading the manuscripts. In the morning I had resolved to buy them, though it took another day before I was able to telephone my Armenian friend and instruct him to inform Feidi Salahi that I was buying the scrolls.

While I was examining these precious documents in my study, the late news on the radio announced that the United Nations would be voting on the resolution that night . . . I was engrossed in a particularly absorbing passage in one of the scrolls when my son [Mati] rushed in with the shout that the vote on the Jewish State had been carried . . .

The scrolls mentioned here by Sukenik and purchased by him for the Hebrew University were three in number; they were "The War of the Sons of Light against the Sons of Darkness," "The Thanksgiving Psalms" (*Hodayot*), and the partial "Isaiah Scroll" (later designated number "2").

There was frustration too. In the midst of all this excitement, Sukenik learned from two independent sources, an official of the Hebrew University and a member of the Syrian Orthodox Christian Community, that several scrolls had come into the possession of Mar Athanasius Samuel, Metropolitan of the Syrian Monastery of St. Mark in the Old City. Briefly put (see pp. 25 ff. of Yadin's account for the fascinating details), Sukenik got to these scrolls and recognized them to belong to the batch that he had acquired in Bethlehem. However, because of the extreme difficulty in communication—thus "One day towards the end of January 1948," Sukenik has noted, "I received a letter from the Arab quarter of Jerusalem. It had taken three days to come from the other side of the city"—and the lack of ready funds for purchasing the new batch of scrolls, negotiations between the Metropolitan and Sukenik dragged. This provided the Metropolitan the opportunity to make contact with the American Schools of Oriental Research in Jerusalem. Assured that the scrolls would fetch considerably higher prices in the United States and fearful of what the consequences of the war between the seven Arab nations and the State of Israel might be for the scrolls, the Metropolitan up and left the country with these documents and came to the United States. He deposited them in a vault of the Trust Company of New Jersey in Journal Square, Jersey City, and waited for a more opportune day to dispose of the scrolls.

Sukenik was broken-hearted that these scrolls were no longer available to Israel; as he put it, "the Jewish people have lost a precious heritage." A pity that when he died in 1953, he had no inkling that exactly one year later his son Yigael would be given the opportunity of acquiring this "precious heritage." And small wonder that Yadkin was determined to make this acquisition.

The scrolls had become a major problem for the Metropolitan. Even though Israel had beaten back the Arab armies that had threatened to annihilate her, she was yet compelled to share the city of Jerusalem with Jordan. But the Metropolitan could hardly return to his Monastery in the Old City, precisely because it was in the hands of Jordan; for the Jordanian Government regarded itself as the sole legal owner of these scrolls and could scarcely be expected to condone what it considered to be the arbitrary and illegal removal of these antiquities from her territory.

On the other hand, it had become increasingly apparent to the Metropolitan that the huge sums that the four scrolls in his possession had been expected to bring from eager buyers—sums in the millions of dollars were talked about, and hardly ever less than a million—would not materialize. An important reason for this, perhaps the major reason, was the widely known fact that any purchaser, be it an institution or an individual person, would immediately be subject to possible legal proceedings by the Government of Jordan, perhaps in one of the International Courts in The Hague, on the grounds of having purchased stolen goods, the property of the Government of Jordan. In the meantime, the cost of storing the scrolls, insuring them, and the like, could not be ignored, and positive steps had to be taken to sell them for whatever reasonable price could be agreed upon. Hence the advertisement in the *Wall Street Journal*.

But would the Metropolitan knowingly sell the scrolls to the Israeli Government? Hardly; and this worried Yadin. And would the Israeli Government purchase the scrolls, knowing that it might well be subjecting itself to a lawsuit at the hands of a Government which had not signed a peace pact with it? Well, yes. For the Government of Jordan would in effect be recognizing the State of Israel as a legal entity if it haled it into court as an equal partner in a lawsuit, plaintiff vs. defendant. That alone might well have prompted Israel to attempt the acquisition of the scrolls.

Yadin was known personally to the Metropolitan. The scrolls had to be examined at first hand and vouched for by someone who had worked on the texts and had direct knowledge of their appearance;

also, he had to be personally unknown to the Metropolitan, so that no link with the State of Israel might be suspected. It was my task, Yadin told me, to examine the scrolls to make sure that they were the ones that had been advertised for sale, the ones that his father had examined in the YMCA building in Jerusalem in January-February 1948 and wanted so desperately to purchase. At the same time, I was to avoid being identified.

The plan was as follows. I was to assume the name "Mr. Green," an expert on behalf of the client. I was to take a taxi to the Lexington Avenue entrance of the Waldorf-Astoria Hotel, where the Chemical Bank and Trust Co. had a branch. I was to make sure that I was not followed. A Mr. Sydney M. Estridge would be waiting there for me; we had been told how to identify one another. He would go with me downstairs to the vault of the Bank. There we would find a representative of the Metropolitan, with the scrolls ready for examination. I was to say as little as possible, and admit to no identification beyond being Mr. Green.

As I remember it, the vault was stuffy and hot, and inadequately lit; I had the feeling that the electric fan in action was distributing a lot of hot air evenly in the closed dusky room. I saw a large black trunk on the floor; it reminded me for some reason or other of the trunk from whose inside Harry Houdini, the great American stage magician, would emerge triumphantly even though both he and the trunk were securely bound. Out of this trunk, however, there emerged four scrolls. The most important and impressive of them was the Isaiah Scroll, all sixty-six chapters of it. It was cleverly set up for display and examination, in the form of a sandwich. The scroll was placed between two transparent plastic sheets so that either end could be unrolled simply by pulling the other end, the parchment sliding through smoothly between the plastic sheets.

The text of this Scroll was far from unknown to me. Several years earlier, even before it was reproduced by the American Schools of Oriental Research (1950), the text had been made available to the members of the Committee that was responsible for the Revised Standard Version of the Old Testament; we were working at the time on the final draft of Isaiah. But, unknown to the Metropolitan's representative (a Christian Arab merchant from Boston), or to Mr. Estridge, there was a problem in the text of the Isaiah Scroll that I was determined to solve; when would I again have the Scroll so directly at my disposal? The problem involved the reading of the final word in 43.19, namely, whether the Scroll read *netivot* or *netivim,* "paths" (in place of traditional *neharot,* "rivers"); for the views of W. F. Albright, M. Burrows, J. C. Trever, and myself (with reference to P. A. H. de Boer and D. Barthélemy, O.P), see my comment on "Photography and Paleography in the Textual Criticism of St. Mark's Isaiah Scroll, 43:19," on pp. 33-35 of the *Bulletin of the American Schools of Oriental Research,* No. 123, October 1951. (Ironically, none of us realized at the time that what could readily have decided whether the word in the Scroll ended in *-ot* or in *-im* was the vowel letter that preceded the final consonant; the vowel letter was clearly a *waw* [o] and not a *yod* [i], but we had not yet learned that the *waw* and the *yod* in the Isaiah Scroll were clearly distinguishable.)

Since our passage (43.19) was to be found two-thirds from the beginning of the scroll, I kept asking the merchant to keep unrolling the scroll, that is, keep pulling the right end. After a while he became impatient, and perhaps suspicious. He wanted to know who I really was, and why I insisted that the scroll be unrolled almost to the end, and couldn't I tell from the increasing number of columns that had already been exposed for me that the scroll was the original Isaiah Scroll that had created such a sensation in the scholarly and lay world when it was first announced six years earlier? In reply I sort of mumbled that I'd like to make sure that the scroll was intact and undamaged.

When I was through examining the Isaiah Scroll, I turned to the scroll known as the *Pesher* (Exposition) of Habakkuk. From the edition of this scroll published by the American Schools of Oriental Research (in the same volume with the Isaiah Scroll) and a number of studies which discussed it, I was aware of the sensational conclusions that had been drawn by some scholars—and popularized far and wide by a journalist, from a couple of passages—verses 7-8 (where the Scroll exhibited a serious gap in the text) and 14-15 (where the text was quite obscure) in chapter 2. The conclusions had it that the text of the passages—when the imagination filled in the gap in the first and forced a certain interpretation upon the second—referred to a person who was crucified under circumstances that paralleled and recalled some aspects of the traditional account of the crucifixion of Jesus. (No one mentions this nonsense any more.)

I examined the Habakkuk Scroll in general and these two passages in particular, but I came away no wiser: the gap in the first passage and the interpretation of the second remained as tantalizing and elusive as before. However, I noted that a piece of the manuscript at the right hand corner and containing several words was missing. Search was made on the spot for the missing fragment, unsuccessfully. (I was informed later that it was found subsequently, amid some cotton batting in the trunk.)

The third scroll that I examined was the Manual of Discipline (sérekh ha-yáḥad). The fourth scroll I could not examine, because it was not possible to unroll it in its current condition. It had been designated by some scholars as the long-lost Apocalypse of Lamech, because a piece of it (about 4¾" x 8½") had been removed several years earlier and the name Lamech (lmk) was inscribed in various contexts on the inner surface. I tried to unroll a bit more of the scroll at the point where the "Lamech" piece had been removed. (For I was most doubtful that sufficient data existed for the identification of the unopened scroll as the Apocalypse of Lamech, and I insisted on adding to the name the qualifying phrase "So-called." This scroll turned out to be what scholars have designated as "The Genesis Apocryphon.") But the merchant intervened angrily, and with justification; after all, I could be damaging a piece of material that was worth thousands of dollars.

After a final but unrewarding search for the piece missing in the Habakkuk Scroll, I left the vault. I went immediately to a telephone booth and phoned the Israeli Consulate at an unlisted number; if everything was as hoped for, I was to use as a code (as I now recollect it) the single word le-ḥayim. I used the code word agreed upon, replaced the receiver, and went outside to take a taxi back to the Consulate. I was to be sure that I wasn't being followed; if I had any suspicion, I was to leave the taxi at some intermediate point and take another taxi.

Meanwhile, back at the Consulate, unknown to me, another bit of drama was taking place. My wife returned from her brief walking-windowshopping trip, saw a "Press" card inside the front windshield of our car, waited a while for me to appear, and then decided to go into the building of the Consulate and wait in the lobby for me to come down from the office upstairs. A bit later, she went outside again to wait for me. Growing increasingly impatient, she went in again, and asked the receptionist to check with Mr. Harman or Dr. Yadin whether Dr. Orlinsky was still with them.

The receptionist telephoned upstairs, and soon Yadin came bounding down the stairs, welcomed my wife enthusiastically, and asked her to come up to the office. My wife was surprised that I was not with Harman and Yadin in the office, having no idea at all as to what had been transpiring. She declined the offer of coffee, and heard Yadin say to Harman that Mr. Green should be calling any minute.

At that very moment the telephone rang, and Yadin jumped up to answer it. It was not, however, the call they had hoped for, and Yadin turned to Harman and told him that it was not Mr. Green; then he turned to my wife and told her that everything was all right and that Mr. Green would call momentarily. My wife could not understand what she had to do with a Mr. Green, and became worried when she was told that everything was "all right." But she said nothing and waited. Yadin in the meantime was pacing restlessly up and down the office. Finally, the phone rang. This time it was Mr. Green, calling from the Waldorf-Astoria. Yadin answered it, heard my rather brief report, and cried out excitedly to Harman, "Mazal Tov!" He then turned to my wife and said, "That was Harry. Everything is OK. He'll be here soon."

Yadin and Harman began to work up a statement for me to sign. Knowing of my independent evaluation of the scrolls, my wife was a bit apprehensive about my readiness to sign a statement not my own. When I arrived at the Consulate and entered the office, there was much rejoicing, and I was handed the statement for my approval and signature. I changed an item or two (e.g., the "so-called" Lamech Scroll) and I indicated that I had not seen the fragment that belonged to the beginning of the Habakkuk Scroll. The statement that I signed read as follows:

Dear Mr Yadin,

This is to inform you that I examined this afternoon the 4 DSS which formed the subject of negotiations between Mr Sydney Estridge and the representatives of the Archbishop Samuel of the Syrian Church, Jerusalem. I made a detailed inspection of the scrolls and compared them with the official reproduction published by the American Schools of Oriental Research, New Haven, edited by Professor Millar Burrows. I am satisfied that the scrolls, which formed the subject of the above negotiations, are the authentic 4 DSS referred to and reproduced in the a/m work by Professor Burrows and that they are complete. There is one reservation to the above, to which I immediately drew the attention of Mr S. M. Estridge, namely that the right hand fragment of the first page of the Habakkuk Commentary reproduced on Pl. 55 ((columns 1, and 2a) of the Millar Burrows volume I is missing. The 4th Scroll, so-called Lamekh scroll, is still unrolled. There are two fragments of it separately.

With that, we bade one another *shalom* and *kol-tuv* and *le-hitra'ot*, and my wife and I drove off, without the "Press" card, for Red Hook and Toronto. We had been sworn to secrecy, absolute secrecy, until all four scrolls had reached their destination in Israel safely. It was not easy for us not to breathe a word about all this to my sisters and brother in Toronto or to our two sons.

The $250,000.00 for the purchase of the scrolls, I was to learn later, was made possible by a substantial loan from the American Fund for Israel Institutions (popularly known as the "Norman Fund," Edward A. Norman being its founder and current president; later it became the America-Israel Cultural Foundation); the loan was arranged by its director, Itzhak Norman, with the considerable assistance of a member of the Board, Samuel Rubin. As for the repayment of the loan, Yadin tells us that Mrs. Rebecca Shulman, noted leader of Hadassah, introduced him to her co-worker in Hadassah, Mrs. Esther Gottesman, who—now also very excited about the whole matter—arranged a meeting with her brother-in-law, Samuel Gottesman, who ultimately agreed to contribute the major part of the money required.

The scrolls were flown by airplane to Israel one at a time. Each scroll was given a code name in Hebrew, and as they reached Israel one by one Harman sent to Yadin—who was then traveling by boat to England—such cables as " 'Simcha leaving today'—Simcha being the Manual of Discipline—followed by 'Simcha arrived safely'; followed in turn by 'Chaim leaving today' and 'Chaim arrived'. By the time I reached London, the whole of my 'family' had arrived in Israel."

As I look back upon the whole episode, what remains uppermost in my mind is the smoothness with which the operation, planned largely by Yadin with the fullest cooperation of Harman, worked. From the very beginning, when he was first informed of the advertisement in the *Wall Street Journal,* until the very end, when he was in London and received a cable from Teddy Kollek (then Director-General of the Prime Minister's office in Jerusalem, now Mayor of Jerusalem), on February 13, 1955, to the effect that

> At this memorable moment the Prime Minister [Moshe Sharett] is telling the country and the world about the homecoming of the scrolls. Excitement and joy are great,

Yadin's plan worked smoothly in the manner that has become his trademark as archaeologist and administrator.

Bibliographical note

Yigael Yadin's account of the Israeli purchase of the scrolls in the United States constitutes Chapter 3 ("Destiny") of his book, *The Message of the Scrolls* (Simon and Schuster, 1957, pp. 39-52); Chapters 1 and 2 (respectively "Discovery: the Hebrew University" and "The Monastery of St. Mark," pp. 15-30 and 31-38) provide interesting and instructive background for the account. Monty Jacobs published his version of "Israel's Purchase of the Dead Sea Scrolls" in The (London) *Jewish Chronicle,* Feb. 18, 1955, pp. 19 f.

15

The Canonization of
the Bible and the
Exclusion of the Apocrypha

THE BIBLE represents the main, but not the total literary output of ancient Israel. For apart from the literary creations which perished in their oral or written form—for example, the major portion of the "Book of the Wars of the Lord" and the "Book of Jashar"—there have been preserved no less than about thirty books which the Jews produced during the approximately five centuries which intervened between the formation of most of the Bible and that of the Mishnah (i.e., between the 3rd century B.C.E. and the 2nd century C.E.).

[My interest in the Hebrew Canon was much stimulated by the formation of a Board of Editors, on December 24, 1946, at the Dropsie College, that was charged with the task of recovering the original Jewish meaning of the non-canonical, Apocryphal literature; thus the series *Jewish Apocryphal Literature* came into being.

A shorter and more popular essay of mine on the Canon appeared in the February 1973 (XVIII, 5) issue of *Keeping Posted,* under the title "The Making of the Hebrew Bible." The present essay begins with the first paragraph of an article that I wrote for the World Encyclopedia Institute of New York—the Encyclopedia never materialized—and which was printed on p. 1 of *In Jewish Bookland,* Vol. 4, 4 (March-April, 1948).]

The Hebrew Bible consists of three main divisions: the Five Books of Moses (Pentateuch), the Prophets, and the Writings (Hagiographa)—in Hebrew, respectively: *Torah* ("the Law"; or *Ḥumash*), *Nevi'im*, and *Ketuvim*—and hence the popular Jewish term for the whole Bible, *TaNaKh* (*Tanakh*). When did these divisions come to be recognized as constituting the Sacred Scriptures, writings that were revealed or inspired by God?

I. *The Canonization of the Hebrew Bible*

The composition of the Torah from the time that its earliest parts came into being orally until most of it was written down—from about the 18th to the 5th centuries B.C.E.—covered a period of over one thousand years. This material came to be regarded as forever binding upon the Israelite community—and upon their descendants after them—in stages, only a few of which are known to us. Thus Exodus 24.3-7 tells us:

> ³Moses went and repeated to all the people all the commands of the Lord and all the rules; and all the people answered with one voice, saying, "All the things that the Lord has commanded we will do!" . . .⁷ Then he took the document (Hebrew *séfer,* traditional "book") of the covenant and read it aloud to (or: in the hearing of; literally: in the ears of) the people. And they said, "All that the Lord has spoken we will faithfully do!" [1]

The Hebrew expression "to read . . . in the ears of the people" (*qara' . . . be-'ozne ha-'am*), sometimes followed by an expression of consent by the people, describes the biblical procedure in designating a document as official and binding, in

---

[1] Scholars have generally designated this document as the "Book of the Covenant," which deals with what we call today civil and criminal legislation, ritual rules, and humanitarian prescriptions; it is found in Exodus 20-23 and 34. The literature on this is very considerable; see, e.g., O. Eissfeldt, *The Old Testament: An Introduction,* ed. P. R. Ackroyd (New York, 1965), § 33, pp. 212-219, 746.

other words, as divinely inspired, as Sacred Scripture. Thus, in line with Ex. 24.7 quoted above, when the document that the priest Hilkiah said he came upon accidentally in the Temple (about 621 B.C.E.) was read by the scribe Shaphan to King Josiah (II Kings 22-23), the king—in order to make it officially binding upon all Israel—summoned

> ^{23 1}. . . all the elders of Judah and Jerusalem. ²The king went up to the House of the Lord, together with all the men of Judah and all the inhabitants of Jerusalem, the priests, the prophets, and all the people (*we-kol-ha-'am*), young and old. And he read aloud to them (or: in their hearing: *wa-yiqra' be-'oznehem*) all the words of the document of the covenant that had been discovered in the House of the Lord. ³And the king . . . confirmed the covenant . . . and all the people entered into the covenant.

Another instructive instance of "canonization" may be noted in Jeremiah 36.1-10, where we read:

> ¹. . . the following command came to Jeremiah from the Lord: ²Get yourself a scroll and write on it all the words that I commanded you concerning Israel, Judah, and all the nations . . .⁴ Jeremiah summoned Baruch son of Neriah. Baruch wrote down in the scroll at Jeremiah's dictation all the words that the Lord had spoken to him. ⁵Then Jeremiah gave this order to Baruch: "I am in hiding; I cannot go to the House of the Lord. ⁶So you go and read aloud from the scroll the words of the Lord that you wrote at my dictation in the hearing of the people (*be-'ozne ha-'am*) in the House of the Lord on the fast day; moreover you shall read them in the hearing of all the Judeans (*be-'ozne kol-yehudah*) who have come from their towns . . ." ¹⁰Baruch read from the document (*ha-séfer*) the words of Jeremiah . . . in the hearing of all the people . . .

Small wonder that the rejection of this official document by King Jehoiakim and his government (about 600 B.C.E.) brought on terrible retribution at the hands of God (vv. 23-24 and 30):

[23]And as Yehudi finished reading three or four columns (of the scroll), he cut it up with a scribe's knife and threw it into the fire that was in the hearth, until the entire scroll was consumed in the fire that was in the hearth. [24]Neither the king nor any of his courtiers who heard all these words were frightened or rent their garments.

[30]Therefore thus said the Lord concerning King Jehoiakim of Judah: He shall have no descendant occupying the throne of David, and his corpse shall lie exposed to the heat of the day and the cold of the night.

From Nehemiah 8.1-6 we learn that the Torah was formally declared Sacred Scripture in the days of Ezra-Nehemiah (5th century B.C.E.):

[1]All the people gathered as one man into the square in front of the Water Gate and asked Ezra the Scribe to bring the document of the Torah of Moses . . . [2]Ezra the priest brought the Torah before the assembly . . . [3]and read from it . . . from early morning until noon in the presence of the men and women . . . and [in] the hearing of all the people . . . [6]Ezra then blessed the Lord, the great God, and all the people replied, "Amen, Amen!" . . .

In this connection the so-called Letter of Aristeas is instructive. After telling the reader in some detail how the Septuagint (Old Greek) translation of the Torah was made, this Alexandrian Jewish document of the early 2nd century B.C.E. goes on to describe how this Greek version was made authoritative, i.e., canonized (§§ 308-311):

When the work (of translation) was completed, Demetrius assembled the community of the Jews . . . and read it out to the entire gathering . . . [Then] the priests and the elders of the translators and some of the corporate body and the leaders of the people rose up and said, "Inasmuch as the translation has been well and piously made and is in every respect accurate, it is right that it should remain in its

present form and that no revision of any sort take place."
When all had assented to what had been said, they bade
that an imprecation be pronounced, according to their
custom, upon any who should revise the text by adding or
transposing anything whatever in what had been written
down, or by making any excision . . .

It will be apparent at once that every important aspect of the
"canonization" of the Septuagint is biblically derived: "the
community of the Jews," the reading out of the translation "to
the entire gathering," the presence of "the leaders of the
people," and the unanimous "assent to what had been said." [2]

The Bible makes reference to and quotes from certain documents that can no longer be identified and whose "canonical"
status is unknown; they might well be called "lost books." Thus
Numbers 21.14-15 reads:

Therefore the Book of the Wars of the Lord (*séfer mil-
hamoth YHWH*) speaks of[f] ". . . Waheb in Suphah, and the
wadis: the Arnon [15]with its tributary wadis, stretched along
the settled country of Ar, hugging the territory of Moab . . ."

And following v. 16 ("And from there to Beer, which is the

---

[2] Even the phraseology is biblical. Thus, e.g., the expression "(. . . and the
leaders of the people) rose up and said" (Greek *stántes... ei'pon),* on which
the comment is sometimes made, "ROSE UP contributes to the solemnity," is
nothing more than Hebrew *wa-yaqúmu wa-yo'mru* "they proceeded to say;
thereupon they said" (lit: they rose and said). The Hebrew verb *qum* does
not imply here that they had been sitting or squatting, nor was it meant to
introduce solemnity—the whole section is solemn enough; it is the occasional
biblical use of *qum* (and similar verbs, e.g., *bo'* "enter," *halakh* "go") as an
auxiliary verb (see, e.g., Orlinsky, *Notes on the New (J.P.S.) Translation of
the Torah* [1969], Introduction, pp. 34 f.).
  The translation of the *Letter* employed here follows essentially that of
M. Hadas, *Aristeas to Philocrates* (Dropsie College Edition, *Jewish Apocryphal Literature,* 1951), pp. 220-223. On the *Letter* and the Septuagint in
recent literature, see my essay "The Septuagint . . ." elsewhere in this volume
and the reference there to S. Jellicoe's work.

well where the Lord said to Moses, 'Assemble the people that I
may give them water' ") we read (vv. 17-18):

> [17]Then Israel sang this song:
> Spring up, O well—sing to it—
> [18]The well which the chieftains dug,
> Which the nobles of the people started
> With maces, with their own staffs.

And finally—apparently still from the Book of the Wars of the
Lord—vv. 27-30:

> [27]Therefore the bards would recite:
> "[k] Come to Heshbon, it is built firm;
> Sihon's city is well founded.
> [28]For fire went forth from Heshbon,
> Flame from Sihon's city,
> Consuming Ar of Moab,
> The dominant heights of the Arnon.
> [29]Woe to you, O Moab!
> You are undone, O people of Chemosh!
> His sons are rendered fugitive
> And his daughters captive
> By an Amorite king, Sihon."
> [30] [m] Yet we have cast them down utterly,
> Heshbon along with Dibon;
> We have wrought desolation at Nophah,
> Which is hard by Medeba.[3]

The famous quotation in Joshua 10.12, when Israel's military
chief sought to complete the defeat of the Amorites:

> Sun, stand still at Gibeon,
> And moon—in the Valley of Aijalon!

---

[3] The translation of the three passages cited from the Book of the Wars of
the Lord is that of the New Jewish Version of *The Torah*. Notes *f, k,* and *m*
warn the reader that the Hebrew text and the meaning of these ancient fragments are obscure and uncertain.

is cited from the Book of Jashar (*séfer ha-yashar,* v. 13). And the same Book is cited for the equally notable Lament of David over Saul and Jonathan (II Samuel 1.17-27). And how marvellous it would be if the Royal Chronicles of the Kings of Israel and Judah came to light, from which the archival data in the Books of Kings and Chronicles were often drawn (see, e.g., II Kings 1.18; 8.23; and frequently).

Some time before 200 B.C.E. the second major division, the Prophets, came into being. This is evident from the Prologue to the Greek translation made about 120 B.C.E. by the grandson of Jesus son of Eleazar son of Sirach (Greek form of Hebrew-Aramaic Sira) of his grandfather's Hebrew work, known as the Wisdom of Ben Sira or Ecclesiasticus (not to be confused with biblical Koheleth-Ecclesiastes). In this Prologue the grandson clearly uses the Greek expressions for "Law" and "Prophets" (Hebrew *Torah and Nevi'im*) in a manner that indicates that he knew of two—and only two—definite divisions of Holy Writ:

> Whereas many great teachings have been given to us through the Law and the Prophets and the other (books) that followed them . . . my grandfather Jesus [the Greek-Latin form of Aramaic *Jeshu'a,* Hebrew Joshua], after devoting himself especially to the reading of the Law and the Prophets and the other books of our fathers . . . You are urged therefore to read with good will and attention, and to be indulgent in cases where, despite our diligent labors in translating, we may seem to have rendered some phrases imperfectly. For what was originally expressed in Hebrew does not have exactly the same sense when translated into another language. Not only this work, but even the Law itself, the Prophecies, and the rest of the books differ not a little as originally expressed . . .

And in his work proper, the section (Chapters 44-49) which begins with the well-known line,

> Let us now praise the famous men
> And our fathers in their generations,

Ben Sira discusses in succession the more famous men in the Torah (Enoch, Noah, Abraham, Isaac, Jacob, Moses, Aaron), Joshua (and Caleb), the Judges, Samuel, Kings (Nathan, David—including a reference to Psalms—Solomon, Rehoboam, Jeroboam, Elijah, Hezekiah, Josiah), Isaiah, Jeremiah, Ezekiel, the Twelve (Minor) Prophets, Zerubbabel, Joshua the High Priest, and Nehemiah.

The same bipartite division is indicated in another document, one whose composition is variously dated from the second century B.C.E. on the one hand to the first century C.E. on the other, namely, II Maccabees. While this document is far less reliable historically than, say, I Maccabees, the following statement is nevertheless pertinent (2.13-14):

> The same things [viz., those dealing with the nature of proper sacrifice] are reported in the records and in the memoirs of Nehemiah, and also that he founded a library and collected the books about the kings and the prophets, and the writings of David, and letters of kings about votive offerings. [14]In the same way Judas also collected all the books that had been lost on account of the war which had come upon us, and they are in our possession.

Having mentioned earlier in the chapter that the prophet Jeremiah, "after giving them the Law, instructed those who were being deported [from Judah to Babylonia] not to forget the commandments of the Lord . . . And . . . exhorted them that the Law should not depart from their hearts" (vv. 2-3), it seems probable that the phrase "the books about the kings and the prophets" refers to Joshua-Kings and Isaiah-Minor Prophets— what we sometimes call the Former and the Latter Prophets— and the "writings of David" refers to the book of Psalms.

This grouping of the Prophets with the Torah and the lack of a tripartite division are to be found also in such varied sources,

covering a period of about three centuries, as the early manuscripts of the Septuagint, the early first century Alexandrian
Jewish philosopher Philo, the New Testament, and Josephus.
With regard to the Septuagint—the data are readily available in
H. B. Swete, *An Introduction to the Old Testament in Greek*
(2nd ed. revised by R. R. Ottley [1914; reissued by KTAV,
1968], "Titles, Grouping, Number, and Order of the Books,"
pp. 197-230)—it has been insufficiently noted in our connection that the earliest manuscripts of this Alexandrian Jewish
product of the last two centuries or so B.C.E., which contain a
number of books not found in the Hebrew Bible, never manifested a tripartite division.

As for Philo—in his treatise *On the Contemplative Life*
(Chapter III, §25), where he deals with a Jewish sect of ascetic
hermits, the Therapeutae, he notes in passing how they brought
into their rooms, for study only,

> the Laws, and the Words (Oracles) prophesied by the
> Prophets, and the Psalms, and the other Writings by which
> knowledge and piety may be increased and perfected . . .

Luke 24.44 put it this way:

> Then he [Jesus, appearing among his disciples after rising
> from the dead] said to them, "These are my words which I
> spoke to you, while I was still with you, that everything
> written about me in the Law of Moses and the Prophets and
> the Psalms must be fulfilled."

Finally, and interestingly, it has not generally been noted that
even Josephus, the noted Jewish historian of the first century,
knows no third division by name—a clear indication that a
specifically named third division either had not yet come into
being or had but recently been designated and was not yet
widely known. This is what Josephus wrote about 90-95 C.E.
in his work *Against Apion* (Book I, §§ 37-40):

> For we do not have myriads of books among us, disagree-
> ing from and contradicting one another [as the Greeks
> have], but only 22 Books, which contain the records of all
> past time and are justly accredited. Of these, 5 are [the
> Books] of Moses . . . the Prophets who subsequent to Moses
> recorded the history of the events of their times in 13
> Books. The remaining 4 Books contain hymns to God and
> precepts for the conduct of human life . . .

(On the identity of—more correctly, the problem of identifying—the 13 Books of the Prophets and the "Remaining 4
Books" that Josephus had in mind, see below.)

The evidence, then, seems clear and consistent that from
about the third century B.C.E. to well into the second half of
the first century C.E. the Bible knew only two main divisions,
the Torah and the Prophets; at the same time, there were other
Books—the book of Psalms is the only one specified by name—
that were already regarded as belonging to the category of
Sacred Scripture.[4]

We are less certain, however, of precisely when and the cir-

---

[4] On p. 140 (and the notes there) of his acute essay, "An Historical Study
of the Canonization of the Hebrew Scriptures" (in *Proceedings of the
American Academy for Jewish Research*, 1931-32, pp. 121-158)—now reproduced in his *Studies in the Early History of Judaism*, 2 vols. (KTAV, 1973/4)
—S. Zeitlin has cited a passage in Tosefta Kelim, Baba Meṣia V, 8 that states:
"The Book of Ezra [=the Torah; sometimes also called "The Book of the
Azarah" *sefer 'zr' / 'zrh*] when it was taken outside the Azarah in the Temple
defiled the hands. This was true not only of the Book of Ezra but also of
any Books of the Prophets or of the Pentateuch (*nevi'im we-ḥumashim*) or
of any of the other Books (*we-sefer 'aḥer*) brought inside the Azarah; they
defiled the hands." Zeitlin has correctly noted the use of *sefer 'aḥer* here in
relation to the phrase "the other books" in the Prologue to Ben Sira (see
above), which may be compared with the expression "the other Writings"
in Philo. In other words, this passage in Tosefta Kelim would, again, point
to the then recognized bipartite division of the Hebrew Bible.

It need scarcely be pointed out that if certain Greek writers made use of
the Septuagint translation of certain Books that later came to be designated
as members of the Third Division (see, e.g., Swete, pp. 369 ff.), that does
not mean—any more than a reference to Nehemiah on the part of Ben Sira,
or a reference to Psalms on the part of Philo or Luke, or the citation of
Ps. 79. 2-3 in II Macc. 7.17—that a third division was in existence.

cumstances under which the third division, *qua* division, came into being. One possibility is the occasion of the meeting of the two main groups in Judea at the time, the Hillelites and the Shammaites, in the home of Hananiah ben Hezekiah, just before the destruction of the Temple (70 C.E.). Another possibility is the occasion, in 90 C.E., when Eleazar ben Azariah was appointed head of the Academy at Jabneh. In any case, our main source for the determination of the third division derives from Mishnah Yadayim, III:5:

> All the Holy Writings defile the hands. (The books of) Song of Songs and Koheleth defile the hands. Rabbi Judah said, "Song of Songs defiles the hands, but Koheleth was in dispute." Rabbi Jose said, "Koheleth does not defile the hands, and Song of Songs was in dispute. ". . . But Rabbi Akiba said, "God forbid! No man in Israel disputed the fact that Song of Songs defiles the hands, for the entire world does not compare with the day that Song of Songs was given to Israel. All the (Books of the) Writings are holy, but Song of Songs is the holiest of all. If there was a dispute, it was only about Koheleth" . . .

But before entering into a discussion of the two Books, Koheleth and Song of Songs, specifically mentioned in the Mishnah and others not mentioned—and before discussing in this connection several problems raised by the statement quoted above from Josephus—two disparate matters might be dealt with.

Firstly, there can be little doubt that in keeping with the book of Psalms, such Books as Proverbs, Job, Ruth, Lamentations, Daniel, Ezra, Nehemiah, and Chronicles had come to acquire widespread authority even though they had not yet become members of a specific division and were referred to—when they were referred to at all—by such vague phrases as "(the Law and the Prophets) and the other [books] that followed them . . . (the Law and the Prophets) and the other books of our fathers . . . (the Law itself, the Prophecies,) and the rest of the books . . ." (Prologue to Ben Sira), and "(the Law, and the Words/Oracles prophesied by the Prophets,) and the Psalms, and the other writings . . ." (Philo), and ". . . (Books of the Prophets or of the Pentateuch) or any of the other Books . . ." (Tosefta Kelim; see n. 4).

For as Psalms was associated with King David (and had become part of the Temple service), so was Proverbs associated with King Solomon, Job with the Patriarchal period, Ruth with the era of the Judges, Lamentations with Jeremiah and the destruction of the First Temple, Daniel with the end of the Assyrian Empire (late 7th century B.C.E.), Ezra and Nehemiah with the restoration of Judah and the Temple and the authority of the Torah, and Chronicles with the canonical Books of Samuel and Kings. At the same time, there was nothing substantive in any of these Books that would arouse opposition on the part of any Judean group, that would preclude canonization.

Secondly, the expression "the Holy Scriptures defile the hands" (*kitbe ha-qódesh metamme'in 'eth-ha-yadáyim*) had come to replace the biblical phrase "and they read in the hearing of the people" to indicate canonization, that the Book in question was indeed divinely inspired, Holy Writ. This change of phrase is already employed in connection with Hillel and Shammai toward the turn of the Era, when the Second Jewish Commonwealth was beginning to come to a close. Since *halakhah,* the rule of law, had become the norm in Jewish life, the new expression accorded more with the new situation than the older phrase did.[5]

Coming back to the Mishnah. The text begins clearly with the statement (in the second century C.E., though the dates of some of the sages create some chronological difficulty): ". . . Song of Songs and Koheleth were part of the Canon (defile

---

[5] On the origin and function of the expression "the Holy Scriptures defile the hands," I know of no discussion that has superseded the brilliant analysis by S. Zeitlin in his "An Historical Study," etc., cited in n. 4 immediately preceding, especially § 3 on pp. 135-141.

the hands)." However, the text continues, at one time there had been a dispute about their qualification for canonicity. Rabbi Judah (Rabbi Jose, in Megillah 7a) said that Song of Songs had been declared canonical, but Koheleth's claim had been in dispute. Rabbi Jose (Rabbi Meir, in Megillah 7a), on the other hand, asserted that Koheleth had been excluded, and that Song of Songs had been in dispute—to which Rabbi Akiba retorted that Song of Songs had never been in dispute, and that if there had been a dispute at the time, it was concerning Koheleth alone. Rabbi Akiba's brother-in-law (lit., the son of R. Akiba's father-in-law), Rabbi Johanan son of Joshua, said that (Simeon) ben Azzai's version was the correct one (viz., according to Megillah 7a: the Shammaites rejected Koheleth, though the Hillelites favored its inclusion). Rabbi Simeon ben Azzai further stated: I have a tradition stemming from the Seventy-two Elders that on the day that Rabbi Eleazer ben Azariah was made head (of the Academy) Song of Songs and Koheleth were declared canonical ("defile the hands").

What emerges from this Mishnah is that the third and final division—in which only Koheleth and Song of Songs proved troublesome—was achieved in the last third of the first century C.E. And this accords perfectly with all the data available from the other sources discussed previously.

But the term for the third division had not yet been determined. As we saw above, three general terms were employed during the several centuries between the third-second centuries B.C.E. and the first century C.E. for books that ultimately became part of the fixed third division, namely, "other (or: the rest of the) books" (e.g., Prologue to Ben Sira; Tosefta Kelim), "other writings" (Philo), and "sacred writings" (e.g., Mishnah Yadayim). Finally, it was the shorter term *ketubim* "writings" that prevailed in the Judean-Palestinian Jewish tradition, whereas the term *kitbe ha-qodesh* "sacred writings," Greek(-English) *hagiographa,* prevailed in the Alexandrian-Jewish—and thence

Christian—tradition. These terms will not become fixed, however, until the second century C.E.[6]

It has too often been overlooked that when Ben Sira's grandson and Philo and Luke and Josephus used the term "Prophets," it is hardly the same Prophets that the Judean Jewish tradition recognized in the Second Division. Josephus talks of thirteen Books in the Prophets (as against the traditional Judean number of eight: Joshua, Judges, Samuel, Kings, Isaiah, Jeremiah, Ezekiel, and the Twelve Minor Prophets). Indeed, Ben Sira himself mentions the book of Psalms (in connection with David) and Nehemiah (immediately after Zerubabel and Joshua the High Priest); and from the order of the books as found in the earlier manuscripts of the Septuagint (see pp. 201-214 in Swete), which—as against the Hebrew original—in practice constituted for them the Bible, it is clear that the Jewish community of Alexandria had a tradition (later to become the Christian tradition) according to which such books as Ruth, Chronicles, Job, Ezra and Nehemiah, and Daniel were listed among the Prophets. Accordingly, since all of them were either part of the Alexandrian (rather than Judean) Jewish tradition or knew the Bible essentially from its—again Alexandrian—Septuagint version, Ben Sira's grandson, Philo, Luke, and Josephus regarded as belonging to the Prophets, the second division, books that came to be listed in the third division of the Hebrew Canon.

Further, no one can be certain which were the 22 Books that Josephus regarded as "justly accredited"; actually, of course, the number of "problem" Books is not 22 but 17 (13 of the Prophets and 4 of hymns to God and precepts), since the 5 Books of Moses are clearly spoken for. As for the number "22," it may well be that scholars have introduced a fiction that has come to be all but accepted as virtual fact, namely

---

[6] A more intensive study of this matter of technical terminology may prove useful, though the pertinent data appear to be few and sporadic.

that by "22" Josephus meant "24," the number of Books in the Hebrew Canon. I have never seen any justification for this juggling of numbers, other than the desire—and hence the assumption—to make Josephus's list accord with subsequent Jewish tradition.

Not only that, but a second assumption—with no authority behind it—had to be resorted to, namely, not only that the 22 were really 24 but that the 2 books not counted by Josephus were Ruth and Lamentations, since "He has probably . . . treated Ruth and Lamentations as appendices to Judges and Jeremiah respectively" (Swete, p. 320). Since neither those (especially H. E. Ryle) upon whom Swete relied for this assumption nor the many scholars who have accepted it after him[7] have made any serious attempt to prove the assumption as reasonably justified, we may well be dealing here with an essentially nineteenth century scholarly fiction.[7]

There does not appear to be much merit in attempting the identification of the 4 Books of Hymns and Precepts and thus also the 13 Prophets. According to most scholars (see the references offered in n.7 above), Josephus's 4 Books consisted of Proverbs, Song of Songs, Psalms, and Ecclesiastes. Zeitlin has suggested that the 4 are Proverbs, Song of Songs, Ruth, and Lamentations. I should prefer Proverbs, Song of Songs, Psalms, and Ezra-Nehemiah—on the grounds that Psalms had an early and consistent tradition as being outside the Law and the Prophets (Prologue to Ben Sira, Philo, and Luke) and Nehemiah was clearly mentioned by Ben Sira—an influential authority—following on the Twelve Minor Prophets (in which Books only Zerubbabel and Joshua the High Priest are mentioned by name;

---

[7] Cf. in general, e.g., H. E. Ryle, *The Canon of the Old Testament* (London, 1895), Chapters VI-VIII, X, XII; F. Buhl, *Canon and Text of the Old Testament* (Edinburgh, 1892), Chapter I; O. Eissfeldt, *Introduction,* 559 ff.; A. C. Sundberg, Jr., "The Old Testament: a Christian Canon," *Catholic Biblical Quarterly,* 30 (1968), 143-155; G. W. Anderson, *The Cambridge History of the Bible,* Vol. I (1970), ed. P. R. Ackroyd-C. P. Evans, "Canonical and Non-Canonical," pp. 113-159.

50.11-13); further, unlike Psalms and Ezra-Nehemiah, neither Ruth nor Lamentations would fall readily into the category of Hymns to God or of Precepts for the proper conduct of human life.

In short, whether Josephus's 22 Books are literally 22 or in reality 24, the problem of identifying his 13 Prophets and his 4 "remaining Books" remains, and it requires a separate solution.[8]

If Josephus's total of 22 Books is taken literally—and there is no inherent reason that I know of for not doing so—it was obviously lacking two Books that ultimately came to constitute part of the Third Division of the Hebrew Canon. Which two Books were they? It would seem that the two Books in question were Koheleth and Esther.

For the book of Esther is not only not mentioned specifically by anyone prior to the second century C.E. as canonical—thus Melito, bishop of Sardis (about 170 C.E.) does not mention the Book,[9] and Esther is the only Biblical Book whose text is not represented even by a fragment of a Dead Sea Scroll—but it is hardly the kind of story that is easily associated with Divine Inspiration. Nowhere in the Book is the name of God

---

[8] Since much work has been done in the attempt to determine the Septuagint text that Josephus employed, I made a cursory examination of the grouping and order of the books as listed in the manuscripts (Swete, 201 ff.; Jellicoe, 286-288, 293); however, I did not become the wiser therefrom.

[9] This is as good a place as any to note Zeitlin's caveat (p. 134, n.53)— for too many scholars keep overlooking this—that the Church Fathers "were outsiders" and that "their testimony ... must be taken with a grain of salt." And where their statements derive from the Septuagint manuscript they happened to have at hand, those statements are less than decisive. Eusebius (*Church History*, IV, 26 end) quotes Bishop Melito to the effect that while in the East he inquired as to which books constituted the Hebrew Bible. Whoever served as his source(s) of information, the fact is that it is not only Esther but also Lamentations that is lacking in his List (at least as it is preserved in the manuscripts of Eusebius's text), and the grouping and order of the Books are foreign to any Jewish tradition otherwise known to us and probably derive from a Septuagint manuscript: The Five Books of Moses; Joshua, Judges, Ruth, Kings 1-4, Chronicles 1-2, Psalms, Proverbs, Ecclesiastes, Song of Songs, Job, the Prophets (Isaiah, Jeremiah, the Twelve, Daniel,

mentioned, and it is not God who is petitioned for help against Haman and his evil group; rather, it is Esther herself and her sex appeal that bring deliverance to the Jews of Susa and the Persian satrapies—Esther, a Jewish girl who became the wife of a Gentile![10] (Contrast, at virtually every single point, the heroine of the book of Judith; as to why this book was excluded from the Bible and had to find a home among the Apocrypha, see below.)

There is additional, independent evidence that Esther had not yet become part of the Third Division during the first century C.E. The argument and data are presented cogently by Zeitlin on pp. 132-134 of his "Study of Canonization." Briefly

---

Ezekiel), and Ezra. If Melito—as preserved in Eusebius—were our only, or chief, source for the absence of Esther from the Hebrew Canon, our argument would be less than convincing. So that when Swete states about Melito's list (p. 221), "Esther does not appear, but the number of the books is twenty-two, if we are intended to count 1-4 Regn. as two," the fact is that Lamentations is likewise missing, and Melito's list comes to only 21 books. There is no scholarly merit, or justification, to make the unprecise data and statements in such sources as Melito conform to our later traditions and fixed beliefs or preferences. Incidentally, Melito is quoted as having used the phrase "the Law and the Prophets"; no third division is designated by him by name. His source was probably not Judean-Jewish but Septuagint-Christian (i.e., Alexandrian-Jewish originally).

[10] The picture would be incomplete and one-sided if it were not pointed out here that the book of Esther is basically not a God-less Book and had long been read by pious Jews annually on Purim. After all, why did "Mordecai the Jew" refuse to bow low in awe before Haman, and to what God was he loyal, if not to the God of Israel from whose Holy Land he derived (Esther 2.5-6; 3.1 ff.)? And when Esther told Mordecai that the Jews of Susa should fast for three days, just as she herself and her maidens would fast, prior to the desperate attempt to confront the king and save her fellow Jews from extermination, to whom were they to fast if not to the God of Israel? And what distinguished the Jews from all other non-Persians in the vast Persian Empire, if not the fact that they worshiped their own and unique God? And to whom did the Jews express their joy at being saved, and how did many of the non-Jewish inhabitants of the land become Jews (*mithyahadim,* 8.17), if the God of Israel wasn't involved? Nevertheless, it is a fact that the name of God has not been preserved in the Book; indeed it seems to have been very carefully avoided. Did the Name come to be expunged by the Jews, for whatever reason, only subsequently? Contrast, e.g., the central role of God, specifically, in the (Jewish) Septuagint additions to the Book of Esther. There seems to be room for interesting research here.

put, the Festival of Purim is mentioned along with the other minor, semi-holidays recorded in Megillat Taanit (first century C.E.); our Festival would not have been recorded there had the book of Esther been canonical. So that when the rabbis of the second century C.E. justified Purim as a day of rejoicing, a day on which fasting was forbidden, it was Megillat Taanit, not the book of Esther (8.15-17) that was cited as authority. It was only later, when the book of Esther had entered the Hebrew Canon that the Book was cited as authority for the Day of Purim as a festival day, one on which no regular work was to be done.

The book of Esther had long been read on the Day of Purim, though it had not been canonized; as put in Megillah 7a, "(the book of) Esther was composed by divine inspiration to be read (berúah ha-qódesh ne'emrah, ne'emrah liqroth) (on the Day of Purim) but not to be written down (we-lo' ne'emrah likhtob)." It offered the sort of tale that naturally became increasingly popular among the Jewish people in proportion to the troubles and disasters they experienced, e.g., during the Maccabean struggle for Judean sovereignty and survival; incidentally, Purim was called "the Day of Mordecai" in II Macc. 15.36. Occasions such as the destruction of the Second Temple and the collapse of the Bar Kokhba revolt at the hands of the forces of Emperor Hadrian set the stage for public pressure to bring the book of Esther formally into the Canon; it is put as follows in Megillah 7a: "Esther petitioned the sages: Record me (i.e., my Book) for posterity (qib'úni le-doroth)."

There was no formal canonization of the Book by the rabbis, and not all the rabbis accepted the Book as canonical at the same time; so that no formal dispute about Esther—as about Song of Songs and Koheleth—is recorded. That is why a sage such as Samuel could assert in the third century C.E. (Megillah 7a): "(the book of) Esther does not defile the hands," i.e., is not canonical; and why Bishop Melito of Sardis a generation or two earlier did not record Esther among the Books of the

Hebrew Canon—since his source of information did not include it.

The Hebrew Canon has remained closed ever since the book of Esther was brought into it.

As for Koheleth, the tone is set in the very first verses:
Utter futility! . . . All is futile!
What gain is there for a man
For all his toil under the sun?
One generation goes, another comes,
But the earth remains the same forever. (1.2-4)

Nature and man—the whole universe—moves unceasingly and aimlessly in circles, with rhyme perhaps but with no reason. This theme is repeated elsewhere in the Book, in various ways, for example, 7.15-17:

In my own futile life I have seen everything: sometimes a just person dies even though he was just, and sometimes a wicked person lives long even though he is wicked. Do not be over-just . . . do not be over-wicked . . .

Or compare 9.3:

That is the sad thing about all that goes on under the sun: that the same fate befalls everyone.

Consequently, as put in 9.7-10:

Go, eat your bread in gladness and drink your wine in joy . . . Enjoy life with a woman you love all the days of your futile life . . . for there is no doing or thinking, no knowing or learning in Sheol where you are going.

Or as mehitabel the alley cat put it to archy the cockroach in the classic by Don Marquis: "wottahell, archy, toujours gai."

If, however, Koheleth succeeded in the end in acquiring the authority to "defile the hands," it was because authorship of the

Book was associated with Solomon, and an acceptable ending was appended (12.13, repeated):

> The sum of the matter, everything having been heard: Fear God and obey His commandments. For this is the duty of all mankind.

The Song of Songs merits a word or two in connection with canonization. Certainly the Book could hardly have been expected to qualify as Holy Writ, as divinely inspired. It is, after all, to begin with a collection of love poems. In this unsophisticated and elaborate language, the physical and emotional qualities of the two lovers are described in some detail:

> Oh that he would give me the kisses of his mouth;
> For your love is better than wine! (1.2)

> Upon my couch at night
> I sought the one I love—
> I sought, but found him not.
> ... When I found the one I love,
> I held him fast, I would not let him go
> Till I brought him to my mother's house,
> To the chamber of her who conceived me. (3.1-4)

> Ah, you are fair, my darling,
> Ah, you are fair.
> Your eyes are like doves
> Behind your veil.
> Your hair is like a flock of goats
> Streaming down Mount Gilead ...
> Every part of you is fair, my darling,
> There is no blemish in you. (4.1-7)

> Eat, lovers, and drink;
> Drink deep of love. (7.1)

But Song of Songs, fortunately, was declared divinely inspired and part of Sacred Scripture on the basis of two arguments: its composition was attributed to King Solomon (as were Proverbs and Koheleth) and the lovers were interpreted to represent God and Israel; that the Book was probably quite popular among the people at large did not hurt the argument.

II. *The Exclusion of the Apocrypha*

The Apocrypha—the twelve-fourteen or so books that became part of the Old Testament in the early Church and have remained so in the Roman Catholic Bible, but which during the 16th-17th centuries came to be excluded by the Protestant Church from its Old Testament—failed to gain canonical status in the Jewish community of some 1900 years ago for one (or both) of two main reasons: the accepted date of composition and the conflict with the *halakhah* as it was interpreted by those who decided the matter of canonicity.[11] The names and order of the books called Apocrypha are listed as follows in the Revised Standard Version:

I Esdras
2 Esdras
Tobit
Judith
Additions to Esther
The Wisdom of Solomon
Ecclesiasticus, or the Wisdom
    of Jesus the Son of Sirach
Baruch

The Letter of Jeremiah
The Prayer of Azariah and
    the Song of the Three
    Young Men
Susanna
Bel and the Dragon
The Prayer of Manasseh
1 Maccabees
2 Maccabees

The matter of chronology at once ruled out books such as

---

[11] The term Apocrypha, from Greek *'apókrupha* ("hidden") and corresponding to the early rabbinic term *sefarim ḥiṣonim* ("books outside [the canon]"), although used, e.g., already by St. Jerome (died 420) and several predecessors and younger contemporaries, became especially meaningful from the Reformation on; see, e.g., the discussion (which deals also with the term "pseudepigrapha," in C. C. Torrey, *The Apocryphal Literature: A Brief Introduction* (New Haven, 1945), Part I (pp. 3-40).

The total number of books constituting the Apocrypha comes to twelve in the Authorized (King James) Version of 1611 and to fourteen in the Revised Standard Version (1957), according to whether some of the smaller "books" are listed separately or combined with one another.

Ecclesiasticus (Ben Sira) and I and II Maccabees from consideration for canonicity. After the priestly group acquired supremacy in postexilic Judea (after the secular head, Zerubbabel, disappeared from the scene and Joshua the High Priest became sole head of the state, with the "advice and consent," of course, of the Persian overlords), the status of anyone who claimed that he received revelation, and hence authority, directly from God—in other words, one who claimed to be imparting prophecy, like the old-fashioned prophets—was drastically diminished.[12] Henceforth, it was the established and growing priestly bureaucracy, deriving its authority from the received Law of Moses, that comprehended and executed the will of God. Subsequently, the Judean community entered a new stage, in the Hellenistic period, when the theocratic state was replaced by a commonwealth and when the Torah constitution was reinterpreted by the liberal Pharisees in accordance with the new conditions. Henceforth it was the *halakhah* as the Pharisees comprehended it, it was the Torah of Moses as the Pharisees interpreted it and applied it in their attempts to introduce changes in Judea's social structure, that prevailed. To underestimate the role of the *halakhah* in Pharisaic thought and activity is tantamount to failing to understand the history of the latter part of the Second Jewish Commonwealth. It is no exaggeration to assert that the Judaism which the Pharisees developed maintained a profound influence on all phases of

---

[12] The following passages may be cited to indicate the dictum that prophecy ceased in Israel early in the Persian period: I Macc. 4.45-46 (see also 9.27 and 14.41), discussing the Maccabean purification of the Temple, describes how "(they tore down the altar and stored the stones in a suitable place on the Temple mount) until a prophet should come to decide what to do with them"; Yoma 9b reads: "...after the last prophets, Haggai, Zechariah, and Malachi died, the Holy Spirit departed from Israel (*nistalqah ruaḥ ha-qodesh mi-yisra 'el*) ..."; and see below the expression *mi-kan we-'elekh* "from that time on"=when prophecy ceased in Israel (Tosefta Yadayim) in reference to the post-prophecy date of composition of Ben Sira.

A description of the Jewish theocratic state in graphic form may be seen on p. 244 of my *Understanding the Bible through History and Archaeology* (KTAV, 1972).

Jewish life during the two thousand years which have followed, and is a potent factor in Judaism and in Israel today.

In the case of Ecclesiasticus (Ben Sira), the book itself—apart from the Prologue by Ben Sira's grandson ("...my grandfather Jesus ... I came to Egypt in the thirty-eighth year of the reign of Eurgetes ...")—is witness to the fact that its date of composition is late; cf., e.g., the reference to "Simon the High Priest, son of Onias, who in his lifetime repaired the House and in his time fortified the Temple..." (50.1 ff.). Having been composed in the Hellenistic period, after prophecy had ceased, the book was inadmissible to the canon; as put by the rabbis (Tosefta Yadayim, II, 13): *sifre Ben Sira we-khol sefarim she-nikhtebu mi-kan we-'elekh 'enan metamme'in eth-ha-yadayim* "the book of Ben Sira and all books composed from then on do not defile the hands."

I and II Maccabees are even more self-evident than Ben Sira. I Maccabees begins with "After Alexander (the Great) son of Philip the Macedonian ... had defeated King Darius of the Persians ...," and II Maccabees 1.7 ff. reads: "In the reign of Demetrius, in the 169th year [= 143 B.C.E.] ..."

Books such as Judith, Susanna, and Tobit, even after several careful readings, do not readily offer adequate reason for failing to achieve canonicity. Thus in contrast to the book of Esther, the book of Judith had every reason to expect to enter the canon.

Because all the nations in the West, Judah among them, had refused to join him in his attack on King Arphaxad of Ecbatana (Media), King Nebuchadnezzar of Nineveh (Assyria) vowed to inflict terrible punishment upon them. He dispatched a powerful army headed by his chief general, Holofernes, and soon it stood, flushed with uninterrupted victory, at "the edge of Esdraelon, near Dothan," ready to continue his mission of revenge, "so that all nations should worship Nebuchadnezzar only, and all their tongues and tribes should call upon him as god" (3.8-9). In fear of the result but with unwavering faith in God, the Jews prepared their defenses. Holofernes was enraged by their refusal to submit to him peaceably, but Achior, leader of the Ammonites who had submitted to the general, explained to him that as long as the Judeans remained loyal to their God, "their Lord will defend them, and we shall be put to shame before the whole world" (5.21). Undeterred by Achior, Holofernes prepared for action against the Jews, stopped their water supply, and gave them five days in which to surrender.

When her fellow Jews decided to capitulate if God did not intervene, Judith, a beautiful widow of whom "no one spoke ill . . . for she feared God with great devotion" (8.8), took it upon herself to fight God's battle rather than put Him to the test. She prayed fervently to the Lord, and then set out with her maid for the camp of the enemy with her own food and drink. She gained access to the private tent of Holofernes, and on the fourth night, when Holofernes lay on his bed in a drunken stupor, she cut off his head and returned with her maid to her community. Needless to add, the Assyrian army, now dispirited, was routed, and Judea was saved. As for Achior, when Judith returned with Holofernes' head and told him what had transpired, "he believed firmly in God, and was circumcised, and joined the house of Israel, remaining so to this day" (14.10).

Judith exhibits virtually every positive Jewish quality that Esther lacked—perhaps that is one of the reasons why it was written in the first place—and the book was, on the surface, composed at a time (in pre-Persian days) when prophecy flourished in the land; that the book was probably composed in the Hellenistic period, when Jewish beliefs and practices were threatened, is something else again. From the preserved Greek text it is clear that the book was composed originally in Hebrew, and the tale is both well told and inspiring in the best tradition of Judaism. Why then wasn't the book canonized?

This is where the principle of *halakhah* entered the picture.

When the books that were to constitute the Third Division were being considered and the Pharisaic view was dominant, conversion to Judaism required baptism in addition to circumcision; Achior was not baptized. To canonize a book—that is, to make it officially a source of doctrine—when its doctrine did not conform to that of the canonizers, was too much to ask. The book of Esther, with all its "faults," offered nothing specific that violated Pharisaic *halakhah,* yet it was not even considered for canonization in the late first century C.E. any more than Judith was; and much public pressure was required for Esther to achieve canonization when it did. The book of Judith, on the other hand, while it may have been read in connection with the Festival of Hanukkah as Esther was with Purim, never attained the favor of the public that Esther did—perhaps in part because Hanukkah itself fell into some disfavor when the Hasmonean Dynasty was overthrown by Herod.[13]

The book of Susanna, reproduced in some anthologies of detective stories as the first of that genre of literature—where Poe's *The Murders in the Rue Morgue* does not appear first—relates how this pious and beautiful wife of the highly respected Joakim refused to commit adultery with two elders of her captive Jewish community in Babylonia. She was threatened by them: "If you refuse, we will testify against you that a young man was with you" (v. 19), a threat that carried with it the death penalty; but Susanna defied them, "rather than to sin in the sight of the Lord."

At the subsequent trial, "The assembly believed them, because they were elders of the people and judges; and they condemned her to death" (v. 41). But the Lord heard Susanna's supplication, and "aroused the holy spirit of a young lad named

---

[13] See Zeitlin, "An Historical Study," etc., pp. 151-154; and now also his "Introduction" (pp. 1-37, especially 24 ff.) in *The Book of Judith,* ed. M. S. Enslin-S. Zeitlin (Dropsie Series, *Jewish Apocryphal Literature,* 1972).

Daniel; and he cried with a loud voice, 'I am innocent of the blood of this woman!" (vv. 45 f.) In no time, the assembly reconvened in judgment, and Daniel so cross-examined the two elders, the one independently and out of hearing of the other, that he proved their evidence false. "Then all the assembly ... rose against the two elders for ... bearing false witness; and they did to them as they had wickedly planned to do to their neighbor; acting in accordance with the Law of Moses, they put them to death ..." (vv. 60 ff.).

Once again *halakhah* played the central role in determining the fate of a book. The Law of Moses stated clearly (Deut. 19.16-21), "If a person appears against another person ... If the person who testified is a false witness ... you shall do to him as he schemed to do to his fellow. Thus you shall sweep out evil from your midst ... You must show no pity: life for life ..." But the Pharisees had adopted a different interpretation of the Mosaic law at this point: witnesses, even though false, if they were present at the scene of the alleged crime— unlike false witnesses who were demonstrably in another place at the time in question—could not be put to death.[14] The book of Susanna, a product of the Hellenistic period, reflected the older, literal interpretation of the law. It was simply not possible to canonize a book which contained a doctrine that ran counter to the new, more liberal *halakhah*. Where such a book was already part of the canon, as in the case of Deuteronomy, interpretation had to be practiced; but why create a problem in the first place for which a solution would then have to be given?

The book of Tobit purports to recount the trials of a pious Jew living with his wife Anna and their son Tobias in the captive Jewish community in Nineveh, Assyria—and secondarily, of a pious Jewess, Sarah, in Ecbatana, Media. The Assyrian

---

[14] See S. Zeitlin, *The Rise and Fall of the Judean State,* vol. I (J.P.S., 1962), pp. 412-415.

government had forbidden, on penalty of death, the burial of Jews who had been executed. But Tobit, who observed scrupulously the dietary laws, fed and clothed the poor, and "walked in the ways of truth and righteousness," ignored this injunction and danger and buried the Jewish corpses secretly. One Succoth night, after burying the corpse of an executed Jew and thus defiling himself ritually, he lay down in the courtyard to spend the rest of the night; but fresh droppings of sparrows above him fell on his open eyes, and he lost his sight. Small reward from God for his selfless devotion to Him! In his subsequent decline and anguish Tobit begged God to take his life.

Meanwhile, farther east, in Ecbatana, a virtuous young woman, Sarah daughter of Raguel, had married seven times and each time her husband died on the wedding night before the marriage could be consummated. In despair, she begged God to take her life. God heard the pleas of Tobit and Sarah, and sent His angel "Raphael to heal the two of them: to scale away the white films from Tobit's eyes, to give Sarah . . . in marriage to Tobias . . . and to bind Asmodeus the evil demon . . ." (3.17). Thereupon Tobit reminded himself that he was once left ten talents of silver in trust with a certain Gabael of Rages, Media, and he decided that his son Tobias should hire a companion and go to Rages to claim the money; the companion, it turned out, was none other than Raphael in disguise.

One evening, on their way to Rages, they stopped at the Tigris River, and a fish leaped out of the water and would have swallowed Tobias. But Raphael ordered him to catch the fish, cut it open, remove its heart, liver, and gall, "and put them away safely" (6.4). Raphael then told Tobias the use to which these would be put, and all about Sarah and the forthcoming marriage between her and Tobias. They then journeyed on to Ecbatana and Tobias married Sarah. On the wedding night, Tobias "remembered the words of Raphael, and he took the live ashes of incense and put the heart and liver of the fish upon them and made a smoke. And when the demon (Asmodeus) smelled

the odor he fled to the remotest parts of Egypt, and the angel
bound him . . ." (8.2-3). After Raphael obtained the money
from Gabael, Tobias and his increased entourage remained fourteen days with Raguel and then set out to return to Nineveh.
Raphael told Tobias how to cure his father's blindness: ". . .
anoint his eyes with the gall; and when they smart he will rub
them, and will cause the white films to fall away, and he will
see" (11.8). Tobias did as told, and Tobit's eyesight was restored. Raphael revealed himself to the family, and everyone
lived happily long thereafter—Tobit to the age of 158 and
Tobias to the age of 127.

Like Judith and Susanna, Tobit manifests the fine qualities
of a truly devoted follower of the God of Israel, even to the
point of endangering one's life. However, like the first two,
Tobit too was denied canonical status, and the reason was,
again *halakhic*. In the earlier, Hellenistic period, a wife could
be acquired in three ways: by purchase, by document, or by
cohabitation (Kiddushin I, 1: *ha-'ishah niqneth bishloshah
derakhim . . . be-khésef, bishṭar, u-be-bi'ah*). The document in
question (*sheṭar*) was written by the bride's father, who gave
away his daughter; as put in Tobit: 'I (Raguel) have given my
daughter (Sarah) to seven husbands . . . Take her right now in
accordance with the law . . .' Then he called his daughter Sarah
and . . . gave her to Tobias . . . And he blessed them. Next he
called his wife Edna, and took a scroll and wrote out the contract; and they set their seals to it. Then they began to eat"
(7.11-15). This law, according to Shabbat 14b, was changed
by Simon ben Sheṭaḥ (early first century B.C.E.), so that henceforth the groom (not the bride's father) wrote the document of
marriage (*ketubah,* rather than *sheṭar*), and thus also gave the
bride greater protection.[15] The Pharisees could not canonize the
book of Tobit when its *halakhah* on marriage contradicted its
own.

---

[15] S. Zeitlin, *op. cit.,* pp. 415-420.

Some of the Apocrypha, e.g., the Wisdom of Solomon (at least in large part), were probably written originally in Greek, rather than in Hebrew (see, e.g., J. Reider, *The Book of Wisdom* [Dropsie Series, *Jewish Apocryphal Literature;* 1957], pp. 22-29), and could not hope for canonization. Furthermore, such Apocrypha as the "Additions to Esther," "The Letter of Jeremiah," "Baruch," "Bel and the Dragon," "The Prayer of Azariah and the Song of the Three Young Men," and "The Prayer of Manasseh" are really not independent books but essentially "Addenda et Corrigenda" to the biblical books of Esther, Jeremiah, Daniel, and Chronicles, and probably never acquired the status even to merit consideration for canonization. Yet most of these works still require close study by scholars who are steeped in the history of the Second Jewish Commonwealth and with direct knowledge of early rabbinic literature.

Just as the Protestant Church from the sixteenth century on designated as Apocrypha books such as Judith, Susanna, and Tobit that had been designated as part of the Old Testament Canon in the early Church, so did it come to designate as Pseudepigrapha many other books that had long been designated Apocrypha by the Roman Catholic Church. (On the artificiality of the term Pseudepigrapha, see the reference to Torrey in n.11 above.) One of the Apocrypha-turned-Pseudepigrapha books is Jubilees, sometimes called "Little Genesis."

This book presents the history of the universe and early Israel, from Creation to the Exodus, in the form of jubilee (49-year) periods. The strict observance of the Sabbath—in an earlier, rather primitive manner—and of the Jubilee is stressed, and the older, solar calendar is defended vigorously against the solar-lunar calendar that had been adopted. Regardless of the merits of the book, it stood no chance of canonization when its *halakhah,* especially in the matter of the calendar, had fallen behind the times.[16]

---

[16] See the discussion of the problem in S. Zeitlin, "The Book of 'Jubilees' and the Pentateuch," *JQR,* 48 (1957-58), 218-235.

There is an ancient Jewish saying (*Zohar, Naso', 134*):
"Everything depends on luck, even the Holy Writings in the
Temple (*ha-kol talui be-mazal wa-'afilu sifre torah ba-hekal*)."
Had the Third Division been closed a century or so earlier or
later, our Hebrew Bible would be different from what it is today.

16

Jewish Biblical Scholarship in America *

IT MAY BE ASSERTED at the very outset that just as Jewish culture in general did not begin appreciably to develop in this country until the end of the nineteenth century and the beginning of the twentieth, so too did scientific biblical research make little headway among Jews on this side of the ocean until just over half a century ago. The reason

[Based on my survey in the Tercentenary Issue of the *Jewish Quarterly Review* (=*JQR*), 45 (1954-55), 374-412; 47 (1956-57), 345-353, and on the revised Hebrew version that appeared in the volume הגות עברית באמריקה / *Studies on Jewish Themes by Contemporary American Scholars* sponsored by ברית עברית עולמית / World Association for Hebrew Language and Culture, ed. M. Zohari-A. Tartakover-H. Ormian (Tel-Aviv, 5732/1972), pp. 131-164.]

* In part for lack of space and partly for other reasons, the present survey is devoted essentially to American Jewish scholars who are no longer among the living. [But see now the last five paragraphs of this essay and my chapter on "Old Testament Studies," in *Religion*, ed. P. Ramsey (Prentice-Hall, 1965, In *The Princeton Studies: Humanistic Scholarship in America*), pp. 51-109 (and the Index there).] I take pleasure in thanking Rabbi I. Edward Kiev and Herbert C. Zafren, librarians respectively of the New York and Cincinnati schools of Hebrew Union College-Jewish Institute of Religion, and the late Dr. Joshua Bloch and his successor as Chief of the Jewish Division of the New York Public Library, Abraham Berger, for their assistance in tracking down and making available some of the bibliographical and biographical items.

for this is clear. The relatively small number of Jews who were domiciled in the United States before about 1890 were no less meager in the quality of their learning. It was not until the Jewish masses of Eastern Europe, with their remarkable knowledge and thirst for knowledge, began to enter this free country, after the pogroms of 1881 and 1905 and the generally deteriorating circumstances in Czarist Russia, that biblical scholarship began to assert itself. It may be observed here in passing that except that the Christian scholarly world was about half a century or so ahead of the Jewish, the situation was generally the same in the two groups; as George F. Moore put it, in 1889, in his excellent survey, "Alttestamentliche Studien in Amerika"[1] (p. 288): "Die Geschichte der Kritik des A. T. in Amerika erstreckt sich also über kaum mehr als ein Jahrzehnt."

Biblical scholarship in America during the earlier part of the nineteenth century was on an elementary level. Libraries and Hebrew type for the printing presses were still in the process of being born, and even journals and important books were not readily available. Thus Moore wrote as late as 1889 (p. 248), "In der Stadt New-York war vor kurzem kein Exemplar des Jâqût zu finden; die vier grossten Bibliotheken Amerika's besassen vor fünf Jahren keine Ausgabe von Kimchi's Mikhlol. Die umfangreiche Litteratur, welche in Zeitschriften, Monographien u. s. w. zerstreut liegt, ist fast absolut unzugänglich . . ." This was to be expected, since the new immigrants, Jewish as well as Christian, had to provide the material necessities of life before they could afford the luxury of culture, even the religious aspects of it. The American author of *New England's First Fruits* (London, 1643) wrote, "After God had carried us safe to New England, and we had built our houses, provided necessaries for our liveli-

---

[1] *Zeitschrift für die alttestamentliche Wissenschaft* (= *ZAW*), 8 (1888), 1-43; 9 (1889), 246-302. See also the chapter by Joshua Trachtenberg, "American Jewish Scholarship," in *The Jewish People, Past and Present*, vol. IV (New York, 1955), 411-455; Joseph Reider, בני־ברית בארצות־הברית בין המקרא בקרת, *Gilvonot*, XXXI, 5714, 131-38; Menahem G. Glenn, " באמריקה העברית הספרות ראשית " in, מועצת הספר הישראלי ספר השנה for 5704 [1943-44], vol. II, part 1), pp. 14-23.

hood, reared convenient places for God's worship, and settled the civil government: one of the next things we longed for and looked after was to advance learning and perpetuate it to posterity; dreading to leave an illiterate ministry to the churches, when our present ministers shall be in the dust." [2]

The earliest biblical works published by Jewish, as by Christian scholars in this country revolved about Hebrew grammar, the means wherewith to learn to read and understand the Hebrew Bible. In 1735 Judah Monis, who had adopted Christianity in America in 1722, published in Boston the first Hebrew grammar, דִּקְדּוּק לְשׁוֹן עִבְרִית, *Dickdook Leshon Gnebreet. A Grammar of the Hebrew Tongue, Being an Essay To bring the Hebrew Grammar into English to Facilitate the Instruction of all those who are desirous of acquiring a clear Idea of this Primitive Tongue by their own Studies; in order to [make?] their more distinct Acquaintance with the Sacred Oracles of the Testiment [sic!] according to the Original. And Published more especially for the Use of the Students of Harvard-College at Cambridge, in New-England.*[3] נֶחְבַּר וְהוּבָא בְעִיוּן נִמְרָץ עַל יְדֵי יְהוּדָה מוֹנִישׁ.

In his article "American Jewish Literary 'Firsts' " [4] Lee M. Friedman reminds us that "when the first printing press, set up in Cambridge in 1639, printed the first book to be published in English in America, the 'Bay Psalms Book,' to convince the public of its authori-

---

[2] *Collections of Massachusetts Historical Society,* 1 (1792); quoted from Moore, pp. 1-2.

[3] On Monis see, e.g., Moore, pp. 7-8; George A. Kohut, *American Journal of Semitic Languages* (= *AJSL*), 14 (1898), 217-226; Frederick T. Haneman's article in *Jewish Encyclopedia* (= *JE*), VIII, 657; Joshua Bloch, "American Jewish Literature," *Jewish Book Annual* (= *JBA*), 12 (1953-55), 18-19; and now also the study by Jerry W. Brown (see n. 9 below). The title page of the grammar is reproduced on p. 37 of A. S. W. Rosenbach, *An American Jewish Bibliography* (American Jewish Historical Society, Publication No. 30, 1926). Rosenbach has reproduced (p. 36) also the prospectus of a דִּקְדּוּק לְשׁוֹן הַקּוֹדֶשׁ *Dickdook Lashon Aukodesh* (1734). [See now also Eisig Silberschlag, "Origin and Primacy of Hebrew Studies in America" [Hebrew], in הגות עברית באמריקה (5732/1972), 15-41.]

[4] *JBA,* 12 (1953-55), 45-50.

tative authenticity, Hebrew words were printed in Hebrew type and the entire Hebrew alphabet was reproduced. The printing was crude and there are those who believe that the Hebrew type was locally handcut . . ." He then proceeds to remind us "that there was not a set of Hebrew type in America until 1735 when Harvard imported such type from England to print Judah Monis' *Hebrew Grammar* . . . that Harvard might educate future clergymen to be able to read the Holy Bible in the language they believed the Almighty spoke" (pp. 46-7).[5]

Moore has observed that while Monis, as was to be expected, depended very much on earlier Jewish grammarians, especially "D. Kimchi, Rabbi Arkivolty (ארוגת [correct to ערוגת] הבושם . Steinschneider Nr. 132) und Rabbi Temple (ראשית חכמה . Steinschneider Nr. 1140)," [6] his *Dickdook* was nevertheless "eine respectable Leistung und dürfte das Studium des Hebräischen in N[ew] E[ngland] seiner Zeit wirklich befördert haben . . ."

For the record mention may be made at this point of several other Jewish scholars who published Hebrew Grammars. In 1815 E. N. Carvalho put out מפתח לשון עברית *A Key to the Hebrew Tongue containing the Alphabet with the various vowel points, accompanied by easy lessons of one and more syllables, with the English translation affixed thereto, so that the learner may understand as he proceeds. To which is added An Introduction to the Hebrew Grammar with points. Intended to facilitate the scholar in his progress to the attainment of the primitive languages* (Philadelphia, 1815. Rosenbach, p.

---

[5] Moore (p. 31 and n. 1) has noted that the first biblical book printed in this country by an American was Fr. Hare's *Liber Psalmorum Hebraïce cum notis selectis* (Cambridge, 1809; title page reproduced in Rosenbach, p. 139), the first Hebrew dictionary that by Clement C. Moore (New York, 1809; Rosenbach, p. 141), and the first complete Hebrew Bible in Philadelphia in 1814 ("2 Bde., eine äusserst schöne Ausgabe"; Rosenbach, p. 156).

[6] Samuel Archevolti (16th cent.; *JE, II*, 85), ספר ערוגת הבשם בדקדוק (Venice, 1602; reprinted Amsterdam, 5670-1730); Solomon Raphael Leon (Leao) Templo (died about 1733; *JE*, VIII, 3), ראשית חכמה, *Principio de Sciencia ou Grammathica Hebrayca*, etc. (Amsterdam, 5463 [1703]). The ראשית חכמה does not appear to be listed on p. 78 in Wilhelm Bacher's comprehensive article on "Grammar, Hebrew," *JE*, VI, 67-80.

159).[7] In 1823 the converted Jew, Joseph Samuel Christian Frederick Frey, published *A New Edition of a Hebrew Grammar* (New York. Rosenbach, p. 212, and cf. pp. 160-162 and Index s. v.). James Seixas did his bit through *A Manual Hebrew Grammar for the use of beginners* (Andover, 1833, Rosenbach, p. 291; p. 299 reproduces the title page of the second edition). A third edition appeared in 1852, including already *"a Vocabulary of Roots, Nouns and Particles of Common Occurrence* (Philadelphia). Joseph Aaron, too, published ספר מפתח אֶל לְשׁוֹן עברִי וְחָכְמַת הַדִקְדוּק מְפֹרָשׁ עִם נְקוּדוֹת שַׁעַר הָרִאשׁוֹן , *A Key to the Hebrew Language and the science of Hebrew Grammar. Explained* (with points). First Part (New York, 1834. Rosenbach, p. 293). Solomon Deutsch published *A New Practical Hebrew Grammar with Hebrew-English and English-Hebrew Exercises and a Hebrew Chrestomathy* (New York, 1868). Moore (p. 35) refers to a "Meyrowitz, Heb. Grammar 1877"; but I do not know it.

Isaac Nordheimer (1809-1842), educated by the noted Talmudist Moses Sofer and recipient of the Ph. D. in Oriental Languages at the University of München, became Professor of Arabic, Syriac, and other oriental languages and Acting Prof. of Hebrew in the University of the City of New York in 1836, and soon thereafter published in two volumes *A Critical Grammar of the Hebrew Language* (New York, 1838, 1841. Rosenbach, p. 327). Moore's high opinion of this work is worth quoting here: "In derselben versucht der Verfasser einen Mittelweg zwischen Gesenius und Ewald einzuschlagen. Mit den alten jüdischen Grammatikern, wie mit den neuesten Arbeiten auf diesem Gebiete durchaus vertraut, und mit rechtlicher Kenntnis der verwandten Sprachen, wie der Versuche auf dem Gebiete der vergleichenden Sprachwissenschaft ausgerüstet, hat Nordheimer ein Werk zu Stande

---

[7] On Emanuel Nunes Carvalho see pp. 19-20 of Bertram W. Korn's Introduction to *Incidents of Travel and Adventure in the Far West* by Solomon Nunes Carvalho (Phila., JPS, 1954-5715), nephew of Emanuel, and p. 318. Korn has noted (p. 19) that Emanuel "published the first Hebrew Grammar to be written by an American Jew . . . He was engaged in compiling another American Jewish 'first,' a Hebrew-English dictionary, when he died in 1817."

gebracht, welches wirklich wissenschaftliche Bedeutung beanspruchen darf und mehr Aufmerksamkeit verdiente, als demselben seitens der europäischen Fachgenossen zu Theil geworden ist . . ." (p. 34). In addition, Nordheimer published one fascicle of a new Hebrew Concordance to the Bible.[8]

In common with so much non-Jewish culture and scholarship in America over a century ago, Isaac Leeser's work in the biblical field derived substantially from European models and sources; fortunately these were the product of the sound scholarship which characterized German research in that period.[9] In 1853 Leeser (1806-1868) published an English translation of the Hebrew Bible[10] which in a short time became the standard Bible for English-speaking Jews, especially in America.[11] Leeser's Bible, as it has come to be known—with "the

---

[8] Nordheimer published a Grammatical Analysis in 1838 (New Haven; Rosenbach, p. 328). Moore noted that Nordheimer left unpublished manuscripts on Arabic grammar, on Aramaic and Syriac grammar, and a commentary on Koheleth.

[9] Cf. Moore (pp. 41-2), "Der gesammten Litteratur dieser Periode haftet mit äusserst wenigen Ausnahmen ein gewisser Mangel an Selbstständigkeit an, welcher besonders in der Abhängigkeit von den deutschen *Autoritäten* zu Tage tritt, oft zwar in der Form der Opposition, aber auch *so* nicht minder deutlich. Es war dies die unvermeidliche Folge unserer Verhältnisse und bedarf keiner weiteren Entschuldigung . . ." There has just appeared a useful study of the influence of German biblical scholarship on the scholars and theologians of nineteenth-century New England; see Jerry W. Brown, *The Rise of Biblical Criticism in America, 1800-1870: The New England Scholars (1970).*

[10] The bibliography on Leeser is reaching rich proportions. See, e. g., Henry Englander's survey in *Yearbook of Central Conference of American Rabbis* (= *YBCCAR*), 28 (1918), 213-252 ("Leeser's *magnum opus* is undoubtedly his translation of the Bible into English . . . ," p. 224); Moshe Davis, יהדות אמריקה בהתפתחותה (The Shaping of American Judaism; New York, 1951), 12-23 and *passim;* Bertram W. Korn, *Eventful Years and Experiences* (Cincinnati, 1954), *passim* (Index, 244), especially in Chap. VII, "The First American Jewish Theological Seminary: Maimonides College."

[11] The Pentateuch, תורת האלוהים *The Law of God,* in Hebrew and English, appeared in 5605-1845 in Philadelphia, in 5 vols. Leeser's Bible, *The Twenty-Four Books of the Holy Scriptures . . . carefully translated according to the Massoretic Text on the basis of the English Version,* as Alexander Harkavy's Bible (*The Twenty-Four Books of the Old Testament. Hebrew Text and English Version* [New York,

affectionate regard of American Jews," Israel Abrahams would add[12] —had considerable merit, and is useful even to this day. Its main fault lay in the style; too much German and Hebrew protruded in the translation. On the other hand, the grammatical niceties of Biblical Hebrew frequently came through successfully, and the scholarship in general was on a consistently high level. Were it not for the appearance of the Jewish Publication Society's Translation in 1917 (on which see below), Leeser's Bible would have retained much of its deserved popularity to this day.

Isidor Kalisch (1816-1886) wrote *Wegweiser für Rationelle Forschungen in den biblischen Schriften*, etc. (Cleveland, 1853), which appeared four years later in Cincinnati in English dress as *A Guide for Rational Enquiries into the Biblical Writings*, etc. During 1851-52 Kalisch published a series of "Exegetical Lectures on the Bible" in the *Occident* (ed. Isaac Leeser).[13]

One should not leave unnoted Adolph Hübsch, *Die fünf Megilloth*.[14] Hübsch (1830-1884) received his Ph.D. in 1857 at the University of Prague, and he came to this country in 1866, the year his *Megilloth* appeared. Later he published *Gems from the Orient* (1885), a collection of Arabic aphorisms.

1916]), appeared with the Hebrew text facing the English translation. After World War I, when the immigration of Jews from Eastern Europe became increasingly limited, the Jews of America began to dispense with the Hebrew text. It is a good sign that *Hebrew*-English Bibles are again becoming popular in this country. כן ירבו! . On Harkavy, see B. J. Richards, *American Jewish Yearbook* (= *AJYB*), 42 (1940-5701), 153-164.

[12] *By-Paths in Hebraic Bookland* (Phila., 1920), 256. Strangely, Leeser's Bible translation seems to have gone unmentioned in Moore's survey.

[13] See *Studies in Ancient and Modern Judaism . . . Selected Writings of Rabbi Isidor Kalisch*, Edited and Compiled with a Memoir by Samuel Kalisch . . . and an Introduction by Joshua Bloch (New York, 1928). See there (pp. 88-109), e. g., also the article on "The Biblical Idea of God."

[14] The full title is *Die fünf Megilloth, nebst dem syrischen Thargum gennant 'Peschito,' zum erste Male in hebräischer Quadratschrift mit Interpunktation edirt, ferner mit einem Kommentare zum Texte, aus einem handschriftlichen Pentateuch-Codex der k. k. Univ. Bibliothek zu Prag, und einem Kommentare zum Thargum, mit sprachlichen Erlauterungen, Nachweisnugen der verschiedenen Lesarten, Vergleichung mit andern alten Versionen, Erklärungen vieler thalmudischer und midraschischer Wörter und Sätze u. s. w.* (Prag, 1866).

Isaac M. Wise (1819-1900)[15] wrote on Jewish history and theology. In 1854 there appeared his *History of the Israelitish Nation from Abraham to the Present Time* (Albany), and in 1880 he published the second volume, *A History of the Hebrews' Second Commonwealth, with special reference to its Literature, Culture, and the Origin of Rabbinism and Christianity* (Cincinnati).[16] Among Wise's other publications in the field may be mentioned *Pronaos to Holy Writ establishing, on documentary evidence, the authorship, date, form, and content of its Books and the Authenticity of the Pentateuch* (Cincinnati, 1891). In 1881-82 Wise published in the *Hebrew Review* (Vol. 2, pp. 107-117) an article on the Massorah and the Massoretic Text; though marked "To be continued," nothing more appeared.

Israel Abrahams in his extremely delightful book *By-Paths in Hebraic Bookland*[17] has some interesting and pertinent things to say about "Wise's learning and originality . . . [so that] it is not possible to withhold from him the crown of scholarship. In particular, his *Pronaos* abounds in acute and fresh contributions to the biblical problem . . ." He has noted further that Wise's *Pronaos* "is among the earliest of the reasoned replies to the Higher Criticism. Wise would have nothing to do with the modern treatment of the Pentateuch. He had as little patience with Graetz as he had with Wellhausen. The Pentateuch is through and through Mosaic. Moses wrote Genesis and Deuteronomy with his own hands; the rest was set down soon after his death from the records which he had left for the purpose. And

---

[15] See, e. g., Max B. May, *Isaac Mayer Wise* (New York and London, 1916); Jacob R. Marcus, *The Americanization of Isaac Mayer Wise* (Cincinnati, 1931); article by George Zepin in *Universal Jewish Encyclopedia* (= *UJE*), X. 539-44; B. W. Korn. *Eventful Years,* etc., Chap. VI and *passim.*

[16] The preface states that ". . . The present volume, though a complete book in itself, is a continuation of the former [*History of the Israelitish Nation,* 1854]. It begins where the first closes." See A. S. Oko, *A Tentative Bibliography of Dr. Isaac M. Wise* (Cincinnati, 1917; reprinted from *Hebrew Union College Monthly,* Vol. 3), items 2, 19 and 39. Moore (pp. 294-5) commented on Wise's volume. "Für uns liegt der Wert des Buches ausschliesslich in der Ausbeutung der talmudischen Quellen . . . Als Geschichtsdarstellung ist dasselbe ganz unbrauchbar." And see now Andrew F. Key, *The Theology of Isaac Mayer Wise* (*Monographs of the American Jewish Archives,* Cincinnati, No. V, 1962 (65 pp.).

[17] " 'The Pronaos' of I. M. Wise," pp. 346-52.

further: 'There exists no solid ground on which to base any doubt in the authenticity of any book of Holy Writ.' With that emphatic assertion the book ends."

Michael Heilprin (1823-1888), along with such others as Isidor Kalisch, Adolf Hübsch, and Benjamin Szold among the "Jewish 'Forty-Eighters' in America," [18] published a two-volume work *The Historical Poetry of the Ancient Hebrews Translated and Critically Examined* (New York, 1879-1880). The work begins with the "brief address of Lamech to . . . Adah and Zillah" and ends with Hosea. It is a learned study, including translation and critical exegetical notes. A forthright person in all his activities, Heilprin exhibited a liberal attitude to the biblical criticism of his time. As Moore put it (p. 293), "Die Anmerkungen bekunden grosse Belesenheit und einen freien Blick; auf der anderen Seite macht der Mangel an Methode das Buch schwer geniessbar . . ." [19] In 1893 Benjamin Szold published Heilprin's "Bibelkritische Notizen" (185 pp., Baltimore; "als Manuskript gedruckt") in which various passages in the Bible are compared.

Alexander Kohut (1842-1894),[20] while not directly a biblical scholar, deserves mention because of his *Aruch Completum,* the last four volumes of which (as also the supplementary volume, 1927) were completed after he had removed to this country.[21] This encyclopedic dictionary of the Talmud is indeed a significant achieve-

---

[18] An interesting chapter in American Jewish history; cf. Korn, op. cit., pp. 1-26. On Heilprin, see Peter Wiernik's article in *JE,* VI, 325; Gustav Pollak, *Michael Heilprin and His Sons, a Biography* (New York, 1912), pp. 3-229.

[19] The book is worth any scholar's perusal today. Unfortunately, there is no Table of Contents or Index.

[20] See M. Davis, op. cit., 71-83, with full references. Kohut's bibliography was compiled by his son, George Alexander Kohut, *Concerning Alexander Kohut, a Tentative Bibliography* (Budapest, 1927). The son (1874-1933) was himself a very distinguished scholar and patron of biblical and Jewish scholarship; as only Stephen S. Wise could have put it (p. X of his Memoir in *Jewish Studies in Memory of George A. Kohut,* ed. Salo W. Baron and Alexander Marx [New York, 1935]), "It is not too much to say that he adopted all Jewish scholars as if they were his Father."

[21] Moore (p. 270) simply noted that "Kohut setzt seine Aruchausgabe in New-York weiter fort. Bd. V soll demnächst erscheinen."

ment, and is "justly characterized as one of the monuments of Hebrew literature" (*JE,* VII, 537-8). Joshua Bloch (op. cit., 24) is correct in stating that "It still maintains its position as a work of reference without which the study of the language of the Talmud would be more difficult than it is now."

Benjamin Szold's[22] Hebrew commentary on the book of Job is a fine piece of scholarship, unfortunately insufficiently consulted and appreciated even by Jewish scholars.[23] Szold (1829-1902) made use of the best Jewish and non-Jewish scholarship of medieval and modern times (*cf.* pp. 497-8 of his Commentary), but yet applied his own learning and ingenuity in unraveling the mysteries in the text of the Book.[24] He correctly recognized two main aspects in the interpretation of the Book: (1) to follow the general argument not only from one chapter to another but from one section to another within a chapter; (2) to clarify each verse *per se* and in context. Very few commentators before or since managed to achieve Szold's success in interpreting the Book. Not least, the Hebrew is a pleasure to read, simple, lucid, partaking of the best features of medieval and nineteenth-century Hebrew. In fine, Szold's commentary is still the best in

---

[22] On Szold, see William Rosenau's eulogy in *YBCCAR,* 13 (1903), 357-62; M. Davis, op. cit., 46-53.

[23] ספר איוב, מבואר מחדש על פי כללי הדקדוק וחוקי המליצה של שפת עבר, מאתי

Baltimore, 1886. בנימין סאלה . . רב ומורה לעדת ,אוהב שלום' בעיר באלטימארע במדינה אמעריקא,

(English Title Page: *The Book of Job* with a New Commentary, by Benjamin Szold, Rabbi of the Oheb-Shalom Congregation of Baltimore.) The commentary is brought to a close with a clever poem (המבאר להמחבר) in which Szold asks the author of Job,

אך כי ישאלני פי המדבר . . .

להגיד לו מה שמך —

מה אשיב לו? הגד, מחבר!

איך קראוך בני עמך?

and the author is made to answer the commentator (המחבר להמבאר),

השב לשואלך בשמי אומר בְּשֶׁלִי

למה זה תשאל לשמי — והוא פלאי!

[24] Ibid., אמנם הקורא המבין לאשורי יבין כי דרכיהם |מכל מלמדי השכלתי|

דרכי, וכי סללתי לי דרך חדש להבנת ספרי קדשנו אשר מנעורי היו שעשועי יום יום . . .

I cannot agree with Moore's low estimate of this commentary (p. 292, where he refers to Karl Budde's review in *Theologische Literaturzeitung* [= *TLZ*], 1887, 293-4).

Hebrew on Job, and very useful alongside the more recent critical commentaries in any language.

Szold published two other works on the Bible. In 1874 there appeared in Baltimore his אמרי בינה , *The Proverbs of Solomon in Hebrew, English and German, arranged according to Different Subjects, forming a Proverbial Companion;* and his analysis of "The Eleventh Chapter of the Book of Daniel" appeared in *Semitic Studies in Memory of Rev. Dr. Alexander Kohut* (ed. G. A. Kohut, Berlin, 1897), pp. 537-600.[25]

The *Randglossen* by Arnold Bogumil Ehrlich (1848-1919)[26] ranks as one of the more important and better known contributions to biblical studies, textual and contextual.[27] Of his Hebrew philological commentary, מקרא כפשוטו ,[28] the Pentateuch appeared in 1899, followed in 1900 by the Prose Books, and in 1901 by the Poetical Books. The *Randglossen zur hebräischen Bibel, textkritisches, sprach-*

---

[25] It is a pity that there remained unpublished commentaries by Szold on several other Books of the Bible; ibid., והיה אם ימצא ביאורי זה חן בעיני קוראיו ויטעמו בו טעם הספר. בכל מאמריו ומליו, יעוררני זה להוסיף להוציא לאור גם שארי הביאורים אשר הם אתי בכתובים. האל ינמור בעדי וינחני באורו ואמתו .

[26] See article on Ehrlich in *UJE*, IV, p. 19 (with reference to David de Sola Pool's sketch in *Dictionary of American Biography*, 6 [1931], 57); "A Great Bible Scholar," by Israel Friedländer, *The Nation*, Jan. 10, 1920, p. 41. Prof. Boaz Cohen (see his *Israel Friedländer, a Bibliography of his Writings with an Appreciation*, New York, 1936, 40 pp.) gave me the latter reference.

[27] Cyrus Adler (in the Paul Haupt Volume, p. 327) linked Szold and Ehrlich as follows, "The production of a work in Hebrew like BENJAMIN SZOLD'S Commentary to the Book of Job, and especially the notable contribution to Biblical study made by ARNOLD B. EHRLICH would have been worthy of any country and any period." On Margolis' stature see below.

[28] מקרא כפשוטו, והוא מקרא מפורש פורש ושום שכל, ומשם יפרד והיה לשלשה ראשים. הראש האחד, דברי תורה. אמרתים מתוך כתבי הקדש בלי משא פני הקדש וכמי שאינו נוגע בדבריו איו שבתי בן יום טוב אבן בודד . . Interestingly, Ehrlich used the concept "in the year 122 of the Independence of the United States" (לחרות.ארצות הברית) instead of "1898" as the date of his Preface. The German title is *"Mikrâ ki-Pheschutô (Die Schrift nach ihrem Wortlaut)*. Scholien und kritische Bemerkungen zu den heiligen Schriften der Hebräer." Ehrlich dedicated the first volume to Franz Delitzsch, and the second to whoever read it (מקדש לקורא בו).

liches und sachliches (Leipzig, 7 volumes) appeared from 1908 to 1914.[29]

In the Preface of the *Mikrâ ki-Pheschutô* Ehrlich set forth clearly the purpose, scope, and method of his *magnum opus*. He began by saying that the Bible had always occupied the central interest of his studies, and that unlike so many other scholars, especially the modern Jewish scholars who frequently imitated their Christian colleagues, he always asked himself two questions when confronted by a biblical text: (1) Whence do we know this? and (2) What does it mean? In this way, Ehrlich asserted, he was able to make original contributions to the correct understanding of the Bible.[30]

Ehrlich, a product of the nineteenth-century European system of education, was a learned scholar. His knowledge of Arabic was excellent.[31] Above all, however, he was a master of the Hebrew language and a trained philologian. This is evident on every page of his monumental *Randglossen*. On the debit side of Ehrlich's work is the casualness with which he introduced emendations of the Hebrew text, sometimes allegedly on the basis of the Septuagint and other ancient versions. It is true that his emendations were consistently of superior quality to those proposed by the vast majority of his contemporaries; but they were too frequently quite unnecessary, and purely conjectural,

---

[29] Vol. VII of *Randglossen* includes "Nachträge und Zusätze" (pp. 387-403), "Verzeichnis der . . . Stellen aus dem Talmud, dem Midrasch und dem Neuen Testament" (405-6), and "Wortregister" (407-476).

[30]   בתוך עמי אני יושב ובין חכמיו נְדלתּי, ולמדתי מקרא ומשנה הלכה והגדה. ומנעורי לא חפצתי כי אם במקרא, ובו כל מעיני למיום היותי לאיש ועד היום הזה. ובחרתי במקרא, מפני שהוא ראשון לכלם, ואב לכלם, וכנגד כלם. וממה שלמדתי ואני נער לא שמרתי מכל משמר כי אם שתים, ונדולות הן אלי. "מנלן?" היא האחת, והשנית "מאי טעמא?" . . . ועל פי הדברים האלה דעת לנבון נקל שלא הלכתי אחרי המפרשים שהיו לפני לאמר כדבריהם כשאין להם יתרון מלבד אשר הם דברי גאוני ישראל ותפארתו, או דברי חכמים מחוכמים מחכמי הגוים, כי חתרתי וירדתי לעמק פשוטו של מקרא להעירות מקורו ולהעלות דברים של טעם. ואני נכון לבי בטוח שחפצי בידי הצליח; ולא מפני שחכמתי מכל אשר היו לפני, כי אם מפני שהלכתי ובטוח אני שלא ימצא ends with The הקדמה. דרך אחרת ורוח אחרת היתה אתי .בספר הזה הקורא בו דברים הרבה שנודעים לו ממקום אחר, כי דרכי דרך חדש

[31] Note *inter alia* his adopted name, שבתי בן יום טוב אבן בודר , and the quotation on the title page from Ibn Mas'ud ("Mas'ud" in Vol. I was corrected in the volumes following.)

rarely based on a sound understanding of the versions.[32] Samuel R. Driver, *Notes on the . . . Books of Samuel,* 2nd ed. (1913), p. XV ("List of Abbreviations"), summed it up in the pithy statement, "Clever; but apt to be arbitrary, and unconvincing."

There is much more that can be said about Ehrlich personally and about his scholarly work, as may be seen readily from my Prolegomenon (pp. IX-XXXIII) in the recent reissue of מקרא כפשוטו by the KTAV Publishing House (New York, 1969, 3 vols.). Thus, e.g., I am inclined to believe that Ehrlich—egocentric and spiteful as he was, and posing as a martyr in the interests of Jewish exegesis— was, for a time at least, a convert to Christianity. He issued his Hebrew commentary, מקרא כפשוטו (contrast his later German commentary, *Rondglossen*), on the order not of the threefold Jewish but of the fourfold Protestant division of the Bible: I. דברי תורה Der Pentateuch; II. דברי סופרים / Die prosaischen Schriften; III דברי נבואה / Die Propheten; but Vol. IV, דברי שיר (see end of the Preface in Vol. II) never appeared. Ehrlich's explanation for the fourfold division is less than clear and forthright when it is noted that Daniel, as in the Christian tradition, was included among the prophets; instead of putting Daniel in Vol. II (Prose Books), along with Ezra and Nehemiah, Ehrlich placed it at the end of Vol. III, directly after the Book of the prophet Malachi, and then followed it with the concluding phrase: (הגם דניאל בנביאים?) ! תמו דברי נבואה

Ehrlich was closely attached to Franz Delitzsch (the מקרא כפשוטו is dedicated to him) and, apparently, to his missionary projects; thus he helped Delitzsch with the Hebrew translation of the New Testament (one recalls the similar efforts of the converts Isaac Edward Salkinson and Christian David Ginsburg before him in the same century). Also significantly, it was in Delitzsch's *Saat auf Hoffnung* (Vols. XXV and XXVI, 1888 and 1889), which was the "Organ des evangelisch-lutherischen Centralvereins für die Mission unter Israel,"

---

[32] Cf. Max L. Margolis' review of Vols. I-III of *Randglossen,* in *JQR,* 1 (1910-11), 575-8. J. Bloch, op. cit., 23, is among those who have a high appreciation of the "Most notable . . . exegetical notes of Arnold B. Ehrlich."

and the *Zeitschrift für die Mission der Kirche an Israel* that Ehrlich
published his reminiscenses. In this light, the acute psychoanalyst
will find significant the manner in which Ehrlich addressed himself to
his Jewish readers (עמי [בני ו]אחי) and began the Preface to Vol. I:
בתוך עמי אני יושב. [32a]

[There is no longer any reason to doubt or deny that Ehrlich was, for a
time at least, a convert to Christianity. In the Sept. 17, 1971 issue of
Hadoar (pp. 665–666), G. Kressel drew attention to his recent discovery
that already in 1935–36 Richard J. H. Gottheil, in his biography of his
father, *The Life of Gustav Gottheil: Memoir of a Priest in Israel* (Bayard
Press, Williamsport, Pa.), in a chapter (VII) devoted to "Arnold B.
Ehrlich" (pp. 75–81), presented clear evidence both for Ehrlich's conversion to Christianity in Leipzig (about 1870: "tempted by prospects
of a better position than I imagined I could ever attain as an Israelite")
and his formal return to Judaism in New York City on March 7, 1876.
Ehrlich's confession (his own German version) and the *Minute* recorded
by Rabbi Gustav Gottheil—who with Rabbis David Einhorn and Samuel
Adler constituted the *Beth-Din* for the re-conversion—may be found on
pp. 76–77.]

The Jastrows, father and son, helped in furthering biblical scholarship. Marcus Jastrow (1829-1903) made his contribution by way of
the well-known and widely-used *Dictionary of the Targumim, the
Talmud Babli and Yerushalmi, and the Midrashic Literature* (London

---

[32a] To the considerable bibliography cited in my above-mentioned Prolegomenon,
add David Hoffmann, in *Israelitische Monatsschrift: Wissenschaftliche Beilage zur
Jüdischen Presse,* No. 42 (Oct. 19, 1899, No. 10, p. 52); *Beilage zur . . . no. 34*
(Aug. 23, 1900, No. 8, pp. 30-31); Jacob Goldstein, "Arnold Bogumil Ehrlich:
Greatest of Living M'forshim," *The Hebrew Standard,* Vol. LII, 5 (Feb. 7, 1908),
including a photograph of Ehrlich; Richard M. Stern, "Arnold B. Ehrlich," *American Jewish Archives,* XXIII (April, 1971), 73-85. In this connection it may be
made known that Dr. Stern has given me, and they will be deposited at the New
York School of HUC-JIR, five notebooks (388 pp. in all) in Ehrlich's handwriting,
filled with *addenda* and *corrigenda* (all in German) to Genesis 1.4—Judges 9.24;
a number of passages in Genesis-Deuteronomy are repeated or discussed twice. [I
have just learned that several additional such notebooks, dealing with other Books
of the Bible, have been on deposit in the Library of the New York School.]

and New York, 1886-1903). This work was severely criticized from the very outset,[33] but its usefulness reached into circles which had no direct access to Jacob Levy's authoritative Wörterbücher in German.

Morris Jastrow Jr. (1861-1921),[34] Professor of Semitic Languages at the University of Pennsylvania, edited two Hebrew grammatical works written in Arabic by the brilliant medieval Jewish scholar, Ibn Hayyuj, dealing with *The Weak and Geminative Verbs in Hebrew* (Leyden, 1897). In addition, he wrote several works on the religion of ancient Mesopotamia which have retained a lot of value to this day; his book on *The Religion of Babylonia and Assyria* (Boston, 1898) went through several editions in English and German (cf. *Die Religion Babyloniens und Assyriens*, 2 vols. [Giessen, 1905-12]), and his *Aspects of Religious Belief and Practice in Babylonia and Assyria* (New York and London, 1911), is still being quoted. His *Hebrew and Babylonian Traditions* (New York, 1914) constituted the Haskell Lectures at Oberlin; nor should his book *The Civilization of Babylonia and Assyria,* etc. (Phila., 1915) go unmentioned.

In the field of Bible proper, Jastrow published an interesting trio of commentaries, *A Gentle Cynic* (Phila. and London, 1919),[35] *The Book of Job* (1920),[36] and *The Song of Songs, being a Collection of*

---

[33] Cf. Moore, p. 270, after the first two fascicles appeared, "M. Jastrow's Wörterbuch . . . ist wesentlich eine durch Weglassung der meisten Belegstellen verkürzte Übersetzung der Werkes Levy's . . . ," and he criticizes Jastrow's curious etymologies; cf. also Margolis, *AJSL,* 18 (1901-02), 56-58. On Jastrow, see M. Davis, op. cit., 54-60, with references on p. 60, n. 12, to a work by Jastrow on Jewish history between 586 and 166 B.C.E. (Heidelberg, 1865). Jastrow published an "Analysis of Psalms LXXXIV and CI" in the Alexander Kohut Memorial Volume, pp. 254-63.

[34] Cf. "In Memoriam Morris Jastrow, Jr." in *Journal of the American Oriental Society (=JAOS),* 4 (1921; part 5), 321-44, with articles by J. Morgenstern (on Jastrow "as a Biblical Critic," 322-33), A. T. Clay (". . . as an Assyriologist," 333-6), and J. A. Montgomery (with Clay; "Bibliography," 337-44); Clay and Montgomery had printed previously a *Bibliography of Morris Jastrow, Jr., Ph. D.,* etc. (Phila., 1910), on the occasion of "the twenty-fifth anniversary of his membership in the Faculty of the University of Pennsylvania." See also James A. Montgomery, "Morris Jastrow, Jr.," *AJSL,* 33 (1921), 1-11.

[35] *Being a Translation of the Book of Koheleth commonly known as Ecclesiastes stripped of later additions; also its Origin, Growth and Interpretation.*

[36] *Its Origin, Growth and Interpretation together with a New Translation based on a Revised Text.*

Love Lyrics of Ancient Palestine (1921).[37] Among his articles may be mentioned "A Babylonian Parallel to the Story of Job" (*JBL*, 25 [1906], 135-191) and "Rô'eh und Hôzeh in the Old Testament" (28[1909], 42-56).

Kaufmann Kohler (1843-1926)[38] dealt with biblical matters primarily as a theologian. Already his doctoral dissertation at Erlangen (Berlin, 1867), *Der Segen Jacobs* (Gen. 49), Kohler asserted, was "a bold effort at reconstructing the entire historic development of the religious views of the Bible, based upon novel mythological research." His *magnum opus* in this field is *Jewish Theology Systematically and Historically Considered* (New York, 1918), the original of which had appeared in German seven years earlier. Kohler was less successful in his textual studies of the Bible.[39]

David Neumark (1866-1924),[40] appointed in 1907 Professor of Religious Philosophy at the Hebrew Union College, wrote a noteworthy work *The Philosophy of the Bible* (Cincinnati, 1918). Joshua

---

[37] *Being a Collection of Love Lyrics of Ancient Palestine. A New Translation based on a Revised Text together with the Origin, Growth and Interpretation of the Songs.*

[38] See Max Kohler's biographical sketch of his father in *Studies in Jewish Literature issued in Honor of K. Kohler*, ed. David Philipson, David Neumark, and Julian Morgenstern (Berlin, 1913), 1-10; other sketches appeared there on Kohler as "Reformer" (11-29) by Philipson, and as theologian (30-38) by Neumark. See also Samuel Schulman's article in *UJE*, VI, 428-30. Adolph S. Oko contributed to the Kohler Festschrift a "Bibliography of Rev. Kaufman Kohler, 1867-1913," and M. J. Kohler compiled a supplementary bibliography for *K. Kohler Studies, Addresses and Personal Papers* (New York, 1931). Cf. also Kohler's conception of *A Living Faith*, ed. Samuel S. Cohon (Cincinnati, 1948). Special mention may be made of Kohler's monograph "The Testament of Job, an Essene Midrash on the Book of Job, reëdited and translated with Introductory and Exegetical Notes," pp. 264-338 of the Kohut Memorial Volume.

[39] Cf. Moore (269), "Kohler's textkritische Versuche zu Jesaias ("Emendations of the Hebrew Text of Isaiah," *Hebraica*, 2 [1885], 39-48) sind klassische Beispiele der unmethodische Willkür, welche die Textkritik schon zu oft in Miskredit gebraucht hat."

[40] On this gifted scholar see the Neumark number of *Hebrew Union College Monthly* (Jan. 1924); L. L. Mann's eulogy in *YBCCAR*, 35 (1925), 240-42; and S. S. Cohon, "The History of the Hebrew Union College," *Publications of the American Jewish Historical Society*, 40 (1950), 43 and n. 50 (which includes bibliography and references to additional data).

Bloch (op. cit., 25-6) has correctly observed that he "daringly ventured to show the historical development of various philosophical problems in Jewish thought and literature. He was more than the historian of Jewish philosophy; he was also an original religious thinker . . ."

Mayer Sulzberger (1843-1923)[41] applied his knowledge and interest in matters of jurisprudence to the Bible. In 1909 appeared his first work, *The Am Ha-Aretz, the Ancient Hebrew Parliament* (Philadelphia), in which the proposition was set forth that, as put by Horace Stern (*UJE*, X, 100-101), "Am Ha-Aretz was in reality the name given to a representative council in the Jewish kingdom which had all the essential qualities of a modern parliamentary body." In his study *The Polity of the Ancient Hebrews* (Phila., 1912) it would appear that Sulzberger had in mind his own United States when "he sought to reconstruct the scheme of government of the Jewish city-states and the federal laws which bound them together." His study of *The Ancient Hebrew Law of Homicide* (1915) was followed eight years later by his analysis of *The Status of Labor in Ancient Israel;* in the latter the attempt was made to prove that already 3,000 years ago the Israelites provided legislation to protect the working class in the land. Judge Stern summed up these works very fairly: "While, perhaps, his theories, thus expounded, have not been generally accepted by Bible exegetes, these studies of the laws and government of ancient Israel amply attest to his Hebraic scholarship as well as the originality of his intellect."

Gabriel Wolf Margolis (1848-1935),[42] an outstanding figure in American Jewish Orthodox life, published a five-volume commentary on the Pentateuch under the title תורת גבריאל,[43] together with a commentary on the Haftarot[44] and the five Megillot.[45]

Herman Rosenthal (1863-1917),[46] among other things Chief of

---

[41] Cf. Horace Stern, *UJE*, X, 100-101; M. Davis, op. cit., 61-70.

[42] Popularly known as Rebbi Velvele. See *Who's Who in American Jewry*, 1926, p. 416. Unfortunately he was omitted in the *UJE*.

[43] ספר חמשה חומשי תורה, ועליהם תרגום אונקלוס ופי' רש"י, ובעל הטורים ותולדות
אהרן. ובאור חדש בשם תורת גבריאל והערות הרבה בשם נחל נבים ... (Jerusalem, 1910-1925).

[44] הַנֵּת אֱגוֹז.

[45] ספר גנזי מרגליות, והוא באור חמש מגלות.

[46] *JE*, 10 (1907), 478-9; *UJE*, 9 (1943), 219-20. I must thank Dr. Bloch for drawing my attention to H. Rosenthal, as well as to G. W. Margolis following.

the Slavonic Department of the New York Public Library (1898-1917), published two items that fall within our scope, *Worte des Sammlers* (*Koheleth*) (International News Co., New York, 1885 [47]) and *Das Lied der Lieder* (New York, 1893, 30 pp.). Both works were described by the author as "aus dem hebräischen Urtext in neue deutsche Reime gebracht."

Cyrus Adler (1863-1940) was the first student to register in the newly-formed Semitics Seminary at the Johns Hopkins University when he heard that Paul Haupt was coming from Germany to head the Department.[48] In 1889 Moore noted (p. 258 and n. 2) that Adler "hat eine Ausgabe der Schriften Edward Hincks angekündigt *(Proceedings of the American Oriental Society,* May, 1888, XXII-XXVI) eine versuchsweise gegebene Bibliographic genannter Schriften enthaltend. Von Adler haben wir auch u. a. The views of the Babylonians concerning Life after Death, Andover Rev. X, S. 92 ff.: The Legends of Semiarmis and the Nimrod Epic, Johns Hopkins Univ. Circulars VI, S. 50 ff. Anderes s. *LBOPh.* II. 910-913." Abraham A. Neuman recalls (pp. 23 f.) that Adler "had the distinction of being the first American to receive the Doctorate in Semitics in an American University . . . A strange mishap marred the fate of his doctoral thesis, 'The Annals of Sardanapalus; a double transliteration, translation, commentary and concordance of the cuneiform text.' For, no sooner had he completed his work, than the text appeared in a German publication, and Adler, consequently, abandoned the idea of publishing his own work." Within three years after graduation Adler had attained the rank of Associate Professor in Semitics at the Johns Hopkins, and was apparently destined for a distinguished career in the

---

[47] Second ed., 1893, 36 pp. Dedicated to Michael Heilprin, on whom see pp. 295 above.

[48] See Abraham A. Neumann, *Cyrus Adler, a Biographical Sketch* (New York, 1942); Walter H. Blumenthal, *UJE,* I, 88-9, with some bibliographical data; Cyrus Adler, *Lectures, Selected Papers, Addresses* (Phila. 1933), with the bibliography compiled by Edward D. Coleman and Joseph Reider, pp. 363-445—where there will be found, e. g., Adler's chapter (162-71) on "The Semitic Seminary of Johns Hopkins University."

field[49], but he came into contact with S. P. Langley and the Smithsonian Institution in Washington and went off to carve out for himself a unique career in much broader scholarly and public circles; the founding of the Dropsie College for Hebrew and Cognate Learning in Philadelphia in 1907, "as a postgraduate institution for Hebrew learning and other branches of Semitic culture," was probably his greatest achievement. But that is another story, to be recounted elsewhere.

Aaron Ember (1878-1926) was another distinguished student of Haupt. He specialized in Egypto-Semitic, attempting to determine the common primitive Semitic stratum in the Egyptian and Semitic languages. Part of his doctoral thesis and major work appeared in the Haupt Volume, "Partial Assimilation in Old Egyptian" (pp. 300-312), and four years later there appeared his *Egypto-Semitic-Studies,* ed. Frida Behnk, with a "Vorwort" by Kurt Sethe (Leipzig, 1930; aided by the Alexander Kohut Memorial Foundation). [50]

The high-water mark of biblical scholarship was achieved in the person of Max Leopold Margolis (1866-1932). Coming to this country at the age of 23, already trained both in traditional and secular learning, Margolis soon began to specialize in Semitics. Three years later, in 1892, he was launched on a career in biblical studies, having been appointed Assistant Professor of Hebrew and Biblical Exegesis

---

[49] Cf. such articles as "The Cotton Grotto — an Ancient Quarry in Jerusalem. With Notes on Ancient Methods of Quarrying," in the Kohut Memorial Volume, 73-82; "The Beginnings of Semitic Studies in America," *Oriental Studies published in Commemoration of the Fortieth Anniversary* (1883-1923) *of Paul Haupt as Director of the Oriental Seminary of the Johns Hopkins University* (Baltimore and Leipzig, 1926), 317-28. This volume was edited jointly by Adler and Aaron Ember. For a number of additional scholarly items by Adler, see *Index to JAOS* (1902), pp. 1-2, s. Adler.

[50] Cf. F[rank] R. B[lake], "In Memorian Professor Ember," p. IX of the Paul Haupt Volume; Kurt Sethe, *Zeitschrift für die ägyptische Sprache und Altertumkunde,* 4 (1926), 130-1; Heinrich Loewe, *Aaron Ember In Memoriam* (Berlin, 1926; privately printed, 8 pp.); *UJE,* IV, 96-7.

at the Hebrew Union College in Cincinnati.[51] This remarkable career was to span forty years, the last twenty-four of which he served at the Dropsie College for Hebrew and Cognate Learning in Philadelphia as Professor of Biblical Philology.

Margolis' scholarship was probably not equalled in this country, just as S. R. Driver was unique in Great Britain and Julius Wellhausen in Germany. As a teacher too he was preeminent. Disciples of his have occupied chairs in such higher Jewish institutions of learning in America as Dropsie College, Hebrew Union College-Jewish Institute of Religion (New York), Jewish Theological Seminary, and at the University of Pennsylvania.

Margolis was unsurpassed as a textual critic. His analysis of "The Scope and Methodology of Biblical Philology"[52] at once stamped it as a model work, which most modern Bible scholars could consult to considerable advantage. In a period when scholars had come to use the ancient versions, especially the Septuagint, rather indiscriminately to support emendations of the Hebrew text, Margolis set for himself the task of determining the true character and usefulness of these versions, above all the Septuagint, in the reconstruction and understanding of the preserved Hebrew text. In a series of articles, among them $\Lambda \alpha \mu \beta \acute{\alpha} \nu \epsilon \iota \nu$ (including Compounds and Derivatives) and its Hebrew-Aramaic Equivalents in Old Testament Greek" and "Studien im griechischen alten Testament,"[53] Margolis laid down once and for all the correct method that the biblical scholar must employ if he wishes to use the Septuagint and other primary versions as an aid in the textual analysis and exegesis of the Hebrew Bible.

Margolis went beyond that. He decided that even before the

---

[51] See Robert Gordis, "The Life of Professor Max Leopold Margolis; an Appreciation," in *Max Leopold Margolis, Scholar and Teacher* (Alumni Association of Dropsie College, Phila. 5712-1952), 1-16; Alexander Marx, *Studies in Jewish History and Booklore* (New York, 5704-1944), 418-30.

[52] *JQR,* 1 (1910-11), 5-41. Margolis used Job 3.3 in this article. It is interesting that Bleddyn J. Roberts used Job 3.2-4 to exemplify textual criticism in *The Old Testament Text and Versions* (Cardiff, 1951), 180-1, unaware apparently of Margolis' study.

[53] Respectively in *AJSL,* 22 (1906), 110-119 and *ZAW,* 27 (1907), 212-70.

competent scholar tried to determine the original text and meaning of the Hebrew Bible on the basis of, say, the Septuagint, he should attempt to recover the original text and meaning of the Septuagint text itself. For "how could one be certain that he had before him the original text of the Greek translation as it left the hands of the translators? After all, there were several Greek manuscripts of various divisions and books of the Bible. These manuscripts differed from each other to a greater or lesser extent. Moreover, the Septuagint itself had been translated in various periods into other languages, into Latin (2nd century C.E.), Sahidic-Bohairic (Coptic; 2nd), Gothic (4th), Armenian (4th?), Georgian (4th-5th), Ethiopic (4th-5th), Arabic 7th-8th), and Slavonic (9th-10th). And a third source of the Septuagint are the quotations made from it in the commentaries and writings of Church Fathers and other writers (e. g., Philo and Josephus)."

The present writer can do no better than to continue to quote from what he had previously written on this subject:

"Thus the textual critic would logically have to study the quotations from the Septuagint, the manuscripts of the secondary versions, and the manuscripts of the Septuagint, and try to get through this mass of material to the original (Proto-)Septuagint. The first scholar to have outlined an approach to this material which would lead to the recovery of the Proto-Septuagint was Paul de Lagarde, and both his theory and his practical work were pursued profitably by Alfred Rahlfs. In commentary form, Lagarde's approach was utilized best (under the influence of Margolis) by J. A. Montgomery (*International Critical Commentary on Daniel,* 1927).[54] It was Margolis however who carried out the Lagardian idea most completely and successfully to its logical conclusion. For two decades he devoted himself to the problem of reconstructing the text of the book of Joshua, providing us with the most exhaustive investigation ever made by any one man or group of men of the entire textual history of any book in the Old Testament . . . In a preliminary study on 'The Groupings of the Codices in the Greek

---

[54] See in general, Harry M. Orlinsky, "Current Progress and Problems in Septuagint Research," *The Study of the Bible Today and Tomorrow,* ed. Harold R. Willoughby (Chicago, 1947), 144-161.

Joshua' [55] he wrote that 'While engaged in a study of the transliterations occurring in the Greek Old Testament[56] . . . I deemed it advisable to include geographical terms . . . and names of places . . . This additional material being particularly abundant in the Book of Joshua, my attention was caught by the frequently recurring collocation of certain sigla in the apparatus of Holmes-Parsons. In one instance where an entire verse had to be investigated, the grouping was unmistakable. With the key found, I set about working up chapters 15 and 19 which are replete with place-names, but also other passages, covering in all one-half of the book. My key proved to work . . .' The following year Margolis published two more exploratory articles along these lines, the superb analysis of 'The K Text of Joshua' [57] and 'The Washington M.S. of Joshua' [58] . . . Margolis began to devote himself increasingly to the unusually complex and laborious task of getting at the original Septuagint text of Joshua. Whenever possible, he gathered from all corners of the earth photographic reproductions of every uncial and cursive manuscript, catena, lectionary, and the like, containing all or part of Joshua. In addition he had before him the various editions of the Onomasticon and of all the secondary versions, such as the Old Latin, Syriac, Sahidic, Bohairic, Ethiopic, Arabic, Armenian, and of all the earlier patristic writers, such as Justin, Origen, Eusebius, and Theodoret. He chose Joshua of all the books in the Bible because it lent itself admirably to textual and exegetical analysis and, what is of supreme importance, because it contained hundreds of proper names in the text. Margolis had come to recognize in 'geographic terms . . . and names of places . . . [the key to the] collocation of certain sigla in the apparatus of Holmes-Parsons' . . . In 1927 Margolis published a brief but comprehensive enough article in which he presented to the scholarly world the conclusions which he had reached in his Greek Joshua, after almost two decades of keen and laborious work. In his own words[59]: 'The sum

---

[55] *JQR,* 1 (1910-11), 259-63.

[56] Cf., e. g., Margolis' discussion "The Pronunciation of the שׁוא according to New Hexaplaric Material," *AJSL,* 26 (1909), 62-70.

[57] *AJSL,* 28 (1911), 1-55.

[58] *JAQS,* 31 (1911), 365-367.

[59] "Specimen of a New Edition of the Greek Joshua," in *Jewish Studies in Memory of Israel Abrahams* (New York, 1927), 307-323. Cf. Margolis' careful and erudite analysis of *"Xwpis"* on the margin of certain Septuagint manuscripts, in *Oriental Studies dedicated to Paul Haupt* (Baltimore-Leipzig, 1926), 84-92.

of the witnesses yields four principal recensions, P, C, S, E, and in addition a number of MSS. variously mixed which I name M. At the outset it must be remarked that all of our witnesses are more or less mixed; the classification has in mind the basic character of a text, which alone is the determinant. P is the Palestinian recension spoken of by Jerome, that is the Eusebian edition of the Septuagint column in Origen's Hexapla-Tetrapla [then, as in the case of CSEM below, follows a sketch of some of the more important manuscripts that belong to this recension] . . . C is a recension which was at home in Constantinople and Asia Minor. We are helped in localizing the recension by the aid of the Armenian version . . . S is the Syrian (Antiochian) recension . . . An outstanding characteristic of the S recension is the correction of the Greek style, as shown by the substitution of Attic grammatical forms for Hellenistic. Otherwise Jerome's description of Lucian as but a form of the common text holds good. But it is a distinct form, as the proper names show with all the desired evidence. The Egyptian recension, E, is reserved with relative purity in B . . . The Coptic and Ethiopic versions unmistakably point to the Egyptian provenance of their text. Hence the designation of the recension. There remains a number of mss. which may be classed together as M, i.e. mixed texts. Mixture is the general characteristic, the elements coming from the four principal recensions in diverse processes of contamination . . . The road to the original text of G leads across the common, unrevised text . . . In his monumental work (all in autograph!), *The Book of Joshua in Greek, according to the critically restored text, with an apparatus containing the variants of the principal recensions and of the individual witnesses* (Parts I–IV, covering 19.38, Paris, 1931-38), Margolis provided at the top of the page 'the nearest approach to the Greek original as it left the hands of the translator(s)' of Joshua. Below the text there was made available the pertinent data of the chief recensions. And lastly, at the bottom of the page, brief notes bearing on the Septuagint in relation to the Hebrew text. It is exceedingly unfortunate that Part V of this great work has not yet appeared, and that the all-important Introduction to it probably never will appear . . ." [60]

---

[60] From H. M. Orlinsky, "Margolis' Work in the Septuagint," in the Margolis Volume, 38-42. [See now also, H. M. Orlinsky, "The Hebrew *Vorlage* of the Septuagint of the Book of Joshua," *Supplements to Vetus Testamentum*, vol. XVII, 1969 (Rome Congress Volume), pp. 187-195.]

Margolis was no less scientific in dealing with the grammar of Biblical Hebrew. Scarcely anyone knew this discipline as thoroughly as he did. In the tradition of the Hayyujes and Janahs of the Spanish Golden Era, as well as in accord with the growth of Comparative Semitic Linguistics in his own day, he tried to comprehend Biblical Hebrew in the light especially of Arabic and Aramaic.[61]

An outstanding achievement to be credited to Margolis was the primary role which he played in the making of the Jewish Publication Society translation of the Hebrew Bible.[62] The only biblical specialist among the seven men on the Editorial Committee, of which he was Editor-in-Chief and Secretary, Margolis was responsible for going through the vast and complex sources and secondary literature, Jewish and non-Jewish, and to draw up for the Committee the first draft of the proposed translation. No one else in this country, or in Europe for that matter, was equipped to perform this exacting and prodigious task. That the translation, which appeared finally in 1917, at once became recognized as the outstanding modern version of the Hebrew Bible was due essentially to the wisdom of Margolis.[63]

In summation, Margolis was the single brilliant star in the crown of biblical scholarship to which American Jewry can point with justified pride.

Solomon Bloomgarden (1870-1927),[64] the great Yiddish poet and

---

[61] Cf. Margolis' *Elementary Text-Book of Hebrew Accidence,* etc. (Cincinnati, 1893) and the Two-leaf Folder containing tables of Hebrew grammar (Jerusalem, 1925), respectively described by Joseph Reider in his "Bibliography of the Works of Max L. Margolis," *Max Leopold Margolis,* etc., pp. 63 (bottom) and 74-5. And see F. Zimmerman, "The Contributions of M. L. Margolis to the fields of Bible and Rabbinics," and Ephraim A. Speiser, "The Contribution of Max Leopold Margolis to Semitic Linguistics," respectively on pp. 17-26 and 27-33 of the Margolis Volume.

[62] See Margolis' (anonymous!) article "The New [*JPS*] English Translation of the Bible," *American Jewish Yearbook,* 5678-1917-18, 161-93. Cyrus Adler was Chairman of the Editorial Committee.

[63] Margolis published commentaries on Micah (Phila., 5669-1908), Zephaniah and Malachi (in Abraham Kahana's series; תנ״ך עם פירוש מדעי, Tel Aviv, 5690); see J. Reider's brief descriptions of them, on pp. 67 and 76 of the Margolis Volume.

[64] The best brief account of Yehoash's life and works may be found in Zalman Raisin's Yiddish *Lexicon fun der Yiddisher Literatur, Presse, un Philologie* (4 vols.,

stylist more popularly known as Yehoash, fascinated as he was from his earliest youth by the Bible, conceived the idea of making available to the Jewish masses a Yiddish translation of the Hebrew Sacred Scriptures that would be both literary and scientific. In 1910 he published the first fruits of his labor, the book of Isaiah in one volume, and Job, Canticles, Ruth, and Ecclesiastes in another.

But Yehoash was not pleased with these efforts; he was satisfied neither with his understanding of the Hebrew—although a *musmakh* (ordained graduate) of the famed Volozhin Yeshivah—nor with his style and choice of words in Yiddish. To prepare himself properly for what now became his life's work, he left America in 1914, after an uninterrupted residence of twenty-four years, to live in Palestine, there to absorb into his sensitive soul the atmosphere of the country which produced the Bible, and to acquaint himself ever more intimately with everything in the way of translations, introductions, commentaries, and analyses which bore on the Book of Books. He acquired a thorough knowledge of Arabic[65] and Syriac, and increased his knowledge of Greek and Latin, in order that he might use the Septuagint, Peshitta, Vulgate, (Judeo-)Arabic, etc., in the original. Like so many other Jewish intellectuals of Eastern Europe, he was quite familiar with the languages and literatures of Russia, France, Germany, and England, to say nothing of Hebrew and Aramaic.

World War I forced Yehoash's return to New York in 1916. During the eleven years which followed, years made long and difficult by the fact and knowledge that his health and life hung on a fine hair,

---

Vilna, 5786-1926), in vol. I, cols. 1244-53. Cf. also Chaim Lieberman, *Dichter un Velten* (1923), 83-136; Z. F. Finkelstein, *Jüdisches Lexikon,* III (1929), cols. 169-70, where reference is made to Yehoash's Yiddish translations of Aesop, La Fontaine and Lessing, "und schliesslich (gemeinsam mit Spiwak) ein Wörterbuch aller Ausdrücke hebr. und aram. Ursprungs, die in jiddischer Sprache gebraucht werden"; Joshua Bloch, *UJE,* II (1940), 413-4. Evlin Yehoash Dworkin has a sketch of "My Father Yehoash" in Isidore Goldstick's English translations of *Poems of Yehoash* (London, Canada, 1952), pp. 11-15.

65 The post-qoranic as well as the classical. Yehoash published a number of old Arabic stories in Yiddish translation.

he devoted himself to his sacred task. He compiled innumerable notes on the Hebrew text and versions; he revised his translation time and again. Yet throughout all this, he could interest no one to finance the publication of his translation. In 1922 he agreed to publish it, at the rate of several chapters per week, in the New York Yiddish daily *Der Tog* (The Day); by the end of 1925 more than half of the Bible, including the book of Jeremiah, had thus been made available to the public. It was, finally, Yehoash's good fortune to raise sufficient funds to publish part of his great work, and he lived just long enough to see in print the first two volumes, constituting the Pentateuch.

Through the tireless efforts of his immediate family, this edition was completed in eight beautifully printed and bound volumes, in special type set up by the Jewish Publication Society of America (1937). In 1938 there appeared a *Folks Oisgabe* (popular edition) in two volumes, which has gone through a number of printings. And in 1941 Yehoash's dream of a bi-glot Bible in two columns, a masoretic text of the Hebrew and his Yiddish translation facing each other, was realized.[66] The entire work was crowned in 1949 by the publication of Yehoash's Notes,   הערות צום תנ״ך.[67]

---

[66] Many of the data given above were drawn from my article "Yehoash's Yiddish Translation of the Bible," *JBL*, 60, 2 (June 1941), 173-7. The best account of Yiddish translations of the Bible or portions thereof, together with excellent historical treatments of their origin and character, may be found in Israel Zinberg's remarkably complete and compact *Die Geschichte fun der Literatur bei Yiden* (in Yiddish), Vilna, Vol. VI (1935), Chaps. II and V; Vol. VII, Book II (1936), Chap. VIII. Samuel I. Feigin reviewed Yehoash's translation in the Yiddish periodical, *Die Tsukunft* (The Future), 1930, 355-60.   And see now Judah Rosenthal's, נ״ע״, "הערות צו יהואשעס תנ״ך-איבערזעצונג", in the Yehoash number of "די גאלדענע קייט" (Tel-Aviv, no. 72, 1971, 107-115. [My article on "Yehoash's Yiddish Translation of the Bible" is reproduced elsewhere in this volume.]

[67]   שנת תש״י — לפ״ק,   שנה ב' למדינת ישראל, New York, Yehoash Farlag Gezelshaft, 4to, 317 pages. Together with the הערות appeared a useful לעקסיקאן פון מפרשים און פירושים אין יהואשעס הערות צום תנ״ך (*Lexicon of Sources and Exegetes in Yehoash's Notes on the Bible*) by the recently lamented Dr. Mordecai Kosover (62 pages, including an Index). Perhaps mention may be made here of Yehoash's Yiddish translation of The Sayings of the Fathers די לעהרען פון די פאטערס (פרקי אבות) (New York, 1912; English translation, revised by Benzion Halper (New York, 1921) on whom see below, p. 320.

Israel Friedlaender (1876-1921),[68] a warm, communally-minded Jew and humanitarian, was primarily an Arabist. Indeed, "He met his death," Prof. Boaz Cohen reminds us in his moving *Appreciation* (p. 3), "at the hands of ruthless bandits, in the prime of his life, while administering to the needs of his stricken brethren in the pogrom-ridden area of the Ukraine . . ." Friedlaender's original intention was to acquire a rabbinical degree, and it was for this purpose that he came to the Rabbinical Seminary in Berlin at the exciting age of eighteen. At the same time, however, he began to study also Semitic languages at the University of Berlin, and this led him ultimately to Strasbourg University and its noted philologian, Theodor Nöldeke. He acquired a Doctorate[69] in the Department of Semitics, received a thorough knowledge of Arabic, Syriac, Ethiopic, and Assyrian, as well as of Hebrew and Aramaic, and even obtained an instructorship in Semitics, "an unusual distinction for a Russian Jew," as Cohen hastens to add. In 1903 Solomon Schechter invited young Friedlaender, then twenty-eight, to come to the Jewish Theological Seminary of America; here he taught Bible and Philosophy, and later also History.

"Friedlaender's approach to Biblical problems," Louis Finkelstein

---

[68] See Boaz Cohen, *Israel Friedlaender, a Bibliography of his Writings, with an Appreciation* (New York, 1936, 40 pages); cf. there (p. 12, n. 3) a select list of notices and tributes on the occasion of Friedlaender's death. Mention may be made here of Alexander Marx, "Friedlaender the Scholar" in his *Studies in Jewish History and Booklore* (New York, 5704 — 1944; reprinted from the *Menorah Journal*, 6 [1920], 344-50), pp. 400-8 (note in the same issue, Mrs. Israel Friedlaender's elegy on "A Chassid's Service to American Judaism" [pp. 337-344] and Judah L. Magnes' account of "Friedlaender the Student" [351-4]); Samuel A. Poznanski, התקופה, 8 (1921 — 5680), 483-8; Jacob Kohn, *American Jewish Yearbook* [= *AJYB*], 23 (1921-22), 65-79; Louis Finkelstein, *UJE*, 4 (1941), 450-2; Max Raisin, *Great Jews I Have Known* (New York, 1952), Index, s. Friedlaender.

[69] *Der Sprachgebrauch des Maimonides. Ein lexikalischer und grammatischer Beitrag zur Kenntnis des Mittelarabischen* (Leipzig, 1901); in its fuller form the dissertation appeared in 1902 (F. a. M., XXI + 199 pages). One of the important results of this study was "the conclusion that the common idea of a special Judeo-Arabic dialect had no real foundation. Maimonides, he showed, wrote the same Arabic as his most cultured Mohammedan contemporaries, only that he was more free from the literary influence of the language of the Koran, which restricted the Mohammedans in their literary expression . . ." (A. Marx, 401-2).

has well said, "was conservative, deviating widely from the dominant Wellhausen school of the day. Friedlaender was less interested in the technical problems of textual criticism than in the clarification of the meaning of the prophetic teaching . . ." And this is precisely why he did not make Bible his major field of investigation. "Much as he loved the Bible (indeed he knew the Hebrew original by heart and had actually every word of it at his fingertips)," wrote A. Marx (p. 407), " 'Biblical science with its bewildering divergence of opinion' did not overmuch appeal to him, and . . . he was too conscientious a scholar to accept its critical dicta uncritically. 'Ignorabimus,' he was convinced, must remain the answer to many of the mooted problems of Biblical criticism and he did not feel a call to add new hypotheses to the large number of those propounded by the Biblical students of our generation. Altogether he felt that we are much more Talmud Jews than Bible Jews. The later literature attracted him more as a subject of study . . ."

It required courage, as well as ability, for Friedlaender to review Charles A. Briggs, *International Critical Commentary on the Book of Psalms* (2 vols., New York, 1906-7), as critically as he did,[70] exposing "the terrible abuse of textual emendation on the part of 'critics' like Briggs, how the liberty toward the biblical text degenerates into license, unrestrained by considerations of philology, criticism or even common sense . . ." (p. 127).[71]

Friedlaender suggested in his article "Das hebräische סֵפֶר in einer verkannten Bedeutung,"[72] that the Hebrew word *séfer* in Isa. 30.8

---

[70] In *The American Hebrew and Jewish Messenger*, Literary Supplement, vol. 81, No. 9, pp. iii-vii, July 5, 1907; reprinted as Chap. VIII, "A New Specimen of Modern Biblical Exegesis" in Friedlaender's *Past and Present, a Collection of Jewish Essays* (Cincinnati, 1919), 113-137.

[71] Seven years earlier Friedlaender had reviewed in the same vein, and no less justifiably, Thomas K. Cheyne's *The Book of the Prophet Isaiah* (in Paul Haupt's so-called Polychrome Bible series), in *Zeitschrift für hebräische Bibliographie* (= *ZfHB*), 4 (1900), 105-8. Other reviews by Friedlaender are those of J. Barth, *Wurzeluntersuchungen zum hebräischen und aramäischen Lexicon*, in *ZfHB*, 7 (1903), 3-5; Max Löhr, *Untersuchungen zum Buche Amos, op. cit.*, 13-14.

[72] *JQR*, O. S., 15 (1903), 102-3.

and Job 19.23 might have not the usual meaning "letter, book" but "bronze" or the like, cognate to Akkadian *siparru* and Arab. صِفْر , and (עַל) כתב (parallel to חקק) might mean not "write" but "carve out" (einhauen); "Zu dem Lautwandel צ = ס vgl. Barth, *Etymologische Studien . . .*" Perhaps, Friedlaender concluded, the original pointing was *sippār* rather than *sefer*.[73] But Friedlaender's better-known writings in the field of Bible were his historical studies, which, as A. Marx observed (pp. 406-7), "maintained a close relationship with the present, as he was always earnestly concerned with the well-being of his people." This is borne out by such essays as "The Political Ideal of the Prophets: a Study in Biblical Zionism," [74] "Were Our Ancestors Capable of Self-Government?" [75] "Hezekiah's Great Passover," [76] and "The Prophet Jeremiah." [77] The following passages from the first-named essay are noteworthy: (pp. 31-2), " 'With the death of Haggai, Zechariah and Malachi,' so our Rabbis declare, 'the holy spirit departed from Israel.' Modern critics, from a diametrically opposite point of view, draw a similar line of demarcation and speak of the period following that of the prophets sneeringly as the 'genesis of Judaism' [with reference to the title of Eduard Meyer's well-known book, *Die Entstehung des Judentums*]. But this demarcation is unjust as well as unfounded. For the scribes were faithful followers of the prophets, and Ezra was the disciple of Isaiah . . . The Jews of the post-exilic age were only a weak, insignificant remnant, surrounded by dangerous foes, and by still more dangerous friends, and absorption stared them in the face. They did not wish to be dissolved . . . And

---

[73] In *JQR*, New Series, 1 (1910), 252-7, Friedlaender published an interesting discussion entitled "The Jews of Arabia and the Rechabites."

[74] *Jewish Comment*, March 11, 1910; reprinted also in Hebrew (היסוד המדיני בהשקפות הנביאים , *Hatoren*, [June-Oct. 1913], pp. 9-10, 64-7, 156-162, 208-212), and finally as Chap. I in *Past and Present*, 1-34.

[75] *American Hebrew and Jewish Messenger*, vol. 84, no. 21, March 26, 1909, pp. 539-40 (= Chap. III in *Past and Present*, 39-49).

[76] *Sunday School Times*, May 27, 1911 (not accessible to me) (= Chap. V in *Past and Present*, 59-66).

[77] *Jewish Exponent* (Philadelphia and Baltimore), Nov. 25 (p. 1), Dec. 2 (p. 8) and 9 (p. 11), 1904 (= Chap. VI in *Past and Present*, 67-94).

when on the twentieth of Kislev 458, the people, shivering from cold and excitement, gathered on the street around Ezra and took a vow to send away their foreign wives and the children born from them, and to separate themselves from the people of the earth, the political ideal of the prophets achieved its final and lasting triumph . . ."

The essay "Self-government" was prompted by a paper published a year previously in which the following statement appeared: "The history of Israel and Judah . . . is on the whole a gloomy record of bad government, tyranny and oppression, such as has been characteristic of every little Oriental state from beginning of history. It is the most incontrovertible proof that Israel's genius does not lie in the field of self-government, that from the first to last as a nation Israel was a most dismal failure." But let the reader go to Friedlaender's spirited reply directly.

Abraham Shalom Ezekiel Yahuda (1877-1951)[78] began his scholarly career as an Arabist, but he devoted the last quarter-century of his life in trying to prove that "higher biblical criticism" was entirely wrong. He received his doctorate at Strasbourg in 1904, having studied Semitics under Nöldeke. From 1904 to 1914 he occupied the chair in Biblical Exegesis and Semitic Philology at Berlin's Hochschule für die Wissenschaft des Judentums, finally leaving for the University of Madrid to fill the special chair in Hebrew Language and Literature of the Jewish Golden Era in Spain (1915-1922). In 1942 he became associated with the New School for Social Research in New York.

Yahuda made Egyptology bear the major burden in his efforts to clarify and substantiate the text and context of the Bible, especially the patriarchal and Mosaic periods. In 1902 he published a study of the "Hapax Legomena im Alten Testament,"[79] and four years later

---

[78] See *Jüdisches Lexikon* (where 1878 is the year given for his birth), 4, 2 (1930), cols. 1519-20; *UJE*, 10 (1943), 583-4; Menachem Ribalow, מָסוֹת בְּקֹרֶת, עִם הַכַּד אֶל הַמַּבּוּעַ (*Essays on Modern Hebrew Literature*, New York, 1950): א.ש.יְהוּדָה אִישׁ הַמִּזְרָח), pp. 188-95; *American Jewish Year Book* (= AJYB), 54 (1953), 541.

[79] *JQR*, 15 (1903), 698-714.

Die biblische Exegese in ihren Beziehungen zur semitischen Philologie.[80] His two major works were *Die Sprache des Pentateuch in ihren Beziehung zum Ägyptische*[81] and *The Accuracy of the Bible.*[82] Biblical scholars generally were not as impressed by Dr. Yahuda's arguments as some lay circles were, and professional Egyptologists were rather critical of his methodology and use of data.

In addition, Yahuda published numerous articles in various journals, here and abroad,[83] and in 1946 the Histadrut Ivrit (*Ogen*) put out a Hebrew volume of his essays and articles in matters biblical, Arabic and *personalia,* עֵבֶר וַעֲרָב,[84] the first section of which was devoted to Biblical Researches (מחקרים במקרא , pp. 1-102), dealing with such topics as Joseph and his Rule (ספּוּרֵי יוֹסֵף וְשִׁלְטוֹנוֹ), the Bondage in Egypt (שֵׁעֲבוּד יִשְׂרָאֵל בְּמִצְרַיִם), the Date of the Exodus (שְׁנַת יְצִיאַת מִצְרַיִם), Sigmund Freud on Moses (זִיגְמוּנְד פְרוֹיְד עַל מֹשֶׁה וְתוֹרָתוֹ), the Book of Esther (. . . כִּתְבֵי־הַקֹּדֶשׁ מֵהַתְּקוּפָה הַפַּרְסִית) and Our Sabbath and the Sabbath of the Bible Critics (הַשַּׁבָּת שֶׁלָּנוּ וְהַשַּׁבָּת שֶׁל מְבַקְּרֵי הַמִּקְרָא).

A notable accomplishment in the field of Bible which reflected great credit on the American Jewish community was the section constituting the articles on Bible in *The Jewish Encyclopedia* (12 volumes, 1901-1905). Under the astute and thoroughly competent

---

[80] Antrittsvorlesung gehalten in der Lehranstalt für die Wissenschaft des Judenthums in Berlin am 2. Mai 1905 (Berlin, 1906, 51 pp.).

[81] Berlin und Leipzig, 1929, 301 pp., and a "Hieroglyphische Beilage" of 16 pp. In its English form: *The Language of the Pentateuch in its Relation to Egyptian* (London, 1933).

[82] Subtitled: *The Stories of Joseph, the Exodus and Genesis Confirmed and Illustrated by Egyptian Monuments and Language* (London, 1934, 226 pp.).

[83] E. g., "Medical and Anatomical Terms in the Pentateuch in the Light of Egyptian Medical Papyri," *Journal of the History of Medicine and Allied Sciences,* 2, 4 (Autumn, 1947), 549-74; "Hebrew Words of Egyptian Origin," *JBL,* 66 (1947), 83-90.

[84] אֹסֶף מַחְקָרִים וּמַאֲמָרִים, שִׁירַת הָעֲרָבִים, זִכְרוֹנוֹת וּרְשָׁמִים (New York, 5706, 307 pp., and 18 reproductions); many of these essays appeared originally in the Hebrew weekly *Ha-Doar,* the Hebrew Annual *Sefer Ha-Shanah Lihudei America,* and the Hebrew monthly *Bitzaron.*

editorship of Cyrus Adler and his associates, among which the name of Louis Ginzberg ought not go unmentioned, the best scholars of the time were drawn in as contributors. Unlike the other biblical and general encyclopedias, the *Jewish Encyclopedia* divided the articles on biblical books and themes into three main parts: the traditional Jewish view, the modern critical views, and the post-biblical views in Jewish, Christian and Moslem circles. In this connection it should be noted that many of the articles on biblical themes which were written by Richard Gottheil (e. g., Bible Translations; Job) are still useful today. They are characterized by a knowledge of the literature and by their sober statements.[85]

Abraham H. Rosenberg (1838-1925; see *JE*, X, 474) compiled an encyclopedic work on the Bible, אוצר השמות (2nd ed., New York, 5683-1923). A wealth of rabbinic material was incorporated in this work.

The family of Rabbi Israel Zeligman (1842-1908) published his אוצר המספרים , *The Treasury of Numbers. A Numerical Compilation, including references of Numbers ranging from One to One Thousand, taken from the Bible, Talmud, Midrash and other Classical Writings of Rabbinical Literature* (Baltimore and New York, 1942).

Caspar Levias (1860-1934), trained at Columbia University and the Johns Hopkins University, and a member of the Faculty of Hebrew Union College (1895-1905) and then of the Jewish Teachers Seminary, was a noted grammarian of Hebrew and Aramaic. Among his works is *A Grammar of the Aramaic Idiom contained in the Babylonian Talmud with constant reference to Gaonic Literature* (Cincinnati, 1900); this work appeared more elaborately in Hebrew in 1930, דקדוק ארמית בבלית (Alexander Kohut Memorial Foundation). In 1914-15 his valuable, but unfortunately uncompleted אוצר חכמת הלשון (Dictionary of Hebrew Philological Terms; Leipzig) appeared. His article "Who Were the Amorites?" (*Studies in Jewish Bibliography and Related Subjects in Memory of A. S. Freidus* [New York, 1929],

---

[85] Cf. George A. Kohut, "Professor Gottheil . . . an Appraisal at Seventy," *Columbia University Quarterly*, 25 (June, 1953), 137-45; *UJE*, V, 70-71.

404-30), wrote Joshua Bloch, "was a bold venture to identify the Amorites as the Amhars" (*UJE*, VI, 628). Levias contributed a number of important articles to the *Jewish Encyclopedia,* e. g., "Massorah" in Vol. VIII, 365-71; he left much unpublished material.

While not a specialist in Bible, William Rosenau (1865-1943),[86] from 1902 to 1932 a member of the Faculty of the Johns Hopkins University, published in 1901 a study of the *Hebraisms in the Authorized Version of the Bible* (Baltimore) and of *Jewish Biblical Commentators* three years later (Baltimore, 1904). His idea of "What Happened to the Ten Tribes" appeared in the *HUC Jubilee Volume* (1925, 79-88).

Phineas Mordell (1861-1934; *UJE,* VII, 644-5) published numerous studies of Hebrew grammar and of the origin of the Hebrew alphabet and numerals. In articles in the *JQR* and in Hebrew periodicals he tried to prove that the Hebrews, rather than the Phoenicians, invented the alphabet. Mention may be made here of "The Origin of Letters and Numerals according to the Sefer Yesirah" (*JQR,* 2 [1911-12], 557-83; 3 [1912-13], 517-44) and "The Beginning and Development of Hebrew Punctuation" (24 [1933-34], 137-49). Mordell died before he could finish working up his concept of a grammar of Biblical Hebrew; preliminary studies appeared in *Leshonenu,* אִמּוֹת וּתְנוּעוֹת (2 [5689-90], 231-56) and הַשְּׁוָא (3 [5690-91], 118-25).

Morris Levine (1881-1936), from 1917 until his death a member of the Faculty of the Jewish Theological Seminary, deserves mention. Seventeen of his essays were published, together with four essays by admirers of his, under the title כִּתְבֵי מֹשֶׁה הַלֵּוִי.[87]

Nathaniel Julius Reich (1882-1943) was an outstanding Egyptologist, until his death a member of the Faculty of the Dropsie College. He was the founder and editor of *Mizraim* (1933), and a contributor to many learned journals in matters relating to ancient Egypt and Israel; his special field of authority was Demotic.

---

[86] See J. Morgenstern, in *YBCCAR,* 54 (1944), 182-4; William F. Rosenblum. *The Life and Work of Rev. Dr. William Rosenau* (Cincinnati, 1946; 15 pp.).

[87] The Matz Foundation, New York, 1937 — 5697 (הוצאת קרן ישראל מץ, בהשתתפות ידידי המנוח).

Benzion Halper (1884-1924; *UJE*, V, 185-6), a noted Hebraist and Arabist, from 1912 a member of the Faculty of the Dropsie College, wrote a comprehensive study "The Participial Formations of the Geminate Verbs" (*ZAW*, 33 [1910], 42-57, 99-126, 201-228). A year later he published an interesting discussion, "The Notions of Buying and Selling in Semitic Languages" (vol. 34, 261-66). Halper's subsequent illustrous career was in the post-biblical field of study.

Israel Eitan (1885-1935) was a fine linguist and textual critic who made many *A Contribution to Biblical Lexicography* (New York, 1924). Utilizing the Semitic languages, especially Arabic, Eitan was able to derive new—or, rather, the original—meanings and nuances of a number of biblical words. Among his other publications may be mentioned here his analysis of Hebrew and Semitic particles (*AJSL*, 1928-30); unfortunately, this did not appear separately, as planned, as a book of 113 pages. Had Eitan been a Professor of Bible instead of a teacher in a Hebrew school, his reputation would have been as great as his scholarly work merited. See Samuel I. Feigin's appreciative essay on Eitan in Chap. III of   אנשי ספר, חוקרים וסופרים *Men of Letters: Scholars and Writers* (New York, 1950), pp. 40-55; the notes on pp. 405-8 constitute also something of a bibliography of Eitan's scholarly work.[88]

C. A. Ben Mordecai (Hyman Starr, died 1942) was a business man turned " 'amateur'—the lover of an art—who found in the study of the Bible the joy of his life." In 1946 there appeared posthumously *A Layman Looks at the Bible* (New York; with an Introduction by Abraham I. Katsh and a Memoir by Solomon E. Starrels), in which Ben Mordecai's two articles in *JBL* ("Chezib" [1939] and "The Iniquity of the Sanctuary" [1941]) were reproduced with thirty-one other "Essays" and "Notes and Jottings."[89]

---

[88] To which may be added, e. g., his articles in *JBL* on "Two Unknown Verbs (חלש, איד)" and "The Identification of תשכח ימיני, Ps. 137.5" (respectively 42 [1923], 21-8 and 47 [1928], 193-5), and special attention drawn to his two articles in *HUCA*, "A Contribution to Isaiah Exegesis" (12-13 [1937-38], 55-88) and "Biblical Studies" (14 [1939], 1-22).

[89] The author also "devised a method whereby it became possible to write both

Max Radin (1880-1950; *UJE*, IX, 65) was Professor of Law at the University of California, but he made two well-known incursions in the field of Bible. In 1915 the Jewish Publication Society of Philadelphia published his volume, *The Jews among the Greeks and Romans,* and in 1929 his study *The Life of the People in Biblical Times.*

Henry Englander (1877-1951), Professor of Medieval Jewish Exegesis at Hebrew Union College,[90] published several studies of Rashi and one of Rabbenu Tam as grammarians of Biblical Hebrew.[91] His discussion of the significance of the Exodus in the Bible (pp. 108-116 of the Kohler Volume)—at a time when the Exodus event was frequently not accepted as historical—is especially worth reading now, when the pendulum has swung considerably in the other direction.

Solomon Gandz (1887-1954; *UJE*, IV, 510), on the Faculty of the Rabbi Isaac Elchanan Theological Seminary and Yeshiva College from 1923 to 1935, and since 1942 Research Professor in the History of Semitic Civilization at the Dropsie College, published several articles dealing with the Bible. Mention may be made here of his discussions of "Oral Tradition in the Bible" (George A. Kohut Volume [1935], 248-69) and "Hebrew Numerals" (*PAAJR*, 4[1932-33], 53-112).

It is not easy to categorize the remaining two Jewish scholars who specialized in the biblical field, Moses Buttenwieser (1862-1939) and Jacob Hoschander (1874-1933). Working from opposite points of

---

in English and in Hebrew on a standard 42-keyboard typewriter . . ." (p. 138), by substituting eleven Hebrew characters for certain other signs.

[90] See M. M. Feuerlicht's Memorial Address, *YBCCAR*, 61 (1951), 247-51.

[91] "Rashi's View of the Weak, ע"ע , and פ"י Roots," HUCA, 7 (1930), 399-437; "Grammatical Elements and Terminology in Rashi's Biblical Commentaries," *HUCA*, 11 (1936), 371-83; 12-13 (1937-38), 505-521; 14 (1939), 387-429; "A Commentary on Rashi's Grammatical Comments," 17 (1942-43), 427-498; "Rashi as Bible Exegete and Grammarian," *YBCCAR*, 50 (1940), 342-59; "Rabbenu Jacob ben Meir Tam as Grammarian," *HUCA*, 15 (1940), 485-95. Mention may be made here also of "The Men of the Great Synagogue," *HUC Jubilee Volume*, 1925, 145-69. He published articles also on "Joseph Kara's Commentary on Micah in Relation to Rashi's Commentary" and "Mendelsohn as Translator and Exegete" in *HUCA* (respectively 16 [1911], 157-62 and 6 [1929], 327-348).

view and sympathies to begin with, both shared the tendency to read into the text and context of the biblical data meanings and theories which many students of biblical history frequently did not care to accept.

Buttenwieser received his Ph.D. at the University of Heidelberg in 1896, and the year following he came to the Hebrew Union College in Cincinnati, where he served as Professor of Biblical Exegesis until his retirement in 1934.[92] At the turn of the century Buttenwieser published two works on the later Jewish Apocalyptic literature, *Die hebräische Elias-Apokalypse* (Cincinnati, 1897) and *Outline of Neo-Hebraic Apocalyptic Literature* (Cincinnati, 1901). From then on, however, he devoted himself to the biblical period proper. In one of his articles, "Are There Any Maccabean Psalms?"[93] Buttenwieser argued—in a period when scholars generally tended to regard a number of psalms as having originated in the Maccabean period—that such was not the case. While scholars today would probably tend to share this view, it is doubtful that Buttenwieser's reasoning would be any more acceptable today than four decades ago. "The main point for our purpose," asserted Buttenwieser, "is that by the time of the Maccabees Hebrew had given way to Aramaic and in the light of this fact it is to be questioned whether there are any psalms dating later than the middle of the third century B.C."

Subsequently Buttenwieser published a *magnum opus, The Psalms, chronologically treated with a New Translation* (Chicago, 1938). The sub-title "chronologically arranged" indicates clearly in what manner this work differed from other commentaries on the book of Psalms. The attempt was made to date with precision most of the 150 psalms, so that Psalm 68B (= 68:8-9, 16-18, 11*c*, 12-13, 14*b*, 15, 19*a-b*, 25-28, 14*a*) emerged as "One of the Ancient Songs of the Wars of

[92] *UJE,* 11, 610-11; "Buttenwieser Anniversary Number" *Hebrew Union College Monthly,* 8 (May, 1922), No. 7, with articles by S. H. Goldenson, S. H. Markowitz, A. Cronbach and E. Starrels, with a bibliography by A. S. Oko.

[93] *JBL,* 36 (1917), 225-48.

Yahweh" (pp. 29-47), whereas 68A (= vv.1-7, 19c, 20-24, 29-36) became one of the "Exilic Psalms of Deutero-Isaiah" (Isa. 40-55. Cf. pp. 257-271). Psalms 73, 139, 39 and 23 were attributed to "The Author of the Job Drama" (pp. 524-554); psalms 118, 103, 138, 149, 40 and 87 were explained as "Psalms Inspired by the Appearance of Alexander the Great" (pp. 659-705); and so on.[94]

Much of Buttenwieser's textual criticism revolved about the shifting around of verses and the emendation of the Hebrew text. It is frequently not possible to locate the chapter and verse of a psalm, or of the text of *The Book of Job* (New York, 1922) without a Cross-Index. On the other hand, Buttenwieser emphasized repeatedly that too many scholars were wont to emend the perfect form of a verb into the imperfect, not realizing the significance and frequency of the precative perfect; he published a long article on this in the Jubilee Volume of the *Hebrew Union College Annual* (1925, "The Importance of the Tenses for the Interpretation of Psalms," pp. 89-111; abridged on pp. 18-25 of the Introduction to *The Psalms*).

Buttenwieser's analysis of *The Prophets of Israel from the Eighth to the Fifth Century, their Faith and their Message* (New York, 1914), is a provocative work. He permitted nothing to deter him from identifying the precise date and meaning of every sentence in the prophetic books which came within his purview.[95] He regarded "the Book of

---

[94] In his survey "The Psalms" in *The Old Testament and Modern Study* (ed. Harold H. Rowley, Oxford, 1951), 162-209, Aubrey R. Johnson has stated (p. 183), "Similarly, the liberal Jewish scholar M. Buttenwieser . . . offered instead an attempt on the grand scale to treat them [the Psalms] in their historical sequence, doing so, for the most part, with an exactness of dating which, as is usual in cases of this kind, fails to carry conviction because of the general terms in which the thought of each psalm tends to be expressed and the fact that history is full of repetition in the lives of both nations and individuals . . ." But see now Nahum Sarna's Prolegomenon (pp. XIII-XXXVIII) in the KTAV reissue of *The Psalms* (1969).

[95] As Buttenwieser himself put it (Foreword, pp. xix-xx), "My treatment of the prophets, though it departs to a certain extent from the chronological order of presentation, is not in opposition to, but is in full harmony with the historico-critical method of modern research. This method means for that province of knowledge which deals with the politico-social and mental development of the human race, what the analytic-genetic method means for the province of science. Like the latter

Nahum [as] an example among the preëxilic prophetic writings, of the national chauvinistic prophecy, the representatives of which the true prophets never tired of denouncing . . . As to Ezekiel, though his importance for the subsequent religious development in Israel must be acknowledged, his place is not among the great prophets . . . In conclusion, just a word on the question on which at present biblical scholars are divided into two camps—the question whether monotheism originated with the literary prophets or was known long before their appearance . . . [I] shall only state here that my study of the prophets has confirmed my conviction that the position of the Graf-Wellhausen school on this question cannot be dislodged. However scant the references of the prophets are to the official religion of their times, in Judah as well as in Israel, they leave no doubt that monotheism was unknown in Israel prior to their advent . . ." (pp. xxi-xxii). Thirteen years later Buttenwieser published a popular sketch of this volume under the title "The Prophets and Nationalism," in the *Yearbook of the Central Conference of American Rabbis* (37 [1927], 271-291). In closing this section I should like to quote from Buttenwieser an assertion whose pertinence is not always realized: "Literary prophecy is not the natural, lineal growth out of the older religious beliefs and usages . . ." (*The Prophets of Israel*, p. 155).

Buttenwieser's last important article appeared in 1930, "The Dates and Character of Ezekiel's Prophecies" (*HUCA*, 7, 1-19). He argued (p. 18) that "Up to 586 B.C. he [Ezekiel] shared the common view of priest and laity that the Temple at Jerusalem was inviolable, that Yahweh could not possibly permit its destruction . . . Ezekiel did not actually at any time before 586 B.C. predict the fall of Jerusalem, that only after that event had happened did he make out that he had prophesied it."

Jacob Hoschander (1874-1933) was a learned and traditionally-minded scholar—indeed of saintly character. He was awarded his

---

it insists that every fact or phenomenon under consideration be minutely analyzed, that is to say, that its relation to its environment be determined, and its development and growth and, if possible, also its genesis, be traced . . ."

Ph.D. by the University of Berlin in 1904, and six years later he became Instructor in Cognate Languages at the Dropsie College in Philadelphia. In addition, for many years he gave weekly lectures at the Jewish Theological Seminary in New York on the archeology, exegesis, etc., of the Bible. In 1923 he was appointed Sabato Morais Professor of Biblical Literature and Exegesis, a post which he held until his death a decade later.

Hoschander was at home in the Akkadian as well as in the strictly biblical field. For over a period of many years his "Survey of Recent Biblical Literature," which included the extra-biblical too, the cuneiform especially, appeared regularly in the foremost Jewish scholarly journal in the world, the *Jewish Quarterly Review*. It was, however, more in the role of a "defender of the faith" that Hoschander functioned in the scholarly world. He opposed the "historico-critical" school of biblical research. He abhorred this school's rejection of so much of the biblical tradition as unhistorical, and the atmosphere of despise for that tradition in which they labored. The Preface to his volume *The Book of Esther in the Light of History* (Phila., 1923) begins at once: "The aim of the present book is to interpret the Book of Esther from the historical point of view and to show the historical origin of the Festival of Purim . . . In placing this novel interpretation of the Book of Esther for the consideration of Biblical and Semitic scholars, I am far from deluding myself into the belief that it will immediately find ready acceptance. As far as the modern critics are concerned, the non-historical character of the Book of Esther is at present with them the standard opinion, and my interpretation would come into collision with what may be properly termed a dogmatic bias . . ."

Very considerable learning was devoted by Hoschander to prove his point. It is a refreshing experience, e.g., to see the talmudic and medieval Jewish material used critically alongside the Persian, Greek, and biblical data—at a time when anything Jewish of post-biblical times was sneered at not only by most non-Jewish but even by Jewish scholars.

It is ironical how scholars, setting out with mutually exclusive sympathies and purposes, will so frequently end up with similar conclusions. Thus very few scholars in modern times betrayed publicly their hostility to what such books as Esther, Ezra, and Nehemiah stood for in the manner that Albert T. Olmstead did, in his detailed *History of the Persian Empire* (Chicago, 1948). His loathing for Zionism, ancient and modern, revealed itself in such an expression as "Ezra . . . did not succeed in stopping permanently the activities of the prophets, whose dreams of a coming national kingdom returned again and again, but he did point the way to the only safe policy for the salvation of Judaism—abandonment of nationalistic hopes, reconciliation to the political rule of foreigners, loyalty to the powers that be, and full acceptance of the unique position of the Jew as the guardian of God's moral law. Fortunately for the world, succeeding generations have generally followed his guiding principle: the reactionary minority which has time and again raised the standard of separate nationality has only increased the woe of their fellow-Jews" (p. 307). One wonders which is greater, Olmstead's ignorance of the simple facts of Jewish history or his malice.

Hoschander, on the other hand, was always the sympathetic Jew. Withal, both Hoschander and Olmstead agreed that these biblical Books constituted basically first-hand and first-class sources for Jewish history.

In 1938 Hoschander published his study, *The Priests and the Prophets* (New York, 1938). There is scarcely a more elusive problem in biblical history than the status and relationship of these two groups, and brave—and arbitrary too, alas!—must be the man who would undertake to reconstruct in detail their origin and development on the basis of the meager and inconclusive data at our disposal. Hoschander courageously attempted just that. In the process, Hoschander expressed opinions that startled those who regarded him as "anti-Wellhausen." Thus Hoschander believed the statement in Deut. 6.4, שמע ישראל יהוה אלהינו יהוה אחד to "express the Unity of the Lord as far as Israel was concerned, and do(es) not imply the doctrine of an absolute Monotheism, which denies the very existence of all other gods" (p. 41). To Hoschander, it was not any of the patriarchs, or

Moses, or the literary prophets, but Deutero-Iṣaiah who was the first rigid monotheist in history (pp. 48 ff.). And when Jeroboam I set up the two bulls in Bethel for Northern Israel to worship, he was not really introducing anything new. "In former days," wrote Hoschander (p. 13), "the Israelites themselves worshipped the Baalim in the images of bulls. Thus the introduction of the Bull-worship was not an innovation but a restoration of the former mode of worship. There was only one difference between the past and present practices. Formerly the image of the bull was the representation of Baal or the Baalim, while now it became the representation of Jahweh."

Samuel I. Feigin (1893-1950),[96] on the Faculties of the College of Jewish Studies and of the Hebrew Theological College in Chicago, and for over fifteen years associated with the Oriental Institute of the University of Chicago, likewise played the role of "Defender of the Faith," and like so many apologetes he emended the Hebrew text freely and reconstructed various events and aspects of biblical history arbitrarily. Many of his articles and reviews were put together in Hebrew form in the volume *Missitrei He-Avar* ("From the Hidden Things of the Past"; New York, 1943). Not uncharacteristic of his method is the article, "Shemesh the Son of Yaweh" (*JQR,* 28 [1937-38], 225-42). The masoretic text of I Sam. 6:19 is so emended and explained as to get "Shamash, the son of Yahweh" out of "And He smote among the men of Bethshemesh . . ." Feigin concludes, "Of course, 'Shamash, the son of Yahweh,' does not refer to a son by birth . . . Shamash was only the agent of Yahweh in Beth-shemesh. Thus this restoration affords us a glimpse of the old popular religious conceptions of Israel. 'Shamash, the son of Yahweh' was apparently not the only son. There were many more sons of this kind. But only 'sons of God' in general on the one hand and 'angels of God' on the other hand were permitted to survive. However, the conceptions of angels and

---

[96] See the 40-page brochure issued by the College of Jewish Studies *In Memoriam Samuel I. Feigin* (Chicago, 1952), which includes a bibliography of Feigin's works by Judah Rosenthal (pp. 12-30).

sons of God were not in agreement with pure monotheism and they were combated in various periods in Jewish history."

Solomon L. Skoss (1884-1953), on the Faculty of the Dropsie College during the last twenty-eight years of his life, since 1934 its Professor of Arabic, was an outstanding authority in the field of Judeo-Arabic. Specializing as he did in the medieval Jewish scholarly understanding of the grammar and exegesis of the Bible, Skoss was able to contribute much of significance toward our own scholarly understanding of the Bible. His doctoral study *'Ali ben Suleiman's Commentary on Genesis* (Philadelphia, 1928) was the first important step in that direction. His major contribution appeared a few years later, in the form of a two-volume edition of *The Hebrew-Arabic Dictionary of the Bible known as Kitab Jami' al-Alfaz (Agron) of David ben Abraham al-Fasi*,[97] a model piece of work. Another major work was in the making, namely, the publication and analysis of Saadia Gaon's studies in the grammar of Biblical Hebrew, the *Kutub al-Lughah*, when death intervened. Four parts have appeared to date,[98] and it is hoped that the material still unpublished will see the light of day in the near future. Every biblical scholar who is wont to use the Biblical Concordance by Solomon Mandelkern—himself, incidentally, a Doctor of Jurisprudence from the University of Jena and a writer of love poems, as well as a fine grammarian and exegete—will appreciate the hundreds of corrections to Mandelkern's Concordance which Skoss published in the *JQR* (40 [1949-50], 173-188).

Eugen Täubler (1879-1953), since 1941 Research Professor in Bible and Hellenistic Literature at the Hebrew Union College (- Jewish Institute of Religion) in Cincinnati, published only a few articles pertaining directly to the Bible[99]; he was, as is well known, an au-

---

[97] New Haven, 1936, 1945 (= Vols. XX-XXI in Yale Oriental Series, Researches).

[98] *JQR*, 33 (1942-43), 171-212; 42 (1951-52), 283-317; *Proceedings of the American Academy for Jewish Research,* 21 (1952), 75-100; 23 (1954), 59-73. Cf. also "The Root בטח, in Jer. 12.5, Ps. 22.10, Prov. 14.16, and Job 40.23," in George Alexander Kohut Volume, pp. 549-553.

[99] "Kharu, Horim, Dedanim," *HUCA,* 1 (1924), 97-123; "The First Mention of Israel," *Proceedings of the American Academy for Jewish Research* (= *PAAJR*), 12 (1942); "Cushan-Rishataim," *HUCA, 20* (1947), 136-142.

thoritative scholar in the Greco-Roman field. But in his "Necrology" by Salo W. Baron and Ralph Marcus (*Proceedings of the American Academy for Jewish Research*, 22 [1953], xxxi-xxxiv) we are "told that a three-volume manuscript of Biblical Studies and another volume entitled *Ideology and Reality, the Jewish Fate to the Return from the Exile* are practically ready for the press." I can but join in the hope expressed there "that some of these studies will before long be made available to the scholarly world."

The rabbi in this country nowadays has to expend so much of his time and energies on the more immediate and mundane tasks of his calling that he can but rarely revel in matters academic. If only for this reason, mention should be made of two works by Rabbi Solomon Goldman (1894-1953), *The Book of Books: An Introduction* (Philadelphia, 5708-1948. Vol. I in *The Book of Human Destiny*), and *In the Beginning* (5710-1949, Vol. II). Vol. III in this series, dealing with the book of Exodus, is in manuscript, ready for posthumous publication. [It appeared in 1958 under the title *From Slavery to Freedom*, edited in part and with an Introduction (pp. xi-xiii) by H. M. Orlinsky. In 1956 Maurice Samuel edited, with an Introduction, Goldman's *The Ten Commandments*.]

The great talmudist of the Jewish Theological Seminary, Louis Ginzberg (1873-1954), made noteworthy contributions to the better understanding of the Bible. The work that he did in conjunction with the *Jewish Encyclopedia* (see above) derived from and developed into the enormous mass of critically sifted data published as *The Legends of the Jews*.[100] Biblical scholars, both Jewish and non-Jewish, would appreciate their discipline even more if they utilized regularly the Jewish and non-Jewish texts and ideas which go to make up these "Legends." Ginzberg himself demonstrated the value of these materials for the biblical scholar in such important works as *Die Haggada bei*

---

[100] 6 vols. (Philadelphia, 1909-1928). Vols. 5 and 6 constitute the very valuable sources and notes, and vol. 7 is the very useful *Index* compiled by Prof. Ginzberg's student and younger colleague at the Jewish Theological Seminary, (the lamented) Prof. Boaz Cohen.

den Kirchenvätern (und in der apokryphischen Litteratur),[101] "The Religion of the Jews at the time of Jesus,"[102] and "Some Observations on the Attitude of the Synagogue towards the Apocalyptic Writings"[103]; his volume on *Students, Scholars, and Saints* (Philadelphia, 1928) will be rewarding reading for anyone.

Yet the reader will realize (see the initial note * of this essay) that the true picture of contemporary Jewish biblical scholarship in America is not to be ascertained from this study. In limiting himself arbitrarily to the works of those Jewish scholars who are no longer among the livnig, the writer has of necessity not been able to present the complete record. Consequently, he has not put the reader in a position to evaluate fully the present characteristics of Jewish scholarly work in the field, nor to hazard a guess about its possible road of development in the forseeable future. The knowing reader, nevertheless, is fully aware that the major contributions that have been made and are continuing to be made in ever increasing quality and quantity, when analyzed in the light of the record submitted here, promise far more good than evil for the future. Jewish biblical scholarship has developed in this country to a level that could hardly have been foreseen fifty years ago. What it needs now, more than ever before, is for Jewish institutions of learning to attract talented young Jewish men— and women too—who will be ready within the next decade and two to replace the present guild of scholars, and raise the level of the discipline to even higher stages of development.

This last paragraph was written almost twenty years ago (toward the

---

[101] See items 3, 4, 77, 84, 90, and 96 in the "Bibliography of the Writings of Prof. Louis Ginzberg" by Boaz Cohen, pp. 19 ff. in Vol. I of the two-volume *Louis Ginzberg Jubilee Volume* (English and Hebrew volumes; New York, 1945). Incidentally, Solomon Goldman sketched there (pp. 1-18) of Prof. Ginzberg a fine "Portrait of a Teacher."

[102] *HUCA*, 1 (1924), 307-321; and reprinted in *Students, Scholars, and Saints* (Phila., 1928).

[103] *JBL*, 41 (1922), 115-136.

end of 1954). I am most happy to assert summarily at this point that Jewish biblical scholarship—and Semitic, and now also Judaic in the widest sense of the term—is currently flourishing in America-Canada as never before. Eight years ago, I published an analytical survey of "Old Testament Studies" in the United States and Canada during the three decades between 1930 and 1960; the study was commissioned by the Council of the Humanities of Princeton University, and it appeared in the volume *Religion,* ed. Paul Ramsey (1965), pp. 51-109, in the series: *The Princeton Studies: Humanistic Scholarship in America.* In this study, I naturally had occasion to deal with the work of living Jewish scholars; a perusal of the study (or see the Index to the *Religion* volume as a whole) will give the reader an idea of the quality and quantity of the work done in that period by such professional American and Canadian Jewish scholars as Sheldon H. Blank, Theodor H. Gaster, H. Louis Ginsberg, Nelson Glueck (died 1971), Robert Gordis, Cyrus H. Gordon, Zellig S. Harris, Samuel Iwry, Samuel N. Kramer, Wolf Leslau, Julius Lewy (died 1963), Leon J. Liebreich (died 1966), Menahem Mansoor, Isaac Mendelsohn (died 1965), Julian Morgenstern, Edward E. Neufeld, A. Leo Oppenheim, Harry M. Orlinsky, Isaac Rabinowitz, Joseph Reider (died 1960), Franz Rosenthal, Ephraim A. Speiser (died 1965), Alexander Sperber (died 1971), Shalom Spiegel, Matitiahu Tsevat, and Frank Zimmermann.

Among the younger scholars—I suppose that those who have not yet reached their fiftieth birthday could be so classed—one calls to mind readily Jacob J. Finkelstein, Stanley Gevirtz, Moshe Greenberg, Jonas C. Greenfield, Samuel Greengus, William W. Hallo, Moshe Held, Baruch A. Levine, David Neiman, Bezalel Porten, Nahum Sarna, Michael H. Silverman, David B. Weisberg—not to mention an increasing number of mostly young scholars such as Herbert C. Brichto, Jacob Milgrom, Yohanan Muffs, Shalom Paul, Jack M. Sasson, and Jonathan P. Siegel, whose doctoral dissertations or other publications indicate promising careers for them.

As chairman of a session on Biblical Studies at the Fourth (1965) World Congress of Jewish Studies in Jerusalem, I opened the session by remarking that the American Jewish community had already begun to experience a "Scholarship Explosion"; and I emphasized this in an interview in the *Jerusalem Post* (August 4, 1965, p. 4), in which I asserted that "This phenomenon may well produce the most promising period of Jewish scholarly learning in all our history. Rooted in the unprecedented social, economic and political status of this major Jewry, the 'Scholarship Explosion' came on the heels of the Holocaust and coincided with the rebirth of Jewish nationhood; both these happenings helped supply *raison d'être* to the tremendous spurt of activity that has electrified the Jewish communities."

Given a relatively balanced social order in America, Israel, and elsewhere, the future for Jewish Biblical scholarship on the American continent, as for Jewish scholarship in Semitics, Judaica, and the like, is bright indeed.

17

American Stimulus
and Jewish Response:
A Challenge to our Youth

YOU, YOUTHFUL MEMBERS of the graduating class of 1957 of the Hebrew Teachers College, share with the Jewish youth of the western world a unique and difficult task, that of integrating your careers and lives as Jews in a non-Jewish world, in a manner that no generation of Jewish youth in the long history of the Diaspora has ever had to face. In the past few years, since some six millions of Jews in Europe were done brutally to death by the Hitler government and since less than one-half million Jews, who had left Europe in time and gone to Palestine, had helped set up a sovereign State of Israel, it has become clear to everyone who knew something about Jewish history that Europe was now going to be replaced by America and Israel as the new world's centers of Jewish activity and culture.

You have heard and read how the Jews of Babylonia eventually took over the social and cultural life of the Jews of Judea when the Second Jewish Commonwealth was destroyed by Rome in the year 70 and during the several Jewish revolts which followed in the second century. You are quite aware that the Babylonian Jewish way of life, covering the entire talmudic and gaonic period, found a new

---

[Commencement Address, Hebrew Teachers College, Brookline, Mass., June 16, 1957. Published originally by Hebrew Teachers College Press.]

home and new expression in Spain, so that in less than 500 years a Golden Era of Jewish activity was established once more. The great catastrophe which struck Spanish Jewry in the fifteenth century, in the form of the Inquisition and the Exile, found a growing Jewish community in Eastern Europe ready to take up and develop further, along its own lines, the Jewish culture of Spain and Babylonia and ancient Judea and Israel. In turn, the largest Jewish community in the world today, our own American Jewry, and the most energetic and learned Jewish community, Israel, are now looked upon as the heirs of the great Jewish traditions and civilization which the Jews of Europe had produced during the past several centuries, for us to develop and to adapt as we see fit, to serve our needs and to express the genius of our generation.

The matter of cultural inheritance and adaptation, however, is not simple; and too many important, even crucial elements tend to be overlooked in the sweeping generalizations which are frequently made. For one thing, Jewish history is not confined to one great center at a time. There have always been several contemporaneous centers, some greater than others, but all of them simultaneously active and mutually beneficial. The Bible itself, the unmatched product of the Jews when they lived in their own land, includes the writings of two great prophets who were active not in the land of Israel and Judah, but in Babylonia, namely, Ezekiel and the author of the second part of Isaiah. When the Second Jewish Commonwealth was at its height, there flourished in Egypt, chiefly in Alexandria, a monumental Jewish civilization, one which produced the Septuagint, the Old Greek translation of the Bible, and the theological and philosophical works of Philo of Alexandria, and several of the books which came to constitute Jewish Apocryphal Literature. The Jewish community of Rome provided the environment for the priceless historical writings of Josephus.

When Babylonian Jewry stood in its fullest glory, there were important Jewish centers of learning and activity in Palestine, and in Egypt, and in northwest Africa, and in southern Europe. During the Golden Era in Spain, notable Jewish communities thrived in Egypt, France, Germany, Italy, Bohemia, and elsewhere. When one talks of Eastern

European Jewry, one cannot even for one moment overlook the very significant Jewish communities in Germany, France, Holland, and Palestine. Consequently, it is a gross mistake to speak nowadays of the United States and Israel, without mentioning in the same breath Canada, and Latin and South America, England and France and, perhaps in the not very distant future, also Poland, Roumania, and Russia. Argentina alone is currently publishing as many Yiddish books as the United States, and our numerous and wealthy American Jewry has not equalled the very much smaller Jewish community of Great Britain in putting out in English dress a commentary on the entire Bible and complete English translations of the *Mishnah*, the *Talmud*, and the *Midrash*.

Of far greater importance, however, are the precise circumstances under which one Jewish center breathed in the life which another outstanding Jewish center was at that time giving up. Some historians, not to speak of popular lecturers and journalists, have turned this historical Jewish transmission into something of a mysterious phenomenon, something inevitable, which will always continue to happen whenever any major Jewish center is about to die out. Yet the facts, properly integrated and analysed, are clear enough. When the general social conditions in a country begin to deteriorate, so as to result in increasingly widespread anti-Jewish feeling and action, the Jews are compelled in approximately corresponding proportion to leave that country. They naturally move to the region or country which is at once sufficiently near and friendly. The fact that the new country is hospitable, is ample indication that its social order and economic system are in good enough shape, that those in power recognized that there was room in their midst for increased commerce and prosperity. Up to our own days this was always the case.

Babylonia was congenial territory for the Jews after the destruction both of the First and Second Temple. Moslem Spain accepted the Jews, and gained very much prosperity from their activities. Poland and Lithuania were relatively good hosts to the Jews when Christian Spain and other parts of Western Europe drove them out. The Jews of Germany played an important role in the tremendous growth of the kingdom of Poland in the fourteenth century under Casimir the Great, who, it is said, "found a Poland of wood and left behind him a Poland of stone." The United States was then a young growing country, eager and able to expand in every direction, and the Jews, like the other immigrants, were welcomed and encouraged to contribute their skills to the growing economy.

This situation no longer obtains. A primary reason for the destruction of six million Jews in Europe is that no country was willing to open its doors to them; the Jews of Europe simply had nowhere to go. The interrelationship of the world is no longer what it was before the depression of 1929 and the subsequent World War II, a collection of relatively independent and individual countries, so that hundreds of thousands of Jews could enter western Europe and Latin and South American countries and that millions of Jews could immigrate into the United States. The economic and social conditions of England, France, Holland, Belgium, Germany, Canada, the United States, Australia, South Africa, Argentina, and the like, no longer make it feasible and useful for those in power to permit widespread immigration. Manufacture, trade, and agriculture in the United States have required only limited immigration ever since 1924. All of Canada, with its vast open spaces, even now has only about 225,000 Jews. Russia and the countries which it dominates allow virtually no one out and no one in. Great Britain and its dominions have long had a *numerus clausus* for Jewish immigrants. Consequently, whereas Babylonia was able to draw on Palestinian Jews when conditions in Palestine began to deteriorate, where Spain and Eastern Europe could receive a continuous flow of Jewish families from the considerable reservoirs of the countries which were failing, we American Jews have been cut off suddenly and completely from our forefathers, from our immediate sources of cultural nourishment, from the *Yeshivot* and *Gymnasiums* of Russia, Poland, Lithuania, Roumania, Austria, Germany, and Hungary. For us, this is an unparalleled catastrophe. At this moment, when we should be receiving the quality and quantity of the millions of Jews who lived in all parts of Europe and Russia, when we should be striving to build our own American Jewish culture with the aid of the best that our European Jewish brothers created during the past several hundred years, at this time we find ourselves to a critical extent cultural orphans, bereft, by the uncouth and uncivilized, of our learned and understanding fathers and mothers, of our stimulating and sympathetic brothers and sisters on the other side of the ocean.

It is not generally recognized that in the earlier epochal changes, the new Jewish centers did not mature and replace the old, dying centers in a matter of a few years, or even decades. The generalizing character of writing and teaching history has given most people the impression that virtually at the very moment that Judea was passing away, Jewish Babylonia became the grown-up father of the household; that no sooner did Spanish Jewry breathe its last, that Poland and Lithuania replaced it in full glory and authority. This is so far from being true that it can harm us if we fail to see the historical development in its proper light.

When Roman imperialism destroyed the Second Jewish Commonwealth in the year 70, the Jews of Judea did not cease to flourish. Numerous Palestinian Jewish communities continued their cultural activities. The *Mishnah* went through several codifications, and received its final codification, under Rabbi Judah ha-Nasi, on Palestinian soil. Five generations of Tannaim, the authoritative Jewish scholars of the period, are recorded for Palestine as well as for Babylonia, and five generations of Amoraim, the successors to the Tannaim, are similarly recorded. It is only when we reach the fifth century of the Common Era that Babylonian Amoraim alone are recorded, followed in the sixth century by the Saboraim, and in the seventh by the Gaonim. One of the last of the Palestinian Amoraim, Ulla II, symbolizes the final transfer of authority when he himself moved from Palestine to Babylonia.

What does this mean for us? Probably the most popular single topic with which public symposiums and lectures have dealt during the past few years is "The Future of American Judaism." It seems to me that a characteristic common to most of these lectures and articles is a feeling of urgency, of foreboding, even of doom. Apparently not aware that the outstanding Jewish centers of the past were not the only great centers of Jewish activity at the time, and that they did not come into being overnight, as it were, writers and lecturers have taken a hasty look about them, have perceived the relatively low level of Jewish cultural activity in this country, and proceeded to foresee a declining American Jewry, a Jewry of some five millions largely unaware of its extended history and traditions, blissful in its ignorance of Jewish literature, departing at an increasingly rapid pace farther away from Jewish interests and living. The lecturers condemn the Jews of America for being uninterested in Judaism, they accuse them of assimilation, and frighten them with the prospect of cultural extinction.

Underlying this attitude is not alone an incorrect understanding and application of our past history, but also a marked lack of respect and appreciation of the actual and potential ability and learning of the Jews of America. There is altogether too widespread an opinion that right now, and for all time to come, the American Jewish community simply lacks the learning and desire to develop into a major Jewish center, on a level with Eastern Europe, or Spain, or Babylonia. Some persons have gone so far as to urge strongly, either that American Jews adapt themselves to, and adopt wholesale the culture of the State of Israel, or better still that they move wholesale to Israel. By what right does anyone take such an attitude toward the present generation of Jews? Certainly there is nothing in history to justify this extreme demand and distorted perspective! Forgotten is the fact that the mass immigration of Jews into America did not begin until about 60 years ago. What did the United States at large amount to culturally during the first sixty, and twice sixty years, of its existence? And what a pessimistic picture would have been painted by our current prophets of doom, of Babylonian Judaism after only sixty or one hundred or more years of existence, or of the Jews of Spain, and of Eastern Europe!

There is more to this, however, than the question of chronology, important as it is. There is the question of quality, of the form and substance of the culture which American Judaism represents and into which it may develop. There is, for example, the question of language. There can be no doubt that the classical language of the Jews always has been, and will always continue to be, so long as there is a significant group of Jews in existence, the Hebrew language. It is the language of the Bible, the greatest religious and literary product of human creativity. It is the language of Jewish prayer for over three thousand years. It is the language of the *Mishnah* and of the *Aggadah.* It is the language of the codifications of Jewish law, the *Mishneh Torah* of Maimonides, and the *Shulhan Arukh.* It is the language of the great Jewish poets, from Kalir, Yehudah Halevi, and the Ibn Ezras, to Tschernichowsky and Bialik. It is the language of the State of Israel and its great writers.

On the other hand, it is casually forgotten that the culture of the Jewish people in their great flourishing epochs was not created exclusively in Hebrew. Already in biblical times, Aramaic was beginning to challenge Hebrew as the vernacular of the Jews, and one-half of the book of Daniel, the original half, was actually canonized as part of Holy Scripture, and it is written in Aramaic. The great and fundamentally important Babylonian *Gemara* is in Aramaic. When Spain came to the fore, Arabic emerged as the vernacular of the Jewish people and of many scholars. The notable Hebrew grammars were written in Arabic. Ibn Gebirol, Yehudah Halevi, and Maimonides wrote their great philosophical works, the *Fountain of Life*, the *Kuzari*, and the *Guide to the Perplexed*, in Arabic. In Eastern Europe the Jewish communities flourished in the Yiddish language, and in Central Europe, Zunz, Frankel, Geiger, Graetz, and the many other great scholars and leaders wrote in German. Bearing this linguistic element in mind, one can well afford not to take too seriously the forebodings of those who insist that American Jews will never create a great culture because their vernacular is English. In one and the same breath, they glory in the Aramaic of Judea and Babylonia, in the Arabic of Spain, in the Yiddish of Eastern Europe and in the German of Western Europe; but they collapse in advance before the "frightening" prospect of English in America. It would appear to be an historical fact that the Jewish people throughout its history was a two-language people, Hebrew and Aramaic, Hebrew and Greek, Hebrew and Arabic, Hebrew and Yiddish, Hebrew and a Western European language, Hebrew and English. It cannot be a non-Hebrew language alone. Nor is it Hebrew alone.

The language of Jewish culture aside, there is the question of quality, the substance, of American Jewish culture. Once again, much that Jewish history is capable and eager to teach us, is disregarded. Every one knows that the culture, the religion, the laws, the prayers, the literature of the Jews in biblical times in Israel and Judah were not at all the same as those which the Jews of Babylonia created, and by which they lived. And apart from the Babylonian *Gemara,* which they adapted to their own needs, the Jews of Spain and the Provence developed a culture which was quite different from that of their Babylonian Jewish predecessors. The gap is even greater between the kind of culture which was created by the Jews of Spain and that which characterized the civilization of the Eastern European Jews. As a matter of fact, the Jews of Eastern Europe did not produce any such great literary masterpieces which characterized the Golden Era in Spain, the travel literature, the chronicles, the ethical works, not to speak of the philosophical works. Even the great mystical Kabbalistic works, such as the *Zohar,* are essentially Judeo-Spanish products. The Jews of Poland, Lithuania, and Russia, on the other hand, lived and organized the kind of daily Jewish life, the likes of which neither the Jews nor the world at large ever knew before, or will, in all likelihood, ever know again. Theirs was essentially a Jewish life all twenty-four hours of the day. Their piety, their devotion to the commandments of Jewish Law, their immersion in learning, the study of the Talmud—all these set the Jews of Eastern Europe apart from all other Jewries and peoples. Never in the history of mankind was so large a proportion of the population able to read and write. Our own United States, or England, or Canada, has not yet achieved the state of literacy that our fathers and grandfathers achieved and practiced in Eastern and Central Europe.

The competent historian does not judge the relative merits and values of the biblical, Babylonian, Spanish and European Jewish cultures, accepting some as worthwhile and rejecting others as worthless. His task is to describe them and to account for them, for their points of agreement and of disagreement. He must identify the elements which are common to them all, the features which mark the cultures of these different centers in time and space as Jewish, the ingredients which go to make up the continuum in Jewish history. In this light, it is false and harmful to underestimate, and well in advance at that, the kind of culture which the Jews of America have been, and will in the future be creating. There is not the remotest possibility that our culture, and the culture of our children and our children's children, can, or will be the same as that of our fathers in Europe. We live under entirely different social conditions.

You, the members of the graduating class, surely understand that the development of a Jewish culture in America is a real personal matter for each one of you, as it is for every young Jewish girl and boy in the country. Our parents and grandparents, escaping as they did from oppressive governments and conditions in Europe, found a welcome haven in this country, and an unprecedented opportunity to live freely. To a very great extent, the generation preceding our own began to feel that they, and their children, no longer had to face the kind of problems which they, as Jews, had to face in most European countries. They were now part of a social order which permitted them to think and to act freely, and to contribute to that social order to the fullest extent of their talents. The first generation of American-born Jews, not finding in the Jewish culture which was developed in Europe and brought over by their parents, anything of value and pertinence for their own life in this country, increasingly abandoned their Jewishness, their interest and participation in Jewish institutions and cultural activities. The Jewishness in the home life of their parents did not attract them; it even repelled them. The religious beliefs and practices of their European-born parents held no meaning for them. Only that which was gentile American, and secular, appeared to interest and to satisfy the needs of the younger generation of American-born Jews. Anti-Jewish acts in Europe, pogroms against the Jews of Palestine in 1921 and 1929, the anti-Semitism of the Hitler regime in the Thirties—these were events in some other part of the world, to certain Jewish groups which may have deserved what they got; in any case, they were not the concern of the young American Jew in the Twenties and Thirties.

The older generation, itself new in the country and new to its ways, was intent on making a living, and on providing for the children the kind of education and career which had been denied to most Jews in Europe. It was in no position to stem the tide of assimilation on the part of its Jewish children. Virtually all the Jewish organizations in this country were dominated by the older generation. They did not attract and train successors to themselves in the leadership of these institutions. They did not, for the most part, stop to think what would happen to the organized forms of Jewish life and activity in this country after they passed on. The tragic upshot of this development was that an entire generation of Jewish youth in America was forever lost to us as leaders and participants in the growth of Judaism in America. No less tragic was the fact that this generation was lost even to itself; it became a confused and confusing generation.

This is the generation which may well go down in history as the generation which required psychoanalysis because it had lost its moorings in Judaism. As any number of recent novels and case-histories have shown, the children who abandoned the fruitfulness of their parents' Jewish home, ended up in a non-Jewish "Wasteland." In the tens of thousands, the young men and women found their gentile, secular life so empty, so meaningless, so distorted, that they ran to psychoanalysts, to Christian Science, to Ethical Culture, to benevolent and purely philanthropic societies. They could not, or would not, see beneath the symptoms of their ills and difficulties; they were unable or afraid to do some serious and penetrating soul-searching. This is the generation which became so upset, which developed inferiority complexes, persecution manias, and even Jewish anti-Semitism, when Hitlerism and its allies began the virtually world-wide attack on the Jews, on their history, mentality, and culture. This generation was not rooted in Jewishness; it was Jewishly rootless. It did not understand the essence, and character, and value of Jewish history. It had tried to escape its Jewish origins, and had failed. It blamed the Jews themselves for anti-Semitism. It blamed everyone but itself for the Jewish problem. It was either not interested in, or was hostile to, the nationalistic, Zionist movement among the Jews. At best, it tolerated Zionism and a National Homeland for some European Jews who wanted it, or needed it. It was no concern of American Jewry, who would never need it or derive any use from it.

This is how the situation stood in the Thirties and Forties. The older generation, men and women, sixty and seventy and more years of age, did not expect, and did not plan for the terrible catastrophe which struck the Jews of Europe. The two sources of future leadership in American Jewish life, the younger American-born generation and the Jewish communities of Europe, were no longer available. Very few Jewish organizations in America today are led or controlled by people who are not sixty and seventy years of age. There are scarcely any Jewish institutions in our country whose leaders honestly tried to attract and educate young men and women twenty and thirty years younger than themselves to succeed them. But you, young graduates, are the first generation which is being raised at a time when American Jewry is beginning to strive consciously and intelligently to set up standards, techniques, and goals for the Judaism to be.

Let me explain this statement by way of concrete examples. The fastest growing areas in the country today are the suburbs of the great cities. Jewish communities are springing up there by the dozens, and our theological seminaries, orthodox, conservative, and liberal, are sometimes hard put to supply these with rabbis. Our graduates have been telling me that what is significant and unique in this development is the fact that the parents who organize the synagogues and community centers are young people, in their twenties and thirties, many of them veterans of World War II. They themselves are a part of our lost generation of Jewish youth. They did not know what it was to be a Jew. They floundered mentally and ideologically through the critical years of Hitlerism and World War II, and the founding of the State of Israel. They were lost souls who are now determined that their children would not have to experience what they had gone through. Consequently, our graduates tell me, the parents organize a synagogue or center, not so much primarily for themselves as a place of worship or for social gathering, but as a means of establishing Hebrew schools for their young children. Our students and graduates are being increasingly interviewed not as orators or public relations men of the synagogue or temple, but rather as educators, as teachers of adult and youth.

The growing maturity of American Jewry may be found also in the field of Jewish education. The earlier, purely secular tendency of many of the Yiddish schools has given way to a more sympathetic approach and appreciation of the Jewish past. The Reform movement in America, which contented itself with a Sunday school, a one-day-per-week schedule, now increasingly supports a minimum of three days a week of Hebrew school for its children and youth. The growth of the all-day schools is further evidence that a number of parents want a maximum Jewish education for their children, alongside the regular public school education. All these are reflections of a healthy, growing Jewish way of life in America, and—no less important—they indicate that far from being a fossil of an extinct civilization, the American Jew, democratically and Jewishly educated and minded, is responding vibrantly to the challenging stimuli of the American scene. This means that the need for educators and teachers is becoming increasingly urgent.

And the same, at long last, now holds true also in the area of Jewish scholarship. Never before have Jewish scholars been needed in this country as now, and this need will continue to grow greater. The existing higher Jewish institutions of learning, the Dropsie College, Hebrew Union College-Jewish Institute of Religion, the Jewish Theological Seminary, Yeshivah College and University, Brandeis University, the several Hebrew colleges in Boston, New York, Philadelphia, Baltimore, Chicago, and elsewhere, are in constant need of younger men to replace the older men on their faculties. Even more, several secular universities are opening departments of Hebraic, Judaic, and Semitic Studies, and Jewish scholars are filling these posts. I have in mind—in addition to New York University—Cornell University, Wayne State University (which has just appointed two men), University of Wisconsin, University of Kentucky (where two Jewish scholars were appointed), and University of California (where three men were appointed). We here can no longer depend on European *Yeshivot* and *Gymnasiums* and universities to produce our Jewish scholars; neither can Israel fill the gap. We must educate our Jewish scholars ourselves. There is indeed a great future for Judaism, and for Jewish educators and scholars in America.

You, honored graduates of this afternoon, are representative of this healthy growth, and stand in its vanguard. This is no platitude, no cliché. As Jews and as Americans, you stand on the threshold of what will come to be known in Jewish history as the American and Israeli Epoch. You will derive the benefits from this great development in proportion to the part that you will actively play in it. Your lives will be much better integrated as Jews and as Americans, than those of any American Jewish generation before you. You have had the advantage of a Jewish education up to this point, and for your own personal good you will continue with your Jewish education, and make use of it. The Babylonian Talmud has it that "Jerusalem was destroyed because the education of the youth was neglected." In time to come it will be said that Judaism in America flourished because you, the Jewish youth, were Jewishly instructed.

ESSAYS IN BIBLE TRANSLATION

18

Wanted: A New English Translation of the Bible for the Jewish People

THE JEWISH PEOPLE were themselves the first to recognize the importance of making the כִּתְבֵי הַקֹּדֶשׁ , "The Holy Writings," available in translation for those of their fellow Jews who could not understand adequately the original Hebrew text. It was about 2200 years ago that the Jewish community in Alexandria, not unlike the manner of our own Jewry in this country at the turn of the century, had grown to such proportions in population and status, and had begun to give up the Hebrew language in favor of the Greek vernacu-

---

[This address was delivered at the invitation of the Jewish Publication Society of America at the Society's Annual Meeting, May 10, 1953, at the Warwick Hotel in Philadelphia. The express purpose of the invitation and address was to influence some reluctant members of the Society into agreeing to sponsor a new Jewish translation of the Bible. Shortly thereafter the project was voted into being, and the New Jewish Version was officially launched in 1955. This address, which triggered the NJV into being, is here published in its original form, as read, for the first time, though parts of it have been used on various occasions in other contexts. A more elaborate treatment of some parts of this address may be found in other chapters in this volume, e.g., "Toward a New Philosophy of Bible Translation" (Chapter 22), "The Septuagint," etc. (Chapter 19), "The Hebrew Text and the Ancient Versions of the Old Testament" (Chapter 21), and "Jewish Influences on Christian Translations of the Bible" (Chapter 24). The "Introduction" (pp. 1–40) of my edition of *Notes on the New Translation of the Torah* (JPS, Philadelphia, 5730– 1969) may also be of interest to the reader.]

lar to such an extent, that a translation into Greek of the Five Books
of Moses, the most authoritative part of what then constituted the
Holy Writings, became necessary. This is the famous Greek translation which came to be called the Septuagint. Translation into Greek
of the other sacred Books, which ultimately came to constitute the
remaining two divisions of the Hebrew Bible, the   נְבִיאִים   and the
כְּתוּבִים , the Prophets and the Hagiographa, took place during
the second and first centuries B.C.E. There are many reasons for
considering this translation the most important ever made by Jews.

In Western Asia, especially in Babylonia and Judea, on the other
hand, Aramaic rather than Greek was the popular vernacular among
the Jews; so much so, as a matter of fact, that the original part of the
book of Daniel is the Aramaic, and this had to be turned into
לְשׁוֹן הַקֹּדֶשׁ , the "Holy Tongue," Hebrew, before the Book
could be incorporated as Holy Writ. By the second century C.E.,
there were in existence several Jewish Aramaic versions of the Bible,
best known among them being the Targum Onkelos on the Pentateuch.

It so happens that as the earlier Christian Jews who, like so many
of the rest of the Jews, had adopted the Septuagint version of the
Bible, became less Jewish and more Christian, and as the sovereign
Jewish state was destroyed by Rome in the year 70, this Old Greek
version came to be rejected by the Jews at large, and to be accepted
by the Christians at large. Early in the second century C.E., a pagan
convert to Judaism, Aquila by name, made a fresh and unique Greek
translation of the Hebrew Bible. He incorporated the sort of Jewish
interpretation which was current in his day. Interestingly, it was still
in use in the synagogue in the days of the Byzantine emperor, Justinian I, in the sixth century, and fell into disuse when Arabic came to
replace Greek and Latin after the seventh century.

There were other Greek revisions made from a Jewish point of
view, but we may not dwell on them here, though mention should be
made of a Jew, name unknown, who probably in the fourteenth century translated the Pentateuch, Megillot, and other parts of the Hebrew Bible into classical Greek (the Attic dialect), using the Doric
dialect for the Aramaic part of Daniel.

In the tenth century, less than 1000 years ago, the Jews of Babylonia and other parts of the great Moslem domains were not altogether ignorant in Hebrew and Aramaic, yet read and spoke Arabic so
much better that the outstanding Jew in their midst, Saadia Gaon,
undertook to provide them with an Arabic translation of the Hebrew
Bible. Saadia, who respected the Hebrew text no less than any of us
today, had but one primary goal before him while working on the
translation, and that was the achievement of *intelligibility*. That was
why the translation, while not a paraphrase, was not yet literal either.
Saadia did not hesitate to add a word not found in the Hebrew original, or to telescope several Hebrew words, if only the Arabic translation made sense to the Jewish reader. I cannot refrain at this point
from citing a poignant passage in the marvellous little book on the
Story of Bible Translations which Professor Margolis wrote, and which
this Society published exactly 46 years ago. On page 54 he wrote,
"Though naturally not free from faults, Saadya's version served as a
mine in the hands of successive generations of Bible students; but it
was intended in the first instance for the people, the Jews in the vast
domain of Arabic culture; to this day it is read by the Yemenite Jews,
who driven from their home by persecution, and employed as common
laborers in the Jewish colonies of Palestine, bring with them the Scriptures in the Hebrew original, the Targum neatly pointed, and Saadya's
Arabic translation"—that was almost 50 years ago, even before the
British Mandate came into being!

About 1400 c.e., a Jew made a Persian translation of all or part
of the Hebrew Bible; and just over a century later, still another Jewish
translation into Persian, of the Pentateuch, was made in Constantinople. As a matter of fact, Jewish translations into several vernaculars
began to come thick and fast in this period, encouraged in no small
measure by the revolutionary invention of printing. In addition to
two Greek translations, there were several Spanish translations. One
of the latter, the Ferrara Bible of 1553, is especially interesting, in that
in the copies intended for Christian readers, the term for "virgin" was
introduced in Isaiah 7:14, whereas the others read either "young
woman" or simply "la alma," the עַלְמָה .

The ladies in the audience this afternoon will be interested to learn
that the Bible of every good Jewish woman, the טַייטְש חומֶש   or

צְאֶינָה וּרְאֶינָה , came into being the following century; there were other Judeo-German, or Yiddish translations of parts of the Bible, among them the Yiddish translation by Joseph Witzenhausen, published in Amsterdam in 1679, which was approved by the וַעַד אַרְבַּע הָאֲרָצוֹת, "the (East European) Council of the Four Lands."

These translations, made by Jews for Jews, were themselves a reflection of the social ferment of the gentile society round about them. Christians too, to whom the Hebrew Bible was the important Old Testament forerunner to the New Testament, made translations and revisions, even more than the Jews, to conform to their needs, in the various vernaculars of Asia, Africa, and Europe, into Latin, Coptic, Armenian, Syriac, Ethiopic, the German of Luther, into Dutch, Danish, Swedish, Norwegian, the English translations of Tyndale and Coverdale, and, finally, the King James, so-called Authorized, Version of 1611. Do not think for one moment that Jewish influence, both direct and indirect, did not play a considerable role in the making of these numerous Christian translations; but this aspect, important and interesting as it is, may not be dwelt upon here. [See Chap. 24 below.]

No translation since the Septuagint and the Vulgate has had such influence on other Bible translations as the King James, even if it did take about half-a-century before it ousted the popular Geneva Bible.

The King James Version, in turn, has had very considerable influence on most subsequent Jewish versions of the Hebrew Bible, on some indirectly and on others quite directly; I shall return to this matter presently.

A very great impetus to the Jewish versions which began to appear increasingly in the 18th and 19th centuries was the renewed study of the Tanakh, with a rationalistic emphasis, in Jewish circles. Since the days of Rashi, Ibn Ezra, and the Spanish school of biblical philology, from the 11th and 12th centuries, this approach did not characterize the Jewish interpretation of the Holy Scriptures. Partly under the influence of the Protestant biblical criticism of the 18th and 19th centuries, and partly as an inner development, parallel to the gentile attitude, both of which were brought about by the advent of the industrial revolution and the new economic and political orders which emerged in its wake, the Jewish study of the Bible, along more scientific lines, once again came into its own. One calls to mind at once Moses Mendelssohn and his school of Biurists; Heinrich Graetz, Samuel David Luzzatto, Meir Leibush Malbim, and others too numerous to mention.

Out of all these new conditions and studies, there came forth the many and varied Bible translations and revisions which culminated in this country in the Jewish Publication Society's translation in 1917. Among the more notable of these was the scholarly *French Bible* which was completed in 1851, and a more popular French version, of which only the Humash appeared, done by members of the French rabbinate. Three translations in German, by Philippson, Herxheimer and Fürst, appeared between 1856 and 1874. Two Dutch versions, one of the entire Tanakh, came out. Luzzatto's pupils did the entire Bible into Italian, in 1875. The Russian, Hungarian, and Yiddish languages were likewise enriched by Jewish versions of the Bible, in whole or in part.

It is, however, the Anglo-Jewish versions which are of more immediate interest today. Isaac Delgado in England,—"teacher of the Hebrew language" he is described somewhere, published in 1789 an English translation of the Humash. He made this version as a correction of the King James, in three main areas—and I quote—"wherever it deviates from the genuine sense of the Hebrew expressions, or where it renders obscure the meaning of the text, or, lastly, when it occasions a seeming contradiction." Fifty years later, Selig Newman published his *Emendations of the Authorized Version*, and 25 years afterwards Abraham Benisch produced a fresh English version of the Hebrew Bible. Michael Friedländer put out in 1884 a somewhat modified revision of the Authorized Version.

In this country, indeed in this very city, where the first Hebrew Bible on the continent was printed, in 1814, a very important English version of the Bible was produced by Isaac Leeser in 1853, exactly one hundred years ago. For over fifty years it was virtually *the English Bible* for English and American Jewry, and it is in use even in our own time. There is much merit in Leeser's Bible, and I myself have, not at all infrequently, found its translation of the Hebrew superior to the one adopted in the JPS translation.

But even in the 19th century "time" was marching on. Forty years after Leeser's Bible appeared, this Society, at its second biennial meeting, resolved to assume the responsibility of producing a new English version of the Bible. A subcommittee worked out the plan in 1893, and in 1894 the Society formally adopted the plan, which revolved about a revision of Leeser's Bible. Within two years each Book in the Bible was assigned to a different Jewish translator, except for Rabbi Joseph H. Hertz in London, England, all of them in America. Marcus Jastrow was made Editor-in-Chief, with Kaufman Kohler and Frederick de Sola Mendes as his two Assistant Editors. The quality of the would-be translators was unusually uneven, with not one Bible specialist in the entire group! Be as it may, the committee and the procedure did not function smoothly and rapidly enough, even when Marcus Jastrow died and was replaced by Solomon Shechter.

In 1908 the entire project was reorganized, Cyrus Adler became Chairman of a seven-man Committee, and the great Bible scholar, the only Bible scholar on the Committee, Max Leopold Margolis, Professor of Biblical Philology at the newly-founded Dropsie College, was appointed Editor-in-Chief. The entire scholarly work was done by Prof. Margolis, probably the only scholar in the world who controlled so many of the pertinent sources directly and methodologically; and his manuscript was the basis for all the Committee's deliberations. (Parenthetically, it must sometimes have been very difficult for Margolis to see a hand being raised in opposition to a rendering of his, when the owner of the hand was voting on a linguistic problem involving the " 'a'id" construction, or on a rendering which revolved about the Coptic and Ethiopic versions, which were Greek to some on the Committee. But that is the penalty which an erudite Bible scholar must be prepared to pay.)

The Translation made its debut in 1917. "It aim(ed)," the Preface asserted, "to combine the spirit of Jewish tradition with the results of biblical scholarship, ancient, mediaeval and modern. It gives to the Jewish world a translation of the Scriptures done by men imbued with the Jewish consciousness, while the non-Jewish world, it is hoped, will welcome a translation that presents many passages from the Jewish traditional point of view."

Now what prompted the idea, first of a revision of Leeser, and then something more independent, in the direction of a new translation? And, to say the same thing but in other words, what exactly did the Jewish Publication Society's Committee intend to achieve in its own projected translation? The answer is on public record, not only in the translation itself, but also in the model Preface to the JPS translation, done mainly, I believe, by Margolis, and in Margolis' little book that I mentioned previously, *The Story of Bible Translations*. I quote: A translator's "principal function is to make the Hebrew intelligible. Faithful though he must be to the Hebrew idiom, he will nevertheless be forced by the genius of the English language to use circumlocution, to add a word or two, to alter the sequence of words, and the like . . . Naturally opinion will differ as to what may be deemed an addition and what may not, but as intelligibility was the principal aim, the Editors have felt justified in making their additions, sparingly it is true, but nevertheless as often as the occasion required." (Preface, p. x.)

The key word in this quotation is "intelligibility." And it is precisely this concept which has brought us together this afternoon. In the past decade or so, Jews all over the world have been complaining increasingly that this great translation, made almost fifty years ago, is no longer as intelligible as it should be. History had begun all over again. Leeser's Bible flourished in usefulness for some fifty years, until new conditions brought the JPS version into being. The JPS version, on the other hand, could not be expected to maintain undisputed popularity for so long a period, and for two reasons: firstly, the English language itself has undergone rapid change, far more since the days of World War I than it did through the entire 19th century preceding; and secondly, our knowledge of the background and text of the Hebrew Bible has increased since World War I by such enormous leaps and bounds that scores of passages in the older translations are now to be understood differently and more correctly than previously. In this respect there is a close parallel that may be drawn between the American Standard Version of 1901 and the Revised Standard Version of 1952, on the one hand, and between the Jewish Publication Society

Translation of 1916 and the inevitably forthcoming revised Jewish version, on the other. From the King James Version to the American Revision, no less than 290 years elapsed; but less than 3 decades had elapsed when serious discussion had begun for another revision. The same three decades had elapsed when Jewish individuals and groups, like their Christian counterparts, likewise began to articulate the ever increasingly urgent need for a new Jewish version of the Holy Scriptures. And the basic cause for this need was precisely that which had brought in to being, first Leeser's Bible, and then the Jewish Publication Society's Bible, namely intelligibility and correctness, the accord with the new English style and the latest scholarly truth.

This is not the occasion for a detailed analysis of the shortcomings of the JPS translation, and of the precise manner in which these shortcomings may be overcome. Nevertheless, several characteristic cases in point ought to be taken up.

So far as the style of the English is concerned, it is surprising that some Jews would retain all or many of the expressions which set the King James and similar versions apart from more modern English expressions. I say "surprising," because so many responsible organizations and individuals in the English-speaking Christian world have not hesitated to sacrifice on the altar of intelligibility the kinds of expressions which are no longer readily recognizable and clear to the modern average person. To them, the English language is not sacred. Nearly everyone recognized the King James Version for "its simplicity, its dignity, its power, its happy turns of expression . . . the music of its cadence, and the felicities of its rhythm"; but the very people who made the statement that I just quoted, were the foremost among those who recognized that new generations of people were growing up whose home and school and church upbringing was such that the English of the King James Version was all too frequently foreign to them, to the point where the Bible in English had become and remained for them quite a closed book. The English of the JPS translation, as is well known, was patterned after that of the King James Version. The Protestants and Catholics have rejected the English of the King James; we Jews are in the anomalous position of clinging to that English.

Precisely what do we mean by the term "English?" Well, in Deut. 24:11, and elsewhere, the older English versions, followed by the JPS, read "Thou shalt stand without," for בַּחוּץ תַּעֲמֹד ; nowadays, in this prose passage, we should say something like "You shall stand outside." In Judges 12:9 we are told that Ibzan of Bethlehem, a Judge in Israel, "had thirty sons, and thirty daughters he sent abroad, and thirty daughters he brought in from abroad for his sons." The word "abroad" to most of us usually means "a foreign country." This is clearly not what Judge Ibzan did; he did not intermarry with the Canaanites. The Hebrew expression הַחוּצָה means in this context simply "outside his clan," and some such idea should be expressed rather than "abroad," which the JPS took over from the King James. In Numbers 12:8 the Lord says to Aaron and Miriam about their brother Moses, פֶּה אֶל־פֶּה אֲדַבֶּר־בּוֹ וּמַרְאֶה וְלֹא בְחִידֹת , which is rendered in JPS, "with him do I speak mouth to mouth, even manifestly, and not in dark speeches." For מַרְאֶה King James rendered "apparently." JPS followed the American Standard Version of 1901 in substituting the term "manifestly." I do not think that this term is particularly clear to the average reader of our own time, and some such term as "clearly" ought to be used instead. There are dozens of such terms, which no longer are able to convey the meaning required by the original Hebrew text.

I do not believe that any English translation of the Hebrew Bible meant for the reader of today has the right to retain the obsolete, Old English forms and endings, such as the second and third singular endings in -est and -eth. When the angel of the Lord, in Genesis 16:8, said to Hagar, Sarai's handmaid, to use the rendering in JPS, "whence camest thou, and whither goest thou?" surely the Hebrew אֵי־מִזֶּה בָאת וְאָנָה תֵלֵכִי , Hagar herself, and the modern reader would be eminently satisfied with something like, "Where have you come from, and where are you going?" The pronoun "thou" and its other forms "thy" and "thine" ought not to be retained, except perhaps where the Deity is involved. No one today would address a maid as "thou"—or would they, in these days of social security benefits, shortage of good maids, etc.? The plural nominative "ye" could stand elimination. Whenever possible, such double prepositions as "unto" and "into" should be replaced by the simpler forms "to" and "in."

The cumbersome forms, "whosoever, whatsoever, according as," and the like, should be simplified to "whoever, whatever, as." The same holds true of such words as "wherein, whereby, thereabout."

In short, the style and vocabulary of the JPS translation must be simplified and modernized, without undue loss of majesty and dignity.

There is the matter of correctness in the rendering of a Hebrew expression. This is the domain of the scholar, into which anyone not a specialist ought not enter. The alert Bible scholar recognizes today the correct meaning and nuance of a word better than his—no less, and sometimes even more—competent predecessors, due largely to the increased knowledge which archeology and refined methodology have made available. We know now that the famous expression in Psalm 137:5, אִם אֶשְׁכָּחֵךְ יְרוּשָׁלִָם תִּשְׁכַּח יְמִינִי, should not be rendered, as in JPS and earlier Christian versions, "If I forget thee, O Jerusalem, let my right hand forget her cunning." There is no word for "her cunning" in the original Hebrew, and the JPS translation does not indicate to the reader the existence of this serious gap. Several emendations have been proposed for תִּשְׁכַּח, such as the passive form תִּשָּׁכַח "my right hand shall be forgotten"— whatever that means— and תִּכְחַשׁ "shall grow (become) lean." It would seem that the preserved reading תִּשְׁכַּח is original and requires no emendation. From Canaanite texts which have come to light in the past two decades it would seem that our Hebrew word can mean "waste away," just as Israel Eitan argued even before these Canaanite texts were discovered. Indeed, it is more than likely that in Psalm 102:5 our יִשְׁכַּח should be translated in this manner. The Hebrew reads הוּכָּה כָעֵשֶׂב וַיִּבַשׁ לִבִּי כִּי־שָׁכַחְתִּי מֵאֲכֹל לַחְמִי and the JPS, following the earlier renderings, translated, "My heart is smitten like grass, and withered; for I forget to eat my bread." The word שָׁכַחְתִּי should here be rendered, "For I am wasted away from not eating my food," or "For I am too wasted away to eat my food." Note that שָׁכַח is used here precisely parallel to יִיבַשׁ, "to wither." Again, the two words כֶּסֶף סִיגִים in Proverbs 26:23, usually rendered "silver dross," are in all likelihood to be read as one word כְּסַפְסָגִים, and to be translated, "like glaze." But there are dozens of expressions in this category which require fresh study and, perhaps, different translation, and I should not bore you with matters which are properly the domain of the competent, well-informed specialist.

Various objects used in the daily life of the Israelites can now be identified with greater certainty than was possible in the pre-archeological and pre-exploration days of World War I, and the results are bound to affect the terms employed in the JPS translation. The word חַמָּן is found 8 times in the Bible, and the JPS translation, in keeping with the American Standard Version, employed for it the term "sun-pillar." "A few years ago there was excavated at Palmyra, in Syria, an altar of incense which had this very word inscribed on it. Accordingly, this word ought to be translated 'incense altar.' " But again, we cannot enter here into these technical minutae, important and numerous as they may be, both for the correct and for the intelligible understanding of the Hebrew text.

I should say a word about this Hebrew text. Until World War I, and the consequent rediscovery of an important part of the ancient Near East by way of exploration and excavation, scholars generally felt justified in reconstructing the history of ancient Israel, even where the biblical record was evidently not altogether clear or adequate. In those days, from about 1875 to 1925, many competent scholars belittled and even disregarded these biblical data. This sceptical, even cynical attitude to the Bible as an historical document was well expressed as recently as 1945 by Bertrand Russell, in his book, *A History of Western Philosophy*, in the following passage, "The early history of the Israelites cannot be confirmed from any source outside the Old Testament, and it is impossible to know at what point it ceases to be legendary. David and Solomon may be accepted as kings who probably had a real existence, but at the earliest point at which we come to something certainly historical, there are already two kingdoms of Israel and Judah in the ninth century. . . ." The first thousand years of Jewish history was so glibly written off as "legendary"!

We know differently today. A mass of archeological and inscriptional material has now turned the Bible into one of the most important and reliable documents in history. (This, of course, is a chapter in itself.) But it is not alone the substantial reliability of the Bible as an historical document of ancient times which has come into prominence. Even the very text of the Hebrew Bible, which Jewish scribes and scholars had copied by hand and transmitted for 1500 years after the Second Jewish Commonwealth was destroyed by Rome in the year 70, is now coming once again to be appreciated. The nineteenth century and the first part of the twentieth witnessed an unprecedented tendency among scholars to emend the Hebrew text of the Bible whenever it did not appear original or satisfactory in their eyes. The best known and widely used critical edition of the text of the Hebrew Bible, Rudolf Kittel's *Biblia Hebraica*, recommended several thousands of changes in the traditional Hebrew text.

In contrast to this tendency, there is now available the evidence of a text of Isaiah which came to public light six years ago, the so-called Dead Sea, or St. Mark's Isaiah Scroll. This manuscript is dated variously by scholars, from about 100 B.C.E. to about 400 C.E. Regardless of its date, the text of this manuscript is so sloppily reproduced, and is so inferior to the text preserved by the Masoretes, the Jewish scholarly scribes of the first millennium and a half of the Common Era, that scholars are now coming increasingly to realize how remarkably careful and trustworthy the Masoretes were in preserving accurately the text of the Holy Scriptures. In my opinion, it is a self-evident proposition that the preserved, masoretic Hebrew text must form the basis of any modern, revised Jewish translation of the *Tanakh*. While it may be necessary sometimes to emend the masoretic text, emendations should be held to a minimum, and in no case should an emendation be introduced if it lacks the support of a pertinent ancient Near Eastern text, or of an ancient primary version, such as the Septuagint. The late Professor Margolis put it this way, "A judicious handling of the ancient versions often brings to light superior readings. But whether by the aid of the versions or by mere conjecture, the business of textual emendation requires a sure tact which few possess."

I have been asked frequently whether the new Protestant Bible, the Revised Standard Version, on which I had worked actively seven years, would be suitable for English-reading Jews. Let me say at the very outset that all translations which shed light on the Hebrew Bible should be utilized. Thus Hai Gaon of Pumbeditha, 900 years ago, when confronted with an exceptional difficulty in Psalm 141:5, did not hesitate to consult the Christian interpretation, on the ground "that scholars in former times did not hesitate to receive explanations from those of other beliefs." On the other hand, it is my opinion that Jews generally should use a translation which relies more on the Jewish scholarly interpretation of the Septuagint, Targum, Rashi, Ibn Ezra, Davis Qimhi, the Malbim, and the like. Thus, e.g., in the very first chapter in Genesis, verse 2, for the expression וְרוּחַ אֱלֹהִים מְרַחֶפֶת עַל־פְּנֵי הַמָּיִם, the RSV reads the "Spirit of God," with capital "S"—as though the Christian concept of the Holy Spirit had been meant by the author of the Hebrew text. The Preface in the JPS translation put it very well: "The repeated efforts by Jews in the field of biblical translation show their sentiment toward translations prepared by other denominations. The dominant features of this sentiment, apart from the thought that the christological interpretations in non-Jewish translations are out of place in a Jewish Bible, is and was [and may I add, should continue to be] that the Jew cannot afford to have his Bible translation prepared for him by others. He cannot have it as a gift, even as he cannot borrow his soul from others. If a new country and a new language metamorphose him into a new man, the duty of this new man is to prepare a new garb and a new method of expression for what is most sacred and most dear to him."

This, ladies and gentlemen, has now become the crux of the situation. The past fifty years have witnessed such great changes in our country and our language that a new man has emerged, one who was not raised on the language of Shakespeare, of the King James, and Leeser, and JPS versions, nor on the Hebrew text of the Bible. It is the duty of this new man to prepare a different garb and a different method of expression for what is most sacred and most dear to him. Saadia did not need a new garb and method of expression for himself; he needed it for his fellow Jews at large. Mendelssohn did not require a new version for himself, and neither did Luzzatto, nor Leeser; it was needed by their Jewish contemporaries who were less learned. Margolis was in no urgent need of a revision of Leeser, or of any translation; but he devoted the most important years of his life to making possible for his fellow Jews a JPS translation. I doubt that the vast majority of my distinguished audience this afternoon requires a revision of the JPS translation to render the Hebrew Bible intelligible to them; but the overwhelming majority of our fellow Jews does require precisely such a revision. In all periods and in all lands, wherever Jews have found themselves, such revisions have been made in the past. The JPS cannot, and should not, shirk its duty—and its privilege—in projecting at once the kind of revision which is already long overdue.

19

The Septuagint:
The Oldest Translation of the Bible

TABLE OF CONTENTS

[This essay appeared originally in 1949 in the *Union Anniversary Series* of the Union of American Hebrew Congregations, to mark the — approximately — 2200th anniversary of the birth of the Septuagint, the most influential translation of the Bible ever made. A few changes have been introduced here.]

1. EGYPT AND ITS JEWS DURING THE THIRD
CENTURY B.C.E.

ABOUT 2200 years ago there were many Jews in Egypt and especially in its capital city, Alexandria. Some of them were the descendants of Jews who had fled from the Kingdom of Judah as a result of
the destruction wrought by the armies of King Nebuchadnezzar of
Babylonia in 597 and 586 B.C.E. Others traced their ancestry to
Jews who emigrated from Judah to Egypt at a later date, during
Persia's rule. Still others were Judean freemen, or their children,
who were taken into Egyptian captivity by Ptolemy I Soter (323-285
B.C.E.) and liberated in the course of time.

This large and important Jewish community retained a deep interest in its parent body in Judea. It sent tithes and made pilgrimages
to the Temple in Jerusalem, and maintained and even strengthened
the bonds of religion and culture between itself and the homeland.

However, conditions in Egypt under the Ptolemies were not the
same as those in Judea during the Second Jewish Commonwealth.
The tremendous military conquests achieved by the Greeks under
Alexander the Great did not fail to bear political and cultural fruit
even after their great leader died in 323 B.C.E. Western Asia (Babylonia, Asia Minor, and Syria) finally fell to General Seleucus, and
Egypt was taken over by General Ptolemy. Judea became a pawn between the Seleucids in the north and the Ptolemies in the south, strug-
gling hard to play off one against the other and to maintain a measure
of independence, as well as to try to increase it. Greek culture, too,
invaded these non-Greek territories. The Hellenic language and civilization came to the direct attention of the peoples of Western Asia,
Judea, and Egypt, and began increasingly to affect them. The way of
life known as Hellenism was on the march. [1]

The Jews of Egypt knew Hebrew and Aramaic, the latter especially

---

[1] A. Tcherikower, *The Jews in Egypt in the Hellenistic-Roman Age* (in Hebrew,
with a 30-page abstract in English; Jerusalem, 1945). [See now also S. Zeitlin,
The Rise and Fall of the Judaean State, 2 vols. (Phila., 1962 and 1967).]

being widespread. Already in the sixth and fifth centuries B.C.E. the Jewish garrison stationed at Elephantine, at the first Cataract of the Nile River, employed Aramaic. However, just as the Jews of Europe who came to this country during the eighteenth and nineteenth centuries found, after a while, that they sometimes had to give up the linguistic vehicles of their culture (e.g., German, Yiddish, Hungarian) for the national language of America, English, so too did the Jews of Egypt come in time to realize that for certain aspects of their culture they had to give up Hebrew and Aramaic in favor of Greek. And just as the Jews of America during the past century found it necessary to render their Bible into English, so did their ancestors in Egypt during the third century B.C.E. find themselves compelled to translate their Bible, the Torah, into Greek. This translation is known as the *Septuagint,* and it is the first translation of the Bible ever made.

II. *THE LETTER OF ARISTEAS*

A. *Contents of the "Letter"*

Most of our information about the origin of the Septuagint comes from a little Greek work known as "The Letter of Aristeas." An Alexandrian who called himself Aristeas addressed a letter to his brother Philocrates, telling him how Demetrius, head of the famous library in Alexandria, persuaded Ptolemy II Philadelphus (285-246 B.C.E.) to send a delegation to Eleazar the High Priest in Jerusalem, with the request that he appoint six Elders from each of the twelve tribes of Israel for the purpose of translating the Torah into Greek. The translation when completed was to be deposited in the library. Eleazar complied with the request. He appointed seventy-two Elders, who proceeded to Alexandria with "the parchments on which the Torah in Jewish characters was inscribed in gold." After a royal banquet which lasted seven days, the Elders departed for the island of Pharos to a building specially prepared for them. There, in seventy-two days, the Elders completed the Greek translation. Demetrius then "assembled the Jewish people on the spot where the translation had been made, and read it through to the whole assembly in the presence of the translators, who received another great ovation from the people." The work was then read to the king, who "made obeisance and ordered that great care should be taken of the Books."

B. *Reliability of the "Letter"*

It has been said of the "Letter" that it lacked all historical validity; that some Alexandrian Jew, wishing to glorify his people and the Torah in the eyes of his non-Jewish neighbors, assumed the Greek name Aristeas, made up the story, and "palmed" it off as true. The well-known German scholar of pre-World War I days, Emil Schuerer, classified the "Letter," together with other works which came to be called Apocrypha, under the heading: "Jewish Propaganda under a Heathen Mask."

We now know better. It is now generally recognized that the "Letter" is far from being unhistorical; that while many of the details are fictitious, there is considerable truth which remains; that many expressions and references in it could hardly have been known and employed in a much later age.[2]

III. THE NAME "SEPTUAGINT"

The term "Septuagint" (frequently abbreviated "LXX") which is applied to the Greek translation of the Bible, is but the Latin word *septuaginta* meaning "seventy." Aristeas tells us, as we mentioned above, that seventy-two Elders took part in the translation; consequently it should have come to be called "The (Translation of the) Seventy-two." While it is no longer possible to determine with certainty the circumstances under which "Seventy-two" became "Seventy" (the Talmud speaks of the "Translation of the Seventy"), it would seem that

---

[2] H. St. J. Thackeray, *The Letter of Aristeas* (London, 1918). [See now also, e.g., *Aristeas to Philocrates* (*Letter of Aristeas*), ed. M. Hadas (in *Jewish Apocryphal Literature*, 1951); and in general, S. Jellicoe, *The Septuagint and Modern Study* (Oxford, 1968), pp. 29-58.]

the change took place in Judea because of some popular association with the "seventy elders" mentioned in Exodus 24:1, 9 (where Moses publicly read and authorized the "Book of the Covenant"), or with the Sanhedrin of Seventy, or in Christian circles with the seventy apostles of Jesus (Luke 10:1).

IV. THE SEPTUAGINT AMONG JEWS AND CHRISTIANS

Here then was an authorized translation of the Hebrew Torah into Greek, the work of Jewish scholars. And within a century or two the rest of the Bible, the Prophets and the other Books which came to constitute the Writings, was likewise done into Greek. It was popular, and widely used in Jewish circles.

But numerous changes took place in Jewish life after 70 C.E. Rome crushed Jewish sovereignty and destroyed the Temple. Christian Jews, one of several Jewish sects toward the end of the Second Jewish Commonwealth, began to move more and more from things Jewish and in the direction of things Gentile, so that by the time the Bar Kochba revolt was crushed in 135 C.E. the majority of Christians were not Jews in origin but Gentiles. The Jewish Greek Bible, the Septuagint, became for them not merely a translation of the Bible but a complete *substitute* for the Hebrew Bible; in fact, in the early church, the Septuagint was not infrequently considered even more inspired than the original Hebrew! In the Western (Roman Catholic) Church it was only after the fifth century C.E. that the Septuagint was replaced by Jerome's Latin translation, the Vulgate. In the Eastern (Greek Orthodox) Church, the Septuagint is still the official Bible.

The Jews, on the other hand, began to shy away from the Septuagint, as from many other Jewish works in the Greek language (e.g., the writings of Philo and Josephus; the Apocryphal literature), especially after the Christians adopted the Septuagint as their own, and here and there even changed an expression to conform to their own theological outlook. Furthermore, in keeping with the current Jewish manner of interpreting Holy Scripture in the first and second centuries, C.E., a new Greek translation of the Bible was made, by Aquila;

it was still in use in the synagogue in the days of the Byzantine emperor, Justinian I (sixth century), and fell into disuse when Arabic came to replace Greek and Latin after the seventh century.

V. SOME EXTERNAL FEATURES OF THE SEPTUAGINT

A. Names of Biblical Books

Those who have read the Bible in the original Hebrew know that the names of the different Books are frequently derived from the first important word or words in the Book. Thus, B^ereshith ("In the beginning of"), Sh^emoth, ("Names"), Va-yiqra ("And He called"), B^emidbar ("In the wilderness of"), and D^evarim ("Words") constitute the Hebrew names of the Five Books of Moses (the Pentateuch; Torah). In the Septuagint, however, the names describe the main contents of each Book, so that these Books are called respectively: *Genesis* ("Creation" of the world), *Exodus* (from Egypt), *Leviticus* (priestly matters), *Numbers* (the census taken of the Hebrews in the wilderness), and *Deuteronomy* (the second giving of the Torah; cf. 17:18). It is clear that the English titles of thee Books derive from the Septuagint (by way of the Latin). However, the Septuagint usage is also Jewish, and we know that *B^ereshith* was sometimes referred to as *Sefer Y^etsirath Ha-Olam* "Book of Creation of the World" (Genesis); *Sh^emoth* was known also as *Sefer Y^etsi'ath Mitsrayim* "Book of the Exodus from Egypt" (Exodus); and *Va-yiqra* was called popularly *Sefer Torath Kohanim* "Book of the Law of the Priests" (i.e., Leviticus); *B^emidbar* was sometimes called *Ḥomesh Ha-P^equdim* (i.e., Numbers); and *D^evarim* had another name, *Sefer Mishneh Torah* (i.e., Deuteronomy). [3]

B. Order of the Books

The Torah came to be canonized, that is, designated as Sacred Scripture, by the time of Ezra in the fifth century B.C.E.; the Prophets (He-

---

[3] On other aspects of the Jewish origin of the Septuagint, see now my Prolegomenon, "The Masoretic Text: A Critical Evaluation," pp. XVIII ff., in KTAV reissue of C. D. Ginsburg, *Introduction,* etc. (1966).

brew: $N^evi'im$), sometime before 200 B.C.E. The third major division, the Writings or Hagiographa (Hebrew: $K^ethuvim$), however, did not become fixed until after 65 C.E., and this resulted in considerable fluidity in the order of the Books.

During the period preceding 65 C.E., when our Bible was known only as "the Law, the Prophets, and the rest of the Books," the Jews who used the Septuagint began to put some of "the rest of the Books" among the Prophets. Thus, the Septuagint (followed by the Latin and English Bibles) listed Ruth after Judges, Lamentations after Jeremiah, Chronicles after Kings; and the like.

C. *The Books Included in the Septuagint*

Until the rabbis fixed the limits of the Hebrew Canon in the first century C.E., learned Jews could regard as sacred any Hebrew book which they believed was divinely inspired. Scores upon scores of works were written by Jews during the Second Jewish Commonwealth, and many others after the subjugation of Judah in 70 C.E. Many of these books were included in the Septuagint. However, when the Hebrew Bible was fixed, and only twenty-four books finally included in the Canon, all the other works were set aside and designated as "Outside Books" (Hebrew: S^efarim $Hitsonim$).

The Christians, however, naturally did not heed the rabbinic edict all the way. The Septuagint was their Bible, and it contained many books never included in the Hebrew Canon and numerous additions to such canonical books as Daniel (Susannah, Bel and the Dragon) and Esther. After considerable debate at various Synods (Church Conferences), the Catholic Church decided that the Christian Canon would include all of the Hebrew Canon (which they came to call the "Old Testament"), the New Testament, and about twelve additional books (I and II Esdras, Tobit, Judith, Wisdom of Solomon, Ecclesiasticus, Baruch, the Additions to Esther and Daniel, the Prayer of Manasseh, I and II Maccabees); these additional books were incorporated into the Old Testament. The remaining books were designated "Apocrypha" (Greek for Hebrew S^efarim $Hitsonim$ "Books Outside the Canon").

In modern times the Protestant Church, following the Hebrew Canon, excluded the dozen books and designated them as Apocrypha, while those books which had been called Apocrypha by the Roman Catholic Church it called, rather arbitrarily, Pseudepigrapha ("False Writings"). Thus it is that while Apocryphal books may be read for spiritual edification, they lack entirely the authority of Holy Writ.[4]

VI. MANUSCRIPTS AND TRANSLATIONS OF THE SEPTUAGINT

A. Manuscripts of the Septuagint

It is not unlikely that even before the Septuagint translation came into being, some individual attempts were made by Alexandrian Jews at translating parts of the Torah into Greek. This was done in the same spirit that several English translations of parts of the Bible were made by Christians in England before the so-called King James version was done and by Jews in England and America prior to the version issued by the Jewish Publication Society of America in 1917. However, all traces of these assumed pre-Septuagint translations have disappeared, leaving only the Septuagint itself. The original Septuagint manuscript, too, has not been preserved. It may have perished during one of the anti-Jewish pogroms which occurred in Egypt under Roman domination, or when the great library in Alexandria burned down. Fortunately, copies of the Septuagint had been made. In our own times, pending a census of what was destroyed in Europe during World War II, there are in existence some twelve manuscripts containing the Septuagint of the entire Old Testament, and many hundreds containing individual divisions (the Pentateuch), or groups of books (the Minor Prophets; the Major Prophets), or individual books,

---

[4] C. C. Torrey, *The Apocryphal Literature* (New Haven, 1945), pp. 3-40; S. Zeitlin, "An Historical Study of the Canonization of the Hebrew Scriptures" in *Proceedings of the American Academy for Jewish Research*, 3 (1945), pp. 121-158. [See now my essay elsewhere in this volume, "The Canonization of the Hebrew Bible and the Exclusion of the Apocrypha," chap. 15, pp. 257ff.]

or fragments of parts of single books. Most of the manuscripts are to be found in Italy, Great Britain and Ireland, France, Russia, and Germany.

The best known manuscript of the Septuagint is Codex Vaticanus (Vatican Library), dating from about 350 C.E. It is an extremely fine quarto volume of the finest vellum, written in an extraordinarily beautiful hand, and containing now 759 leaves (of which 617 belong to the Old Testament) out of an original total of about 820 leaves. Another of the famous manuscripts of the Septuagint is Codex Sinaiticus. Some readers will remember that in 1933 the British Museum purchased this fourth-century Codex from the Soviet Government for a reported price of some $500,000. The same Museum is the owner of another fine and noted specimen of the Septuagint, the fifth-century Codex Alexandrinus.

Since the end of World War I there have been discovered and published a group of Septuagint manuscripts known as the Chester Beatty Papyri, dating in part from the second century C.E. Numerous fragments of individual books have also been brought to light in recent years, some of them (the Rylands fragments of parts of some chapters in Deuteronomy) dating as early as about 150 B.C.E. [5]

B. *Translations of the Septuagint*

Early in the Common Era (probably second century), Latin-speaking Christians in Africa and Italy translated the Septuagint into Latin. This is known as the Old Latin version. At about the same time, other Christians in Egypt translated the Septuagint into Coptic (various dialects). After Christianity became the official religion of the Roman Empire (in the fourth century), different linguistic groups of Christians needed translations of the Christian Bible, the Septuagint, in their own tongues. Thus there came into being during the fourth and fifth centuries such versions as the Armenian, Georgian, Gothic,

---

[5] J. Finegan, *Light from the Ancient Past* (Princeton, 1946), pp. 305-352. [See now Jellicoe, *op. cit., passim.*]

and Ethiopic. An Arabic translation followed about 700, and a Slavonic about 900.

The Septuagint exerted an influence upon most Bible translations, even such as were not direct translations of the Septuagint itself. Thus the Syriac (Peshitta) translation made from the Hebrew Bible (probably during the second century C.E.), the Greek translations made by Theodotion, Aquila, and Symmachus at about the same time (incorporated by Origen early in the third century in his six-columned Bible called "Hexapla"), and the Vulgate (Latin) translation by St. Jerome during the fourth and fifth centuries (to become the official Bible of the Roman Catholic Church)—all of these were considerably influenced by the Septuagint. [6]

VII. EDITIONS OF THE SEPTUAGINT

A. *The Earlier Period* (to about 1850)

Most manuscripts of the Septuagint are not readily accessible; moreover, in the course of copying the text of the Septuagint, various kinds of errors and alterations were introduced by scribes and scholars. Consequently, the text of no one manuscript of the Septuagint is completely identical with that of any other. Thus it became necessary to put out a handy edition of the Septuagint for scholars and students.

In 1517 printing was completed of a three-columned Bible in four volumes (publication of which was withheld until the New Testament volume was completed in 1520-1), known as the Complutensian Polyglott. Column I contained the Hebrew text, with the Targum at the foot of the page; Column II consisted of the Vulgate; and Column III constituted the Septuagint, with an interlinear Latin translation of it. It is the first printed text of the Septuagint. Among the other editions of the Septuagint, the best known are the Aldine (1518-19), Sixtine (1587),

---

[6] S. R. Driver, *Notes on the Hebrew Text and Topography of the Books of Samuel,* 2nd edition (Oxford, 1913), Introduction, especially pp. lv-lxix; J. A. Montgomery, *International Critical Commentary on Daniel* (New York, 1927), Introduction, especially pp. 35-38.

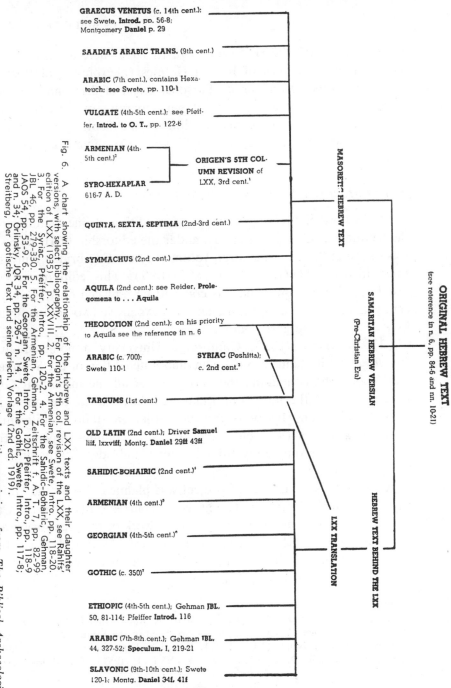

GRAECUS VENETUS (c. 14th cent.); see Swete, **Introd.** pp. 56-8; Montgomery **Daniel** p. 29

SAADIA'S ARABIC TRANS. (9th cent.)

ARABIC (7th cent.), contains Hexateuch; see Swete, pp. 110-1

VULGATE (4th-5th cent.); see Pfeiffer, **Introd. to O. T.,** pp. 122-6

ARMENIAN (4th-5th cent.)[2]

ORIGEN'S 5TH COLUMN REVISION of LXX, 3rd cent.[1]

SYRO-HEXAPLAR 616-7 A. D.

QUINTA, SEXTA, SEPTIMA (2nd-3rd cent.)

SYMMACHUS (2nd cent.)

AQUILA (2nd cent.): see Reider, **Prolegomena to . . . Aquila**

THEODOTION (2nd cent.); on his priority to Aquila see the reference in n. 6

ARABIC (c. 700); Swete 110-1

SYRIAC (Peshitta); c. 2nd cent.[3]

TARGUMS (1st cent.)

OLD LATIN (2nd cent.); Driver **Samuel** liif, lxxviff; Montg. **Daniel** 29ff 43ff

SAHIDIC-BOHAIRIC (2nd cent.)[4]

ARMENIAN (4th cent.)[5]

GEORGIAN (4th-5th cent.)[6]

GOTHIC (c. 350)[7]

ETHIOPIC (4th-5th cent.); Gehman **JBL,** 50, 81-114; Pfeiffer **Introd.** 116

ARABIC (7th-8th cent.); Gehman **JBL,** 44, 327-52; **Speculum,** I, 219-21

SLAVONIC (9th-10th cent.); Swete 120-1; Montg. **Daniel** 34f, 41f

MASORETIC HEBREW TEXT

ORIGINAL HEBREW TEXT (see reference in n. 6, pp. 84-6 and nn. 10-21)

SAMARITAN HEBREW VERSION (Pre-Christian Era)

HEBREW TEXT BEHIND THE LXX

LXX TRANSLATION

Fig. 6. A chart showing the relationship of the Hebrew and LXX texts and their daughter versions, with select bibliography. 1. For Origen's 5th col. revision of the LXX, see Rahlfs' edition of LXX (1935) I, p. XXVIII. 2. For the Armenian, see Swete, Intro. pp. 118-20. 3. For the Syriac, Pfeiffer, Intro., pp. 120-2. 4. For the Sahidic-Bohairic, Gehman, JBL 46, pp. 279-330. 5. For the Armenian, Gehman, Zeitschrift f. A. T., 7, pp. 82-99; JAOS 54, pp. 53-9. 6. For the Georgian, Swete, Intro., p. 120; Pfeiffer, Intro., pp. 118-9 and n. 34; Orlinsky, JQR 34, pp. 296-7 n. 14. 7. For the Gothic, Swete, Intro., pp. 117-8; Streitberg, Der gotische Text und seine griech. Vorlage (2nd ed. 1919).

[Reprinted, with permission, from *The Biblical Archaeologist*, 9 (1946), 30. For an explanation of the notes and other data, see the original article there.]

[I would now extend the line between LXX TRANSLATION and HEBREW TEXT BEHIND THE LXX straight up, to indicate that the Hebrew *Vorlage* behind the LXX did not always derive from the ORIGINAL HEBREW TEXT from which the (so-called) MASORETIC HEBREW TEXT derived. The books of Joshua, Samuel, Jeremiah, and Job are cases in point.]

and Grabe (1707-1720). From 1798 to 1827 there appeared in five large volumes the work of Robert Holmes (a Professor of Poetry at Oxford University) and James Parsons, a text of the complete Septuagint and, what is more important, an apparatus of variant readings culled from 297 separate manuscripts of the Septuagint as well as from the Old Latin, Coptic, Arabic, Slavonic, Armenian, and Georgian versions.

B. *The Modern Period* (from about 1850)

(1) A portable, relatively inexpensive edition of one manuscript of the Septuagint, Codex Vaticanus, under the editorship of H. B. Swete, was issued in three normal-sized volumes by the Cambridge University Press in 1887-94 (revised in 1895-1899). This edition was very widely used in its time, and has come to be replaced only in very recent years by the more accurate and less expensive two-volume edition by A. Rahlfs (Stuttgart, 1935).

(2) In March, 1883, Cambridge University announced in its *Reporter* that it planned to issue an elaborate edition of the Septuagint and Apocrypha containing the variations of all the important Greek manuscripts, of the more important versions, and of the quotations made by Philo and Josephus and the earlier and more significant ecclesiastical writers (Church Fathers). Nine volumes appeared from 1906 to 1940. [Apparently this "Larger Cambridge Septuagint" will not be resumed.]

A generally similar kind of project was planned also by the University of Göttingen Septuagint Commission, spurred on (as was the Cambridge University) by the keen analytical work of the great orientalist, Paul de Lagarde. So far there have appeared Psalms, I Maccabees, Isaiah, and the Minor Prophets—the latter two exceptionally well done. [7]

---

[7] *Psalmi cum Odis* (X; 1931) was edited by A. Rahlfs, and I Maccabees (IX, 1; 1936) by W. Kappler. All the Prophets — as listed in the Septuagint — were edited ably by J. Ziegler: Isaiah (XIV; 1939), Jeremiah, Baruch, Lamentations, and the Epistle of Jeremiah (XV; 1957); Ezekiel (XVI, 1; 1952), the Minor Prophets

(3) A great work which deserves notice here is "The Book of Joshua" in Greek (Paris, 1931 ff.) by Max L. Margolis (1866-1932) of the Dropsie College in Philadelphia. Margolis obtained photostatic copies, wherever possible, of all manuscripts of the Septuagint and of the translations made from or influenced by the Septuagint. Then he compared these translations with the manuscripts of the Septuagint, and the manuscripts of the Septuagint with one another, and with the citations of the Septuagint in the writings of the early Church Fathers. He found that all this material could be distributed among four major groups (called recensions) and one mixed group which arose during the first few centuries C.E. in Egypt (especially Alexandria), Syria (especially Antioch), Palestine (the work of Origen, the noted Christian scholar), and Asia Minor (especially Constantinople). In his monumental work (all in autograph!), Prof. Margolis provided at the top of the page "the nearest approach to the Greek original as it left the hands of the hands of the translator(s)" of Joshua. Below the text he made available the pertinent data of the chief recensions, and, at the bottom of the page, brief notes bearing on the Septuagint in relation to the Hebrew text. [8]

VIII. THE LANGUAGE OF THE SEPTUAGINT AND ITS INFLUENCE

A. The Language of the Septuagint

It used to be thought that the sort of Greek used in the Septuagint never really constituted a living dialect in Alexandria, that it was essentially an artificially contrived literary production consisting of

---

(XIII; 1943); and Susanna, Daniel, Bel and the Dragon (XVI, 2; 1954). In the Wisdom Literature J. Ziegler edited The Wisdom of Solomon (XII, 1 1962) and Ecclesiasticus (XII, 2; 1965). R. Hanhart edited II and III Maccabees (IX, 2 and 3; 1959 and 1960). Genesis, edited by J. W. Wevers, is due to appear soon; and he will probably edit other Books of the Pentateuch as well.

[8] See my chapter on "Margolis' Work in the Septuagint" (preceded by a photograph of p. 1 of Margolis' *Joshua in Greek*) in *Max Leopold Margolis: Scholar and Teacher* (Philadelphia, 5712-1952), pp. 35-44.

Greek words (many of them created on the spot) put together after
the manner and in the spirit of the Hebrew original.

We know quite differently now. The Greek dialects spoken in and
around Alexandria from about the third century B.C.E. on have become known largely through the discovery of papyri and other writing
materials since the beginning of the century. There can no longer
be any doubt that while the Jews who made the Septuagint translation
did adapt the Greek language to the Hebrew original (in essentially
the same manner as English was adapted to the Hebrew in the now
classical King James version of the Bible), they were nevertheless
using a living dialect of Alexandrian Greek (called the *Koine*), a dialect which they knew very well indeed. As a matter of fact, the Septuagint has now become an important source for the reconstruction of
that dialect.

B. *The Influence of the Language of the Septuagint*

What is more important is that the Jewish translator, sometimes
lacking a Greek word to reproduce exactly the nuance of the Hebrew,
gave the closest Greek word a new meaning, one that came to influence
Latin and other languages thereafter (e.g., English, French, German).
Thus, when the Jews had to translate the Hebrew word *barakh* "bless"
into Greek, they found themselves at a loss; such a concept, and hence
the word for it, was unknown to Greek culture. So they took the
nearest Greek word, *eulogeō,* which meant "speak well of, commend,"
and adapted it to the Jewish concept "bless." In turn, when the Christians came to translate into Latin the Septuagint word for "bless"
(eulogeō), they too found themselves at a similar loss. So they took the
nearest Latin word, *benedico* "speak well of, commend," and adapted
it to the now Jewish-Christian concept "bless." The result was that
Greek *eulogeō* and Latin *benedico* acquired the meaning of Hebrew
barakh "bless," and from them there developed the concept "to bless"
in English, *bénir* in French, *bentshen* in Yiddish, and *segnen* in German.

In the same way, the English word "angel" developed the special meaning of "messenger of God" (as did French *ange* and German *engel*) from Greek *angelos* (by way of the Latin *angelus*) only because the Greek word, which had only the simple meaning of "messenger," came to take on in the Septuagint the technical meaning of "messenger of God" to correspond to the Hebrew expression *mal'akh Adonay*. (The reader may pursue this fascinating subject, e.g., the expressions "Lord," "Devil," and "paradise," in the fine chapter by A. Meillet, "Influence of the Hebrew Bible on European Languages," in *The Legacy of Israel,* ed. E. R. Bevan-C. Singer [Oxford, 1927], pp. 473-81.)

IX. THE IMPORTANCE OF THE SEPTUAGINT FOR THE STUDY OF THE HEBREW BIBLE

A. *The Septuagint in Relation to the Hebrew Text*

Far and away the greatest importance of the Septuagint lay in the proper use of it for the study of the Hebrew text of the Bible.

It so happens that the oldest dated manuscript of the Hebrew text of the Bible does not antedate the tenth century C.E. This text is the product of Masoretes, Jewish scholars who labored devotedly during the first millennium to transmit the Holy Scriptures in the form in which they received them. The Septuagint translation, on the other hand, is represented by one manuscript of the second century and several of the fourth and fifth centuries; and with the method employed by Margolis in the book of Joshua, it is possible to get back to approximately the original text of the Septuagint. From this text, in turn, it is generally possible to determine the character of the Hebrew text used by the translators. [9]

It has long been recognized that the Hebrew text from which the

---

[9] On the biblical texts of the Dead Sea Scrolls, see now my essay, Chapter 21 below, on "The Hebrew Text and the Ancient Versions of the Old Testament" (with special reference in n. 1 there to my chapter on "The Textual Criticism of the Old Testament" in the Albright Volume [Doubleday Anchor Book A431; 1965]).

Septuagint translation was made differed in many respects from the preserved Hebrew text.

Overwhelmingly the Hebrew text preserved by the Masoretes agrees with that underlying the Septuagint, or is superior to it when the two do not agree. The use of the Septuagint comes into play when its Hebrew text differs from the Masoretic and there is uncertainty as to which of the two represents the original reading. This is where the competent textual critic of the Bible can show his mettle.

The average biblical commentary of three or four decades ago was filled with a wealth of changes of the Hebrew text which were believed to be indicated and even demanded by the Septuagint. A great change began to take place after World War I, induced in part by archeology. The latter discipline has helped considerably in revolutionizing the attitude of the scholarly world toward the Bible. We are now less inclined to be skeptical of something merely because extra-biblical data supporting it are lacking. Until demonstrated otherwise, the benefit of the doubt must be entered on the credit side of the biblical ledger. The same attitude is now generally being taken toward the reliability of the traditional text of the Hebrew Bible in relation to the Septuagint and to its *Vorlage,* i.e., to the Hebrew text from which the Septuagint translation was made.

B. *The Septuagint as a Jewish Work*

An important reason for the older attitude of skepticism toward the Hebrew text of the Bible was the failure on the part of scholars to bear in mind the fact that the Septuagint is a Jewish work, resulting in an enormous amount of time and effort being wasted in its unscientific use for the "elucidation" and "restoration" of the Hebrew text.

(1) The Hebrew Bible was read, studied, and interpreted by the Jews during the Maccabean, Mishnaic, and Talmudic periods no less than it was before the second century B.C.E. and after the sixth century C.E. It is only reasonable to assume that where the Septuagint points or appears to point to a Hebrew reading which differs from that preserved in the traditional text, there may be involved not two variants

of which only one can be original, but one reading of which the Septuagint is simply an interpretation. And parallels to this interpretation should be sought in the vast literature which the Jews produced from the second century B.C.E. through the sixth century C.E., a literature which is a mine of information for the discerning scholar. It is the great contribution of Rabbi Zecharias Frankel of Breslau (1801-75) to one phase of correct Septuagint study that he collected and classified material of this kind, demonstrating the manner in which the Septuagint exhibits the kind of exegesis found in the Targumim, Mishnah, Tosefta, Midrashim, and Gemara. Had this important approach been kept in mind, many of the best-known critics of the past generations would never have emended the preserved Hebrew text so recklessly and indiscriminately. [10]

(2) The Hebrew Bible was to the Jews a collection of sacred books. The Bible was translated into Greek precisely because the Sacred Scriptures had to be made accessible to those Jews who no longer knew enough Hebrew to read the original. The Aramaic Targums, Saadia's Arabic translation, and the modern English version sponsored by the Jewish Publication Society were made for the same reasons. Is it reasonable to suppose that these same Jews willfully or negligently altered and corrupted their Hebrew Bible between the third century B.C.E. and the second century C.E. to the extent that so many scholars assumed, to the extent, say, that the footnotes in the second and third editions of the most widely used critical edition today, R. Kittel's *Biblia Hebraica,* would indicate? Scholars should first have made an independent and thorough study not only of the Hebrew text of whatever book in the Bible they were commenting on, but also of the Septuagint. Had they done so, they would not have abused the Septuagint so frequently and unjustifiably as to create from it a Hebrew text which never existed outside of their own imagination.

---

[10] See, e. g., R. Marcus, "Jewish and Greek Elements in the Septuagint" in *Louis Ginzberg Jubilee Volume,* English Volume (New York, 1945), pp. 227-245.

X. THE NEED TO RECLAIM ANCIENT JEWISH CULTURE

One of the most important periods in the vast range of Jewish his
tory is the Second Jewish Commonwealth, which came to an end ir
70 C.E. Much of the literary creativity of the Jews during this period
both in Judea and in the Diaspora (especially Alexandria) took on
from the very beginning, or came to take on in time, Greek form.
Among this extensive literature there were many scores of works of
which the thirty or so which have been preserved acquired the designation "Apocrypha." There are also the writings of the Jewish philosopher of Alexandria, Philo (flourished during first half of the first
century C.E.), and of the Jewish politician and historian of Judea and
Rome, Flavius Josephus (about 37-100 C.E.); and there is the Septuagint.

After the loss of their sovereignty and the failure of the Bar-Kochba
revolt, the Jews lost all interest in these "Greek" works; but thanks to
the Catholic Church these works have been preserved. Jewry today is
better off and in a different mood compared with those catastrophic
days. There is hardly a single important language in the world in
which the Jews have not been culturally active during the past two
millennia. One has merely to call to mind the great Jewish cultures in
Aramaic, Latin, Arabic, Yiddish, German, French, Russian, English,
and the like, to realize the truth of this statement. There is no longer
any reason to withhold "recognition" from the significant culture produced by the Jews of Judea and the Diaspora around the turn of the
Common Era.

There is, however, something more at stake here than merely re-
claiming Jewish literature in Greek form. For some eighteen hundred
years, ignored as it was by the Jews, this literature was utilized by
Christian scholars chiefly to reconstruct the Christian aspect of the
New Testament period. On the other hand, the vast range of the fundamentally important literature produced by the Jews in Hebrew and
Aramaic in the post-biblical period (especially the Midrashim and
the Talmud) has scarcely been touched by Christian scholars. Such a
procedure is tantamount to utilizing only the rabbinic sources for a

study of the New Testament period in the Greco-Roman world! Yet the fact remains, and it is becoming increasingly recognized in recent years, that for the correct understanding of this literature, one must study it in the light of the Jewish history of the times, a history that can be reconstructed essentially only by the proper study of the Jewish post-biblical sources. For the period between the third century B.C.E. and the second century C.E. this kind of study is absolutely indispensable for the correct understanding of Judaism, of certain aspects of Hellenism, and of early Christianity.

Let us hope that the Third Jewish Commonwealth, the modern State of Israel, with the active aid of Jewish scholarship and patronage in other parts of the world, will help us understand significantly better the culture of the Second Jewish Commonwealth.

GENERAL BIBLIOGRAPHY

SWETE, H. B.: *An Introduction to the Old Testament in Greek* (Cambridge, 2nd edition, 1902; revised by R. R. Ottley, 1914 [and reissued by KTAV, 1968]). Although there is now much to correct and add, this excellent survey is still the standard introduction to the Septuagint. [This is now supplemented by a most useful survey and analysis by

JELLICOE, S.: *The Septuagint and Modern Study* (Oxford, 1968). Furthermore, there now appears the *Bulletin* of the International Organization for Septuagint and Cognate Studies (IOSCS), edited by S. Jellicoe; the Organization came into being in 1968.]

OTTLEY, R. R.: *A Handbook to the Septuagint* (London, 1920) A useful and readable popularization of Swete's more technical work. [But to be supplemented by Jellicoe's volume.]

MARGOLIS, M. L.: *The Story of Bible Translations* (Philadelphia, 1917). This little book of 135 pages is a thoroughly authoritative and readable treatment of the subject by one of its greatest authorities.

ORLINSKY, H. M.: "The Septuagint—its Use in Textual Criticism" (in *Biblical Archaeologist*, 9 May 1946, pp. 21-34; followed by F. V. Filson's fine article on "The Septuagint and the New Testament," 34-42); "Current Progress and Problems in Septuagint Research" (Chap. VIII in *The Study of the Bible Today and Tomorrow*, ed. H. R. Willoughby, Chicago, 1947).

20

The Septuagint:
A Little Known Fact about the
First Translation of the Torah

WHEN THE NEW JPS version of the Torah appeared early in 1963, some of the rather meager criticism directed against it derived from a statement found in the Rabbinic Literature about the Septuagint translation, namely: "The day on which the Greek translation was made, was as difficult for Israel as the day on which Israel made the Golden Calf in the wilderness; for the Torah could not be translated adequately." What was true about the Septuagint, some of our critics said, was hardly less true of the new JPS version. But let us look into the facts a bit more closely.

Some 2,200 years ago (about 200 B.C.E.) there flourished in Alexandria, Egypt, a large Jewish population which had become Egyptianized (Americanized?), that is to say, had forgotten much of its Hebrew. The daily language of this Jewry was Greek, the vernacular that spread all over Asia as a result of Alexander's great conquests of that continent.

[This note was written in response to some critics who opposed the new JPS translation of the Torah on the grounds that no translation was adequate, not even the Septuagint. The note appeared originally on pp. 2-3 of the *JPS Newsletter of the New Translation of the Holy Scriptures,* No. 1, February 1964.]

The Jews of Egypt recognized the authority of the Bible, which for them consisted only of the Torah, the Five Books of Moses; the books that later came to be designated as the Prophets and the Writings were not yet recognized.

Unable to read their Bible in the Hebrew original, they translated it into Greek. Because legend had it that 72 elders—6 from each of the 12 tribes of Israel—participated in the project, the translation came to be called "The Seventy-two," and then simply "The Seventy"; *Septuagint* is the Latin word for "seventy."

The Septuagint soon swept over Jewish Egypt. It became their Bible, hardly lower in authority than the Hebrew from which it derived. In this respect, the reader will note at once a parallel with our own situation here. In this country, too, translations of the Bible into our vernacular, English, have acquired official status alongside the Hebrew original; this was true of Isaac Leeser's fine translation of the Bible a little over a century ago, and of the Bible that came to replace it, the JPS version of 1917.

The Jewish literature of two thousand years ago is lavish in its praise of the Septuagint translation. In the apocryphal book called *The Letter of Aristeas* we read (§§308-311) of the "great ovation" that the translators received from the entire Jewish community, "inasmuch as the translation has been well and piously made and is in every respect accurate." Both the great Jewish philosopher Philo (died about 50 C.E.) and the historian Josephus (died sometime after 100 C.E.) used the Septuagint as their Bible and praised its great merits; Philo described the translators as "inspired prophets."

The Greek language was highly regarded by the rabbis. Whenever mention is made of the language in which phylacteries, mezuzot, and the Torah may be written, Greek is regularly held in esteem second only to Hebrew. Thus, when expressing their satisfaction with the fact that the Torah had been translated into Greek, the rabbis quoted Genesis 9.27:

"May God enlarge Japheth,
And let him dwell in the tents of Shem"—

that is, since Japheth is the ancestor of the Greeks and Shem of the Israelites, the rabbis cleverly interpreted the verse to mean that it was good that Israel's Torah was rendered into Greek (cf. Megillah 8b-9a).

An anti-Septuagint statement appears only much later, in the extra-talmudic tractate *Masseket Soferim* ("Tractate of Scribes"). We read there (chapter I, 7)—as quoted in our first paragraph above—about the translation of the Torah into Greek being as calamitous an event for Israel as the making of the Golden Calf, "for the Torah could not be translated adequately." To understand this complete change of at-titude toward the Greek language and the Septuagint, one must recall the dire events that had in the meantime befallen the Jews of Judea and some of the Jewish communities in the diaspora. For in the year 70 the Second Temple was destroyed and Judean sovereignty was reduced to nought. Coupled with this catastrophe was the fact that the originally Jewish sect of Christians had begun increasingly to part from Judaism, the pace of estrangement increasing after the year 70. For the Chris-tian Jews, as for so many Jews in general, the Septuagint rather than the original Hebrew was *the* Bible; and this attitude was fortified after 70, when Christianity turned to the Gentiles for support and for fol-lowers.

The Jews, in turn, proceeded to give up what they had themselves created in the Greek language. They rejected the Septuagint; they neglected the Greek works of Philo and Josephus, and the apocryphal books composed in or translated into the Greek language.

Had it not been for the Church, these great Jewish creations would have perished long ago. Interestingly, these very works are in our own day being reclaimed by Jewish scholarship.

Thus it becomes clear that only by ignoring and misinterpreting the facts of history and the totality of the data to be found in the rabbinic literature may reflection be cast upon the Jewish Septuagint translation of over two thousand years ago and, through it, upon the new JPS ver-sion of the Torah. The Septuagint was highly regarded by the Jewish people from the very beginning, and continued to be respected for several centuries. It is only because of the combined effects of the loss of sovereignty, the destruction of the Temple, and the rise of Christianity that the attitude toward the Septuagint changed as it did.

It is already clear that the new version of the Torah is being received enthusiastically by the Jewish community of the English-speaking world, in the spirit of its first ancestor over two millennia ago. Let us hope that its usefulness and influence for good will exceed that attained by its illustrious ancestor, the Septuagint.

21

The Hebrew Text
and the Ancient Versions
of the Old Testament

DURING THE FIRST MILLENNIUM A.D. there labored in Palestine and in Babylonia generation after generation of Jewish scholars, known as Masoretes, whose concern it was to preserve the text of the Hebrew Bible exactly as it had been received by them. Printing and other forms of mechanical reproduction were then unknown, and unless skilled and reliable scribes copied texts accurately, errors would result. The Masoretes counted every letter of every Book in the Hebrew Bible. They knew the middle letter and the middle passage of the Five Books of Moses, and the middle letter and the middle passage of the entire Old Testament. They made note of nearly every unusual form and word in the Hebrew text. They compiled regulations and hundreds of lists, the observance and knowledge of which helped the scribes to determine and follow the accuracy of the Hebrew text before them.

The Masoretes did not labor in vain. Biblical scholars recognize now more clearly than ever before that during the past nineteen hundred years, since the destruction of the Jewish State in 70 A.D. at the hands

---

[Reproduced with minor changes from *An Introduction to the Revised Standard Version of the Old Testament* (by Members of the Revision Committee, Luther A. Weigle, Chairman; 1952), where it constituted Chapter IV, pp. 24-32.]

of Rome, the consonantal text of the Hebrew Bible has remained virtually unchanged. This achievement on the part of the Masoretes becomes all the more remarkable when one recalls the number and severity of the persecutions and exiles which the Jews of western Asia, and later also of western and eastern Europe, experienced.

Before about 600 A.D. the Hebrew Bible was not vocalized. The consonants alone were written, sometimes in conjunction with two consonantal letters used as vowel letters (*waw* and *yod,* to indicate respectively *u* or *o,* and *i*); but a complete system of vowels had not yet been devised and integrated into the consonantal text. Thus the consonants *mlk* could be read to mean "king" (*mélek*), "he ruled" (*malák*), "Molech" (the god *mólek*), "to rule" (the infinitive *mᵉlok*), "rules, is ruling" (the participle *molék*), and "Rule!" (the imperative *mᵉlok*). It stands to reason that occasionally a word in the consonantal Hebrew text, especially if the context permitted, would be read incorrectly. Yet even this kind of error is extraordinarily rare. This is so because the Jews, who read and studied the Hebrew Bible in postbiblical times with unabated fervor and scholarship, always pronounced the Hebrew text even though an acceptable and authoritative system of vocalization did not emerge until later in the second half of the first millennium. Scholars sometimes tend to forget this fact, so that the vowels of the Hebrew text are considered by them less authoritative than the consonants.

In reality, there is no one manuscript or printed edition of the Hebrew text of the Bible which can trace the history of its transmission back to an authoritative manuscript in the days of the Second Jewish Commonwealth. There is a Talmudic tradition that authoritative texts of the Hebrew Bible were "on file" in the Second Temple, and several authoritative codices were known by name during the Talmudic period (to about the sixth century A.D.). Except for a few fragments, the overwhelming majority of the eight hundred or so manuscripts of the Hebrew Bible which have been studied, derive from the twelfth, thirteenth, and fourteenth centuries A.D.; after that the printed editions begin. No two of these manuscripts agree with each other in every detail; but the differences are virtually always so few and insignificant, and the origin of the differences usually so clear, that no competent scholar denies to all these manuscripts, and to the printed editions which are ultimately based upon them, a single text-tradition. No one manuscript or printed text is superior to another, and every variant must be studied for its own sake, to determine its origin and worthiness. In this connection it should be noted that the scroll of Isaiah, said to have been discovered in 1947 in a cave near the Dead Sea, has limited value for the reconstruction of the Hebrew text.[1]

Even from this brief sketch it will be clear that the faithful and competent work that the Masoretes accomplished was such that the preserved text of the Hebrew Bible, the consonantal text with full vocalization, became commonly known in learned circles as the "Masoretic Text." [2]

Max L. Margolis, the chief translator of the Jewish Publication Society's authoritative translation into English of the Hebrew Bible, has a well-written and pertinent chapter on "The Difficulties Inherent in all Bible Translations" in his excellent little book, *The Story of Bible Translations* (Philadelphia, 1917). "The translator's preface," Margolis points out, "has a stereotyped content. Everywhere we meet with the same diffidence and anticipation of unfavorable criticism. The prototype of all prefaces to Bible translations, the Prologue to the Greek Sirach (chapter II), tersely expresses the difficulties when it observes that 'things originally uttered in Hebrew have not the same force in them, when they are translated into another tongue,' and the translator

---

[1] On the methodology to be employed, see, *e.g.*, the writer's articles in *Jewish Quarterly Review*, 30 (1939-40), 33-49; 31 (1940-41), 59-66; *Journal of Near Eastern Studies*, 11 (July 1952). [See now my chapter on "The Textual Criticism of the Old Testament," in *The Bible and the Ancient Near East* (the Albright Volume), ed. G. E. Wright (Doubleday Anchor Book A431, 1965), pp. 140-169, with reference to several additional articles of mine on the Isaiah Scroll and to such studies as M. Burrows, *The Dead Sea Scrolls* (N.Y., 1955), chap. XIV (pp. 301 ff.); *More Light on the Dead Sea Scrolls* (N.Y., 1958), chap. XIII (pp. 146 ff.)]

[2] See article "Masorah," by C. Levias, in *Jewish Encyclopedia*, Vol. VIII, 1904 (pp. 365-71); B. J. Roberts, *The Old Testament Text and Versions*, Part I (Cardiff, University of Wales Press, 1951, (pp. 1-100). [See now my Prolegomenon, "The Masoretic Text: A Critical Evaluation," in the KTAV reissue (1966) of C. D. Ginsburg, *Introduction to the Massoretico-Critical Edition of the Hebrew Bible*.]

is quite certain that the same fault attaches to the Greek version of 'the law, and the prophets, and the rest of the books,' which preceded and guided his own effort. Likewise the rabbis in Palestine were very much troubled about the difficulty of adequately rendering the Torah into any language . . ." (pp. 117-8).[2a]

The Hebrew text of the Bible is very ancient. Parts of it, for example, the Song of Deborah (Judges 5), are some three thousand years old. Large portions of the Pentateuch, long preserved in oral form, were written down in substantially their present form about twenty-eight hundred years ago. The other parts of the Old Testament came to be written down between about 800 and 165 B.C., so that no part of the Hebrew Bible is less than about twenty-one centuries old. The plain meaning of the Hebrew text would be completely clear to us were it not primarily for two reasons: (1) the forgotten meaning of individual words and expressions, and (2) the corrupted form of the text.

In Biblical times, the Israelites did not devote their time to the study of the Pentateuch or to the writings of the prophets. The overwhelming majority of the people were too taken up with the daily onerous task of eking out an existence, of providing food, clothing, and shelter for themselves and their households, to have the leisure, energy, and interest for such study. The literary creations remained, by and large, the property of the relatively few, often only in oral form. Furthermore, the kind of conflicts which existed among the more cultured and influential groups did not make for the continued study and preservation of the text of these literary productions. Thus, for example, the priestly hierarchy of the Temple and the court scribes were not ordinarily interested in the pronouncements of the prophets so as to preserve their original form and meaning. The classical prophets were themselves not members of guilds or other organized groups; consequently, their oral statements were not infrequently altogether lost, or else were preserved inexactly. Jeremiah dictated his speeches to his secretary Baruch after the original copy was burned by the king. It is not known when

---

[2a] [See now my brief essay, immediately preceding, "The Septuagint: a Little Known Fact about the First Translation of the Torah," chap. 20, pp. 383 ff.]

and by whom the speeches of Amos, Isaiah, Hosea, Micah, and the other prophets were collected and edited. If the writings of these prophets were edited after their death, perhaps several centuries later, it is not surprising that not everything in the text which was clear and pertinent to the prophets themselves and their listeners was equally clear and pertinent to the editors and readers of later generations. The original tradition of the text was therefore sometimes made "more intelligible," to the point where it was for ever lost.

In the earlier Biblical period, the precise wording of the text of what later came to be regarded as Sacred Scripture was apparently not respected in the same degree as the message which the text conveyed. In addition, very few copies of these texts circulated at any one time. The Hebrew text was written consonantally, without any vowels. The misreading or mispronunciation of a single letter in a word, especially in the poetic parts where the average clause consisted of three words, made the correct understanding of the entire sentence unclear, and sometimes brought on an editorial revision of another word in the clause or sentence, to make new sense in the new context.

Biblical Israel experienced numerous invasions and several destructions. It was inevitable that some of the literature of the northern kingdom of Israel perished as a result of the destruction of the kingdom in 722-721 B.C., and that even more of the literature of the southern kingdom of Judah was lost as a result of the Babylonian devastation of this area in 586 and the exile of many of its cultured and prominent citizens to Babylonia. Another major destruction of Israel's literature took place about 170 B.C., when Antiochus IV Epiphanes of Seleucia, Syria, tried to impose his brand of Hellenistic religion and culture upon Judea. Accordingly, while the Hebrew text of about 70 A.D., when Judea's sovereignty was destroyed, has been preserved very creditably by the Masoretes, and while the condition of the text is remarkably pure for the period which preceded, the fact does remain, as several medieval Jewish students of the Bible recognized in anticipation of their more recent Christian and Jewish colleagues, that many words and passages in the Hebrew Bible are unintelligible to us, and that some of them are undoubtedly in need of emendation.

By far the most important and fruitful source for the understanding and restoration of the Hebrew Bible when its text is not clear as it stands, is the Old Greek translation of the Old Testament, known as the Septuagint. This version was made by Alexandrian Jews during the third and second centuries B.C., to satisfy the needs of the Greek-speaking Jews of Egypt whose knowledge of Hebrew was too inadequate to read and understand the original. There are hundreds of instances where the Septuagint version differs from the traditional Hebrew text. Most frequently this is due to the fact that the translators paraphrased the text. Thus in Isaiah 32.6, whereas the Hebrew text reads literally, "and his heart will do iniquity," the Septuagint (with the same Hebrew words before it) rendered freely, "and his heart will devise iniquity." A number of scholars failed to evaluate the Septuagint here properly, and used it as a basis for emending the Hebrew word "to do" into another Hebrew word "to devise"; but the present translation (RSV) has recognized the original character of the Hebrew, and has rendered it, in the spirit of the Septuagint, "and his mind plots iniquity."

On numerous occasions, the text of the Septuagint differs from the preserved Hebrew text because the former, rather than the latter, has experienced corruption. Thus in Job 8.16 the Hebrew text reads "and over his garden his shoots go forth," whereas the Septuagint reads "his corruption" for "his shoots." Some scholars explained the Septuagint as deriving from a Hebrew word *rimmah*, in place of the Hebrew word *gannah*. Actually, the Septuagint text itself probably read originally *prasia* "garden-plot," and this word became accidentally corrupted into *sapria* "corruption." The Revised Standard Version has wisely accepted the Hebrew reading.

There remain many scores of instances where the Septuagint text differs from the Masoretic because the former derives from a Hebrew text which was different from the latter. Thus in Job 5.8 the Septuagint is one of four independent arguments in favor of changing preserved *el* "God" to *"shaddai"* "the Almighty." In Numbers 24.9 the Septuagint (supported by the Samaritan translation) constitutes one of three independent reasons for substituting *rabaṣ* "to lie down, crouch" (used for animals) for Masoretic *shakab* "to lie down" (used for human beings). In many of these instances, however, it is possible for an English translation to make perfect sense and at the same time to retain the Hebrew text, so that in neither of these two instances did the RSV give up the traditional Hebrew text in favor of the Hebrew text indicated by the Septuagint. There are many other passages, however, where the translator must choose between an improbable or impossible reading in the traditional Hebrew text and a much more sensible reading in the Septuagint translation. In Genesis 4.8 the Hebrew text reads, "And Cain said to Abel his brother. And when they were in the field," etc. The Septuagint text, however, reads, "And Cain said to Abel his brother, 'Let us go out to the field.' And when they were in the field," etc. The RSV has acted correctly in inserting this clause from the Septuagint. In Jeremiah 15.11, an unclear verse, the Hebrew seems to say, "The Lord said." The Septuagint reads, "So let it be, O Lord," where the difference between the two renderings involves but one letter. The RSV has chosen the reading of the Septuagint.

There are several other translations, into Greek, Aramaic, Syriac, and Latin, which were made shortly after the turn of the era directly from the Hebrew Bible. Early in the second century A.D. Aquila, a convert to Judaism, made an independent and unique Greek translation of the Hebrew Bible. He incorporated the kind of Jewish interpretation which was current in his day, and he avoided the Christological elements which had been introduced in the Septuagint text. Thus Aquila rendered the Hebrew word *ha-almah* in Isaiah 7.14 literally, "the young woman," in place of the term which had acquired the meaning "virgin" in Christian circles.[2b] Unfortunately, only fragments of Aquila have survived.

In western Asia, especially in Babylonia and Judea, Aramaic was a popular vernacular among the Jews. The early history of the Aramaic translation of the Pentateuch and of the Prophets and Hagio-

---

2b [My original statement read: ". . . in place of the word 'virgin' which the Christians had substituted for it." What I meant to indicate is that the Greek word *parthenos,* when it was employed in the Septuagint and elsewhere in pre-Christian times, did not necessarily mean "virgin." I hope to publish soon my analysis of *"Almah* in Isaiah 7.14 and the Plain Meaning of the Verse."]

grapha is obscure. In any case, by the second century A.D. there were in public use the Targum Onkelos on the Pentateuch, the Jerusalem Targum (so-called Targum Jonathan) on every Book in the Bible but Daniel, and other Aramaic translations now known to us only in fragmentary form.

During the latter part of the second century there was still another translation made from the Hebrew Bible, the Syriac, called popularly the Peshitta. Whether this version, like the Septuagint, Targum, and Aquila, was also made by Jews for Jews, to be later worked over by Christians, or whether it was made originally by a (Judeo-?) Christian group and later came under the influence of Jewish exegesis, can no longer be determined. This version reflects influence on the part of the Septuagint.

By the fourth century, much of the Christian world had come to employ Latin as its vernacular. Jerome set to work turning the Hebrew Bible ("The Hebrew Truth" he called it) into this language. Thus the Vulgate came into being.

These five translations, the Septuagint, Targums, Aquila, Syriac, and Vulgate, constitute the five ancient primary versions which are basic for the understanding and occasional reconstruction of the Hebrew text of the Old Testament. All five, moreover, being essentially Jewish in origin, stand close to the spirit of the Hebrew Bible; that is to say, Jewish scholars participated in the making of four of these versions, and Jewish exegesis and teachers (as well as the Septuagint and Aquila) influenced Jerome to a very considerable extent in the making of the fifth. Many translations were subsequently made from these primary versions; but they do not concern us here. Suffice it here merely to note that none of the secondary versions has any direct importance for the Hebrew text of the Bible; they are important for determining only the text of the primary versions from which they derive. Thus it has become a common practice to cite the Old Latin translation of the Old Testament as an independent authority for some reading or interpretation; this lacks all justification. The Old Latin translation merely reflects the Septuagint text from which it was made.

None of the four primary versions which were made subsequent to the Septuagint has the authority that the Septuagint has. This is because they were made after the destruction of the Second Temple, by which time the Hebrew text of the Bible had been more or less fixed. Accordingly, these four versions should be used sparingly, and only when all other attempts, short of emendation, have been made to make sense of the Hebrew text. As for the Septuagint, only one who has made a thorough study of the character of this Greek translation, of the entire Book of which his own troublesome word or passage is a part, is in a position to use it for interpretation and reconstruction of the Hebrew text. He must know and "feel" the stylistic, lexical, exegetical, and theological characteristics of the Septuagint translator.

Not infrequently, neither the Hebrew text nor any of the ancient versions makes for a clear context. The need for an emendation of the Hebrew text is obvious. But, as Margolis has bluntly put it, "whether by the aid of the versions or by mere conjecture, the business of textual emendation requires a sure tact which few possess." [3] A generally misleading work in this respect is the widely used *Biblia Hebraica* edited by R. Kittel (third edition, 1937). Nearly every line of the footnotes in Kittel's Bible has errors of omission and commission, as regards both the primary and the secondary versions, and the quality of the Hebrew emendations there proposed is all too frequently inferior. One scholar put it this way, "The apparatus of Kittel's *Biblia Hebraica* contains very many readings erroneously supposed to be attested by the Greek versions, readings gathered blindly from the commentaries . . ." The Hebrew text in Kittel's Bible is, moreover, no more authoritative than any of the numerous manuscripts and printed editions of the Old Testament. [4] In general, considering their much greater use of the versions, the translators of the RSV have been circumspect in the matter of emending the Hebrew text of the Old Testament.

---

[3] *The Story of Bible Translations* (p. 126).

[4] For references and bibliography, see H. M. Orlinsky, "The Use of the Versions in Translating the Holy Scriptures," *Religious Education*, Vol. 47 (July, 1952, pp. 253-259). [See now my essay "Whither Biblical Research?" reproduced above in this volume.]

22

The New Jewish Version of the Torah: Toward a New Philosophy of Bible Translation

THE RAGE TO TRANSLATE—really to retranslate—the Bible is more widespread today than it has been since Protestantism burst upon the European scene in the sixteenth and seventeenth centuries. Nearly every country in Western Europe—Germany, England, France, Switzerland, Norway, Hungary—is experiencing this social phenomenon, just as the United States and Canada are. This is no accident.

The eighteenth and nineteenth centuries, and the earlier part of our own twentieth, are not unfairly labeled by historians as the age of reason, enlightenment, ideology, and analysis—in short, the age of science. In this extremely exciting epoch man began increasingly to reject, and then to ignore the Bible, the revealed word of God for more than two thousand years preceding, as the ultimate source of knowledge by which the problems of society could be resolved. Man began to depend upon his own powers of observation and analysis to probe into the secrets of the universe and its inhabitants: Why do we have wars and crises? Why do so many people have so little, and so few people so much? Are these basic problems really caused by divine intervention, or are they within the control of man himself?

[Reprinted—with some slight changes—from *Journal of Biblical Literature,* 82 (1963), 249-264.]

Rationalists, political scientists, economists, historians, philosophers, psychologists—the two centuries preceding our own time are full of great minds who grappled with societal problems, and proposed for them solutions of various kinds. If only the oppressed and impoverished many could be protected against the greed and power of the few, if only groups and nations learned to arbitrate and tolerate, if only man learned to use the brains and experience which were his inherently and by acquisition—in short, if only reason prevailed in man's relations to his fellow man—the kind of universal peace and personal contentment that religion had been promising humanity for over two thousand years would finally come to pass.[1]

Alas, this has not come to pass. If anything, the opposite seems to prevail. Ever since World War I in the teens, the world depression of the early thirties, the rise of fascism in Europe, the horrors of World War II, the cold and hot and lukewarm wars of the past decade and a half, increasing unemployment and automation, and the rather frequent recessions, it has become ever more clear that reason alone was unable to bring our problems closer to solution. And so, people have begun to come back to Holy Scripture, to the Bible.

But to what Bible? Well, ever since the seventeenth century the English reader had known chiefly the King James Version (KJ); more recently, since 1885, the British Revised Version (RV) had also become popular, more so than the American Standard Version (ASV; 1901). Twentieth-century man, however, is different from his counterpart of the three centuries preceding. For one thing, the style, the words, the very atmosphere of King James and the Revised Version are utterly foreign to him. He was not raised in a Bible-reading home, and old-fashioned "Bible" English was not his literary meat. Moreover, the Bible frequently enough does not lend itself to "do-it-yourself" com-

---

[1] The symposium of the 1960 annual meeting of the American Council of Learned Societies ("The Bible and the Humanities") revolved about this general theme; of the *Five Essays on the Bible* (New York, 1960) that were published, see especially E. R. Goodenough on "The Bible as Product of the Ancient World," R. H. Bainton on "The Bible and the Reformation," and M. S. Enslin on "Biblical Criticism and its Effect on Modern Civilization."

prehension, and the modern would-be reader found himself doubly frustrated in his attempt to understand what he was reading. As so often in other matters too, the late Benjamin Franklin knew what he was talking about when he said—about 1770, two centuries ago!— of the King James Bible: "The language in that time is so much changed and the style, being obsolete and thence less agreeable, is perhaps one reason why the reading of that excellent book is of late so much neglected."

There is, too, the matter of archeology. Ever since the tomb of King "Tut" was cleared, half a century ago, the reader of the daily press has been told regularly that excavation and discovery have brought to light many, very many documents that shed light on the Bible, that enable—indeed compel—the student of the Bible to translate and interpret the text quite differently from the traditional manner. Our understanding of the Bible had been revolutionized by the newly uncovered data from the Bible lands of the Ancient Near East, and none of these data was to be found in King James or the Revised Version.

And finally, the modern reader of the Bible is not the naïve believer that his ancestors were. After all, he was the proud possessor of the knowledge and outlook that reason and science had made available to him. He was not coming to the Bible to discover the whole Truth; he was not ready to give up reason and science. Rather, he was approaching the Bible as one source of information, along with several other sources, that might help him comprehend man and the universe. The Bible, to him, was now a guide to the truth, a repository of worthwhile information; but not the Truth itself.

Aware of this new interest in the Bible—for groups and individuals were clamoring in increasing numbers and with ever greater intensity for the satisfaction of their biblical desires—all three great faiths, the Protestant, the Roman Catholic, and the Jewish, embarked on new, official versions of the Bible for their followers, both in Europe and on this side of the ocean.

In 1937, after several meetings held in preceding years, the Inter-

national Council of Religious Education authorized the making of a
new translation of the Bible. The Council, consisting of the educational
boards of forty major Protestant denominations of the United States
and Canada, truly represented American and Canadian Protestantism.
The Council (the religious-educational arm of the National Council
of the Churches of Christ) proceeded to appoint a committee of scholars to produce a version that would "embody the best results of modern
scholarship as to the meaning of the Scriptures, and express this meaning in English diction which is designed for use in public and private
worship and preserves those qualities which have given to the King
James Version a supreme place in English literature." The Revised
Standard Version of the New Testament appeared in 1946, the Old
Testament in 1952, and the Apocrypha in 1957.

At about the same time, in 1941 to be exact, the Roman Catholic
community was presented with a revised New Testament. The Episcopal Committee of the Confraternity of Christian Doctrine then
authorized a new translation also of the Old Testament, to be made by
members of the Catholic Biblical Association of America. "The supreme goal to be sought in rendering the word of God into the vernacular," says the letter of the Episcopal Committee, "is rigorous
fidelity to the meaning of the original, expressed in simple and intelligible language." Three of the four volumes of *The Holy Bible Translated from the Original Languages* have appeared to date. [The entire
Bible appeared in 1970 under the title *New American Bible*.]

Back in 1917, the Jewish Publication Society of America, with
headquarters in Philadelphia, issued an English translation of the
Hebrew Bible. For several decades this version satisfied the needs of
the Jewish community of this country and abroad. But by the forties
it had become apparent that a new version was needed; just as the
Protestants—and for essentially the same reasons—had published the
Revised Standard Version (RSV) to "supplement" KJ, RV, and ASV,
and the Roman Catholics had added the new Confraternity Bible to
the old Challoner-revised Douay Version (1750), so too did the Jewish community demand a new translation to succeed the 1917 version.
For, in truth, the 1917 Jewish version was essentially but an extremely

modest revision of the English Revised Version of 1885, a revision that probably did not exceed more than a very few percent of the whole. [2]

In 1955 the Jewish Publication Society appointed a committee of seven scholars to prepare the new translation. [3] Late in 1962 the first part appeared, *The Torah* תורה , *The Five Books of Moses: A New Translation of the Holy Scriptures according to the Masoretic (or: Traditional Hebrew) Text.*

The new Jewish version (NJV) differs considerably from the new Protestant and Catholic versions—not to speak of King James, Revised Version, and Douay; and the very first three verses of Genesis indicate clearly and characteristically the nature of the differences.

New Jewish Version (1962)

I When God began to create[a] the heaven and the earth—[2]the earth being unformed and void, with darkness over the surface of the deep and a wind from[b] God sweeping over the water—[3]God said, "Let there be light"; and there was light.

[a]*Others "In the beginning God created"*   [b]*Others "the spirit of"*

Revised Standard Version (1952)

1 In the beginning God created[a] the heavens and the earth. [2]The earth was without form and void, and darkness was upon the face of the deep; and the Spirit[b] of God was moving over the face of the waters. [3]And God said, "Let there be light"; and there was light.

[a]Or *When God began to create*   [b]Or *wind*

---

[2] N. D. Dow has written a useful survey of "Twentieth Century Translations of the Bible in English," *Austin Seminary Bulletin: Faculty Edition,* 77, 3 (Nov., 1961), pp. 36-82.

[3] Viz., H. M. Orlinsky (editor-in-chief), H. L. Ginsberg and E. A. Speiser (fellow editors), Dr. M. Arzt (member of the Rabbinical Assembly — Conservative), Dr. B. J. Bamberger (member of the Central Conference of American Rabbis — Reform), Dr. H. Freedman (member of the Rabbinical Council of America — Orthodox), and Dr. S. Grayzel (editor of Jewish Publication Society of America) — the last-named serving also as secretary of the committee.

Catholic Confraternity Version (1952)

I 1. In the beginning God created the heavens and the earth;
   2. the earth was waste and void; darkness covered the abyss, and the spirit of God was stirring above the waters.
   3. God said, "Let there be light," and there was light.

The Revised Standard Version is the first authorized translation to introduce "When God began to create . . ." and "wind" (of God), even if only as alternate readings in the margin; yet it retained the "Spirit" (with capital "S") of KJ and ASV, as against "spirit" (small "s") of RV; the former points to something of the Holy Spirit of God, the latter simply to "a spirit of God."

The new Jewish version has done just the opposite. It has introduced "When God began to create . . ." into the text proper, and offered the reader as an alternate reading in the margin *("Or")* the traditional: "In the beginning . . ." [4]; furthermore, it embodied "a wind from God" in the text, and excluded altogether as an alternate rendering *("Others";* viz., the translators reject this traditional reading as unacceptable even as an alternate reading): "the spirit of." Why these sharp differences of opinion?

Scholars have long recognized the fact that the vowels of the first word in the Hebrew, *b^ereshith,* indeed the very word itself (as against, e. g., *barishonah),* points to the meaning "In the beginning *of* (God's creating)," that is, "When God began (to create)." Secondly, when the story of creation is resumed, in 2.4, it is again the temporal ("when") construction that is employed: "When the LORD God made earth and heaven." [5] Again, anyone recognizes the Ancient Near Eastern background of the biblical account of creation. The best known parallel is the Babylonian account of the rise of Marduk and creation, *Enuma elish,* and it likewise begins with the "when" sentence structure:

---

[4] The first edition of NJV underwent a number of changes in subsequent printings; thus original *"Or 'In the beginning God created'"* was soon altered to *"Others . . ."* These changes are given in my edition of the *Notes on the New Translation of the Torah* (5730-1969).

[5] . . . *b^eyom c^asoth YHWH 'elohim,* lit., "in the day of the Lord God's making of . . ." Cf. also 5.1 *b^eyom b^ero' 'elohim 'adam.*

When above, the heaven had not been named [i.e., did not yet exist],
(And) below, the earth had not been called by name. . . .[6]

And so the evidence is cumulative—lexical, syntactical, contextual, comparative—in favor of "When God began to create the heaven and the earth" and against traditional "In the beginning God created . . ."

The implications of the new, correct rendering, are clear. The Hebrew text tells us nothing about creation *ex nihilo* or about the beginning of time; it has nothing to say about the order of creation, so far as heaven, earth, darkness, deep, wind, or water are concerned. Indeed, the last four elements are not even described as having been created by God; all that the text informs us is that these elements were present when God's act of creation began! This becomes even clearer when it is noted that vs. 2, traditionally rendered as a separate sentence: "The earth was unformed and void . . .," must be understood as a circumstantial clause, that is, a sentence which describes the circumstances under which God began to create the universe. For the Hebrew word order, subject-verb as against normal verb-subject (*we-ha-'áres ha-yethah* as against *wa-tehi ha-'áres*), indicates at once that the verse should be translated: "—the earth being unformed and void . . ."; cf., e. g., the verbs in the parallel version of creation, 2.5-6. [7]

We are now, finally, in a position to understand exactly what the writer of the first three verses of the Bible meant to convey to his reader: [1]"When God began to create the heaven and the earth . . . [3] God said, 'Let there be light'; and there was light." In other words, the first thing that God did when He created the world was to create light. And the circumstances under which He began the act of creation with the creation of light was: [2] "—the earth being unformed and void, with

---

[6] For "Related Babylonian Creation Stories" that begin with the "when" construction, see ch. 2 in A. Heidel, *The Babylonian Genesis, the Story of Creation*[2] (1951), pp. 61 ff., *passim*.

[7] "([4] . . . When the Lord God made earth and heaven—[5] no shrub of the field) being yet *térem yihyeh* (in the earth and no grains) having yet sprouted *térem yişmaḥ* (because the Lord God had not sent rain upon the earth and there was no man to till the soil,) [6]but a flow would well up *we-'ed yaʿaleh* (from the ground) and water *we-hishqah* (the whole surface of the earth—[7]the Lord God formed man from the dust of the earth . . .)."

darkness over the surface of the deep and a wind from God sweeping over the water."

Interestingly, this is precisely how these verses were explained already a thousand years ago by the outstanding Jewish commentator, Rashi (R. Solomon son of Isaac; 940-1005). This is what he wrote: ". . . But if you come to explain the passage in its plain sense, thus explain it: At the beginning of the creation of heaven and earth, the earth being unformed and void, and darkness, etc., God said, 'Let there be light,' etc. For the passage did not come to teach the order of the (acts of) creation, to say that these (namely, heaven and earth) came first, for if it had come to teach us that, it would have written *barishonah*, 'In the beginning' . . ." [8]

Naturally, many people are upset by this old-new interpretation. "When did time begin?" they ask. "What existed in the beginning? Who created the darkness and the water and the deep?" And so on. Now every committee that assumes the responsibility of producing an authorized translation of the Bible for members of a church is always aware of the difficulties that may arise as a consequence of the translation decided upon for such "delicate" passages as Gen. 1.1-3. But the reply by the biblical scholar to such questions can only be: We know only what the biblical text tells us; and that is all that anyone can know from the Hebrew Bible itself. If the ancient Hebrew writer did not bother to think about these things, or if he did, did not bother to pose these questions and give us his answers, it is unfortunate. But we cannot read into his text what he simply did not say; and anyone who does this is simply not being faithful to his biblical, Hebraic source.

More than one person, scholar as well as layman, has been disturbed by the rendering of "a wind from God" in place of the traditional "the Spirit (or spirit) of God" for *ruᵃh ʾelohim*. The former is materialistic,

---

[8] Cf. *The Pentateuch and Rashi's Commentary, a Linear Translation into English,* by A. Ben Isaiah-B. Sharfman-H. M. Orlinsky, 5 vols. (1949-1950), Vol. I: *Genesis,* pp. 1 ff.

[9] The verbs *epiféromai* (in the Septuagint) and *menash-sheba* (in the Targum) indicate that their respective subjects (*pneuma* and *ruḥā*) denote "wind" (rather than "spirit; breath").

they assert, or flat, or tasteless; whereas the latter is spiritualistic, majestic, soaring, and the like. It is not easy for those not acquainted with scholarly procedure to comprehend the real problem here, as elsewhere in translating the Bible, namely, that it is not the task of the Bible translator to improve upon the original, to gloss over the difficulties and obscurities in it, to depart from the original for esthetic or theological reasons, so that recognition of the original is lost.

In our passage, if the Hebrew word *ruᵃh* was intended by the author to convey the meaning of "wind," then "wind" is the term that must be employed for it here, regardless of the arbitrary wishes and predilections of the theologian, or philosopher, or literary stylist. In a translation of the biblical text, no one has the right to read into that translation ideas and views that came into being after the Bible was composed.

It so happens that it is now possible to prove beyond reasonable doubt that "wind" is precisely the original meaning of the Hebrew, and that "S/spirit" is really a Christian interpretation that originated in the postbiblical period. The argument may be presented here only briefly. Scholars have long been perturbed by the fact that if *ruᵃh*, here in vs. 2, meant "S/spirit," what was the function of this living being when God began to create the world? The "spirit of God" did nothing at all; it participated in no activity whatever. Furthermore, whatever the Ancient Near Eastern background there was for the biblical story of creation, the fact is that the latter is entirely free of the polytheism of the former. The God of the Bible, unlike the male and female gods elsewhere in the Fertile Crescent of old, had no sex and no mythology. He existed from time beyond comprehension, and was alone among living beings when He began creation. Such inanimate elements, then, as earth, water, sun, and darkness pose no problem for Hebraic monotheism. But what about the living being, "spirit"? What was it doing alongside God Himself? Did it really coexist with God at creation, if not prior to it?

The word *ruᵃh* occurs about 380 times in the Hebrew Bible, having the meaning "breath, wind, spirit." Thus when Adam and Eve partook of the forbidden "fruit of the tree in the middle of the garden" and hid, God came into the garden "at the breezy time (traditional "in the cool") of day" (Gen. 3.8); the term for "breeze; cool" is ru^ah. In 8.1 we are told, "God remembered Noah and all the beasts and all the cattle that were with him in the ark, and God caused a wind to blow across the earth and the waters subsided"; again it is ru^ah that represents "wind." In 6.3,17 and 7.15, 22 ru^ah means "breath," that which God blew into Adam's nostrils to bring him to life. And so on. It is actually not until Gen. 41.8, when Pharaoh had his well-known "double-feature" dream and "his spirit was agitated," that our word ru^ah means "spirit."

Already some 2,200 years ago the considerable Jewish community of Alexandria had achieved a Greek version of its Sacred Scriptures, the Torah; the other two major divisions, the Prophets and the Writings, had not yet achieved that status. In this Jewish translation, the Septuagint, our ru^ah was translated *kai pneûma* "and the wind (of God was sweeping across the water)." Again, within a century or so of the making of the Septuagint in Egypt, the large Jewish community of Syria and Mesopotamia, whose vernacular was Aramaic, acquired an Aramaic translation of the Torah, the "Targum." And the translation of our word reads again $w^eruhā$ "and a wind (from before God was blowing over the face of the water)."

Even more. A Jewish sage of Babylonia, toward the end of the third century, Rab Judah by name, said in the name of his teacher, Rab: "Ten things were created (by God) on the first day. These are: heaven and earth, *tohu* and *bohu*, light and darkness, wind and water, and the duration of day and of night. . . ." [10] And finally: scholars have long recognized that the biblical version of creation has great affinity with what we know of the Mesopotamian versions, that the former—whether directly or indirectly—derives ultimately and in significant measure from the latter; and the wind plays a recognized rôle in the latter! Thus in *Enuma elish,* Anu the sky god begot the four winds; and it is they,

---

[10] Bab. Hagigah 12a: *'Amar Rab Yehudah 'amar Rab:* ^casarah d^ebarim $nibr^e'u$ b^eyom *rishon,* $w^e'elu$ *hen:* *shamáyim wa-áres, tóhu wa-bóhu, 'or* $w^ehoshekh,$ ru^ah *u-máyim, middath yom u-middath láylah.*

along with seven more that Marduk himself created, that later enabled mighty Marduk to slay terrible Tiamat and bring order into the chaos of the world.

An unusually clear and consistent picture has thus emerged, one that begins in the second millennium B.C. and extends to the fourth century A.D., according to which our *ruᵃḥ* was understood from the outset to mean "wind" and was thus understood throughout the biblical period and well into the first millennium A.D. Whence, then, "spirit" or "Spirit"?

In the first half of the first century, in Alexandria, the great cosmopolitan city that had produced the Septuagint, lived the noted Jewish philosopher, Philo. A firm believer in the literal truth of the Torah and at the same time alive to the truth of Greek philosophical thought, Philo developed a systematic comprehension of the Bible according to which the Jewish and the Greek views of the universe complemented each other fully, to constitute the perfect explanation of the universe. Thus, e. g., when the Bible asserts (Gen. 2.10-14) that "A river issues from Eden to water the garden, and from there it divides and becomes four branches . . .," that is literally true; at the same time, however, Philo interprets Eden as "the Wisdom of the Existent," and "the divine Logos descends from the fountain of Wisdom like a river to lave and water the heaven-sent celestial shoots and plants of virtue-loving souls which are as a garden; and this holy Logos is 'separated into four heads,' which means that it is split into four virtues." [11] To Philo, then, with his allegorical interpretation of Scripture, the Hebrew truth and the Greek truth both derive ultimately from the God of Israel, representing both the internal and the external meaning of Hebrew scripture, faith and reason.

In the matter of creation, Philo naturally accepted the biblical ac-

---

[11] From H. A. Wolfson, *Philo: Foundations of Religious Philosophy in Judaism, Christianity, and Islam*, I, p. 260. Wolfson goes on (pp. 260 f.) to cite and analyze a second interpretation of our verse by Philo, according to which " 'River' is generic virtue, goodness. . . . And generic virtue waters the garden, that is, it waters the particular virtues. . . ." But this problem in Philo is not our immediate concern.

count in the first chapter of Genesis: God literally created the universe
and all that is in it. On the other hand, he recognized the truth of
Plato's belief that before any concrete element could come into being,
the idea or the concept of that element had to exist, that the spiritual
counterpart of that physical element had to be conceived beforehand.
Thus "earth" is explained as "invisible earth," i.e., the idea of the element earth; "water" is explained as "the incorporeal essence of water,"
i.e., the idea of water; and so on. [12] Consequently, "wind" derived
from the incorporeal essence or idea of wind, i.e., spirit.

But what began as a purely philosophical interpretation of our *ruᵃḥ*
in Philo soon became something else altogether. For Christianity had
begun to develop within Judaism, and then—after the Roman destruction of the Judean state and the Second Temple in A.D. 68-70—increasingly outside of and in opposition to Judaism. And the more it
found itself confronted by the Hellenistic-Roman world, the more it
had to face the arguments and criticisms of the pagan philosophers.
Since Philo the Jew had already done much in harmonizing biblical
revelation and Greek reason, what was more natural than that Philo
should become the main philosophical-theological source for Christian
self-defense and countercriticism. When Christianity came to develop
the concept of the Trinity, so that the Holy Spirit shared with Father
and Son the unity of the Godhead, what was more natural than for
Philo's allegorizing idea of "spirit" for *ruᵃḥ* in Gen. 1.2 to have become "Spirit" and, in time, to have pushed out original "wind." [13]

That "wind of (or from) God" may not be aesthetically or theologically attractive to many readers of the Bible is not of primary concern
to the Bible translator. [14] He is first of all a philologian, not a theolog-

---

[12] See Wolfson, *op. cit.*, I, ch. 5, "Creation and Structure of the World," pp. 295
ff., especially pp. 306-07. Cf. p. 289, "The starting point of Philo's philosophy is
Plato's theory of ideas. . . ."

[13] On the Holy (or Divine) Spirit (*rúᵃḥ ha-qódesh*) in Judaism, see Wolfson,
op. cit., I, pp. 286-87; II, ch. 9, pp. 3 ff. (especially 24 ff.).

[14] That is true even if one should accept the reasoning of J. M. P. Smith in "The
Use of Divine Names as Superlatives" (*AJSL*, 45 [1928-29], pp. 212 f. This is an
addendum to his article, "The Syntax and Meaning of Genesis 1:1-3," 44 [1927-28],

ian, or a philosopher, or an aesthete. In any case, the new Jewish version of the Torah is the first official translation to read "When God began to create . . . and a wind from God. . . ."

Particles, the *waws,* and the like, are the bane of the Bible translator. Hitherto he has been content with reproducing them literally, mechanically, without regard to idiom. Thus, e. g., Hebrew *hinneh* has been regularly turned into "behold," a term which would ordinarily but rarely be employed in English, for it is essentially a hebraism. In Gen. 1.29 the traditional [15] "And God said, 'Behold I have given you . . .'" has become in the new Jewish version: "God said, 'See, I give you. . . .'" In 9.9 the traditional "Behold, I establish (my covenant with you . . .)" has become "I now establish." In Ex. 4.23 the traditional "(. . . if you refuse to let him go,) behold, I will slay (your firstborn son)" has become "(. . . yet you refuse to let him go.) Hence, I will slay. . . ." In Num. 20.18 the traditional "But Edom said to him, 'You shall not pass through, lest I come out (with the sword against you)'" now reads "But Edom answered him, 'You shall not pass through us, else we will go out . . .'"—where "answered" has replaced mechanical "said" for Hebrew *'amar,* and "else" has replaced mechanical "lest" for *pen.*

Unlike the ordinal numerals employed for the remaining days of creation ("a second day," "a third day," etc.), it would seem at first sight that the Hebrew used the cardinal in Gen. 1.5 for the first day, *yom 'ehad,* traditionally rendered "one day." But Hebrew *'ehad* means "first" no less than "one" (cf., e. g., 8.5 *be-'ehad la-hodesh,* "on the first day of the month"), and "a first day" is not only as correct *per se* as

---

pp. 111-14). I for one have remained unconvinced. It would prove nothing for the justification of some such rendering as "a tempestuous wind" (T. J. Meek, *An American Translation*). Neither should the Bible translator permit himself to get involved in "overinterpretation"; cf. B. S. Childs, *Myth and Reality in the Old Testament*[2] (*Studies in Biblical Theology,* No. 27), ch. 3, "Myth in Conflict with Old Testament Reality," pp. 31-43.

[15] The term "traditional" refers to KJ, RV, ASV, RSV, when they agree on the rendering under discussion.

"one day" but accords better with "second," "third," etc. (*sheni, sheᵉlishi*, etc.). By the same token, the well-known exhortation in Deut. 6.4, *Shᵉma' Yisra'el YHWH 'Elohénu YHWH 'eḥad*, is usually, and mechanically, rendered "Hear, O Israel: the LORD our God, the LORD is one" (1917 JPS) or "the LORD our God is one LORD" *(KJ; RSV,* with three alternate renderings in the margin). But not only is "one LORD" or "the LORD is one" only mechanical for *'eḥad*, it itself requires clarification and justification. What does "is one" mean? Clearly in the polytheistic society which the Near East then constituted, it was Israel's boast that it believed in and worshiped one God alone—leaving aside the question whether it did or did not acknowledge the existence of other deities. And if monotheism was the issue, then surely something like "Hear, O Israel! The LORD is our God, the LORD alone" (so NJV) is what the Hebrew intended. This is supported by the pertinent statement in Zech. 14.9 *(wᵉhayah YHWH lᵉmélekh ᶜal-kol-ha-'áreṣ ba-yom ha-hu' yihyeh YHWH 'eḥad ushmo 'eḥad*, where the idea is clearly expressed that Israel's God will be recognized as the *only* deity in the world ("[And the Lord shall be king over all the earth; in that day] there shall be the Lord alone and His name alone"—where traditional "the Lord will be one and his name one" is without meaning; was the Lord YHWH more than one?).

For it is precisely the deliberate rejection of the mechanical word-for-word approach to the problem of Bible translation that sets off the new Jewish version of the Torah from its predecessors. In Gen. 3.15b, e. g., where God pronounces curses upon serpent and man alike, and upon their offspring (. . . *hu' yᵉshufᵉkha ro'sh wᵉ-'attah tᵉshufénnu ᶜaqeb),* the traditional renderings run: "he shall bruise your head,//and you shall bruise his heel," as against NJV: "They shall strike at your head,//And you shall strike at their heel." Everyone recognizes that *hu'* and the suffix in *tᵉshufénnu*—exactly like *'attah* and the suffix in *yᵉshufᵉkha*—are singular collectives; the rendering of these pronouns as "he" and "his" rather than "they" and "their" (fortunately "your" and "you" are both singular and singular collective) is a hebraism. Or take the idiomatic use of the root *nasa'* in such expressions as *wa-yissa' 'eth-ᶜenaw wa-yar'* and *wa-yissa' 'eth-qolo wa-yébk*. Traditionally they are rendered—mechanically—"he lifted up his eyes and saw" (Gen. 22.4) and "he lifted up his voice and wept" (27.38); in reality, however, all that the Hebrew means is "he looked up and saw" and "he wept aloud" (or "he broke into weeping")—so NJV. The Hebrew idiom was traditionally avoided only when the result would have been ludicrous, e. g., in 29.1 where *wa-yissa' yaᵃᶜqob raglaw wa-yélekh* could hardly be rendered "And Jacob lifted up his feet and went"!

In being the first official translation to eliminate "Thou" and "Thy/Thine" in favor of "You" and "Your" even where God is addressed, NJV has done simple justice to the Hebrew text. The biblical writers made no distinction between God and man or animal so far as the pronoun *'attah* or verbal form (e. g., *nishbá'ta*) was concerned. Both God and Pharaoh are addressed directly by *'attah*. Why should misleading and incorrect "Thou" be used for God and "you" for Pharaoh? And since the argument has been advanced that "Thou" is more "pious" than "You," the reply is twofold: (1) the primary purpose of NJV—as of any scholarly translation—is to reproduce as exactly as possible the meaning intended by the Hebrew original; and (2) hardly anyone would really insist that the "Thou" of the previous authorized versions had brought very much "piety" into this world of ours.

The traditional translations of the Bible could well be designated "And" Bibles; hardly a sentence goes by without an "and" or two, often more. The fact that English, unlike biblical Hebrew, is not co-ordinate in its sentence structure was pretty rigorously ignored by former translators. It is, however, more than merely a question of rendering the *waw* by "When" or "So" or "Then" or "Thus" or "Although" or "But" or "Yet" or the like, rather than automatic "And"; there are many scores of instances when the *waw* should not be translated at all. Thus, e. g., the traditional translations all rendered initial *wa-yó'mer 'Elohim* for each of the six days of creation in Gen. 1 (vss. 3, 6, 9, 14, 20, 24) by "And God said"; NJV reads simply "God said."

As a result of this over-all view, NJV has tended to break up sentences and combine sentences through subordinating clauses far more frequently than previous official translations have done, where "and" mechanically joined clause to clause and sentence to sentence. Cf., e. g., Gen. 1.1-3 discussed above, or Deut. 1.46-2.1: "Thus, after you had remained at Kadesh *h*-all that long time,-*h* ¹we marched back into the wilderness, toward the Sea of Reeds, as the LORD had spoken to me, and skirted the hill country of Seir a long time," with note *h-h* reading: *Lit. "many days, like the days that you remained."* The traditional rendering is "So/And you remained at Kadesh many days, the days that you remained there. ¹Then we turned, and journeyed into the wilderness in the direction of the Red Sea, as the LORD told me; and for many days we went about Mount Seir." ¹⁶

On the new philosophy of translation, the reader is no longer denied knowledge of the fact that the translation is not seldom sheer conjecture, based on learned guesswork in the context. Many theories, alas, are based on official translations that lack real philological justification. Of course, when some previous official versions offered the reader alternate readings in the margin, that in itself indicated that the correct rendering was not certain, or else a matter of individual taste. But I have in mind here the frequent warning that NJV gives its reader: *"Meaning of Heb . . . uncertain"* or *"Heb obscure."* (And our committee of translators could readily have doubled the number of such caveats). Whatever was responsible for withholding this important

---

¹⁶ NJV has not hesitated to ignore the chapter division—itself a medieval innovation—when the Hebrew syntax required it. Thus the last verse of Gen 7 and the first of ch. 8 have been combined to form the beginning of a paragraph, to read: "²⁴ And when the waters had swelled on the earth one hundred and fifty days, 8¹ God remembered Noah and all the beasts. . . ." This is exactly what Saadia did at this point; as a matter of fact, in Gen 1 he even ran together the verses containing "And it was evening," etc., with those following: 4 and 5a, 5b and 6, 8 and 9, 13 and 14, 17 and 18, 23 and 24 — not to mention 1.31 and 2.1 (cf. *Oeuvres Complètes de R. Saadia ben Iosef al-Fayyoumî*, ed. J. Derenbourg, vol. I: *Version Arabe du Pentateuque* [1893], pp. 5-6).

information in the past, there can surely be no valid reason now for continuing to do so.[17]

NJV, unlike, e. g., RSV, Confraternity, and *La Sainte Bible,* was made "according to the Masoretic text"—so the title page; but "the traditional Hebrew text" on the dust jacket and in the blurb. The reason for the two terms, "masoretic" and "traditional," as the scholar realizes, is that no two "masoretic" manuscripts or printed editions of the Hebrew Bible are identical and that there is, in reality, no such thing as "the masoretic text." [17a] On the other hand, the better manuscripts and printed editions of the Bible agree to such an extent that for all the intents and purposes of the translator they constitute a single Hebrew text. After all, apart from masoretic minutiae and the variant readings that constitute *kethib-qere, sebirin,* and the like, how often will tradition offer a case like (*wa-yissa' 'abraham 'eth-cenaw wa-yar' we-hinneh-'áyil) 'ehad;* Gen. 22.13 alongside *'ahar*—where, incidentally, NJV reads "(When Abraham looked up, his eye fell upon) a[a] ram, (caught in the thicket by its horns . . .")" as against traditional "(And Abraham lifted up his eyes and looked, and behold), behind him was a ram (caught in a thicket by its horns . . . .")." Note *a* in NJV:

---

[17] M. L. Margolis (*The Story of Bible Translations,* p. 54), in commenting on Saadia's desire to provide his Arabic-reading Jewish community with a lucid translation of the Bible, noted that ". . . With a view to the same end a positive Arabic equivalent is introduced where the meaning of the Hebrew is doubtful, in order not to awaken in the laity the thought that there are obscure expressions in the Scriptures. . . ." The scholar need hardly be reminded that this "concern" for the laity has characterized all official Bible translations prior to NJV — even though the use of emendation in the text proper is one way of revealing to the reader that the received text is incorrect. The translators of KJ noted in their Preface that ". . . it hath pleased God in his divine providence, here and there to scatter words and sentences of that difficulty and doubtfulness, not in doctrinal points that concern salvation, (for in such it hath been vouched that the Scriptures are plain) but in matters of less moment, that fearfulness would better beseem us than confidence, and if we will resolve, to resolve upon modesty. . . ." [It should have been noted in the original article that RSV frequently resorts to emendation of the text (indicated in the footnotes by "Cn") and warns the reader "Heb obscure/uncertain."]

[17a] I have discussed this subject in my Prolegomenon, "The Masoretic Text: A Critical Evaluation," to the KTAV reissue of C. D. Ginsburg's *Introduction to the Masoretico-Critical Edition of the Hebrew Bible* (1966), especially pp. XVIII ff.

Reading 'aḥad [*correct to* 'eḥad] *with many Heb. mss. and ancient versions; text* 'aḥar *"after."* [18]

There was good reason for the decision to adhere to the so-called masoretic text. All official translations are meant for the community at large, Protestant, Catholic, or Jewish, as the case may be; they are not meant primarily for scholars, who can control the pertinent data at the source and who comprehend the canons of textual criticism. The general community has the right to expect the most accurate and intelligible translation possible of the best text handed down through the ages. Not only that; once a committee of translators begins to resort to emendation, it is difficult to draw the line. Every Bible scholar has his own collection of favorite emendations, some of which originate with him, with or without versional support; and it is only natural that in a committee translation hundreds of emendations would be proposed, many of them purely conjectural, many of them based on allegedly pertinent roots and meanings in the cognate languages. [19] It is not easy, mere mortals—even biblical scholars—being what they are,

---

[18] In Gen. 49.10 difficult (ᶜad ki-yabo') shiloh was rendered in NJV "(So that) tribute (shall come) to himᵇ," with note *b* reading: "Shiloh, *understood as* shai loh *"tribute to him," following Midrash; cf. Isa. 18.7 Heb obscure; lit. "Until he comes to Shiloh."* While following a midrash, *shay loh* is not yet *shiloh*, and this must be considered an emendation. In a brief study of "A Modern Translation of the Hebrew Bible compared with Ancient Versions" (*JBL,* 66 [1947], pp. 311-14) — in this case, the Jewish Version of 1917, so far as the book of Job is concerned — J. A. Montgomery speaks of the "conservative spirit" of the JV and the ASV and notes the manner in which they not infrequently depart from the Hebrew text without divulging this to their readers.

[19] M. L. Margolis, *op. cit.,* pp. 125 f., has observed: "That the received text is in need of correction, or, as the technical term goes, emendation, is recognized by the medieval Jewish students of the Bible. None perhaps went so far as Ibn Janah and his admiring follower Tanhum of Jerusalem, who have frequently anticipated the suggestions now going by the name of modern emendations. In the nineteenth century, Krochmal and Luzzatto fearlessly emended the received text. The tendency among modern scholars, Jews and Christians, lightly to distrust the text of the Synagogue is discountenanced by more serious students. A judicious handling of the ancient versions often brings to light superior readings. But whether by the aid of the versions or by mere conjecture, the business of textual emendation requires a sure tact which few possess."

to vote against another's proposed emendation and expect his support
in return; nor is it always easy, personal relationships aside, to decide
when an ancient primary version has been comprehended correctly or
when a purely conjectural emendation is sufficiently probable to de-
serve a place in the text of an official translation. Take, e. g., RSV's
thirteen emendations of the traditional text of Isaiah which were based,
largely or only, on the major Isaiah scroll. Of these, M. Burrows has
now written *(The Dead Sea Scrolls,* p. 305). ". . . A brief review will
show that even in these thirteen places the superiority of the manuscript's reading is not always 'certain. For myself I must confess that
in some cases where I probably voted for the emendation I am now
convinced that our decision was a mistake, and the Masoretic reading
should have been retained. . . ." [20]

It would seem that the best solution of this problem is the one
reached in NJV, viz., translate the Hebrew text directly, and offer in a
footnote the proposed emendation and its translation, with minimum
pertinent data. A case in point: some scholars recognize that *wa-yélekh
mosheh waydabber* (*'eth-ha-debarim ha-'élleh 'el-kol-yisra'el*) in
Deut. 31.1 is an accidental error of original *waykhal mosheh ledabber*
(interchange of *k* and *l*), which is the reading in the LXX-*Vorlage*
(*kai sunetélese Mousēs lalŵn*) and now in a Deuteronomy fragment
from Cave 1. [21] On the other hand, other scholars hold that ". . . the
textual change which it implies is not a very probable one" (Driver,
Deuteronomy (ICC), p. 334), and such translations as AT ("Then
Moses proceeded to speak"), RSV ("So Moses continued to speak"),
and *La Sainte Bible* ("Ce ch. est composite. Il est probable que les vv.
1-3ª, 14ª, 15 et 23 appartiennent au document ancien déjà rencontré
au ch. 27 . . .")—all of which, in principle, resort to emendation—
follow the received text, as does, e. g., J. Hempel in Kittel's *Biblia*

---

[20] See in general my chapter, "The Hebrew Text and the Ancient Versions of the
Old Testament," in *An Introduction to the Revised Standard Version of the Old
Testament* (1952), pp. 24-32. [Reproduced above in this volume, chap. 21.]

[21] D. Barthélemy-J. T. Milik, *Discoveries in the Judaean Desert,* I, pp. 59-60 and
plate X:13.

Hebraica[8] (who merely notes the LXX-*Vorlage*).[22] What NJV has done—as regularly—is to follow the received text, "ᵃ-Moses went and spoke-ᵃ these things to all Israel," and inform the reader, through note a-a, that *"An ancient Heb ms. and the Sept. read: Moses had finished speaking; cf. 29.1."*[23]

Even the matter of format is significant. Why must a Bible be bound in black, with the edges red, the pages printed in double column, the type relatively small, the margins hardly noticeable? The popular ($5 buckram) edition of NJV, with good will aforethought, is the opposite in conception and execution. The dust jacket is rather lively, the binding is an attractive blue, the edges are white, the type very clear and running across the width of the page, the margins ample—all in all, a pleasure to handle and read. Let the reader compare, e. g., Num. 1-2 in NJV and in the other official versions, noting the improved appearance and clarity of the text which has been made possible by extensive paragraphing and the use of numerals in place of spelling out the numbers.

---

[22] In Kittel's *BH²* (1909), S. R. Driver recorded: 1 frt C G *waykhal mosheh leḏabber*. Whether the above-cited translators would have emended *wa-yélekh . . . waydabber* to *waykhal . . . leḏabber* had they known of the reading in the Deuteronomy scroll fragment, I don't know. After all, the scroll merely helped confirm *waykhal . . . leḏabber* as the reading in the LXX-*Vorlage,* a fact known previously.

[23] At Gen. 10.10 NJV reads "The mainstays of his kingdom were Babylon, Erech, Accad, and Calnehᶜ in the land of Shinar." Since many scholars regard Calneh as quite out of place here geographically (see most recently W. F. Albright, *JNES*, 3 [1944], pp. 254 f. — but contrast now C. H. Gordon, *Interpréter's Dictionary of the Bible,* "Calneh"—AT, RSV, and SB have all emended the vocalization of received *we-khalneh* to *we-khullánah* ("and all of them"); NJV, on the other hand, through note ᶜ on "Calneh," informs the reader: *Heb.* we-khalneh; *better vocalized* we-khullannah *"all of them being."* RSV (see its Preface, p. v) does not inform the reader of emendations of vocalization, "because the vowel points are less ancient and reliable than the consonants"; the present writer has expressed another view, on pp. 25 f. of his chapter in *An Introduction to the R.S.V. of the O.T.* (see n. 20 above).

At Gen. 4.8 NJV has rendered "And Cain said to his brother Abelᵉ . . . and when they were in the field, Cain set upon his brother Abel and killed him," with note *e* informing the reader: *Ancient versions, including the Targum, read "Come, let us go out into the field."* AT, RSV, and SB insert into the text proper the reading of the versions.

Whence the traditional philosophy of translation? It all goes back to the Septuagint. The Jewish translators of this version regarded the Hebrew text of the Torah as Sacred Scripture, every word of it, revealed by God to Moses. They knew well the admonition in Deut. 4.2: "You shall not add anything to what I command you or take anything away from it . . ." (cf. 13.1). Indeed, the so-called Letter of Aristeas, after noting that the new translation was authorized (". . . Demetrius assembled the community of Jews at the place where the translation was executed, and read it out to the entire gathering . . ."), [24] proceeds with the statement that the leaders of the Jewish community and the translators ". . . bade that an imprecation be pronounced, according to their custom, upon any who should revise the text by adding or transposing anything whatever in what had been written down, or by making any excision. . . ." [25]

This word-for-word translation of Hebrew Scripture became standard thereafter. Not many translators deviated from the norm as did Saadia (892-942) in his great Arabic translation of the Hebrew Bible, of which M. L. Margolis *(The Story of Bible Translations,* pp. 53f.) wrote: "Though not a paraphrase [as the literal Targum sometimes becomes], the version is by no means literal. Where necessary a

---

[24] § 308. "To read a document in the hearing of the people" is the equivalent of authorization; cf. Orlinsky, "The Septuagint — its Use in Textual Criticism," *Bib. Arch.,* 9 (May 1946), p. 23, n. 2, with reference there to Moses and the Law (Ex. 24.17), Joshua and the Law (Josh. 8.34-35), Josiah and the Law (II Kings 22.10 and 23.1-2), and Ezra and the Law (Neh. 8). Note the same procedure also in Jer. 36 and 51.60-64. [See further the essay on "The Canonization of the Hebrew Bible and the Exclusion of the Apocrypha," printed in this volume as chap. 16.]

[25] §§ 310-311. Translation by M. Hadas, *Aristeas to Philocrates.* The *caveat* about adding or transposing or excising anything (cf. Deut. 4.2; 13.1), like reading in the hearing of the people, is conventional procedure in authorizing a document. In his zeal to bolster a theory of previous and independent Greek translations of the Torah — a theory that is as dead as his student F. X. Wutz's transcription theory — P. Kahle has interpreted these sections of the *Letter* (including § 30 and the term *sēmeiṓn)* improperly; cf. e. g., Orlinsky, *Crozer Quarterly,* 29 (1952), pp. 204 f. (review of M. Hadas, *Aristeas to Philocrates*); and "The Textual Criticism of the Old Testament" in *The Bible and the Ancient Near East,* p. 121 and n. 33 on pp. 129 f.; *JBL,* 78 (1959), p. 33, n. 16.

word is added to bring out the sense clearly; several verses are frequently joined together in a syntactical nexus, and thus, though the
original coloring is lost, the translation gains in lucidity. . . ."

This word-for-word procedure was reinforced—as if reinforcement
were needed—in the sixteenth and seventeenth centuries, when the
rise of Protestantism give impetus to new Bible translations in the
vernaculars of Western Europe. For now, more than over a thousand
years preceding, the Bible as the literal Word of God once again became pre-eminent. To such an extent was God's own Hebrew speech
considered sacred that in the version which became associated with
the name of King James, the words for which a direct equivalent was
lacking in the Hebrew were italicized. Thus, while the predicate is
clearly understood in the Hebrew, even though verbally absent, the
version of King James, as is well known, italicized the English correspondents: ". . . and darkness *was* upon the face of the deep . . .
And God saw the light, that *it was* good . . . And God made the firmament, and divided the waters which *were* under the firmament from the
waters which *were* above . . . and let the dry *land* appear . . ." (Gen.
1.2 ff.)—as though God's Hebrew did not include "was . . . it was . . .
were . . . were" and as though *yabbashah* means "dry" rather than "dry
land"!

It is precisely this philosophy of translation which NJV has set out
to discard. It is generally agreed that the Jewish philosopher Philo,
1900 years ago, laid the ideological foundation of Christianity; and
H. A. Wolfson has argued that it was another Jewish philosopher,
Baruch Spinoza (1632-1677), some 1600 years later, who was mainly
responsible for destroying Philonism and for giving Christianity a new
direction. In Bible translation, it was the Jewish Septuagint version,
some 2200 years ago, that set the norm for a word-for-word reproduction of the Hebrew. The translation committee of NJV, reflecting the
verve, growing maturity, and optimism of today's great American
Jewish community, would like to believe that its new version of the
Torah, in its internal and external break with the past, has set a new
pattern which authorized Protestant and Catholic translations of the
future will tend to follow.

23

Yehoash's Yiddish Translation of the Bible

STRANGE AS IT MAY SEEM, until a few years ago the "People of the Book" did not possess a translation of the Bible worthy of the name in their language of the past few centuries, Yiddish. The primary reason for this phenomenon would appear to be as follows: the average Jewish lad of 5-7 years of age, immediately on entering the *ḥéder* (elementary school), learned the Hebrew alphabet and began to translate the *ḥúmosh* (Pentateuch) into Yiddish, suchwise: *wa-yiqra un er hot gerufen, 'el tsu, mosheh Móshe, waydabber un er hot geredt, Adonay Got, 'elaw tsu ihm, me-'óhel fun dem getselt, moˁed fun móˁed, le'mor azoi tsu zogen,*[1] After a few years the student was well on his way to become a master of his mother-tongue, Yiddish, as well as of Hebrew and Aramaic. Accordingly, there was no widespread need felt for a Yiddish translation of the Bible. It is primarily because

---

[This article appeared originally in *Journal of Biblical Literature,* 60 (1941), 173-177.]

[1] Lev. 1.1. It was usually the classical biblical book of halakhah, Leviticus, that served to initiate the young boy into his studies. Cf. in general, E. Gamoran, *Changing Conceptions in Jewish Education,* New York, 1925. For a recent popular summary of "Jewish Education in Eastern Europe at the Beginning of the Seventeenth Century," cf. J. Trachtenberg, *Jewish Education,* XI (1939-40), 121-137. For our manner of transliteration, see below n. 7.

of the Jewish woman, who received no formal education, that attempts
at translations into Yiddish were made, so that she could read and
understand the weekly portions of the Pentateuch read in the Synagogue (the *sédrah*), the *Haftarot,* and the *Megillot.* These translations
came to be called familiarly *Tsénah ve-Rénah* (from *ṣeʾénah
u-reʾénah,* Cant 3.11).[2]

Over forty years ago the great Yiddish poet and stylist, Yehoash
(Solomon Bloomgarden, 1870-1927), who already from his earliest
youth had been fascinated by the Bible, conceived the idea of making
available to the Jewish masses, within the framework of the masoretic
text, a Yiddish translation that would be both literary and scientific.[3]
In 1910 there appeared the first fruits of his labor, the book of Isaiah
in one volume, and Job, Canticles, Ruth, and Ecclesiastes in another.
However, Yehoash was not pleased with these first efforts; he was
satisfied with neither his understanding of the Hebrew nor his style
and choice of words in Yiddish. He decided that this task deserved all
the ability and energy he possessed; it became the most cherished goal
in his life, to the exclusion of practically everything else. To prepare
himself properly for his life's work Yehoash went to live in Palestine
(January 1914), there to absorb into his sensitive soul the atmosphere
of the country which produced the Bible, and to acquaint himself with
everything in the way of translations, introductions, commentaries, and
analyses which bore on the Bible. He acquired a thorough knowledge
of Arabic and Syriac, and increased his knowledge of Greek and Latin,
in order that he might use the Septuagint, Peshitta, Vulgate, (Judeo-)

---

[2] The best account of Yiddish translations of the Bible or portions thereof, to-
gether with excellent historical treatments of their origin and character, is to be
found in I. Zinberg's remarkably complete and compact *Die Geshichte fun der
Literatur bei Yiden* (in Yiddish), Vilna, Vol. VI (1935), Chaps. II and V; Vol.
VII, Book II (1936), Chap. VIII. R. Gottheil's treatment of the subject in the
Jewish Encyclopedia (s. "Bible Translations," III, 191-2) may be found useful.

[3] It appears to me that Yehoash's conception of a translation of the Bible coincided essentially with that of the Committee responsible for the Jewish Publication
Society Translation of 1917 (cf. the Preface in the latter). I personally find
S. R. Driver's idea of a Bible translation for the layman more acceptable; cf., e. g.,
his *Notes on . . . Samuel*[2], p. XVII ("List of Abbreviations"), under "R. V."

Arabic, etc., in the original. Like so many other Jewish intellectuals of Eastern Europe, he was quite familiar with the languages and literatures of Russia, France, and Germany, and even of England, to say nothing of Hebrew, Aramaic, and Yiddish.

The Great War forced his return to New York in the summer of 1916, but this did not deter him from his work. During the eleven years which followed, years made long and difficult by the fact and knowledge that his health and life hung on a fine hair, Yehoash devoted himself to his sacred task. [4] He compiled thousands of notes on the Hebrew text and the versions; he revised his translation time and time again. From informal talks with friends in the course of their visits to his work-room and from private letters, we gather a most vivid picture of Yehoash's problems and temptations as translator (-commentator).

Yet throughout all this Yehoash could interest no one in his translation to the point of financing the publication of it. In order to acquaint the people at large with his work, Yehoash agreed in 1922 to publish it, at the rate of several chapters per week, in the New York Yiddish daily, *Der Tog* (The Day); by the end of 1925 the book of Jeremiah had thus been made available to the public.

At long last Yehoash succeeded in raising enough funds to pay for the publication of part of his work, and it was his good fortune and supreme joy to see the first two volumes of his translation (constituting the Pentateuch) in print before he died. Through the tireless efforts of his immediate family this edition was completed in eight beautifully printed and bound volumes, in special type set up by the Jewish Publication Society of Philadelphia, from 1926 to 1936. In 1938 there appeared a *Folks Auflage* (popular edition) in two volumes,

---

[4] The effects of tuberculosis and the concentrated efforts of 14-16-18 hours a day on the translation for a decade or so, led to his early death. In this connection I may refer to an interesting book that appeared recently, Dr. Lewis J. Moorman's *Tuberculosis and Genius*. The best account of Yehoash's life and works is to be found in Zalman Raisin's *Lexicon fun der Yiddisher Literatur, Presse, un Phililogie* (in Yiddish), 4 vols., Vilna, 1926 ff., s. v. [See now the rich Yehoash issue of *Die Goldene Keyt*, No. 72, 1971.]

which has since gone through six printings and of which about twenty thousand sets have been distributed through *Der Tog* and *Der Fórverts* (The Forward). Yehoash's daughter, Mrs. E. Dworkin, informs me that within a few months there will appear a bi-glot Bible in two columns, the Hebrew text and Yehoash's Yiddish translation. And there is every likelihood that Yehoash's notes will likewise be published in a separate volume soon. [5] [These Notes appeared in 1949 under the Title *Hecaros tsum Tanakh fun Yehoash,* together with a *Lexicon of Sources and Exegetes in Yehoash's Notes on the Bible* by the editor, the now lamented Mordecai Kossover.]

The translation proper, as is to be expected from Yehoash, is as much a literary masterpiece in its own right as any translation of the Bible could be. It not only captures the Jewish feeling and rhythm of the original, but it is a delight to read for its own sake. [6] Whether this translation will play the same role for and occupy the same niche in the Yiddish language and literature as the King James version with respect to English—and this is what Yehoash hoped—is quite problematical. Yiddish is far too advanced as a language and as a bearer of culture to be thus influenced today as compared with the English of four centuries ago.

I cite here two short sections from Yehoash's translation that the reader may see for himself its general character. Those not acquainted with Yiddish will find it surprisingly easy to understand the translation with the aid of German and the Hebrew original [7]

---

[5] I take this opportunity to thank Mrs. Dworkin [alas, recently lamented] for setting me right concerning a number of details in her father's life which, both in printed and oral form, already have been handed down incorrectly. A definitive biography of Yehoash would be very welcome. [The bi-glot Bible has now (1941) appeared.]

[6] For a critical discussion of the Yiddish in relation to the Hebrew, I may refer the interested reader to Dr. S. Feigin's thoroughly competent review (in Yiddish. There is none in English, so far as I know) in *Der Tsukunft* (The Future), 1930, 355-360. I owe this reference, as well as other bits of information, to the kindness of Dr. I. Fein.

[7] The problem of transcribing Yiddish into English is complex. There are, e. g., the questions of dialect (Lithuanian, Polish, etc.) and orthography (etymological,

Ich vell zingen tsu YHWH,
Vorum er iz hoich derheicht,
Dem ferd mit zein reiter,
Hot er geshleidert in yam.
Mein shtarkeit un gezang iz Yah,
Un er is mir geven a yeshu'ah.
Dos iz mein Got,
Un ich vell ihm bashenen;
Der Got fun mein foter,
Un ich vell ihm derheben.

                          (Ex. 15. 1-2)

Dernoch hot Iyov ge'efent zein moil, un hot gesholten zein tog.
Un Iyov hot zich opgerufen, un hot gezogt:

Untergen zoll der tog,
Vos ich bin in ihm geboren gevoren,
Un die nacht vos hot ongezogt:
A ingel iz antfangen gevoren.
Yener tog zoll zein ḥoshech,
Nit fregen zoll oif ihm Got fun oiben,
Un nit sheinen zoll oif ihm a lichtikeit.

                          (Job 3. 1-4)

-----

phonetic, etc.). I have used the following system of transliteration in the hope that
it will serve best the readers of the *Journal*.

Consonants

   ḥ for ח (Yiddish uses ח only in words of Hebrew and Aramaic origin; otherwise
כ); *ch,* as in German *ich,* for כ; *k* for both פ and כ (Yiddish makes use of ק only
in Hebrew and Aramaic words); *ts* for צ; *z* for ז; *v* for ו (Yiddish, like its German
ancestor, does not operate with the sound of English *w*. To reproduce the *v* sound
of German *w,* Yiddish resorted to the orthography וו[= Heb. *waw* written twice;
cf. biblical   "hook"]); *s* for both ס and שׂ (Yiddish uses שׂ only in Hebrew and
Aramaic words).

Vowels

   a as in *far; e* as in *fell; e* as in *prey; o* as in *for; o* as in *note; oi* as in *boil; ei* as
in German *kein.*
   [See now § 4, Spelling and Pronunciation, pp. XX-XXV of "Guidelines for Use of
the Dictionary" in Uriel Weinreich, *Modern English-Yiddish Yiddish-English Dictionary* (YIVO, McGraw—Hill, N. Y., 1968.]

24

Jewish Influences on Christian Translations of the Bible

MAY I AT THE VERY OUTSET pay personal tribute to the Chairman who introduced me so graciously. Raised in an Orthodox home, Reform Judaism was quite alien to me throughout my youth. My first direct contact with the Liberal interpretation of Judaism came when Rabbi Brickner's reputation had spread so widely in Toronto, Canada, that even I felt it necessary to hear him preach. It was not easy for me to enter the Holy Blossom Temple, where the men sat with the women, and with heads uncovered, and prayed in English. If my reactions after the services were mixed, rather than altogether unfavorable, it was due to the kind of sermon which Rabbi Brickner preached that day.

[This essay appeared originally as "Jewish Scholarship and Christian Translations of the Bible," in *Yearbook of the Central Conference of American Rabbis,* 63 (1953), 235–252. It constituted the Conference Lecture of 1953, at Estes Park, Colorado, at the invitation of the Conference's President, Rabbi Barnett R. Brickner. It had come into being a year previously as a lecture at the Institute on Judaism for Christian Scholars and Clergy, the annual series excellently conceived by Rabbi Harry Joshua Stern of Temple Emanu-El, Montreal. This might be designated a Canadian product, what with Rabbis Stern and Brickner and myself being involved in its making.]

My talk for this afternoon revolves about the Jewish Influence on Christian Bible Translations. I propose, in addition, to say a few words about the need and character of a new English translation of the Tanakh for Jewish usage.

Our talk begins naturally with a discussion of the fundamental rôle which was played by the Hebrew language itself, the language of the Holy Scriptures. Up to about the 18th century, it was generally believed that the oldest, as well as the most sacred language in the world was Hebrew, Biblical Hebrew. Thus one of the noted physicians in Germany during the 17th century, a certain Francis Mercurius, Baron van Helmont, not long after it had begun to be realized that "the ancient tradition that the deaf and dumb (were) without intelligence was without foundation," published a Latin work in 1667 under the title, "A brief description of the truly natural Hebrew alphabet, supplemented by a method according to which those born deaf can be so instructed as not only to understand the speech of others, but also to come to the use of speech themselves."[1] "Helmont began with the popular assumption that the Hebrew language was the language of God, and that through Adam He endowed mankind with the natural means of articulating human thought. If one were to teach the deaf by gradual, well-defined steps to arrive at a knowledge of Hebrew, then they could readily develop into regular members of human society." That Helmont was wrong, and that his contribution to the development of lip-reading has been depreciated, do not alter for us the fact that Hebrew held an exalted position in Christian circles at the time.

An immortal contemporary of Helmont was John Milton. He too, among others, valued highly the Hebrew language, and acquired a very good knowledge of it. True, there are a number of errors in the vocalization and accentuation of the Hebrew words cited in his treatise *De Doctrina Christiana*; but a recent study has made it clear that these errors are to be charged not to Milton himself, but to one of his two assistants.[2]

---

1. The references to Van Helmont derive from B. Schwartz, *Jewish Quarterly Review*, 29 (1938–39), 389–395.
2. H. S. Gehman, *Jewish Quarterly Review*, 29 (1938–39), 37–44.

No one whose theology derived in whole or in part, directly or indirectly, from the Hebrew Bible could fail to recognize and revere the Hebrew of the Bible. Joseph Ernest Renan, the renowned French scholar of the 19th century, who was suspended and then dismissed from his professorship of Hebrew at the Collège de France for the purely historical attempt to recreate the career of Jesus, to be restored to his post several years later by the Republic of France, may or may not have waxed too enthusiastic when he described the Hebrew of the Bible in the following, melodramatic manner:

"A quiver full of steel arrows, a cable with strong coils, a trumpet of brass crashing through the air with two or three sharp notes— such is the Hebrew language. The letters of its books are not to be many, but they are to be letters of fire. A language of this sort is not destined to say much, but what it does is beaten out upon an anvil. It is to pour floods of anger and utter cries of rage against the abuses of the world, calling the four winds of heaven to the assault of the citadels of evil. Like the jubilee horn of the sanctuary, it will be put to no profane use, but it will sound the notes of the holy war against injustice, and the call of the great assemblies; it will have accents of rejoicing, and accents of terror. It will become the trumpet of judgment."

Renan was here expressing emotionally what numerous illustrious pietists and humanists had asserted in earlier times. Thus the most illustrious Humanist that Germany produced, Johannes Reuchlin, in his book *De Verbo Mirifico* (1494), where the supremacy of Jewish wisdom and of the Hebrew language is maintained, described Hebrew as "the language in which God, angels, and men spoke together, not through the ambiguous murmur of a Castalian spring, Typhonian Cave or Dordonian wood, but as friends talk face to face."[3] And Reuchlin, be it remembered, was not only the first Christian to write a Hebrew grammar, and introduced anew the study of Hebrew into Western Europe, but he vigorously supported also the study of Greek.

The idea that God and the angels spoke Hebrew is, of course, biblically derived—what other language was employed in the Garden of Eden, and before the Fall and Dispersion of Man?—and reference

---

3. From M. Lowenthal, *The Jews of Germany* (Philadelphia, 1936), 145.

to this fact is found also, e.g., in the book of Jubilees, one of the oldest books in the Jewish apocryphal literature. So that we should not be surprised when we learn that an 11th century monk, who was getting old enough to realize that his days on this earth were numbered, began hurriedly to study Hebrew, for he knew that after he died and went to heaven, he would have to speak and understand Hebrew, Biblical Hebrew, if he wanted to converse with the angels and with the notable worthies who had preceded him from this earth.

The study of Hebrew on the part of Christians is, clearly, a very important aspect and medium of Jewish influence on Christian thought, and on the Christian understanding of the Old Testament, and, of course, on the numerous Christian translations of the Hebrew Bible, down to, and including the Revised Standard Version. It is worthwhile tracing a bit of the history of this phenomenon.

The influence that Jewish scholarship has had on every Christian translation of the Bible through the medium of the Septuagint translation (LXX) can scarcely be overestimated. This version was made by Jews for Jews in Greek-speaking Alexandria during the last three centuries B.C.E.[4] In it is to be found not merely the meaning of the Hebrew as it was understood in Jewish Alexandria at the time, but also a considerable body of traditional Jewish exegesis, which in time became an integral part of Christian exegesis. Among the better studies made in this area, mention may be made of the work of Zechariah Frankel, Chief Rabbi of Saxony in Germany, who just over a century ago published his analysis of "The Influence of the Palestinian Exegesis on the Alexandrian Hermeneutics," and a recent work (1948) by a young Swiss Jew, Leo Prijs, on "Jewish Tradition in the Septuagint." Let me give you two cases in point.

In Prov. 24:28 we read in the Hebrew, "Be not a witness against your neighbor without cause." The Hebrew word generally rendered "without cause" is חִנָּם . But since the LXX at this point reads ψευδὴς μάρτυς "a false witness," many scholars emended חִנָּם to חָמָס . It becomes clear, however, that the LXX really preserved חִנָּם , and interpreted it as ψευδής "false," when one consults the

---

4. See H. M. Orlinsky, *The Septuagint, the Oldest Translation of the Bible* (Union Anniversary Series, Cincinnati, 1949). [Reprinted in this volume as Chapter 19 .]

ancient Rabbinic homiletical commentary on the Pentateuch and the Five Scrolls, the Midrash Rabbah. At Deut. 3:12 the rabbis explain the word חִנָּם as שָׁקֶר "false," precisely the term used by the Jewish LXX translator of Proverbs; and thus no variant reading is really involved.

In Job 23:13 Job says of God, "But He is at one with Himself" (so Jewish Publication Society Translation), or "But he is unchangeable" (Revised Standard Version). The expression in the Hebrew is obscure: וְהוּא בְאֶחָד , literally "and He is in one" or "and He is essentially one." The Septuagint rendered, "And if He judges thus" (εἰ δὲ καὶ ἔκρινεν οὕτως). Many attempts have been made to explain the term "judges" in relation to the Hebrew, without success. The explanation is now forthcoming from the Midrash Rabbah on Deut. 1:7, where our passage in Job is interpreted thusly, " 'And He is One.' What does this mean? That unlike the legal procedure on earth, God is the sole judge on high." There are many scores of such instances.[5]

Probably the two most influential Christians in biblical scholarship up to the fifth century were Origen and St. Jerome. Together they left a heritage in scholarship and exegesis which cannot be isolated from the very fabric of Christian theology and philology without destroying it. Origen, whose Jewish ancestry by way of his mother the Nazi-minded Gerhard Kittel, the learned son of Rudolf Kittel, tried hard to disprove, took it for granted that the Hebrew text of the Bible was original, and he proceeded to edit the Septuagint text of his time, during the first half of the 3rd century, so as to bring it into perfect accord with it. What he did, was to compile a many-columned Bible, later to become known as the Hexapla, usually ranging from 6 to 9 columns, in which Col. I consisted of one or two words of the Hebrew original; col. II transcribed col. I into Greek characters so that the Hebrew could be pronounced through the Greek letters; the most literal translation of the Hebrew, that of Aquila, constituted col.

---

5. The importance of the Septuagint, which is to this day the official Bible of the Greek Orthodox Church, may be gauged from the frequency—perhaps too great frequency—with which it has been made to serve the Revised Standard Version as the basis for a rendering or interpretation different from the Masoretic text.

III; a more idiomatic translation of the Hebrew and of Aquila, that of Symmachus, formed col. IV; the Septuagint, revised to conform to the Hebrew of col. I, formed col. V; and in col. VI was to be found the best all-around Greek translation of the Hebrew, that of Theodotion. Three other Greek translations, known only by the terms Quinta, Sexta and Septima, that is, by the number of the Greek column they occupied in Origen's Bible, and two other translators known only as "The Syrian" and "The Hebrew," where they were available, completed this monumental Bible. I have described this Bible, if only so briefly, for a purpose. There appears to be good enough reason to believe that Origen arranged the columns of this Bible so as to make it possible for Christians to learn by themselves to read and understand the Hebrew of the Bible. Col. II enabled them to read col. I, Aquila in Col. III enabled them to translate the Hebrew literally, and sometimes even provided the etymology of the Hebrew word; Symmachus in Col. IV made intelligible the ofttime unintelligible Hebraized Greek of Aquila. By then, the Christian reader was ready to tackle the all-important Septuagint in Col. V. Theodotion was put in Col. VI only because his translation did not serve Origen's pedagogic purpose earlier.[6]

The Jewish LXX exerted very considerable influence in other forms. The Christian communities of Africa, Syria, Rome, Byzantium, and elsewhere, knew the Hebrew Bible not directly, and frequently not even by way of the LXX, but by way of translations made of the LXX. Thus the Old Latin, the Coptic, the Syriac, the Gothic, Armenian, Arabic and other translations of the LXX were the Bibles of their Christian communities, and the textual basis for their theological reasoning. The Old Latin, especially, made a lasting impression. Many important biblical commentaries, which in those days meant much more to the ideological development of Christianity and Christian institutions than commentaries do nowadays, were written on and around not the LXX text, but the Old Latin translation.

St. Jerome in the 4th and 5th centuries deserves at the very least an entire session to himself. It is simply not possible to discuss our

---

6. See H. M. Orlinsky, "The Columnar Order of the Hexapla," *Jewish Quarterly Review,* 27 (1936–37), 137–149.

subject, or any other in relation to the Bible and its subsequent history, without having to fall back in one way or another on the labors and influence of this Church Father. His private letters constitute an interesting source for us. They reveal a very dramatic, even melodramatic personality, who was determined to learn the Hebrew language if it killed him, and it very nearly did. Jerome tells us how he would study the difficult—to him at least—Hebrew language, all day, and then go to sleep exhausted. Lo, the morning came, and with it the realization that he had forgotten during the night all that he had learned the day before. He knew that it was the work of evil spirits who wanted to keep him from learning the ways of God. And he persisted, deep in the wilderness of Judea, until he had begun to master it. There was, however, very much yet to learn. So Jerome would hire Jews to teach him, and to study with him. Many a time he makes reference to *Hebraeus meus*, "My Jewish teacher." From these Jews, Jerome acquired a considerable knowledge of the rabbinic exegesis current in his time in Palestine. This has been studied pretty exhaustively, especially by one of the great talmudic authorities of our time, Prof. Louis Ginzberg of the Jewish Theological Seminary, author of the six-volumed work, *The Legends of the Jews*; the footnotes in vols. V and VI are a mine of information unequalled elsewhere. [Vol. VII, Boaz Cohen's most exhaustive and useful *Index*, appeared in 1946.]

St. Jerome's Latin translation of the Hebrew Bible, the Vulgate, up to the Protestant revolution the official Bible of all Western Christendom, and to this day official in the Roman Catholic Church, is predominantly Jewish in spirit. It could not be otherwise. While in his commentaries and other works he could and did argue theologically as a Christian, in his translation he was far more limited by the Hebrew text itself. The LXX, Aquila, Symmachus, and the other translations to which he frequently had to resort for guidance and assistance, were all, as we saw, Jewish sources.

With St. Jerome an entire era in the study of Hebrew came to an end. An excellent article on "Hebrew Learning" by Elliot in the *Dictionary of Christian Biography* makes it clear that Hebrew ceased to be studied by Christians, just as Greek too came to be neglected.

The period of the Middle Ages had set in, so far as Christian Europe was concerned.

The study of the Bible in the latter part of the Middle Ages, from the Carolingian period (10th century) through the 13th century, formed recently the subject of a book by an unusually fine scholar. In 1940, Miss Beryl Smalley, Fellow of St. Hilda's College at Oxford, published the First Edition (the Second, revised edition appeared in 1951) of an extraordinarily learned and fascinatingly written book on *The Study of the Bible in the Middle Ages*. I do not know how this lady's work could be improved upon, except to ferret out and make public, manuscripts which have not seen the light of day since they were put away by their authors hundreds of years ago. Miss Smalley concluded her brief "Preface to the Second Edition" with an expression of debt "to those at home and college who have stood between me and the cooking and cleaning that eats up the leisure of most women today." Those in charge of the Guggenheim, Rhodes, Rockefeller, Ford and other such foundations, yea, even the American Marshall Plan, could do very much for brilliant scholarship and international relations if they awarded a Fellowship to an able housekeeper who would release Miss Smalley to devote herself more fully to her research.

Miss Smalley's researches have made it clear that "The Bible was the most studied book of the middle ages. Bible study represented the highest branch of learning." In this period, it was not Biblical Hebrew as a language, but the Bible in its Vulgate form and, in some interesting instances, in the form in which Jewish scholars explained it to Christians at the request of the latter, which dominated the scene. Thus the Venerable Bede, in the 8th century—"the last writer whom Roger Bacon was prepared to accept as an 'authority,'" Miss Smalley reminds us—"had no knowledge of Hebrew beyond the few scraps of information he was able to glean from the writings of St. Jerome," and he knew Greek even less.[7]

The situation in England began to undergo some change at the

----

7. Cf. E. F. Sutcliffe, "The Venerable Bede's Knowledge of Hebrew," *Biblica*, 16 (1935), 305; cf. further pp. 141–2 of my article cited in n. 6 preceding.

beginning of the 12th century. There is evidence of some friendly contacts between Christian and Jewish scholars. At least in his work *Disputatio Judaei cum Christiano,* published about 1100, Gilbert Crispin, abbot of Westminster, would indicate that there were actual conversations with Jews. Peter Abailard a little later wrote a *Dialogus* involving "a Christian, a philosopher and a Jew . . . (showing) a tolerance and appreciation of the Jewish point of view." Abailard also tells us "that he once listened to a Jew commenting on a text of (the book of) Kings"; and a pupil of Abailard "refers to his master's questioning the Jews." This same pupil, while interested "in refuting Jewish arguments," gave expression to the following statement concerning "the Jewish love of letters": "If the Christians educate their sons, they do so not for God, but for gain in order that the one brother, if he be a clerk, may help his father and mother and his other brothers . . . But the Jews, out of zeal for God and love of the law, put as many sons as they have to letters, that each may understand God's law . . . A Jew, however poor, if he had ten sons, would put them all to letters, not for gain, as the Christians do, but for the understanding of God's law, and not only his sons, but his daughters" (from Smalley, p. 78).

Abailard and his school had good precedent for consulting Jews in matters biblical, exegetical, and textual. Thus a certain Benedictine, Sigebert, who taught at Metz about 1070, "was very dear to the Jews of the city because he was skillful in distinguishing the Hebrew truth from other editions; and he agreed with what they told him, if it were in accordance with the Hebrew truth." The abbot of Cîteaux in France, about the year 1100, corrected the text of the Old Testament with the help of Jews. And Nicholas Manjacoria of Trois Fontaines, who died in 1145, rejected the various Latin versions of the Psalter in favor of the Hebrew text, which he ascertained partly by learning some Hebrew, and mostly by consulting Jewish rabbis, among them one who introduced him to the existence of the notable commentaries by Rashi. In this period of the Crusades, it has been well stated that "If scholars could go to Spain, southern Italy and Sicily in search of Arabic learning, the student of Scripture might well consult the Jew on his doorstep" (Smalley, 81).

Far more than these illustrious scholars did Hugh of St. Victor (died 1141), and his successor, Andrew of St. Victor (died 1175), consult Jews and study Hebrew at the source, and they sometimes preferred the Hebrew text to the Vulgate. Miss Smalley reminds us that Hugh's teachers belonged to the contemporary North French school of rationalist exegetes founded by Rashi (died 1105), and does not exclude the possibility that this Christian mystic had actual conversations with the Rashbam, grandson of Rashi.

As for the significance of Andrew and the extent to which that significance was made possible by Jews, I can do no better than quote from p. 149 of Miss Smalley's book: "The Jewish tradition, which Andrew cites in explanation of his text, has brought us to his chief importance as a commentator. Had Andrew relied simply on his own mother wit and his knowledge of antiquity, he would be an arresting, but not a very significant, figure. For his purpose, these were not enough. The 'literal exposition,' as he conceived it, was a real science. A scientific work is bound to date quickly. It ceases to be valuable in itself; it is remembered for having opened up fresh lines of inquiry and fresh sources which later scholars have followed up. Probably the more successful it is, the sooner it will be old-fashioned. So the literal exposition to which Andrew devotes himself demands research work, and would be pointless without it. He would be like a person rattling energetically at a locked door.

"In fact, he had a key provided for him by his masters, St. Jerome and Hugh of St. Victor; and he had the courage to turn it. He went into the vast uncatalogued store-room of Hebrew learning, whose contents had been barely fingered, gingerly and at rare intervals, for the past seven hundred years. The metaphor gives a poor idea of his adventure. His archives were living scholars. The learning that he asked from them was no dead tradition, but something growing. A movement was in process in the Jewish schools as in the Christian. The Jews were developing new ideas and a new technique for the study of their sacred books; they combined conservatism and originality in much the same way as the Christians. Andrew had to take his Hebrew lore as it was presented to him by contemporary French rabbis. He hardly collected his material from them without making some kind of intellectual contact."

So great was the Jewish influence on Andrew that he was even accused by his colleague, Richard of St. Victor, of "Judaizing":

". . . I have found many things stated rashly," asserted Richard, "and discussed in an uncatholic sense. In many places the Jewish opinion is given as his own, and as though it were true. On that passage: *Behold a virgin shall conceive and bear a son* he gives the Jewish objections or questions without answering them; he seems to award the prize to them, since he leaves them as though they were unanswerable."

It is the rationalist school exemplified by Rashi which had the greatest effect on Andrew and on Christian exegesis in general. Previously, there were current in Jewish exegesis two main tendencies, the *halachic* or legalistic, and the *haggadic* or homiletical. The former approach saw in the biblical text primarily a means of working up the legal structure of Judaism, the rules by which the Jew should live. Of course, *eis*egesis went hand in hand with *ex*egesis, since the changing conditions of Jewish life necessitated rules which the biblical writers could not have foreseen. The *haggadic* or *midrashic* approach, used the biblical text as little more than a storehouse and an excuse for moralizing and edifying.

With the advent of Rashi, a more literal, rational approach to the biblical text came into being. Biblical exegesis is becoming scientific. The, unfortunately only occasional modern scholar who consults Rashi regularly at the source, will ofttime marvel at his exact philology, at his sober attempt to reconstruct the chronological and geographical elements in some historical event. Of course, Rashi and his school continued to operate with both the *halachic* and *midrashic* exposition. But they have added something new and vital, the *peshat* or rational, simple, straightforward approach, one which will in time push out the other two, both in Jewish and in Christian learned circles.

Rashi's followers were less patient than he. Thus Joseph Kara (died about 1135) curtly opposed the *midrashic* approach: " . . . Whosoever is ignorant of the literal meaning of Scripture," Joseph wrote, "and inclines after the Midrash of the verse, is like a drowning man who clutches at a straw to save himself. Were he to set his mind to the work of the Lord, he would search out the true meaning of the verse and its literal purpose . . ." Joseph Bekhor Shor (in the middle of the 12th century), a disciple of Rashi's grandson, the Rashbam, goes farther than his predecessors, not alone in rejecting non-rational exposition but in debunking the non-natural, that is, the miracles. Thus, e.g., he explains very simply and naturally the interpretation of the dreams of Pharaoh's cupbearer and baker, which the Bible credits to Joseph only with the aid of God, as due to the fact "that Joseph dreamt of future greatness because such thoughts were in his mind during the day; he needed no divine insight for their interpretation. Any clever man could have interpreted them (correctly); Pharaoh himself ought to have understood them . . ."

The Big Three in medieval Jewish biblical exegesis were Rashi, Abraham ibn Ezra, and David Kimchi, and their influence, both direct and indirect, on subsequent Christian exegesis and Bible translations, was considerable. Of particular importance to us is the fact that Rashi's acceptance of the literal sense of the Hebrew text was taken over bodily, among others, by Nicolas de Lyra, (1270–1340), a Jewish convert to Christianity.

De Lyra applied Rashi's exegesis freely, using essentially none other, in his analysis of the Hebrew Bible, as well as of the New Testament and the Apocrypha. He not infrequently copied Rashi into Latin word for word. It would not be easy to find another scholar whose biblical analyses were as widely read in the Middle Ages as those of de Lyra. And when Martin Luther began his "Protestant" career, one of the aspects of which was the translation of the Hebrew Bible into the current German vernacular, it was Rashi's commentary, even if by way of de Lyra, which was used more than any other. Many of you will recall the famous ditty:

| *Si Lyra non lyrasset,* | If Lyra had not played the lyre, |
| *Lutherus non saltasset;* | Luther would not have danced; |

to which someone could have added:

| *Si Rashi non composuisset,* | If Rashi had not composed (the music), |
| *Lyra non lyrasset.* | Lyra would not have played the lyre. |

To go but one step farther, Rashi's influence on all authorized and most unofficial English translations of the Old Testament becomes evident when it is recalled that no one person had more influence on

William Tyndale than Martin Luther, and Tyndale, more than any other person, is central in every English translation of the Bible down to and including the Revised Standard Version.

Abraham ibn Ezra was a traveling salesman of Biblical scholarship: ". . . from his native city Toledo in Spain through North Africa and the Orient, to Rome, to France to England, 'sojourning everywhere, composing works and laying bare the secrets of knowledge.' "[8] What may turn out to be a fruitful chapter in the study of the Bible in medieval France and England is the careful search through Christian biblical studies for possible influence on the part of Ibn Ezra.

"The influence of David Kimchi (1160–1235)," Professor Max Margolis has asserted sweepingly, "may be traced in every line of the Anglican version of 1611." Abraham ibn Ezra's sojourn in the Provence did much to further scientific biblical exegesis among the Jews there, and it is no mere coincidence that the Kimchi family, Joseph the father, and Moses and David the two sons, flourished in that region and period. David Kimchi's grammatical works and commentaries were eagerly sought out by the Christian scholars of the early 16th century, when the Reformation was to come into its own. Christian Hebraists, who were so relatively plentiful in Europe at this time, among them Sebastian Muenster and Paul Fagius, acquired most of their Hebrew from Elijah Levita, who in his turn was imparting to them so much of David Kimchi. Muenster's Latin translation of the Bible was one of Miles Coverdale's chief aids in his revision of Tyndale's English Bible, the revision being known as the Great Bible. It is interesting to note that in recognizing the difficulties in understanding and translating Psalm 68, "The poet Immanuel of Rome (about 1300) made King David in heaven summon all the commentators of the Psalter . . . and their worth was to be tested by the staggering task of expounding the eight and sixtieth psalm."[9] This very numerous and impressive body of commentators was to be headed, in Immanuel's opinion, by none other than David Kimchi.

With the advent of the era of printing, together with the social revo-

---

8. M. L. Margolis, *The Story of Bible Translations* (Philadelphia, 1917), 58–9.
9. Margolis, p. 123.

lutions which brought about dozens of translations of the Bible directly from the Hebrew and Greek into the vernaculars of Europe and the Moslem area of Western Asia, Jewish influence on Bible studies and translations became increasingly direct and frequent. Protestantism, especially, was interested in the authority of the Hebrew Bible, in what the authors of the different Hebrew Books of the Bible meant to convey to their listeners and readers over three and two thousand years ago. Christian scholars, more than ever, began to welcome scholarly assistance, regardless of its source, towards the correct interpretation of the Bible. Hebrew became fashionable, and the teachings of the Jews, the Talmud and the Cabala no less than the Holy Scriptures, attracted attention everywhere. This is evident enough even if one content himself with consulting the pertinent chapters in the excellent volume on *The Legacy of Israel* which E. R. Bevan and C. E. Singer edited in 1927, and the chapter on "Royal Hebraists" which George Alexander Kohut contributed in the same year to the *Israel Abrahams Memorial Volume*, with its rich bibliography,—including references to "Female Christian Hebraists," an interesting study in itself.

This enthusiastic attitude towards Hebrew, as towards the Bible, the classical Greek literature, and to the Humanities in general, characterized the several centuries between the advent of printing and the Reformation until the 19th century. There is already in existence a very considerable body of data about matters Hebraic in the United States during that period. In the New England region especially, the Hebrew language was popular. In 1680, at the second session of the Synod of the Elders and Messengers of the Churches, Article VIII was drawn up to provide for the study of the Old Testament in Hebrew, "the native language of the people of God of Old."[10] From the very beginning Hebrew ranked with Latin and Greek at such universities as Harvard and Yale. President Ezra Stiles of Yale himself taught Hebrew, and in 1781 he delivered the entire com-

---

10. So Cotton Mather, from A. I. Katsh, *Hebrew in American Higher Education* (New York, 1941), p. 18, n. 46. See also Abraham A. Neuman's stimulating essay on the "Relation of the Hebrew Scriptures to American Institutions," in his recently published *Landmarks and Goals* (Philadelphia, 1953), 255–275.

mencement address in Hebrew! Hebrew was compulsory for all fresh-
men at Harvard, and their first textbook was written by one, Wilhelm
Schickard, who called it *Horologium Hebraeum*, "The Hebrew Sun-
Dial," because it claimed to teach the essentials of Biblical Hebrew in
twenty-four hours. And H. L. Mencken has reminded us, in his
well-known study of *The American Language* (New York, 1938, p.
79), that when the Colonies broke with England, many in this country
advocated the substitution of Hebrew for English as the official American language.

With the coming of the Industrial Revolution, the significant rôle
of the Humanities began to diminish, and with it, Hebrew, as well
as Greek, Latin, and related disciplines. And while Hebrew has become a living language once again, in Israel and among thousands
of Jews in other countries, as well as a modern foreign language in
scores of high schools and in more than 1,000 colleges, seminaries,
and universities in the United States, it is otherwise by and large a
learned language. The modern scientific study of the Bible, consequently, revolves about a guild of scholars, whose nationality and
religion are secondary to the worthwhileness of their scientific contributions. There is a direct rôle, it is true, that Jewish scholarship
played in the making of the Revised Standard Version, in that a Jewish scholar was an active member of the Committee which did the
translation proper. Jewish commentaries were consulted more frequently than would otherwise have been the case; and there is no need
to keep secret the fact that more than half of the Committee purchased
Rabbinic Bibles, containing the Targum, Rashi, Ibn Ezra, and David
Kimchi.

At this point one could well ask: If there is so much that is Jewish
in the Christian translations of the Bible, up to and including the Revised Standard Version, could not then the Revised Standard Version
be read by Jews everywhere as freely as, say, the Jewish Publication
Society Translation of 1917, made expressly by Jews for Jews? The
answer to this query is "No." And let me tell you why.

The Jewish people have always been alert to the need of making
their Holy Scriptures available to the common people, who knew
Hebrew only inadequately, in their own vernacular. The Septuagint

of some 2200 years ago is a case in point. The Aramaic Targumim, the Greek translation of Aquila, the Arabic of Saadia in the 10th century, and the numerous translations in more recent times, into Persian, Spanish, Yiddish, Italian, French, German, Russian, Hungarian, and, of course, English, are eloquent testimony of that fact. "The repeated efforts of Jews in the field of biblical translation," reads the Preface of the Jewish Publication Society Translation, "show their sentiment toward translations prepared by other denominations. The dominant feature of this sentiment, apart from the thought that the christological interpretations in non-Jewish translations are out of place in a Jewish Bible, is and was [and may I add, should continue to be] that the Jew cannot afford to have his Bible translation prepared for him by others. He cannot have it as a gift, even as he cannot borrow his soul from others. If a new country and a new language metamorphose him into a new man, the duty of this new man is to prepare a new garb and a new method of expression for what is most sacred and most dear to him." [See Chapter 18 above, "Wanted: A New English Translation of the Bible for the Jewish People."]

We take it for granted that *all* translations which shed light on the Hebrew Bible should be utilized. Thus Hai Gaon of Pumbeditha, 900 years ago, when confronted with an exceptional difficulty in Psalm 141:5, did not hesitate to consult the Christian interpretation, on the ground that "scholars in former times did not hesitate to receive explanations from those of other beliefs." On the other hand, it seems to me that Jews generally should use a translation which relies more on the Jewish scholarly interpretation of the Septuagint, Targum, Rashi, Ibn Ezra, David Kimchi, the Malbim, and the like. Thus, e.g., in the very first chapter in Genesis, verse 2, for the expression ‫וְרוּחַ‬ ‫אֱלֹהִים מְרַחֶפֶת עַל־פְּנֵי הַמָּיִם‬ , the Revised Standard Version reads the "Spirit of God," with capital "S"—as though the Christian concept of the Holy Spirit had been meant by the author of the Hebrew text.

There is also the important matter of the Hebrew text itself. Until World War I, and the consequent rediscovery of an important part of the ancient Near East by way of exploration and excavation, scholars generally felt justified in reconstructing the history of ancient Israel, even where the biblical record was evidently not altogether clear or adequate. In those days, from about 1875 to 1925, many competent scholars belittled and even disregarded these biblical data.

We know differently today. A mass of archeological and inscriptional material has now turned the Bible into one of the most important and reliable documents in history. But it is not alone the substantial reliability of the Bible as an historical document of ancient times which has come into prominence. Even the very text of the Hebrew Bible, which Jewish scribes and scholars had copied by hand and transmitted for 1500 years after the Second Jewish Commonwealth was destroyed by Rome in the year 70, is now coming once again to be appreciated. The nineteenth century and the first part of the twentieth had witnessed an unprecedented tendency among scholars to emend the Hebrew text of the Bible whenever it did not appear original or satisfactory in their eyes. The best known and widely used critical edition of the text of the Hebrew Bible, Rudolf Kittel's *Biblia Hebraica*, recommended several thousands of changes in the traditional Hebrew Text.

In contrast to this tendency, there is now available the evidence of a text of Isaiah which came to public light six years ago, the so-called Dead Sea, or St. Mark's Isaiah Scroll. This manuscript is dated variously by scholars, from about 100 B.C.E. to about 400 C.E. Regardless of its date, the text of this manuscript is so sloppily reproduced, and is so inferior to the text preserved by the Masoretes, the Jewish scholarly scribes of the first millennium and a half of the Common Era, that scholars are now coming increasingly to realize how remarkably careful and trustworthy the Masoretes were in preserving accurately the text of the Holy Scriptures. In my opinion, it is a self-evident proposition that the preserved, masoretic Hebrew text must form the basis of any modern, revised Jewish translation of the Bible. While it may be necessary sometimes to emend the masoretic text, emendations should be held to a minimum, and in no case should an emendation be introduced if it lacks the support of a pertinent ancient Near Eastern text, or of an ancient primary version, such as the Septuagint. The late Prof. Margolis put it this way, "A judicious handling of the ancient versions often brings to light superior readings. But whether by the aid of the versions or by mere conjecture,

ESSAYS IN BIBLE TRANSLATION

the business of textual emendation requires a sure tact which few possess."

I wonder whether the inevitably forthcoming Anglo-Jewish revision of the Hebrew Bible will follow a certain Jewish interpretation of a classical Hebrew word, in the manner that the Revised Standard Version accepted it. In Proverbs 8:18 we read עֹשֶׁר־וְכָבוֹד אִתִּי הוֹן עָתֵק וּצְדָקָה usually rendered, "Riches and honor are with Me,/Enduring wealth and righteousness." It has long been recognized that the term "righteousness" is hardly appropriate here. If one is righteous and faithful to the Lord, he will receive as his reward riches, honor, and enduring wealth, but surely not additional righteousness. At my very first session with the American Standard Bible Committee, exactly 8 years ago, I found myself confronted by a first draft of the proposed revision of the Book of Proverbs, in which the member of the Committee charged with this draft proposed to render the Hebrew term צְדָקָה not by "righteousness" but by "prosperity." The Committee as a whole did not react favorably to this change in the traditional translation, and argued against it. I could not make up my mind, when I glanced at Ibn Ezra in my Rabbinic Commentary and noted with interest his comment, צדקה, כלומר הצלחה. I immediately advised the Committee that Ibn Ezra had anticipated the newly proposed interpretation of צדקה , and that the change had good Jewish tradition behind it. The atmosphere cleared at once, and the Committee voted to accept "prosperity" as the rendering for צדקה. And for the first time in the history of authorized translations of the Bible, Proverbs 8:18 reads "prosperity" instead of "righteousness."

And the reason that I chose this passage at this point, ladies and gentlemen, is that I have got to stop somewhere, and "Righteousness" and "Prosperity" form an ideal combination and theme on which to bring this talk to a conclusion.

GENERAL INDEX OF SUBJECTS, AUTHORS, ETC.

441

INDEX OF BIBLICAL AND OTHER PASSAGES

456

APOCRYPHAL AND JEWISH-HELLENISTIC LITERATURE

NEW TESTAMENT

RABBINIC LITERATURE